Action, Contemplation, and Happiness

Action, Contemplation, and Happiness

AN ESSAY ON ARISTOTLE

C. D. C. Reeve

Harvard University Press

Cambridge, Massachusetts

London, England

2012

Library of Congress Cataloging-in-Publication Data

Reeve, C. D. C., 1948–
Action, contemplation, and happiness : an essay on Aristotle / C. D. C. Reeve.
p. cm.
Includes bibliographical references and indexes.
ISBN 978-0-674-06373-0 (alk. paper)
1. Aristotle. Nicomachean ethics. De anima. Metaphysics.
2. Ethics, Psychology, Metaphysics, Ancient.   I. Title.
B430.R45 2012
171'.3—dc23   2011036369

For Ina

CONTENTS

PREFACE

When a philosopher has been as much discussed as Aristotle, sometimes the best way forward is to go back to the beginning and start over. I have learned much from already developed views, recording such significant debts as I can remember in the pertinent footnotes, but I have not discussed them in any systematic way or explained my disagreements with each one. I have tried to think everything out afresh for myself, as if I were the first to attempt the task.

An Aristotelian text often admits of multiple interpretations. Consequently, holism soon becomes a reader's default position. His art becomes one of assemblage—of selecting supporting texts in such a way that collectively they all but interpret themselves, ideally leaving nothing to believe except the view in whose defense they are mustered. The many texts assembled in translation here are (imperfect) exercises in that art. In one way, then, this is a naive book, which allows Aristotle's philosophy to emerge in its own terms. Any committed reader of Aristotle should feel at home in it.

Holism needn't be incompatible, of course, with the view that an author's thought develops over time, and may contain fundamental changes in doctrine, and real or apparent inconsistencies. Yet the two are to some degree in tension, especially when, as in the case of Aristotle, independent dating of texts is difficult or impossible, so that developmentalist hypotheses depend on interpretative ones. No doubt some of Aristotle's writings do represent earlier stages of his thought than others, but on the central questions with which I am concerned, I see little evidence of any changes of mind—signally, none are explicitly recorded.

It is, perhaps, also important to say that my book is itself best approached holistically. The paths it takes frequently crisscross, and, at the nodes of maximal intersection, interpretations and arguments developed in one connection on one path will be seen to support those made in a different connection on a different path. In the concluding chapter, many of the major roads meet, often not for the first time. A reader should see the journey through to the end, therefore, before deciding to redraw the map of the Aristotelian world it develops. God, as always, is in the details, but he is also in the whole the details constitute.

A word now about structure and topics. Desire, perception, and understanding, which control action, contemplation, and truth, are the topics of Chapter 2. These involve the transmission of form either to the soul or from it, which transmission is the topic of Chapter 1. Chapter 3 discusses theoretical wisdom, which is the virtue ensuring truth in contemplation, the sort of truth it controls, and the sort of control it exerts in being the most rigorous form of scientific knowledge of the most estimable things. The virtues of character presupposed by practical wisdom are discussed in Chapter 4. Chapter 5 explores practical wisdom itself, which is the virtue ensuring practical or action-related truth. The happiest life, which is practical wisdom's ideal target or goal, is the topic of the final three chapters, with Chapter 6 providing the metaphysical underpinnings for the discussion of happiness in Chapter 7, and of the happiest life in Chapter 8.

As will be plain to anyone familiar with my earlier books on Aristotle, I have sometimes retraced lines of argument first developed in them, often silently modifying them to reflect new understandings. For me, at least, getting Aristotle right—or more nearly so—has proved an asymptotic process. In keeping with my determination to start afresh, however, I have tried to rethink even those things on which my mind has ended up not having changed very much. This is particularly true in parts of Chapters 1, 2, 3, 6, and 8, which rework, and I hope improve, some material first presented in *Substantial Knowledge* (Indianapolis: Hackett, 2000), as part of a different exploration, aimed at a different audience, that focused exclusively on Aristotle's metaphysics. A few ideas from *Practices of Reason: Aristotle's Nicomachean Ethics* (Oxford: Clarendon Press, 1992) and from the introduction to my translation of Aristotle's *Politics* (Hackett, 1998) reappear in Chapters 4 and 5.

Finally, some debts I want to acknowledge explicitly. Richard Kraut, it doesn't need me to say, is a wise and distinguished writer on Aristotle. He was one of the Press's readers of this book, and his comments—constructive, precise, and in some instances transformative—were a model of their genre. For this, and for his good offices on many other occasions, going back now over twenty years, I offer him warm thanks. I am lucky to have him as *sunergos* (*NE* X 7 1177ª32–34). Thanks to an anonymous referee, who, faced with a much longer manuscript, suggested, among other useful things, that I reserve some of the material for a second book. Thanks to Pavlos Kontos, whose astute comments on a late draft saved it from at least three errors, none of them merely typographical. Thanks to Allan Silverman for catching an error of substance in Chapter 2. And thanks, especially, to Lindsay Waters for his unflagging support of my work.

As Aristotle was well aware, philosophy requires leisure. In a world of business, it is a scarce commodity. That I have enjoyed so much of it in the past two years is due to one person and two nonpersons. The person is Geoffrey Sayre-McCord, (now ex-)chairman nonpareil of my department, who granted me a study leave in spring 2009. The nonpersons are the University of North Carolina at Chapel Hill, which awarded me a W. N. Reynolds research leave in the fall of 2009, and its Institute of Arts and Humanities, which awarded me an Espy Family Fellowship for the spring of 2010. To the donors of these fellowships, and those who administer them, I extend my thanks. I extend them, too, to ΔKE, the first fraternity in the United States to endow a professorial chair, and to the University of North Carolina for awarding it to me. The generous research funds, among other things, that the endowment makes available each year have allowed me to travel to conferences and acquire books, computers, and other research materials and assistance, without which my work would have been much more difficult.

ABBREVIATIONS AND EDITIONS

Citations of Aristotle's works are made to Immanuel Bekker, *Aristotelis Opera* (Berlin: de Gruyter, 1831 [1970]), in the canonical form: abbreviated title, book number (when the work is divided into books), chapter number, page number, column letter, and line number. An asterisk indicates a work whose authenticity has been seriously questioned. The abbreviations used are as follows.

APo.	*Posterior Analytics*
APr.	*Prior Analytics*
Cael.	*De Caelo*
Cat.	*Categories*
DA	*De Anima*
EE	*Eudemian Ethics*
Fr.	*Fragments* (Rose)
GA	*Generation of Animals*
GC	*On Generation and Corruption* (Joachim)
HA	*History of Animals*
IA	*De Incessu Animalium*
Insomn.	*On Dreams* (Ross)
Int.	*De Interpretatione*
Juv.	*On Youth and Old Age* (Ross)
Long.	*On Length and Shortness of Life* (Ross)
MA	*Movement of Animals* (Nussbaum)
Mem.	*On Memory* (Ross)
Met.	*Metaphysics*
Mete.	*Meteorology*

MM	*Magna Moralia** (Susemihl)
Mu.	*De Mundo**
NE	*Nicomachean Ethics*
PA	*Parts of Animals*
Ph.	*Physics*
Po.	*Poetics*
Pol.	*Politics*
Pr.	*Problems**
Protr.	*Protrepticus* (Düring)
Resp.	*On Respiration*
Rh.	*Rhetoric*
SE	*Sophistical Refutations*
Sens.	*Sense and Sensibilia* (Ross)
Somn.	*On Sleep* (Ross)
Top.	*Topics*

I have used the *Oxford Classical Texts* editions of these works, where available, otherwise Bekker or the editions noted here:

Düring, Ingemar, *Aristotle's Protrepticus: An Attempt at Reconstruction* (Göteborg: Studia Graeca et Latina Gothoburgensia, 1961).

Joachim, H. H., *Aristotle on Coming-to-Be and Passing-Away* (Oxford: Clarendon Press, 1926).

Nussbaum, Martha C., *Aristotle's De Motu Animalium: Text with Translation, Commentary, and Interpretative Essays* (Princeton: Princeton University Press, 1978).

Rose, V., *Aristotelis Fragmenta* (Leipzig: Teubner, 1886).

Ross, W. D., *Aristotle Parva Naturalia* (Oxford: Clarendon Press, 1955).

Susemihl, F., *Aristotelis Magna Moralia* (Leipzig: Teubner, 1883).

All translations—including those of Plato—are my own.

Action, Contemplation, and Happiness

1

THE TRANSMISSION OF FORM

Action and contemplation involve desire, perception, and understanding, which are functions of the soul. Each of these, in turn, involves the transmission of *form*, either from the world to the soul, as in the case of perception and understanding, or from the soul to the world, as in that of desire and action. Our task in this chapter is to explore the underlying processes by which Aristotle conceives such transmission to take place. Since the soul is itself a sort of form, its nature, too, falls within the scope of our exploration. This begins on earth with animal reproduction, but it takes us to the outermost reaches of the universe. Cosmos and microcosm, universe and soul, involve similar processes and similar explanatory devices.

The Role of Pneuma

We find in nature an apparently continuous scale of beings, in which animate beings—those with souls—differ only very slightly from inanimate ones in their level of formation:

> Nature proceeds from the inanimate to the animals by such small steps that, because of the continuity, we fail to see to which the boundary and the middle between them belongs. For the first kind of thing after the inanimate is the plant kind, and, among these, one differs from another in seeming to have a greater share of life; but the whole kind, in comparison with the other inanimate bodies, appears almost as animate, while in comparison with the animal kind it appears inanimate. The change from plants to animals is continuous, as we said before. (*HA* VIII 1 588^{b}4–12)

The sublunary elements (earth, water, air, fire) aside, the simplest beings on this scale are homoeomerous or uniform stuffs, such as water, wood, olive

1

oil, flesh, and bone, whose parts have the same account as the whole (*GC* I 1 314ª20, 10 328ª10–12). These are constituted out of the elements in some ratio, when the productive potentialities (hot, cold) in the elements master the corresponding passive ones (dry, moist):

> We must describe the operations of the productive potentialities and the forms taken by the passive ones. First, unconditional coming-to-be generally and natural change and the corresponding natural passing-away are the function of these productive potentialities; and these processes occur in plants, animals, and their parts. Unconditional natural coming-to-be is a change produced by these potentialities, when present in the right ratio, in the underlying matter of a natural thing, and this is determined by the passive potentialities we mentioned. The hot and the cold cause the thing to come-to-be when they master the matter. (*Mete.* IV 1 378ᵇ26–379ª1)[1]

The fundamental form of such mastery is concoction (*pepsis*), which is responsible for producing a uniform stuff, and for preserving its nature thereafter:

> Concoction is a completion effected by a thing's own natural heat from the corresponding passive potentialities, these being definitive of the matter proper to the thing. For when a thing has been concocted it has been completed and brought into being. Moreover, the starting-point of the completion is its own proper heat . . . The end of the process of concoction is the thing's nature— but nature in the sense of form, that is, substance. . . . Concoction, then, is what everything undergoes when its matter—that is, its moisture—is mastered; for this is what is given definition by the thing's natural heat, and as long as the defining ratio exists in it, it possesses its nature. (*Mete.* IV 2 379ᵇ18–35)

Natural heat is thus *formative* heat—the principle in nature partly responsible for the coming-to-be and preservation of hylomorphic or matter-form compounds.[2]

---

1. The term "potentiality" is used to capture the two different but related things that *dunamis* signifies in Aristotle. First, as in ordinary Greek, it signifies a power or capacity something has, especially one to cause movement in something else (productive *dunamis*) or to be caused to move by something else (passive *dunamis*). Second, it signifies a way of being F, potentially being F as distinguished from actually being F. These are discussed in *Metaphysics* IX, and explained in Jonathan Beere, *Doing and Being: An Interpretation of Aristotle's Metaphysics Theta* (Oxford: Clarendon Press, 2010).

2. My views on natural heat owe much to Gad Freudenthal, *Aristotle's Theory of Material Substance: Heat and Pneuma, Form and Soul* (Oxford: Clarendon Press, 1995).

Uniform stuffs, as minimally formed, have a low level of such heat. As form is added, so that stuffs come to constitute the structural parts of animals (such as hands and eyes), and these to constitute whole animals of different degrees of complexity, natural heat increases: "the more complete animals are those that are hotter in nature and more fluid—that is, not earthy" (*GA* II 1 732^{b}31–32). Such animals more completely pass on their form to offspring (*GA* II 1 733^{a}33–^{b}2). Since human beings are the most complete or most perfect animals (*GA* II 4 737^{b}26–27), they are also hottest and most estimable:

> All animals with lungs breathe. . . . The reason some have this part, and why those having it need to breathe, is that the more estimable of the animals are hottest; for at the same time their soul must have been made more estimable, since they have a more estimable nature than the cold ones. Hence too . . . that animal in which the blood in the lung is purest and most plentiful is the most upright, namely, man. The reason he alone has his upper part directed to the upper part of the universe is that he possesses such a part. (*Resp.* 13 477^{a}13–23)

Male and female human beings both have formative heat, but it is not the same in each. This is revealed by the different roles played by their respective seminal products—seed (*sperma, gonê*) in the case of males, menses (*katamênia*) in that of females—in reproduction: "what the male contributes to generation is the form and the efficient cause, while the female contributes the material" (*GA* I 20 729^{a}9–11).

What seed does to menses to form it into a fetus is likened to what a carpenter does to wood to make it into a piece of furniture:

> Nothing comes away from the carpenter to the matter of the timber, nor is any part of the craft of carpentry in the product, but the shape and the form are produced from the carpenter through the movement in the matter. His soul (in which the form is) and his knowledge move his hands or some other part in a movement of a particular kind (different when the product is different, the same when it is the same), the hands move the instruments and the instruments move the matter. Similarly, the male's nature, in those that emit seed, uses the seed as an instrument containing movements, just as in craft productions the instruments are in movement; for the movement of the craft is in a way in them. (*GA* I 22 730^{b}12–23)

In the way the movement of the carpenter's hands has its source in the form of the product present in his soul, the movement in the seed has its source in a form—namely, that of the male progenitor. Hence the very same formal constituents exemplified as potentialities in his form are exemplified as movements in his seed, guaranteeing that these movements are (at least to begin with) formally identical to the potentialities that transmit them: "When seed comes into the uterus it causes the female's menses to take shape and moves it in the same movement in which it itself is moving" (GA II 3 737ª20–22). Were this not so, their transmission to seed could not result in the transmission of the male's form to the offspring.

What enables the transmission of such movements to seed is that they are present in the male's blood—where, encoded in formative heat, they are responsible for the preservation of his form—and that seed itself is a very concentrated or concocted blood product:

> In blooded animals, blood is the final form of the nourishment . . . and since seed too is a residue from nourishment, that is, from its final form, surely it follows that seed will be either blood or something analogous to it or something constituted out of these. Every one of the parts of the animal is constituted out of blood as it becomes concocted and somehow divided into portions . . . Therefore, seed is evidently a residue from that nourishment which is a type of blood—that which is finally distributed to the parts. This is why seed has great potentiality . . . and why it is reasonable that offspring should resemble their parents. For that which goes to all the parts [namely, blood] resembles what is left over [seed]. Hence the seed of the hand or of the face or of the whole animal is in an undifferentiated way a hand, or a face, or a whole animal—that is, what each of the latter is in actuality, such the seed is in potentiality. (GA I 9 726ᵇ1–18)

When the male's formal movements are transmitted by concoction to menses, therefore, they first initiate the formation of the fetal heart. Once the heart is formed, the fetus grows automatically, drawing its nourishment from its mother through the umbilicus, and in the process transmitting formative movements via the blood to the other developing parts (GA II 1 735ª12–26).

Menses is also a type of seed—"seed that is not pure, but needs working on" (GA I 20 728ª26–27). For a female's formative heat is cooler than a male's, and so cannot complete the final stage of forming or concocting menses into pure seed (GA I 20 728ª18–21). Nonetheless, a female can concoct her menses (or the seminal residue in it) to within that last stage of becoming pure seed, so that for each actual movement in seed, there is a corresponding potentiality stemming from the female form (GA IV 3 768ª11–14). While menses has the potentiality to move in such a way as to become a fetus, therefore, it cannot do so until it is set moving by seed, since "so far as things formed by nature or by human craft are concerned, the formation of that which is in potentiality is brought about by that which is in actuality" (*GA* II 1 734ᵃ29–31). Just which movements will underlie the offspring's form—whether, for example, it will be male or female—depends on the interaction between the movements in the seed and the potential movements in the menses (*GA* IV 3 768ᵇ5–12). If a male movement is transmitted successfully to the menses, the offspring will have the corresponding component of the male form. If it fails to be transmitted, it may be wholly resisted, in which case it is replaced by the opposing movement in the menses, or resisted to a lesser degree, with different consequences in each case (*GA* IV 3 768ᵃ7–9, 768ᵇ7–8).

While seed, as a concocted blood product, is a very purified type of nourishment, its vital heat, in which its formative movements are encoded, is of a quite special sort: "The potentiality of all soul seems to be associated with a body different from and more divine than the so-called elements. . . . For within the seed of everything there is present that which makes the seeds be fertile, the so-called hot. This is not fire or that sort of potentiality, but the *pneuma* enclosed within the seed and within the foamy part—more precisely, the nature in the *pneuma*, which is analogous to the element that constitutes the stars" (*GA* II 3 736ᵇ29–737ᵃ1). Characterized as "connate" (*sumphuton*), because it is not drawn in from outside but generated and maintained inside the body (*PA* II 2 648ᵃ36–649ᵇ8), it is the sort of *pneuma* that plays a fundamental role in nutrition and reproduction (*GA* II 6 741ᵇ37–742ᵃ16). The reproductive system, indeed, is in many ways simply a means of transmitting the form-preserving digestive system (of which blood and the heart are parts) into new matter, thereby initiating the formation of a new self-maintaining creature. That is why both functions are assigned to the *threptikon* or nutritive part of the soul (*DA* II 4 416ᵃ19–20, 416ᵇ11–12).

Although many natural beings (for example, inanimate ones) do not preserve their form by means of nutrition, or transmit it by means of sexual reproduction, *pneuma* has a fundamental role to play in their existence too:

> Democritus omitted to mention that for the sake of which [or final cause], and so thought that all the things that nature uses are due to necessity. And they are. At the same time, however, they are for the sake of something, that is, for the sake of what is in each case better. Thus nothing prevents the teeth from being formed and lost in the way he says, but it doesn't happen because of these, but because of the end. The [things he cites] are causes in the sense of

being movers, instruments, and matter, since it is reasonable, indeed, for nature to make most things using *pneuma* as instrument. For just as some things have many uses where the crafts are concerned—for example, the hammer and the anvil in blacksmithing—so does *pneuma* in those constituted by nature. (*GA* V 8 789^{b}2–12)

Despite its importance, no focused discussion of *pneuma* occurs in Aristotle's extant works. While this makes it difficult to determine his views with confidence, by piecing together what he does say, a reasonably clear picture emerges.

From its role in embryology alone, for example, we can see that *pneuma* transmits movement by being itself in movement. The role accorded to it in animal movement confirms this fact: "[*Pneuma*] is evidently well disposed by nature to impart movement and supply strength. At all events, the functions of movement are pushing and pulling, so that its instrument must be capable of expanding and contracting. And this is just the nature of *pneuma*, since it contracts and expands without constraint, and is able to pull and push for the same reason" (*MA* 10 703^{a}18–23). Moreover, because the movements it imparts are formative, they must be complex and various—able, as geneticists now put it, to *code for* all of an animal's parts. Since movements are "either in a circle or in a straight line or in a combination of the two" (*Ph.* VIII 8 261^{b}28–29), all the complex movements *pneuma* can produce must be some such combination. What makes this possible is that by actively expanding and contracting, and so pushing and pulling, it can cause not just rectilinear, but also circular movements: "spinning in a circle is a compound of pushing and pulling, since what causes something to spin must be pushing one part of it and pulling another, for it draws one part away from itself and another part toward itself" (*Ph.* VII 2 244^{a}2–4). Hence all movements—rectilinear, circular, or a combination of the two—can be caused by *pneuma* (*DA* III 10 433^{b}25–26).

The element that constitutes the stars, which is *ether* (*aithêr*) or primary body (*sôma prôton*), is a body "different from and additional to the elemental ones met with here, more divine than, and prior to, all of them" (*Cael.* I 2 269^{a}30–32), and is both transparent and in eternal circular movement (*Cael.* I 3 270^{a}12–^{b}25). Hence *pneuma* is a "body more divine than the so-called elements," because it is analogous to ether, which is in fact more divine than they. Initially *pneuma* is assigned a role in the transmission of form to uncontroversially animate beings. As ether's sublunary analogue, however, its role becomes extended to explain other phenomena, such as transparency:

"It is not qua water or air that these are transparent, but because there exists in them a certain nature, which is the same in both of them and in the eternal body above" (*DA* II 7 418ᵇ7–9); "what we call transparent is not something special to air, or water, or any other of the bodies usually called transparent, but is a common nature or potentiality present in these, and in all other bodies in a greater or lesser degree, and does not exist separately" (*Sens.* 3 439ª21–23). Then, because *pneuma* is soul-transmitting, soul is to some extent itself attributed to anything in which *pneuma* is present: "in water *pneuma* is present, and in all *pneuma* there is soul-involving [= formative] heat (*thermotêta psuchikên*), so that in a way all things are full of soul" (*GA* III 11 762ª18–21). When "the potentiality of all soul" is associated with "the nature in the *pneuma* that is analogous to the element that constitutes the stars," then, the point of analogy is that the nature in question is both transparent and—as itself in movement—an appropriate transmitter of soul and life.

The fact that soul is transmitted in this way has consequences for what a soul is. Menses is a complex structure of potentialities to move. As such, it is lifeless and soulless—unmoving. When the pneuma-imbued male seed enters it and causes ongoing movements within it, the resulting embryo acquires nutritive soul (*DA* II 1 412ᵇ27, *GA* II 3 736ª35–36). Hence the seed has the *potentiality* to take in nourishment and grow when it is in a functioning female uterus where menses are available to it. And because it does Aristotle can define soul of every sort—whether nutritive or perceptive or rational—as "the first actualization (*entelecheia*) of a natural body that has life in potentiality" (*DA* II 2 412ª27–28) or, more expansively, as "the first actualization of a natural instrumental body" (*DA* II 2 412ᵇ5–6).[3] For a first potentiality is the potentiality someone has, for example, to acquire theoretical knowledge. When that potentiality is actualized through the acquisition of such knowledge, that is its *first* actualization—the first stage in the actualization of the potentiality. The acquired potentiality he now has to exercise his acquired knowledge in actual contemplation is a second potentiality—a second stage in the development of the original first potentiality. Actualizing that second potentiality in actively contemplating something, in turn, is a *second* actualization (*DA* II 5 417ª21–29) or activity (*energeia*) (*DA* III 4 429ᵇ6–7). In a mature animal, the potentiality for nutrition and

---

3. Since *entelecheia* (actualization, fulfillment) and *energeia* (activity, actuality) are intimately related (*Met.* IV 3 1047ª30–32, 8 1050ª21–23), the soul is also "the activity (*energeia*) of some sort of body" (*Met.* VIII 3 1043ª35–36).

growth is always possessed as a *second* actualization as long as the animal is alive. It is only in the seed from which it develops that nutritive soul is present as a *first* actualization (*DA* II 1 412^{b}26–27).

Pneuma is the vitalizing factor, the one that brings life and soul into the right sort of body, equipping it with the starting-points of the various life or soul functions. In the case of seed, the right sort of body is a natural one with parts that can serve as instruments of nourishment and growth. In the case of potentialities, such as the potentiality to walk, whose actualization requires feet as instruments, the natural instrumental body in which they can be present must obviously be of a different sort from seed. Similarly, to have sight as a first actualization, a body needs to have functional eyes. And what makes an eye functional, what makes it a living eye, is that like a seed, it is vitalized by *pneuma*. For that to be possible, however, the eye must be part of the vitalized body of an autonomously functioning whole animal—one in whose blood *pneuma* is being carried to all the various functional parts. Hence it isn't *pneuma* that is the instrumental body of perceptual soul but the right sort of pneumaticized body.[4] That is why soul can also be defined as the "form of a natural body that has life potentially" (*DA* II 1 412^{a}19–21). If the life in question is simply vegetative life, the requisite type of body can be that of a seed, and its form, the structure of informing movements that code for nutrition and growth. If the life is that of perception, the requisite body must contain a structure of such movements that is correspondingly more complex.

Celestial Animals

The outermost translucent sphere of the fixed stars is finite in size (*Cael.* II 4 286^{b}10–11), with a fixed center coinciding with the center of the universe (*Cael.* II 14 296^{b}6–18) and a fixed periphery coinciding with the outermost boundary (*Cael.* I 6 273^{a}7–13). In common with the other celestial spheres, to which the various heavenly bodies are affixed, this outermost one is not a lifeless object but one that otherwise intractable puzzles make it reasonable to consider a living being—a being with a soul (*Cael.* II 12 292^{a}14–22).

In the case of sublunary animals, up and down, front and back, right and left are not just spatially or relationally distinguished but functionally and absolutely so: "the part from which the distribution of nourishment and growth derives in each living thing is up and the last part toward which this travels is down—the one is a sort of starting-point, the other a limit; and up

---

4. Contrast A. P. Bos, *The Soul and Its Instrumental Body: A Reinterpretation of Aristotle's Philosophy of Living Nature* (Leiden: Brill, 2003).

is a starting-point" (*IA* 2 705ᵃ32–ᵇ2). Similarly, the front is a starting-point, because it is where the organs of perception are located (*IA* 4 705ᵇ10–13). Even in earthworms, where right and left are more difficult to distinguish perceptually, the functional difference between them still exists: "the starting-point of the movement is the same in all animals and by nature has its position in the same place; and it is from the right that the starting-point of movement derives" (*IA* 5 706ᵃ10–13; also *Cael.* II 2 285ᵃ23–24). Thus human beings put their left foot forward, unless they accidentally do the opposite, since "they are moved not by the foot they put in front, but by the one with which they step off" (*IA* 5 706ᵃ8–9). In the case of the sphere of the fixed stars, the same applies not just to right and left but to all six functionally defined directions:

> We should not be puzzled, because the shape of the universe is spherical, about how there will be a left and a right of it when all its parts are similar and all the time moving. We should instead understand it as being just like a thing in which there is a difference between right and left, and other shape-related aspects, about which a sphere has then been placed, since it will possess the difference in function, but will seem not to, because of the uniformity of the shape. It is the same way with the starting-point of movement. For even if it never began moving, all the same it must have a starting-point from which it would have begun if it had begun moving, and, if it were to come to a stop, from which it would start moving again. (*Cael.* II 2 285ᵃ31–ᵇ8)

Animals are animals, after all, no matter where they are, or how strange they might initially seem.

It is these functionally defined directions that determine unconditional or absolute locations or places in the universe. The place that is unconditionally up, for example, as opposed to being up relative to something else, is at the periphery of the sphere of the fixed stars; the one that is unconditionally down is at its center (*Cael.* IV 2 308ᵃ17–29). It is absolute places, in turn, that figure in the essential definitions of the five elements, making them the closest analog of form that these elements possess (*Ph.* VIII 4 255ᵇ13–17).[5] Thus earth, for example, is what is unconditionally heavy, since unless it is opposed, it naturally moves toward the place at the center. The center of the universe, therefore, is its *proper place*—the place where it would be unless something else prevented it. Earth's active (cold) and passive (dry) potenti-

5. A point made and developed in Mohan Matthen, "Why Does Earth Move to the Center? An Examination of Some Explanatory Strategies in Aristotle's Cosmology," in *New Perspectives on Aristotle's De Caelo*, ed. Alan C. Bowen and Christian Wildberg (Leiden: Brill, 2009), pp. 119–138.

alities, by contrast, define it more in relation to the other elements than intrinsically (*GC* II 2 329ᵇ20–24).

Because place is "the limit of the surrounding body at which it is in contact with the thing surrounded" (*Ph*. IV 4 212ᵃ6–6a),⁶ the *place* that is the center of the universe is not a geometrical point but rather a sphere, whose size is determined by the amount of unmixed earth the universe contains. Hence Aristotle describes its place as "the one *around* the center"(*Cael*. I 8 277ᵇ15–16). If *all* the elements were in their proper places, then, earth would be in the innermost sphere. Moreover, all the earth within that sphere would be at rest in its proper place, and so none would be actively striving, so to speak, to get closer to the place's center point. Water (as the next heaviest element) would surround earth, and its contact limit with it would define earth's proper place. Similarly, air would surround water, and fire air, determining their proper places in the same way. The place of fire, finally, would be the contact limit with it of ether, were ether too in its proper superlunary place. Since the sublunary elements are all contained within the sublunary sphere, this limit would coincide with the sphere's boundary.

Just as the center of the universe is not a geometrical point, so its outermost boundary is not a geometrical surface but a spherical shell whose thickness is determined by the total amount of ether that exists. That is why Aristotle can define the proper place of fire—the one toward which it naturally moves—as "the extremity of the universe" (*Cael*. IV 1 308ᵃ21–30) and as "the extremity of the place within which the movement [of the sublunary elements] is produced" (*Cael*. IV 4 311ᵇ27–312ᵃ6). Because of the thickness of the ethereal shell that surrounds fire, these two descriptions pick out the same place. Since there is no body external to this outer shell, no surrounding body is its contact limit (*Cael*. I 9 278ᵇ18–279ᵃ11). Like the universe itself, therefore, there is a sense in which it does not have a proper place (*Ph*. IV 5 212ᵇ8–10). Nonetheless, once the proper places of the other elements are determined and imagined as entirely occupied, the only remaining place or location for ether is "the highest place" (*Cael*. I 3 270ᵇ22). For every body that exists is somewhere (*Ph*. IV 1 208ᵃ29), and no two bodies can be in the same place at the same time (*Ph*. IV 7 213ᵇ33).⁷

---

6. Reading καθ' ὃ συνάπτει τῷ περιεχομένῳ with W. D. Ross, *Aristotle's Physics: A Revised Text with Introduction and Commentary* (Oxford: Clarendon Press, 1936).

7. Some of the puzzles these different doctrines generate—such as the places or locations of places themselves—are discussed in Benjamin Morrison, *On Location: Aristotle's Concept of Place* (Oxford: Clarendon Press, 2002), especially pp. 133–173.

The sublunary elements, as passive rather than active starting-points of movement, are at rest when in their proper places; but this is not true of ether. For ether is an active starting-point that is in perpetual movement "around the center" (*Cael.* I 2 268^{b}24), and so must be moving in that way even when in its proper place. A question arises, therefore, as to the *direction* its circular movement naturally takes, since there is more than one available:

> It is possible to move in two ways on a circle, from A toward B [forward or clockwise] or toward C [backward or counterclockwise]. . . . But if nothing may be a matter of luck or chance among eternal things, and the heaven and its movement are eternal, what can be the reason why it moves in one way rather than the other? (*Cael.* II 5 287^{b}22–27)

Acknowledging that any answer must be speculative in the absence of perceptual data, Aristotle nonetheless ventures what he takes to be a reasonable answer to a related question, namely, the direction of revolution taken by the sphere of the fixed stars or primary heaven:

> If nature always produces the best among the things that admit of being otherwise, and . . . forward movement is more estimable than backward, the heaven, if indeed it possesses left and right . . . , also possesses front and back, since this explanation solves the puzzle. For if things are in the best condition possible, this will indeed be the explanation of the fact we mentioned, since it is best to undergo a simple, eternal movement, and to move in the more estimable direction. (*Cael.* II 5 288^{a}2–12)[8]

He thinks this is a reasonable answer because he thinks that in the sublunary world, where nature also produces the best, animals naturally move forward, just as they naturally have the starting-points of their movement on the right side. As a result, the front is better or more estimable than the back, the right better or more estimable than the left (*IA* 5 706^{b}11–13). The question is why does the sphere of the fixed stars move in this way? Is it because it is constituted of something whose own natural motion is circular and forward? Or is it for some other reason?

8. In fact a sphere has two intrinsic movements, namely, "rolling and spinning" (*Cael.* II 8 290^{a}9–10), so that besides moving (rolling) forward the primary heaven can also spin either clockwise or counterclockwise. For the sake of simplicity of exposition, I have focused on only one of these movements.

In Aristotle's view circular movement does not have a contrary, so that backward movement is not the opposite of forward (*Cael.* I 4 271ᵃ5–22). For contrary movements must have opposite starting and ending places (whereas circular movements are to and from the same places) and must impede one another. Hence if backward and forward movements were contraries, there would have to be an element whose natural movement was one of these and a different element whose natural movement was the impeding other. But this is something Aristotle thinks impossible on quite general grounds:

> If [backward] movement in a circle were contrary to [forward] movement in a circle, one of them would be pointless. For if they were equal, no movement would arise from them, while if one was stronger, the other would not occur. Hence if one of them exists, the other body would be pointless and would not move with its own [natural] movement. For we would say that a sandal is pointless which cannot be worn as a sandal, but God and nature do nothing pointlessly. (*Cael.* I 4 271ᵃ22–33)

The natural motion of ether, we may infer, may be either backward or forward. If it is forward, as in the case of the sphere of the fixed stars, this must be because something else causes it to be that way. Usually when this happens the movement of the element is unnatural to it, and so is forced or constrained. But because ether's natural movement is simply circular, no constraint is involved. "It would be a wonder and entirely absurd," Aristotle can therefore say, for a movement unnatural to ether to be alone "continuous and eternal" (*Cael.* I 2 269ᵇ7–9).

For reasons we shall be exploring, natural sciences treat the existence of moving or changing material things as a fact or posit, obvious on the basis of perception or induction, which it is no part of their task to demonstrate or explain (*Ph.* I 2 184ᵇ25–185ᵃ5). Movement, however, involves the actualization of a potentiality, which can always be possessed without being actualized (*Ph.* III 1 201ᵃ10–11, *Met.* XII 6 1071ᵇ13–14). To explain why there is movement, therefore, there must be a mover that actualizes the potentiality things have to move without itself being in movement. This unmoved mover is the first or *prime mover*, the explanatory starting-point of all movement or change (*Cael.* I 9 279ᵃ15–22, II 6 288ᵃ27–ᵇ7). Hence it must be what explains the forward motion of the primary heaven. The problem now is to explain how as not itself in movement the prime mover can play this role.

Aristotle's answer relies on the already established status of the primary heaven as an animate being, equipped with understanding and wish, and so possessing "a share in the actions and life activities (*praxeôs kai zôês*)" that these make possible (*Cael.* II 12 292ª20–21). For this allows the primary heaven to be moved in the requisite way:

> Objects of desire and intelligible objects move in this way: they move without being moved. Of these objects, the primary ones are the same. For that of appetite is the apparent good, and the primary object of wish is the real good. . . . And understanding is moved [activated] by intelligible objects, and intrinsically intelligible objects are in one of the two columns [of opposites], and in this column substance is primary, and in this, the simple one and an activity. . . . But the good—that is what is choiceworthy because of itself—is also in the same column, in that a best thing is always analogous to a first one. (*Met.* XII 7 1072ª26–ᵇ1)

As a type of desire, wish is efficiently caused or aroused by something's seeming good: "we desire something because it seems [good] rather than its seeming [so] because we desire it" (*Met.* XII 7 1072ª9). Hence it is because the prime mover seems (correctly) to be good to its understanding that the primary heaven wishes for it and is moved by it. What is "in the best state [namely, the prime mover]," however, "possesses the good without performing actions," while "what is nearest to it [that is, the primary heaven] does so by means of a small action and a single one" (*Cael.* II 12 292ª22–24). The reason this action must be circular and forward, we have already seen: nature always acts for the best and, of circular motions, forward circular movement is better and more estimable (*Cael.* II 5 288ª2–12). Hence it is forward circular motion that the primary heaven's wish will cause.

Wish moves the primary heaven as its efficient cause, just as desire moves us. But wish, of course, is a moved mover, not an unmoved one, so its status as efficient cause is unproblematic. What moves wish, in turn, is the good—that is to say, the good is wish's teleological cause, the end or goal it wishes for. Its efficient cause, on the other hand, is the good as grasped by understanding. But of that grasp the good is the efficient cause (*DA* III 10 433ª9–21). That is why Aristotle contrasts his view with Anaxagoras's in the way he does:

> Anaxagoras makes the good his starting-point in the way of mover [or efficient cause]. For understanding [the good] moves things. But it moves them for the sake of something, so that it is different [from the good for whose sake it moves them], except in the way that we say, since the craft of medicine is in a way health. (*Met.* XII 10 1075ᵇ8–10)

Here medicine is the form of health existing in the understanding of the doctor (*Met.* VII 7 1032ᵇ11–14), which is like the form of a house existing in a builder's understanding. Its pertinent analog is the intelligible object grasped by the primary heaven's understanding, namely, the prime mover.

As existing in the doctor's understanding, medicine is the efficient cause of health: "We should always seek the ultimate cause of each thing, just as in other cases. Thus a man builds because he is a builder, and a builder builds in accord with the craft of building. The craft of building, then, is the prior cause, and similarly in other cases" (*Ph.* II 3 195^{b}21–25). The prime mover, then, is not just the teleological cause but the ultimate efficient cause of the primary heaven's movement. But just as the craft of medicine is not itself something moving, and so isn't an efficient cause of movement for that reason, in the same way, the prime mover is not an efficient cause because it is itself in movement: "Nothing prevents the first mover from being unmoved during the movement, and indeed this is necessarily so in some cases, the last in the series is always a mover that is itself moved" (*GC* I 7 324^{a}30–32).[9] In the case of the primary heaven, the first mover is the unmoved prime mover, and the (relevant) last in the series is wish.

What explains the shape of the simple forward circular movement of the primary heaven, as what explains the vastly more complex shape of the movements of a carpenter's hands as he makes a piece of furniture, is the form existing in the understanding—the form these movements code for and transmit to the relevant matter, whether wood or ether. It follows that the form existing in the primary heaven's understanding—the form of the prime mover—must be a very simple one.

Of the two columns Aristotle refers to in introducing the prime mover and its way of moving, one consists of the intrinsic beings in the various categories, the other of privations, whose accounts involve them (*GC* I 3 319^{a}11–17, *Met.* XI 9 1066^{a}13–26). Thus dark, for example, is in the second column, since it is the privation of light, which is in the first. Located in the column of intrinsic beings is the subcolumn of substances, which is further divided into substances of different degrees of primacy, with unconditional primacy assigned to a substance that is both simple and an activity. As a substance, an activity, an intelligible object, and the mover of understand-

---

9. In attributing efficient and not just final causality to the unmoved mover, I have been influenced by Lindsay Judson, "Heavenly Motion and the Unmoved Mover," in *Self-Motion: From Aristotle to Newton*, ed. Mary Louise Gill and James G. Lennox (Princeton: Princeton University Press, 1994), pp. 156–171, and by David Bradshaw, *Aristotle East and West: Metaphysics and the Division of Christendom* (Cambridge: Cambridge University Press, 2004), pp. 24–44.

ing, the prime mover must be this simple substance. As the mover of wish, it must be the good, which thus belongs in the same subcolumn. The identity of the prime mover is now readily established:

> This [the prime mover], then, is the sort of starting-point on which the heavens and the sphere of nature depend. And its activity has the same character as ours has for the short time it is at its best (for it is always in this state [of activity], whereas we cannot be), since its activity too is pleasure (that is why perceiving and understanding are most pleasant, and expectation and memory because of them). Understanding is intrinsically of what is intrinsically best, and so the kind that is in the highest degree best is of what is in the highest degree best. And understanding understands itself in partaking of the intelligible object; for it becomes an intelligible object in touching and understanding its objects, so that understanding and the intelligible object are the same. For that which can receive the intelligible object (that is, the substance) is the understanding. And it is an activity when it possesses it, so that this [active understanding] rather than the former [passive understanding] seems to be the divine thing understanding possesses, and theoretical understanding seems to be most pleasant and best. If, then, that good state [of activity], which we are sometimes in, God is always in, that is a marvelous thing; but if he is in it to a higher degree, that is still more marvelous. But that *is* his state. And life too certainly belongs to him. For the activity of understanding is life, and he is that activity; and his activity is intrinsically life that is best and eternal. We say, then, that God is a living being that is eternal and best, so that continuous, eternal life and duration belong to God, since it *is* God. (*Met.* XII 7 1072^{b}13–30)

Like the primary heaven, then, the prime mover is a living being, God, whose sole life activity is understanding, which life activity just is what he is. Thus, though God is the prime mover, this fact about him is no part of his essence or essential definition. What he is essentially is a kind of understanding, not a kind of mover.[10]

If God is an eternally active understanding, the question naturally arises of what he understands. Aristotle's answer is that he understand himself, making him "an active understanding that is an active understanding of active understanding" (*Met.* XII 9 1074^{b}15–35). However we are to interpret this opaque formula, it must be as something without any of the sort of complex inner articulation that would need a complex set of movements to code

---

10. A view more elaborately defended in Michael Bordt, SJ, "Why Aristotle's God is Not the Unmoved Mover," *Oxford Studies in Ancient Philosophy* 40 (2011): 91–109.

for it. For when the primary heaven understands God, the intelligible object or form present in its understanding, and guiding its own movements, gives rise only to forward circular movement. But this movement isn't something that its understanding gives rise to as an additional product, in the way the carpenter's understanding of the form in his soul moves his hands; rather it is the very thing that codes for that understanding. For the good the primary heaven achieves just is its understanding of God. That is why the way it achieves that good, namely "by means of a small action and a single one," is only a second best one (*Cael.* II 12 292ᵃ22–24). God himself, by contrast, as an unmoved mover, achieves it without any movement at all: "God always enjoys a single simple pleasure. For there is activity not only of movement but of nonmovement (*akinêsias*), and pleasure lies more in rest than in movement" (*NE* VII 14 1154ᵇ26–28). As himself the activity of understanding, he needs no movement, like that of the primary heaven, to code for it.

Were the intrinsic potentialities of the elements the only causal factors present in the universe, all the elements would be in their proper places, and the universe itself would be a nested set of concentric spheres, each constituted of different elemental material. But the universe is not like that. Instead it contains a vast array of causes beyond these intrinsic potentialities, including a mover who, as unmoved, figures in the explanation of all movement. As a result, we have the rich variety of beings, beyond the elements themselves, that make up the universe. What we also have is a universe in which the elements are *not* in their proper places. True of the sublunary elements, this is also true, as we are about to see, of ether itself.[11]

A Puzzle Case

Understanding is unique among psychological functions in having no sublunary bodily correlate: "bodily activity is in no way associated with its activity" (*GA* II 3 736ᵇ28–29). The problem immediately arises of how what is without such a correlate can develop in a fetus as a result of movements in the *pneuma* contained in male seed:

> We must make clear whether that which is constituted in the female takes over anything from that which enters, or nothing; concerning soul, for example, in virtue of which it is called an animal, . . . whether it is present within the seed and the fetus or not, and where it comes from. . . . It is plain enough that seed

11. The generally accepted view is that ether is confined to the superlunary sphere.

and fetus have nutritive soul . . . but as they develop they also have the perceptual soul in virtue of which they are animal. For they do not become simultaneously animal and man, or animal and horse, and so on; for the end is the last thing to be produced, and the end of each animal's coming-to-be is what is special to it. That is why, where understanding is concerned, it is a very great puzzle as to when and how and from where it is acquired by those who share this starting-point, and we must try hard to grasp its solution according to our abilities and to the extent possible. (*GA* II 3 736ª27–ᵇ8)

Now psychological functions can be present as potentialities in seed or fetus in only a certain number of ways:

> [1] Either they must all be produced in the menses without existing there beforehand, or they must all preexist, or some must, but not others; and [2] they must be produced in the matter [that is, the menses] either without having entered in the male's seed, or having come from there; and [3] in the male they must either all be produced [in the seed] from outside it, or none from outside, or some but not others. That they cannot all be present beforehand is clear from the following. [4] All starting-points whose activity is bodily are clearly unable to be present without body (for example, walking without feet). [5] And hence they cannot enter [the seed] from outside. For they can neither enter by themselves, not being separate, nor enter in as the starting-points of an already formed body; for the seed is a residue produced by a change in the nutriment. [6] It remains then that understanding alone enters additionally from outside and alone is divine; for bodily activity is in no way associated with its activity. (*GA* II 3 736ᵇ15–29)

[1] concerns the menses and what it contributes to the fetus; [2] concerns the seed and what it contributes; and [3] concerns the male progenitor and what he contributes to the seed. For the line of descent, as we know, is from formative movements in the *pneuma* contained in the male progenitor's blood to his seed, from seed to menses, and so to fetus. [4] restricts our attention to starting-points of psychological functions whose active varieties are bodily, in that they require bodily organs, as walking requires feet and seeing requires eyes. [5] tells us the two conditions under which these could enter something "from the outside." This signals, as [3] makes clear, that the something in question is the male seed. [5] then shows that the starting-points cannot meet either of the conditions: they cannot enter by themselves, apart from body, because they are not separate from it; they cannot enter the body of the seed as the starting-points of an already formed body, because seed, as a residue produced by nutriment, doesn't contain things like

feet and other bodily parts. On the other hand, [6] because bodily activity is in no way associated with the activity of understanding, understanding does enter the male seed from outside.

Just how understanding manages to do this is left unexplained. All that we are told is that in embryogenesis it is transmitted along with the seed yet separate from it: "Consider now the body of the seed, in and with which is emitted the starting-point of soul, part of which is separate from the body and belongs to those beings in which something divine is included (and this is what is called understanding), while the other is not separate from the body" (*GA* II 3 737^{a}7–11). As a result of being transmitted in this way, it "seems to be born in us as a sort of substance, and not to pass-away. . . . Understanding and contemplation are extinguished because something else within passes-away, but it itself is unaffected" (*DA* I 4 408^{b}18–25). Moreover, it is "in substance an activity," and so is not "sometimes understanding and at other times not," but rather of all the constituents in the human soul "it alone is immortal and eternal" (*DA* III 5 430^{a}18–23). These characteristics, especially when combined with the way understanding operates in such celestial animals as the primary heaven, make it reasonable to suppose that understanding is transmitted along with the male seed as movements in ether that code for it. The following description of ether makes the supposition all but certain:

It is reasonable to assume that ether is ingenerable, imperishable, and incapable of growth or alteration, because everything that comes-to-be does so from a contrary and some underlying subject into a contrary by the action of a contrary, as we said in our initial accounts [in *Ph.* I 7–9]. The movements of contraries, however, are contraries. So if there cannot be a contrary to this body, because there cannot even be a movement contrary to movement in a circle, nature seems to have rightly exempted what was to be ingenerable and imperishable from contraries, since it is in contrary things that generation and perishing occur. Again, everything that grows does so as a result of something of the same kind being added to it and dissolving into matter. There isn't anything, however, from which ether comes-to-be. Yet if it is nongrowing and imperishable, the same line of thought leads us to suppose that is also inalterable. For alteration is change with respect to quality, and qualitative states and dispositions, such as health and disease, do not come-to-be without changes in affection. All natural [sublunary] bodies, however, that change with respect to an affection admit, we see, of growth and decrease. . . . Hence if the body that moves in a circle cannot admit of growth or decrease, it is reasonable to suppose that it is also inalterable. (*Cael.* I 3 270^{a}12–35)

Were understanding coded for by anything other than the circular movements in ether, it could not itself be immortal, eternal, or ever active.

If the direction of the circular movement of the ether transmitted along with the male seed were a matter of indifference, the story of understanding's transmission might end at this point. But because nature always acts for the best, that direction is as important in embryogenesis as it is in explaining the primary heaven's forward movement. That is why Aristotle assigns a role in embryogenesis to the heavenly bodies, especially the sun: "Man owes his coming-to-be to man and the sun" (*Ph.* II 2 194^{b}13); "The cause of a man is his constituents, namely, fire and earth (say) as matter, and the form special to him, and the external cause whatever it is, for example, the father, and besides these, the sun and its inclined circular course, which are not matter, form, or privation, or of the same species as man, but moving [or efficient] causes" (*Met.* XII 1071^{a}13–17; also *GC* II 10 336^{a}31–337^{a}15). Just as ether's forward circular movement causes movements in male seed, so the primary heaven's forward circular movement affects all the other heavenly bodies, including the sphere of the sun, which, in turn, affect the coming-to-be and passing away of sublunary beings (*GC* II 11–12).

Automata

In a number of different contexts, Aristotle appeals to the notion of a mechanical automaton. One such context, which is in *De Mundo*, a work generally considered to be dubiously attributable to him,[12] is cosmic or theological:

> God needs no contrivance or the service of others, in the way that rulers among us need many helping hands because of their weakness. Indeed, this is what is most divine, to be able to accomplish multifarious kinds of things with ease and by a simple movement, just as consummate craftsmen, using as their instrument a single release mechanism, accomplish many different operations. (*Mu.* 6 398^{b}10–16; compare *Met.* I 2 983^{a}12–21)

Here the analogue of the consummate craftsman is God, who is the prime mover, and the analogue of the simple release mechanism is the primary heaven, which by being moved in a single forward circular movement produces all other cosmic movements, because of the way the internal parts

---

12. Many of the grounds for doubt are skeptically examined in Jonathan Barnes, review of Giovanni Reale, *Aristotele: Trattato sul Cosmo per Alessandro* (Naples: Loffredo, 1974), *Classical Review* 27 (1977): 40–43.

of the cosmos are connected and arranged. But unlike in the automaton, where the release mechanism is tripped or triggered at a particular moment, God's influence on the primary heaven is eternal, never beginning and never ending.

A second context is embryological, and the question under discussion is whether the parts of an animal offspring can be made by something external to the male seed:

> In a way they can, and in a way they cannot. Now, whether we're talking about the seed, or that from which the seed comes, makes no difference, insofar as the seed has within it the movement initiated by the one from which it comes. It is possible, then, that A should move B and B move C, as happens in those amazing automata. For the parts of such automata, even while at rest, somehow have a potentiality to move, and when some external mover sets the first part in movement the adjacent part immediately comes to be moving in actuality. As, then, in the case of these automata the external mover is in a way moving them, namely, not by touching any part of them now, but by having touched one previously, so it is in the case of that from which the seed came (or that which produced the seed), it moves not by touching still but by having once touched. In another way, however, it is the internal movement that does this, as the activity of building builds the house. (GA II 1 734^{b}9–17; also II 5 741^{b}5–24)

Here the analog of the automaton's external mover, the one who triggers its release mechanism, is the male progenitor. For his *pneuma*-imbued seed and the ether that accompanies it set the menses moving by transmitting formative movements to it, so that it then continues moving because of its own internal structure, and without needing to be in contact with him.

A final context in which the analogy with automata is employed is in explaining the movement of animals:

> The movement of animals is like that of automata, which are set moving when a small movement occurs: the strings are released and the pegs strike against one another. . . . For animals have instrumental parts that are of the same kind as these, namely, sinews and bones; when these are relaxed or loosened movement occurs. . . . In an animal, however, [unlike in an automaton] the same part has the potentiality to become both larger and smaller and to change its shape, as the parts expand because of heat, contract again because of cold, and undergo alteration. Alteration, however, is caused by appearances, sense perceptions, and intelligible objects. For sense perceptions are an immediate kind of alteration, and appearances and intelligible objects have the power of the things themselves [that gave rise to them]. For in a way the intelligible form of the pleasant or painful is like the thing itself. That is why

we shudder and are frightened because of understanding on its own. All these are affections and alterations; and when things in the body are altered, some become larger and some smaller. And it is not hard to see that a small change occurring in a starting-point produces great and numerous changes at a distance from it—just as by shifting the rudder a hair's breadth you get a large shift at the prow. Besides, when under the influence of heat or cold or some other similar affection, an alteration is produced in the region of the heart, even in an imperceptibly small part of it, it produces a large difference in the body—blushing, for example, or turning white, as well as shuddering, trembling, and their opposites. (*MA* 7 701^{b}1–32)

What enables bodily parts, but not parts of automata, to become larger or smaller is the presence of *pneuma*, which is a constituent of the blood, and has its origin in the heart. When we perceive, imagine, or understand something pleasant or in some other way good, therefore, small motions that code for it—that transmit its perceptual or intelligible form—are produced in the relevant part of the soul, whether sense organ, imagination, or understanding. From there they are transmitted to other parts of the soul, such as the desiring part, where they trigger movements of the sinews and joints that are relevantly like those produced in automata by the small movement of the release mechanism that sets them moving:

All movement involves three things, the mover, second, that by means of which it moves, and third the thing moved. And the mover is twofold, the unmoved one, and the one that moves and is moved. The one that is unmoved is the good done in action, and the one that moves and is moved is the desiring part (for the mover is moved insofar as it desires, and active desiring is a sort of movement), while the thing moved is the animal; and the instrument by which desire moves is then a bodily one. (*DA* III 10 433^{b}13–19)

That the good done in action is an unmoved mover is something to bear in mind.

In a sentence in the *De Anima* that has caused much controversy, because it seems incompatible with the overall hylomorphic account of the soul as the form of a natural body developed there, Aristotle turns not this time to rudders but to entire ships: "Moreover, it is not clear whether the soul is the actualization of the body in the way that a sailor is of the ship" (*DA* II 1 413^{a}8–9). A ship typically has many sailors, of course, organized to perform in harmony the various functions involved in sailing it, including steering it by imparting small movements to the rudder. Collectively, these sailors transform the "dead" ship, incapable of autonomous sailing, into a functional ship, possessed of the second potentiality (or first actualization) to sail. The collective organization of the sailors is the "animating" form of the functional ship, the analogue of the soul considered as the form of the body. The dead "ship" is not the analogue of the *pneuma*-imbued living body, then, but of the menses or the unmoving automaton. The sailors performing their various functions in harmony are like the various functioning parts of the living body, which are jointly organized to work in harmony together. Yet for the body to do anything, as for the ship to sail, something has to actualize its potentiality to do it. In the case of the soul, what does this is some visible or intelligible object coming into contact with the relevant instrumental part of the soul. It is this that sets up small movements in it, which code for, because they are formally identical to, the form of the object itself, and which, when transmitted by the *pneuma* in the blood through the action of the heart, set the whole animal moving in the appropriate way (*MA* 8 701ª33–34).

The thrust of Aristotle's use of automata, then, is threefold. First, the movement that sets them going can be very small and simple. Second, what enables this small movement to produce the many complex movements of the automaton itself is the automaton's inner organization. Third, the initiator of the small movement doesn't have to do anything else to keep the automaton in complex movement. By appealing this time to the analogy with a city, Aristotle makes this point again:

> We should consider the constitution of an animal as being like a city well-governed by laws. For once order (*taxis*) is established in a city, there is no need of a separate monarch to preside over each thing that happens, rather each individual does his own task as the order prescribes, and one thing follows another because of habit. In animals, the same thing happens because of nature, and because each part of them, since they are so constituted, is naturally suited to perform its own function. Hence there is no need of a [separate] soul in each part, but rather, because it is in some starting-point of the body [namely, the heart], the other parts live because they are naturally attached to it, and perform their own function because of nature. (*MA* 10 703ª29–ᵇ2)

As in the earlier analogy of the soul to the sailor of a ship, there is no conflict here with the picture of the soul as the form of the body, since it is blood-borne *pneuma*, with its internal formative motions, that is responsible for the vitalizing ensouling of the body as a whole. As a result, it is by being connected to the heart, which is the source of the *pneuma*, and not by having independent, disconnected souls of their own, that the various other parts of the body are vitalized and vitally linked. Pneuma, then, is the string that links the parts, in the way that a string can link the parts of a puppet, so that puppeteers can make "the neck, hand, shoulder, eye, and sometimes all the parts of the puppet move with a certain harmony" by "pulling a single string" (*Mu.* 6 398^{b}16–19).

In characterizing the relationship of the good to the "nature of the whole" universe, Aristotle has recourse to a closely related analogy:

> We must also consider in which way the nature of the universe as whole (*hê tou holou phusis*) possesses the good and the best—whether as something separate and intrinsic, or as its organization (*taxis*). Or is it rather in both ways just like an army? For the good of an army is in its organization and is also the general. And more so the latter, since he does not exist because of the organization, but it does exist because of him. All things (even swimming creatures, flying creatures, and plants) are jointly organized, though not in the same way, and are not of such a character that one thing has no relation to another. Instead, there is one, since all things are jointly organized in relation to one thing. . . . I mean, for example, that each of them must at least come to be dissolved [into its elements]; and similarly there are other things which they all share for the sake of the whole. . . . The beings, however, must not be governed badly. "The rule of many is not good; let there be one ruler."[13] (*Met.* XII 10 1075^{a}11–1076^{a}4)

As with an automaton or a city, an army has an organization or structure, and a ruler or general. The general gives orders to the second in command, and so on down the line. For this to be possible, information must flow down from the general to all the soldiers. That is to say, forms present in his understanding and coded for by formative movements in ether and in his blood-borne *pneuma* must be transmitted from him to them via all the intermediaries, all the analogues of the parts of the human body. As in the body, it is the presence of ether and *pneuma* in these intermediaries—it is the cosmic equivalent of the bloodstream—that makes this possible. Just as the possession of such a bloodstream gives one soul rather than many to a sublunary animal, it seems likely that the same is true of the universe, whose nature would, therefore, just be that soul.[14] Neither what gets transmitted

13. Homer, *Iliad* II 204. Odysseus is arguing that the Achaians should have one commander-in-chief, just as the universe does.

14. This is the view, most notably, of David Sedley, "*Metaphysics* Λ 10," in *Aristotle's Metaphysics Lambda*, ed. Michael Frede and David Charles (Oxford: Clarendon Press, 2000), pp. 327–350. Others—for example, Mariska Leunissen, *Explanation and Teleology in Aristotle's Science of Nature* (Cambridge: Cambridge University Press, 2010), pp. 45–47—see the nature of the whole as simply supervenient on (or emergent from) the natures of various constituents of the universe.

nor the organization of the parts would be good, however, unless—to put it in these terms—the ether involved were caused to move in the good or forward direction by God as prime mover. It is because he is good—indeed, *the* good—that the organization of the nature of the whole is good.

"What is the starting-point of movement in the soul?" Aristotle asks. The answer, he replies, is clear: "Just as in the whole it is God, so it is too in us. For the divine constituent in us [that is, understanding] in a way does all the moving. Of reason, however, the starting-point isn't reason, but something superior. But what besides God is superior to [reason, that is, to] both scientific knowledge and understanding, since virtue [of character] is an instrument of understanding?" (*EE* VIII 2 1248ª25–29). As the universe owes its movement to God, so our understanding owes its movement to the same source. Animals, to repeat, whether cosmic or sublunary, all have their movements—formative and otherwise—explained in the same way.

2

TRUTH, ACTION, AND SOUL

"Three things in the soul control action and truth—perception, under-standing, and desire" (*NE* VI 2 1139ª17–18). The goal of this chapter is to begin decoding this laconic sentence by exploring Aristotle's account of perception, understanding, and desire—a task that will also occupy Chapters 3, 4 and 5. In Chapter 1, our approach to these was from beneath, since we were looking at the more or less material processes that coded for them, enabling them to be transmitted in embryogenesis, and at the sorts of changes in those processes that occur when the potentialities are actualized by perceptible or intelligible objects. In this chapter, we switch perspectives. Our focus, as in *De Anima* and the short treatises, such as *On Sense and Sensibilia*, associated with it, will be on desire, perception, and understand-ing themselves (*DA* I 1). In Chapter 3, we will be looking at the bodies of scientific knowledge they enable us to develop, and in Chapters 4 and 5 at their roles in practical enterprises, such as ethics and politics.

Desire

Characteristic of animal souls is the possession of two potentialities, which must occur together (*DA* II 2 413ᵇ23–24), one "to discern things and the other to cause movement with respect to place" (*DA* III 9 432ª15–17). The potentiality for discernment is due, first, to the possession of a "perceptual part" (*aisthêtikon*) (*DA* III 9 432ª30), responsible for perception proper and various other functions, such as imagination. In human beings, this part consists of the *primary perceptual part,* located in the heart, as well as the various special senses—sight, smell, hearing, taste, touch—and the com-mon sense. The part responsible for movement is the desiring part (*orek-tikon*). It consists of appetites, such as hunger and thirst, as well as other desires and emotions of various sorts, which cause movement or action by being modes of receptivity or responsiveness to aspects of reality discerned as pleasant or painful or, in some other way, good or bad, end-furthering or end-frustrating (*DA* III 7 431^{b}8–10). Finally, the human soul also contains a rational part, comprising the scientific part (*epistêmonikon*) and the calculative (*logistikon*) or deliberative (*bouleutikon*) one (*NE* VI 1 1139^{a}5–15), as well as the understanding, which, as responsible for knowledge of scientific and deliberative starting-points (*NE* VI 6 1141^{a}7–8), is involved in both of them.

While the desiring part of the soul is responsible for causing movement with respect to place, it does not do so without help from the perceptual part, in the shape of imagination, or from the rational one, in the shape of deliberation (*DA* III 9 432^{b}15–16, 433^{a}6–9). The very presence of rational parts in the soul raises a puzzle, however, about the desiring part. The deliberative subpart of the rational part of the soul can oppose appetite and cause action or movement that frustrates it (*NE* I 13 1102^{b}13–25). Hence it must contain a desire of some sort to do the opposing. This desire is wish (*boulêsis*; *DA* III 10 433^{a}23). At the same time, to "break up" the *orektikon* into separate parts is absurd (*DA* III 9 432^{b}4–6). Yet this is what now seems to have occurred, since wish is in the deliberative part of the soul, not the desiring one (*Top.* IV 5 126^{a}13).

The proposed solution is to treat the desiring part as one not in number, but "in species" (*Met.* V 6 1016^{b}33), in that a single account or definition applies to all its members:

> Since desires arise that are opposed to one another, as happens when reason and appetites are opposed, which takes place in those that have a perception of time (for the understanding commands us to hold back on account of the future, while our appetites command on account of what is immediately available; for what is immediately pleasant seems both unconditionally pleasant and unconditionally good because we do not see the future), it follows that what produces movement, that is, the desiring part qua desiring part, must be one in species . . . , although the things that produce movement are in number many. (*DA* III 10 433^{b}5–13)

What this solution leaves unclear is why wish was excluded from the *orektikon* in the first place, since if the *orektikon* is one only *in species*, conflicts cannot pose any threat to the weaker sort of unity it has. What has presumably happened is this. Wish is excluded from the animal *orektikon*, which is a numerical unity, and is as much a part of the nonhuman animal soul as of the human, but is included in the more loosely unified *orektikon* found only in the human soul. In one sense, then, the *orektikon* is a numerical unity, and Aristotle thinks of it as such, while in another it isn't, so that he thinks of it as being one only in species.

One reason for excluding wish from the animal *orektikon* and including it in the calculative part of the soul has to do with its intentional objects, and the distinctive way in which these are constructed or presented to the mind:

> In so far as an animal has a desiring part, so far is it capable of moving itself. A desiring part, however, cannot exist without an imagination,[1] and all imagination is either calculative or perceptual. . . . Perceptual imagination the other animals have too . . . , but the deliberative sort exists [only] in those with calculative parts. For when one comes to whether to do this or that one at the same time comes to a task for calculation. And one must measure by a single [standard], since one is pursuing the greater [good]. And so one must be able to make out of many appearances a single one . . . the one resulting from a syllogism. (*DA* III 10–11 433ᵇ27–434ᵃ11; also *MA* 7 701ᵃ10–11)

Because its intentional objects are constructed syllogistically, wish is a "desire involving calculation" (*Rh.* I 10 1369ᵃ2), so that whenever "movement is produced in accord with calculation it is also in accord with wish" (*DA* III 10 433ᵃ23–25). Since deliberation is a type of calculation (*NE* VI 1 1139ᵃ12–13), the "desire involving deliberation" that constitutes deliberate choice is wish (*NE* III 3 1113ᵃ10–12).

Besides its distinctive location in the calculative part of the soul and its distinctive relation to calculation and deliberation, wish is also distinctive in being the sort of desire we have for happiness or the good, or what appears to us as such (*Met.* XII 7 1072ᵃ28, *NE* III 4 1113ᵃ22–33). We wish for the end or target, we "deliberate about and deliberately choose what furthers it" (*NE* III 5 1113ᵇ3–4). Deliberate choice (*prohairesis*) is thus a matter of choosing (*haireisthai*) one thing before or in preference to (*pro*) another (*NE* III 2 1112ᵃ16–17), and so of deliberating about what things should be done *earlier than* or *in preference to* others to further the desired end:

---

1. Sometimes perception, even without imagination, seems to be all the desiring part requires. If living things have "a perceptual part, they also have a desiring part" (*DA* II 3 414ᵇ1–2); "perception is invariably present [in animals], but not imagination" (*DA* III 3 428ᵃ8–9); "many animals have perception, but are stationary and unmoving throughout their lives" (*DA* III 9 432ᵇ19–21); also *Ph.* VIII 7 261ᵃ15–17, *PA* IV 7 683ᵇ9–10. Hendrik Lorenz, *The Brute Within* (Oxford: Clarendon Press, 2006), pp. 138–147, discusses.

"someone with understanding chooses the better of two things in all cases" (*EE* VII 2 1237ᵇ37–38).

A second reason for not locating wish in the animal *orektikon* is that the rational part of the soul would not otherwise be capable of causing action— since without desire of some sort, it cannot do so (*NE* VI 2 1139ᵃ35–36). This would make continence (self-control) and incontinence (weakness of will) difficult to explain, since they seem to presuppose a motivational conflict between appetite and rational part, which the latter can either lose (incontinence) or win (continence). It is by appeal to such conflict, in any case, that the nonrational *orektikon* is distinguished from a rational part already conceived as a source of motivational impulses:

> Another natural constituent in the soul [besides the nutritive part] would also seem to be nonrational, though it shares in reason in a way. For we praise the reason of the continent and incontinent, that is to say, the part of the soul that has reason, because it exhorts them correctly toward what is best; but evidently they also have within them another natural constituent besides reason, which conflicts with and resists it. For just as paralyzed limbs move off to the left when their owners decide to move them to the right, so it is in the case of the soul, since the impulses of incontinent people are contrary to each other. In the case of the body, however, we see the part that is moving wrongly, whereas we do not see it in the case of the soul. But presumably we should suppose that the soul too there is something besides reason, opposing it and going against it. (*NE* I 13 1102ᵇ13–25)

With wish located in the rational part, the way is clear to recognizing a type of *reason* that is distinctively practical, and a virtue that is related to both thought and action—namely, practical wisdom.

Perception

In blooded animals, the perceptual system is part of (or piggybacks on) the digestive system, the senses being set on channels connected to small blood vessels around the brain, which are connected to the heart by larger vessels in the neck.[2] The heart, as a result, not the brain, is the locus of the "pri-

---

2. My account of the perceptual system and its workings has benefited from David Charles, *Aristotle on Meaning and Essence* (Oxford: Oxford University Press, 2001), especially pp. 110–129, Pavel Gregoric, *Aristotle on the Common Sense* (Oxford: Clarendon Press, 2007).), and Thomas K. Johansen, *Aristotle on the Sense Organs* (Cambridge: Cambridge University Press, 1998).

mary perceptual part" (*Somn.* 1 454ᵃ22–24). Where there is perception, however, there is "both pleasure and pain, and where these, there is necessarily appetite" (*DA* II 2 413ᵇ23–24). Hence the heart is also the locus of pleasure and pain (*PA* III 4 666ᵃ11–13), and of the animal movement to which appetite gives rise:

> The potentialities for perception, movement, and nutrition in animals are in the same part of the body, hence . . . there must be a primary part with starting-points such as these. And insofar as it is receptive of all the perceptibles, it must be one of the simple [that is, uniform] parts, while insofar as it initiates movement and action, it must also be one of the nonuniform ones. It is because of this, indeed, that in blooded animals the heart is such a part, and in bloodless ones its analogue. (*PA* II 1 647ᵃ24–31)

In human beings, the perceptual part consists of the primary perceptual part, which is divided in its functioning between perception proper and imagination. Thus sleeping and waking are both affections relating to perception by the primary perceptual part, whereas dreaming "is the function of the perceptual part, that is, of it qua imaginative part (*phantastikon*)" (*Insomn.* 1 459ᵃ21–22), since the senses are inactive during sleep, but the imagination isn't (*NE* I 13 1102ᵇ6–11). Perception proper encompasses the special senses (sight, smell, hearing, taste, and touch), whose primary objects are *proper perceptibles*, such as colors, odors, sounds, and so on, which only a single sense can detect. In addition, the perceptual part includes the common sense (*DA* III 7 431ᵇ5, *Mem.* 1 450ᵃ10–11). It is responsible for the simultaneous perception of two or more proper perceptibles in a single act, the perception of two or more proper perceptibles as distinct, the control of waking up the special senses or letting them sleep (*Somn.* 2 455ᵃ12–26), the awareness of the activity or inactivity of the various special senses (*DA* III 2 425ᵇ12–25), and perhaps also the perception of common perceptibles (*koina aisthêta*), which are features accessible to more than one sense, such as change, rest, shape, size, number, unity, and perhaps others (*DA* III 1 425ᵃ14–20). The sphere of perception, therefore, and the one in which it has control and does the discerning, is that of particulars (*kath' hekasta*), which are perceptible because they possess attributes that are special or common perceptibles (*NE* II 9 1109ᵇ22–23, VII 3 1147ᵃ26).

Aristotle's account of perception, as indeed of thought and understanding, is dominated by the idea of the transmission of form through imprinting—of something like wax taking on something like the impression of a seal or signet ring: "We should take it as a general truth about all perception that a sense is what can receive perceptible forms without their matter, just as wax receives the imprint of the ring without the iron or gold" (*DA* II 12 424ᵃ17–20). Since sight is "perception par excellence" (*DA* III 3 429ᵃ2–3), we shall focus on it, only occasionally referring to the other senses.

As with any psychological faculty or potentiality, sight must be explained in terms of its characteristic activity (seeing), and so of the proper perceptible object (color), which alone actualizes it (*DA* II 4 415ᵃ14–22). For potentialities are explained by what actualizes them, effects by their causes (*Met.* IV 5 1010ᵇ35–1011ᵃ2). What is directly affected by color is the eye, the organ or instrument of sight, whose form is seeing and whose matter is eye-jelly (*korê*): "seeing . . . is the eye's substance, that which corresponds to its account," and an eye is "the eye-jelly plus sight, [just as] an animal is soul plus body" (*DA* II 1 412ᵇ18–413ᵃ3). The effect color has on the eye-jelly—which is the part of the eye specifically affected by it (*Sens.* 2 438ᵇ16)—is determined by its nature, which is determined by its relation to light, whose own nature is determined, in turn, by its relation to transparency:

> What is visible is color, and it is on top of what is intrinsically visible—intrinsically visible not in account, but because it has in itself the cause of its own visibility. Every color has the potentiality to produce a change in what is in actuality transparent—that is the nature of color. For this reason it is not visible without light, rather the color of each thing is seen only in light. Hence we must first say what light is. Now there is, surely, something transparent. And I call transparent what is visible—not intrinsically and unconditionally visible, but visible because of the color of something else. Of this sort are air, water, and many solid bodies. For it is not qua water or air that these are transparent, but because there exists in them a certain nature, which is the same in both of them and in the eternal body above. Light is the actualization of this—of what is transparent qua transparent. And wherever this is, in potentiality there is dark also. Light is a sort of color of what is transparent, when it is made in actuality transparent by fire or something such as the body above. (*DA* II 7 418ᵃ29–ᵇ13)

The certain nature referred to, which is present in all transparent things, is *pneuma*. It is also present "in all other bodies to a greater or lesser degree" (*Sens.* 3 439ᵃ24–25). That is why opaque objects can be colored. For color just is the surface envelope that such *pneuma* acquires by being in a bounded body:

> The nature of light is to be in what is transparent as indefinite. But it is clear that what is transparent in bodies must have an ultimate boundary, and it is

evident from the facts that this is color. . . . For color is *in* the limit of the body, but is not a limit *of* the body, rather we must suppose that the same nature that, when existing outside, is colored also exists inside. So both air and water are plainly colored; for their sheen is such. . . . Hence color is the limit of what is transparent in a body with a well defined boundary. (*Sens.* 3 439ᵃ26–ᵇ12)

The very same thing that is dark or light when in an indefinite or unbounded transparent mass, then, is black or white when it is the limit of a bounded one (*Sens.* 3 439ᵇ14–18). Hence the surface of an object is white just in case the *pneuma* in it is illuminated (light) and is black when the *pneuma* is not-illuminated (dark), either because no light is present or because other sub-lunary matter occludes it, since the "same nature is sometimes dark and sometimes light" (*DA* II 7 418ᵇ31–419ᵃ1).

With white and black defined in terms of light and dark, other colors are defined in terms of them:

It is possible that the white and the black should be so juxtaposed that each is invisible because it is very small, but that what is composed of both is visible. This can appear neither as white nor as black. But since it must have some color, and cannot have either of these, it must be some kind of mixture, that is, some other kind of color. Such, then, is a possible way of conceiving of the existence of a plurality of colors besides white and black, but which are a plurality because of the ratio [of white to black that constitutes them]; for they [white and black] may be juxtaposed in the ratio 3:2 or 3:4, or in ratios express-ible by other numbers, or they may be in no numerically expressible ratio, but in some incommensurable relation of excess or deficiency. (*Sens.* 3 439ᵇ19–30)

For the surface of an object to be colored, therefore, is just for the transpar-ent material within it to be dark (unactualized) or light (actualized) in the appropriate way. While the form of a color is some pattern of black and white, its matter is this dark or light transparent material.

"To have the potentiality to cause a movement in what is in actuality transparent is just what it is to be a color. . . . Color causes a movement in what is transparent, for example, the air, and the sense organ is moved in turn by this when it extends continuously [from the colored object to the organ]" (*DA* II 7 419ᵃ9–15). In transparent eye-jelly, this movement results in its taking on the visible form of the color without its matter. Thus the eye-jelly takes on a pattern of black and white similar to the one present in the colored surface that is being seen, but without the corresponding dark and light material that is in the body itself. More precisely, that is what the *surface* of the eye-jelly takes on because the transparent *pneuma* in its interior takes on the corresponding pattern of dark and light.

The reason eye-jelly must be transparent, then, is that it must be able to take on patterns of dark and light in order for the eye to discern colors. For if eye-jelly is to be able to take on any arbitrary pattern of dark and light corresponding to a color, it must be in a mean or intermediate condition between dark and light. And this is the condition transparent material is in, since it is light when illuminated and dark otherwise:

> [A sense] is a sort of mean between the opposites present in perceptible objects. That is why it discerns objects of perception. For the mean is capable of discerning, since it becomes to each extreme in turn the opposite extreme. And just as what is to perceive white and black must be neither of them in actuality, although both in potentiality (and similarly too for the other senses), so in the case of touch that which is to perceive hot and cold must be neither. (*DA* II 11 424ª5–10; also III 2 426ª27–ᵇ7)

The "similarity or kinship" between the transparent material in eye-jelly and that in all colored objects is thus what enables the one to know or discern the other (*PA* II 1 647ª5–9).

By taking on a pattern of dark and light, the eye-jelly becomes in "a way colored" (*DA* III 2 425ᵇ22–23). Moreover, it can remain in this condition even when color itself is no longer being seen: "Each sense organ is receptive of the perceptible object without its matter. That is why perceptions and appearances remain in the sense organ even when the perceptible objects are gone" (*DA* III 2 425ᵇ23–25). There is no question of the eye-jelly's being colored simply because a color can be seen through it, as through a lens or windowpane. Rather, it is dark and light in the very same way as is the transparent material in the interior of a visible object.[3]

As the actualization of what is transparent qua transparent, light is present whenever a fiery body illuminates transparent material. The same applies to dark (since it is this transparent material unilluminated) and so to patterns of light and dark, black and white. Thus if there were no perceivers, there would be "neither perceptible objects nor perceptions, since they are affections of what can perceive, but that the things that underlie—the ones that produce the perceiving—should not exist without perception is

---

3. Contrast M. F. Burnyeat, "Is an Aristotelian Philosophy of Mind Still Credible?" in *Essays on Aristotle's De Anima*, ed. M. Nussbaum and A. Rorty (Oxford: Clarendon Press, 1992), pp. 15–26.

impossible" (*Met.* IV 5 1010^{b}35–1011^{a}2). When transparent material takes on the right pattern of dark and light, its surface takes on the corresponding pattern of black and white. As a result, it—or the determinately bounded object it is in—acquires the potentiality to be seen as red (say) by a person with an appropriately situated functioning eye. For such a person has from birth a correlative potentiality to see red when his eye-jelly is rendered in actuality transparent by fire or the sun, and an object with the correct pattern of black and white on its surface is appropriately situated in his visual field. Eye-jelly, in other words, is the matter required by an organ whose form is seeing, and its taking on a pattern of light and dark constitutes—but is not identical to—seeing a color.

Perception's Control of Truth

On this account of how perception operates, it might seem that—in the case of proper perceptibles, at least—the control of truth attributed to it must be almost absolute (*NE* VI 2 1139^{a}17–18). And we do find Aristotle claiming that: "By a proper perceptible I mean one that cannot be perceived by another sense and about which we cannot be in error. . . . Each sense is discerning about its proper perceptibles, at any rate, and does not make errors about whether there is color or whether there is sound, but rather about what the colored thing is or where it is, or what the thing making the sound is or where it is" (*DA* II 6 418^{a}11–16). But these confident claims presuppose that the senses are functioning properly in conditions that do not impede their achieving their end (*NE* VII 12 1153^{a}15). For people "do not perceive what is presented to their eyes, if they happen to be deep in thought, or afraid, or hearing a lot of noise" (*Sens.* 7 447^{a}15–17) and cannot perceive accurately what isn't presented at the right distance (*Sens.* 7 449^{a}21–24) or in the right way: "each thing is more readily perceptible when presented simply by itself than when mixed with others—for example, pure rather than unmixed wine, or honey, or a color, or a single rather than one in a chord—because they tend to obscure one another" (*Sens.* 7 447^{a}17–20).

In a discussion of pleasure, both sets of conditions are summed up:

Every sense is active in relation to its perceptible object, and completely active when the sense is in good condition in relation to the finest (*kalliston*) of the objects falling under (*hupo*) the sense (for this seems to be above all what complete activity consists in—whether it is the sense itself we say is active, or the subject in which it exists, makes no difference). In the case of each sense, then, the activity that is best is the one whose subject is in the best (*ariston*) condition in relation to the strongest (*kratiston*) of the objects falling under the sense. (*NE* X 4 1174ᵇ14–19)

Kalliston and *kratiston*, more specific in their connotation than the *ariston* used to characterize the state of the sense or the perceiving subject, suggest that the most perceptible objects possess both clarity and liveliness or forcefulness. The fact that they "fall under" the senses, like the subsequent use of "sights and sounds" as examples (*NE* X 4 1174ᵇ27–28), makes it plain that they are proper perceptibles.

Even when conditions of these sorts are met, room for error still remains. For "perceptions persist after the external perceptible object has gone" (*Insomn.* 2 460ᵇ2–4), with the result that things appear to us as they do "when the perceptible object produces the movement [in the sense], but also when the sense is moved by itself, provided it is moved in a similar way to the one in which the object falling under the sense moves it" (*Insomn.* 2 460ᵇ22–25). When, for example, we "have looked for a long time at a single color—such as white or green—any object to which we shift our gaze appears to be of that very color" (*Insomn.* 2 459ᵇ11–13). So we can be deceived even about whether the color is there in front of our eyes. It is presumably with such cases in mind that Aristotle modifies his bold claims about inerrancy. Perception of the proper perceptibles is "true or has the least possible degree of falsity" (*DA* III 3 428ᵇ18–19), at any rate, "while the perception is present" (*DA* III 3 428ᵇ27–28), that is to say, while the perceptible object continues to affect the sense in the right way.

What we typically perceive isn't one isolated proper perceptible, but an array of many different ones. This raises a problem Aristotle discusses in some detail. A single (act of) perception must have a single object at a single unified time, since that is just what makes it *one perception*. Thus it isn't possible to have "one perception of two things at the same time," since the perception "of one thing is itself one thing, and what is one thing occurs at the same time as itself" (*Sens.* 7 447ᵇ9–11). It seems to follow that we cannot see and taste the same thing simultaneously, and so cannot perceive that bile is "bitter and yellow" (*DA* III 1 425ᵇ1–2). Nonetheless, access to complexes of proper perceptibles *is* directly perceptual:

If then, as is in fact the case, the soul perceives sweet with one part and white with a different part, what is constituted of these parts is either one thing, or it isn't. But it must be one thing, since the perceptual part is one thing. What one object, then, is its perception of? For nothing constituted of those two [sweet, white] is one object. There must, therefore, be one part belonging to the soul, with which any proper perceptible is perceived . . . but each kind [of proper perceptible] by means of a different sense. Is it by being undivided as regards its activity, then, that the perceptual part, when its perception is of sweet and white, is one thing, but when it becomes divided in its activity, different ones? Or just as is possible with the things themselves, is it the case with the soul, too? For the same numerically one thing is white, sweet, and much more—even if its qualities are not separable from one another, each of them is different in being. The same, then, should be supposed to be the case with the soul—the perceptible part is numerically one and the same [when its perception is] of any [proper perceptible], but its being is different [when its perception is of different ones]—[when] of some things, different in genus, and [when] of others, different in species. So there can be simultaneous perception with a part that is one and the same, but not the same in account. (*Sens.* 7 449ª5–20)

When we see the yellow of the bile, while simultaneously tasting its bitterness, we do so by means of one part of the soul—the perceptual part. Because yellow and bitter differ in genus (one a color, the other a taste), the account we give of this part qua perceiving yellow will refer to one genus of it (sight), while the account we give of it qua perceiving bitter will refer to a different one (taste). If, instead, the perception were of a yellow and black wasp, the accounts of the perceptual part qua seeing yellow and qua seeing black would refer to different species (yellow, black) of the same genus (color).

The different senses are not numerically distinct parts of the perceptual part, then, but different aspects of its functioning, just as the different attributes of a single substance (the wasp, the bile) are different aspects of it—different in being, but not separate from it. Hence when we perceive bitter and yellow bile or a black and yellow wasp, we do not infer or construct the perceived object from the simple proper perceptibles involved but perceive it directly as one single thing by using two or more distinct senses simultaneously (*DA* III 1 425ª22–24, 425ª31–ᵇ1). Although Aristotle doesn't say that such perception cannot make errors, there is no reason to think that it is any more prone to them than the perception of simple proper perceptibles: a wasp's color isn't a confusion of black and yellow, after all, but a clear pattern of black and yellow stripes. Consequently, perception's control of truth should be the same in both cases.

As the objects to which "the substance or essence of each sense is naturally related," proper perceptibles are the most basic objects of perception—those on which the perception of other things depends (*DA* II 6 418ª24–25). They are not the only objects that are intrinsically perceptible, however, since common perceptibles, such as shape, that are accessible to more than one sense are also such: "Perceptible objects are spoken of in three ways; of these, two are said to be intrinsically perceptible, one coincidentally so. Of the two, one is special to each sense, the other common to all" (*DA* II 6 418ª8–11). Complexes of special and common perceptibles—of the sort presented by substantial particulars—are thus directly perceptible: no inference is required. Included among these are various universal forms of species or natural kinds:[4]

> The first things that are clear and perspicuous to us are above all inarticulate wholes. It is only later, when we make these distinct, that their constituents and starting-points become known. That is why we must advance from universals to particulars, for the whole is better known by perception, and the universal is a sort of whole, since it includes many things as parts. The same in a certain way holds of names in relation to definition. For a name such as "circle" signifies a sort of whole and does so indefinitely, whereas the definition [of a circle] makes the particular [parts of it] distinct. Indeed children first call all men "father" and all women "mother," only later coming to discern different ones of each. (*Ph.* I 1 184ª21–ᵇ14)

It is universal forms that are imprinted on the senses (as patterns of black and white are on the eye-jelly), not the hylomorphic particulars whose forms they are: "we perceive particulars, but perception is of universals—for example, of man and not of Callias the man" (*APo.* II 19 100ª16–ᵇ1). These forms are presented to the sense as wholes, because the task of articulating them—of defining them in terms of their constituents and explanatory starting-points—belongs to science, not perception. When we perceive Callias, the various special and common perceptibles constituting his perceptible form are imprinted on the various senses constituting our perceptible part, so that the structure of the one—a single subject possessed of various universal attributes—is mirrored in the structure of the other.

In his discussion of place (location), Aristotle claims that place "would not be a subject of inquiry if there were not movement with respect to place" (*Ph.* IV 4 211ª12–13). For we become aware of places by perceiving the replacement of one thing by another: "That there is such a thing as place seems clear from the fact of replacement, since where water exists now, there—when the water has gone out as from a vessel—air next exists, and

---

4. *DA* III 8 431ᵇ28–29 mentions the form of a stone.

at another time some other body occupies this same place" (*Ph.* IV 1 208^{b}1–4). Place, however, seems to be a common perceptible, since movement, which is a common perceptible, is change with respect to it. Presumably, it is by appeal to analogous considerations that movement is assigned a fundamental role in the perception of all common perceptibles:

> There cannot be any proper sense organ for the common perceptibles, the ones we perceive coincidentally by each sense[5]—such as, movement, rest, shape, size, number, and unity. For we perceive all these by perceiving movement. For example, we perceive magnitude by movement (and so also shape, since shape is a sort of magnitude), rest by the absence of movement, number by the absence of continuity, and by the proper perceptibles (since each perception perceives one thing). (*DA* III 1 425^{a}14–20)

In the case of place, the change or movement at issue is change in the object of perception. It is also the sort at issue in the case of continuity—anyway, of the sort possessed by the complexes of special and common perceptibles that constitute the perceptible forms of substances:

> Even more continuous is that which is a whole, and has a certain shape and form, especially if it is such by nature, and not by force (like things that are such by being glued or nailed or tied together), but has in itself the cause of its being continuous, and a thing is of this sort because its movement is one and indivisible in place and time. (*Met.* X 1 1052^{a}22–26)

Here the perceptual analogue of the substance's own cohesiveness and continuity of movement is the continuous multi-sense perception of it that constitutes our perceptual tracking of it though space and time. For the temporal unity of a single (act of) perception needn't be that of a temporal point but may be an extended period whose unity is (in part) determined by—or offloaded onto—that of its object: "that which is undivided not with respect to quantity, but in form, is understood in an undivided time and with an undivided part of the soul" (*DA* III 6 430^{b}14–15; also *Sens.* 7 448^{b}19–20). Perceptible forms, we may infer, are not static gestalts, or fixed arrays of special and common perceptibles, but dynamic unities, more akin to films than photographs. They are analogues, too, it is worth noting, of the forms existing in the agent's soul that give unity to his complex actions.

5. They are perceived noncoincidentally or intrinsically by the senses working collectively (*DA* III 1 425^{a}16, *Sens.* 4 442^{b}5–7).

The discussion of time, and our awareness of it, implies that change or movement internal to the soul also has a role to play in the perception of common perceptibles:

> Time does not exist without change; for when our own thoughts do not alter, or we do not notice them alter, it does not seem to us that time has passed. . . . So just as if the now were not different, but one and the same, there would be no time, in the same way even when the now is different but the difference isn't noticed, what is in between [the first now and the second one] does not seem to be any time. If, then, it happens that we do not think there is any time when we do not distinguish any change, but the soul seems to remain in one indivisible [state], but when we do perceive and distinguish a change, then we do say that some time has passed, it is evident that without movement and change time does not exist. (*Ph.* IV 11 218^{b}21–219^{a}2)[6]

In the case of number, indeed, both types of movement seem to figure as its sources (*DA* III 1 425^{a}14–20), one—the perceived absence of continuity—traces back to movement or change in the objects of perception, whereas the other appeals to the perceived change in the soul when what is one perceptual state (because it is the perception of one proper perceptible) is replaced by what is another (because it is the perception of a different proper perceptible).

When we perceive white, our perception is quite reliable, but when we perceive that the white thing "is this, or something else, error is possible" (*DA* III 3 428^{b}21–22). In these cases, the "this, or something else" is a *coincidental perceptible*, such as the son of Cleon, whom we perceive "not because he is the son of Cleon, but because he is white, and the white thing is coincidentally the son of Cleon" (*DA* III 1 425^{a}25–27). It is a person's perception of coincidental perceptibles that fear or some other appetite or feeling can distort, so that he "seems, even from a very slight resemblance, to see his enemy" (*Insomn.* 2 460^{b}6–7). Though errors of this sort are frequent, perception is less prone to make them about coincidental perceptibles than about common ones, since "it is most possible to be deceived by perception" where common perceptibles are concerned (*DA* III 3 428^{b}24–25).

While Aristotle doesn't elaborate on why this is so, the overall context makes the rationale fairly clear. The focus of the discussion is the imagina-

---

6. Discussed in Ursula Coope, *Time for Aristotle: Physics IV.10–14* (Oxford: Clarendon Press, 2005), pp. 37–41.

tion, and the deception at issue is the sort made possible, first, because imagination-based appearances can have the very same content as the perceptions that cause them. Second, because the perceptual part of the soul can operate in isolation from the rational part:

> Imagination is a movement that takes place as a result of the activity of perception . . . , and because its objects persist and are similar to perceptions, animals act largely in accord with them, some, such as beasts, because they lack understanding, and others, such as human beings, because their understanding is sometimes obscured by feeling, disease, or sleep. (*DA* III 3 429^{a}1–8; also 8 432^{a}9–10, 10 433^{a}9–10)

The resulting deception is, therefore, of two types, one occurring when the perceptible object is present to the senses, the other when it is absent (*DA* III 3 428^{b}27–29). When the perceptible object is a proper perceptible, no deception of the first type is possible: only an appearance of *white* sufficiently resembles a perception of white to lead the perceptual part to take it for such an appearance. Hence deception is possible only about the presence of the object to sight, not about its identity.

In the case of coincidental perceptibles and common perceptibles, both types of deception are possible, but there are important differences between them. Even when a white thing that is being perceived is the son of Cleon, neither the resulting perception nor the longer-lasting appearance may be precise enough to distinguish him from many other people. Nonetheless, when the perception or appearance *is* sufficiently detailed and precise it can, like an accurate portrait, provide a reliable basis for identification—although not, of course, when the object is "far away" (*DA* III 3 428^{b}29). In the case of common perceptibles, by contrast, even a very detailed and precise perception or appearance will not provide a reliable basis for discerning between sizes, shapes, numbers, and speeds, if they differ from one another in ways the senses alone, in isolation from the rational part, cannot detect. The point goes back to Plato:

> The same object, viewed from nearby, does not appear the same size, I presume, as when viewed from a distance. . . . And the same things appear bent and straight when seen in water or out of it, or concave and convex because sight is misled by colors, and every other similar sort of confusion is clearly present in our soul . . . And haven't measuring, counting, and weighing proved to be most welcome assistants in these cases, ensuring that what appears bigger or smaller or more numerous or heavier does not rule within us, but rather

what has calculated or measured or even weighed? . . . And that is the task of the soul's rational constituent? . . . [And it] believes in accord with the measurements. (*Republic* X 602d–603e)

Aristotle's thought is presumably similar. Perception's failure to control truth where common perceptibles are concerned is thus its failure to do so when operating in isolation from the rational (calculative) part of the soul, and the measuring instruments, calculating devices, and various sorts of scientific theories that cannot exist without it.

In human beings and in other animals, the fact that perception gives rise to imagination and appearances leads to various sorts of deception and error. That is the downside, as it were, of having an imagination. There is also a substantial upside. Appearances are crucial to memory, since they make up its contents (*Mem.* 1 451^{a}14–16); memory is crucial to induction and the development of scientific knowledge. They are also crucial to thought of all sorts, including understanding: "appearances serve as perceptions to the soul that involves thought (*dianoêtikê*)," since when "someone understands, he must simultaneously understand an appearance" (*DA* III 7 431^{a}14–16). Hence while the control that perception has of truth is limited, the *influence* it has extends to the very highest reaches of knowledge (*APr.* I 30 46^{a}17–22, *DA* III 8 432^{a}7–8). Once scientific knowledge has been acquired, moreover, its application in particular cases reinvolves perception, since we have to perceive that this particular thing is a *b* in order to know what the science of *b*s has to say about it. When the particular thing in question is an action to be done, the "perceptual knowledge" (*epistêmê aisthetikê*) of it, embodied in the minor or particular premise of a piece of deliberation, is deliberative perception, which is the sort that has "controls actions" (*NE* VII 3 1147^{b}9–17).

The form the eye-jelly takes on in any sort of perception is a universal, but what is perceived is the particular that has the form: "coincidentally sight sees the universal color, because this particular color which it sees is a color" (*Met.* XIII 10 1087^{a}19–21). Thus, in contrast to scientific knowledge, which is knowledge of universals, perception is the potentiality of the soul, which, by discerning and controlling particulars, gives us cognitive access to them and thereby to the universals we reach by induction from them (*APo.* I 18 81^{a}38–^{b}6).

Practical Perception

Although not a starting-point of deliberately chosen action (*NE* VI 2 1139^{a}19), perception is a starting-point of action in the broader sense of intentional animal movement or behavior. In this regard, a species of it that we may call *practical perception* is particularly important:

[1] Perceiving, then, is like bare announcing (*phanai monon*) and understanding (*noein*). [2] But when [the perceived object] is pleasant or painful, [the soul], as if asserting or denying (*hoion kataphasa ê apophasa*), pursues or avoids (*diôkei ê pheugei*) [the perceived object]. [3] In fact, to feel pleasure or pain is to be active with regard to the perceptual mean in relation to what is good or bad, as such. [4] Both aversion and desire are the same (*hê phugê kai hê orexis tauto*) as regards the activity, [5] and the desiring part or potentiality (*to orektikon*) and the aversive one (*to pheutikon*) are not different either from one another or from the perceptual one, although their being is different. (*DA* III 7 431ᵃ8–14)

When [1] we perceive a proper perceptible, as when we understand a form or essence, we announce its existence, as we announce a guest, as opposed to predicating something of it, as we do in assertion or denial (*Met.* IX 10 1051ᵇ24–25). When [2] what is perceived is pleasant or painful, the soul pursues or avoids it, as if asserting something or denying it, since "what assertion and denial are in the case of thought, that, in the case of desire, is precisely what pursuit and avoidance are" (*NE* VI 2 1139ᵃ21–22). What turns annunciation into assertion, then, isn't that now something is predicated of the perceptible object (for example, being pleasant) but that an action-causing or movement-causing desire is formed relative to it. It is to signal the arrival of this desire on the scene that two transformations occur in [4–5]. First, *diôkei* is replaced with *hê orexis*. Second, *pheugei* is replaced with *hê phugê*—where *pheugei* is the negative equivalent of *orexei* (that is, active avoiding) and *hê phugê* is the negative equivalent of *orexis* (that is, aversion). Hence in [5] *to pheutikon* is the aversive part or potentiality, as *to orektikon* is the desiring one. Since both are usually referred to as *to orektikon*, [5] points out that *to pheutikon* and *to orektikon* are the same, although their being is different, since one is desire considered as being for something, and the other is desire considered as being against something, or as an aversion to it.

What [4] says about desire and aversion is that they are the same "as regards the activity." This doesn't mean that active avoiding is the same as active pursuing, but that the actualization of the two potentialities is the same, in that they are actualized in the same way, namely, by pleasant or painful objects of perception. This point is reinforced by [5], which reminds us, as we saw, that the two potentialities are also the same, differing only in their being. The other point made in [5], following on [3], is that the perceptual part or potentiality, considered as or qua activated by a pleasant or painful object, is the same as the desiring or avoiding (aversive) one—again, differing from these only in its being. What this difference amounts to is explained in [1–2]. Considered as a kind of perception, practical perception or the perception of pleasure and pain is just annunciation; considered as practical (as directly giving rise to action or animal movement) it involves desire, and is the sort of assertion or denial that is pursuit or avoidance.

The perceptual mean mentioned in [3] is the constituent in a sense that functions like a laboratory balance or weighing scale enabling it to detect differences in proper perceptibles, which activate it by tilting it, as it were, one way or another (*DA* II 11 424^{a}5–10). Depending on the makeup of these perceptibles, the actualization of the sense is either pleasant or painful:

> If voice is a sort of consonance, and voice and hearing are in a way one, and in a way the same thing is not one,[7] and if consonance is a ratio, hearing must also be a sort of ratio. And it is because of this that excess destroys each one, as excess of either the sharp or the flat destroys hearing—similarly, excess in flavors destroys taste, colors that are too bright or too dark destroy sight, and a too strong odor, whether sweet or bitter, destroys smell, since the sense is a sort of ratio. It is also because of this that proper perceptibles are pleasant as well, when brought pure and unmixed to the ratio, for example, acid, sweet, or salt, for they are pleasant then. Generally, though, a mixture, a consonance, is more pleasant than either sharp or flat. The sense and the ratio are the same; whereas excess is painful or destructive. (*DA* III 2 426^{a}27–^{b}7 also *Sens.* 4 442^{a}16–17, 5 443^{b}11–444^{a}3)

The perception of a proper perceptible is pleasant, provided it is within the limits determined by—or consonant with—the structural ratio of the sense (and is painful otherwise). More precisely, since a sense functions better within some areas of its range of operation than others, so that we see better in brighter light than in dimmer, perception is pleasant in the optimal range, the range of *maximal* consonance (*NE* X 4 1174^{b}14–19). What actualizes the sense is the proper perceptible, such as a sweet or salt flavor. And the feature of it that makes that actualization pleasant—the relevant good-making feature—is that it is maximally consonant with the ratio that defines or is the sense. [3] alerts us to the fact that it is when a sense is activated by a perceptible object with this feature that its being activated constitutes

---

7. "The activity of the perceptible object and of the sense is one and the same, although their being is not the same" (*DA* III 2 425^{b}26–27).

feeling pleasure, or, when the object is discordant with the sense's defining ratio, feeling pain. At the same time, [3] reminds us that what is being said about pleasure and pain applies also to good and bad generally. For pleasure "accompanies every object of choice" (*NE* II 3 1104[b]35) and so is woven into every good, as pain into every bad.

The account of practical perception in [1–5] applies to animal action and movement generally, not just to deliberately chosen action, so that there is a certain *suggestio falsi* in calling it *practical* perception. Nonetheless, there is an advantage to using the same term for both, since it preserves an important continuity between animal and human perception. When the animal in question is a human being possessed of understanding, in any case, the account doesn't stop at [5]:

[6] To the understanding soul appearances (*phantasmata*) are like sense-perceptions (*aisthêmata*). And when it asserts (*phêsê[i]*) or denies (*apophêsê[i]*) good or bad, it avoids or pursues, because the soul never understands without an appearance. [7] Just as the air made the eye-jelly such-and-such, and it in turn something else, and hearing likewise, the last thing is one, and a single mean, but its being is manifold. What the thing is by which it discerns that sweet and hot differ has been stated before, but we should also say the following. It is indeed one thing, but in the way a limit is, and, since they are one by analogy and in number, it is with respect to each of them as they are with respect to each other. . . . [8] The part that understands, then, understands the forms in the appearances (*eidê . . . en tois phantasmasi*), and, as in the previous cases, what is to be pursued or avoided is distinguished for it, and so, even outside of perception, when it is dealing with appearances, it is moved to pursuit or avoidance. For example, [9] perceiving the beacon that is a fire, by the common sense, seeing it moving, it recognizes that it is the enemy, [10] but sometimes, by means of the appearances or intelligible objects that are in the soul, it calculates and deliberates about future things on the basis of present ones. And when it [the soul] says, as there, pleasant or painful, here it pursues or avoids—and so in cases of action[8] generally. (*DA* III 7 431[a]14–[b]10)

The goal of the passage is to explain how practical perception is involved in understanding. [6] picks up from [2], explaining that understanding functions in the same way in relation to good or bad that perception does in relation to pleasant and painful. For *phantasmata* are structural analogues of *aisthêmata*, and so have an effect on understanding similar to the one

8. Reading ἐν πράξει with the mss.

aisthêmata have on perception. [7] picks up from [3]. The problem, as in the case of the perception of complexes of proper perceptibles to which Aristotle refers, is that some mean must discern the sorts of arrays of perceptibles that substances present to practical perception, and thus to understanding. The solution proposed is therefore the same as in the case of perception generally. The mean must be like a limit—a point where many different simpler means, corresponding to each of the senses involved, can meet and register the effects of all their perturbations. It will thus be one in number, but its being will be manifold. What is different in this case is just that some constituents of the array will be pleasant or painful, so that understanding, instead of just registering or announcing the existence of the array when activated by it, will do the kind of asserting or denying that is pursuing or avoiding.

Thus far understanding seems to be functioning just like a later stage in perception, but [6] has already alerted us to one way this is not so: understanding, because it makes use of *phantasmata* rather than *aisthêmata,* can function even "outside perception," or when perception is not involved. That is one difference. The other is that what understanding understands isn't the *phantasmata* themselves but the forms that are in them, which are the *noêmata* mentioned in [10]—intelligible objects, then, not perceptible ones, and yet accessible to understanding only as presented in perceptible ones, or in the *phantasmata* that are their structural analogues.

The examples in [9–10] illustrate two different ways in which the understanding is moved by *phantasmata* (or the *noêmata* in them): [9] when it is perception that gives rise to them, and [10] when it isn't. In [9] the first step is the perception of a proper perceptible, light or fire—and perhaps also of a coincidental perceptible, the beacon. The second is the seeing of the moving fire (beacon), which is an exercise of the common sense. The third is the recognition, presumably by the understanding, whose operations the example is supposed to illustrate, that the moving beacon is the enemy—that is, something not good. The final step, left implicit, is understanding's act of denial (as we may suppose)—an act that consists in denying of the enemy that it is good by avoiding it. Although *noêmata* are not explicitly mentioned in [9], [8] has assured us that forms are the understanding's stock in trade. We can be confident, then, that they are being employed when the moving fire is recognized as the enemy, and goodness is denied of it.

In [9] the transition from perception to understanding is direct, in that understanding engages in no explicit reasoning but produces an action directly on the basis of perceptual input and its own extraction of intelligible objects therefrom: in other words, the extraction of the form *enemy* from moving beacons, like a doctor's recognition of some spots as measles, is direct. In [10], by contrast, the understanding does engage in explicit calculation or deliberation. Here it uses *phantasmata* retained in memory, or the *noêmata* in them, to construct practical syllogisms. In this case, since the conclusion of such a syllogism is an action, pursuit or avoidance follows. Since such actions result from deliberation, [10], not [9], is the model for how perception and understanding functions in them.

In subsequent elaboration of the account expressed in [1–10], Aristotle makes two things explicit. First:

[11] Understanding evidently does not move anything without desire—for wish is a desire, and when movement is in accord with calculation, it is in accord with wish. . . . Hence what moves us in every case is the desired object, which is either the good or the apparent good; and not every good but the good done in action. (*DA* III 10 433ª22–29)

Second, intelligible objects, though understood in *phantasmata*, are importantly different from them:

[12] Without perception, no one could learn or comprehend anything, and when one contemplates, one must at the same time contemplate an appearance; for appearances are like perceptions, except that they are without matter. However, imagination is different from assertion and denial; for truth and falsity involve a combination of intelligible objects. The primary intelligible objects (*ta prôta noêmata*), though, what distinguishes *them* from appearances? Or isn't it that neither they nor the others are appearances, although they will not exist without them? (*DA* III 8 432ª7–14)

The *prôta noêmata* are those involving no combination, whose existence understanding announces on being activated by them but neither asserts nor denies. Truth *and falsity* involve a combination of *noêmata*; truth alone does not. Here, as described in [1–5], an *aisthêma* consisting of a pleasant sweet taste (a proper perceptible) leads directly to a *phantasma*, which activates understanding. What understanding grasps is not its perceptible content, but the *noêma* in it—its intelligible form [8]. It is the active grasp by understanding of this *noêma* that is [6] assertion of (apparent) goodness in the shape of pursuit. It can take this shape, however, only because of the presence of desire, signaled by the transformations in [4–5]. Nothing changes in this regard, as [9] makes clear, when we move from an *aisthêma* of a simple pleasant (painful) proper perceptible to the multi-sense perception of a moving enemy beacon, except that now annunciation has become assertion (or denial) of goodness (or badness)—that is, the assertion that this moving beacon is the bad enemy. When, as in [10], calculation or deliberation is involved, the desire that joins with understanding in asserting or denying, pursuing or avoiding, is wish.

In a text related to [1–12], but especially to [1–5], Aristotle rejoins the topic of practical perception and understanding:

> Objects of desire (*to orekton*) and intelligible objects move in this way: they move without being moved. Of these objects, the primary ones (*ta prôta*) are the same. For that of appetite is the apparent good, and of wish the primary object is the real good. But we desire something because it seems [good] rather than its seeming [so] because we desire it; for the starting-point is active understanding. And understanding is moved [activated] by intelligible objects. (*Met.* XII 7 1072ᵃ26–30)

Understanding is moved by intelligible objects. That is to say, when the intelligible objects are primary ones, it is moved to announce their existence. This movement of understanding is the starting-point. For we desire the object in question because it seems a certain way to our understanding, not the other way around: "That which produces movement will be one in kind, the desiring part qua desiring—and the primary [mover] of all is the object of desire. For this produces movement without being moved, by being understood" (*DA* III 10 433ᵇ10–12). Yet how the object will seem depends on two potentially opposed factors: appetite, which responds to the apparent good, and wish, which responds to the real good. It is when they have done their respective work that a resultant something, which seems a certain way, is produced. It is this—the thing that causes the action—that desire is for. That is why the primary objects of understanding and of desire are the same: what desire is for (or against) is what (as a result of the operations of appetite and wish) seems a certain way to understanding.

What we have in [1–12], then, is a somewhat complex picture that is best explained as partly developmental in character. [1–5] deals with the perceptual and imaginative precursors of the primary intelligible objects, and applies as well to beasts and infants as to mature human adults. In all of them, the perception of something pleasant and the desire for it are distinguishable only in being. Hence what is subsequently presented to understanding soul, in such animals as have it, is [6] just what appears to perception, so that it asserts it to be good (pursues) or denies it to be good (avoids) accordingly. At this stage, then, perception, desire, and understanding operate seamlessly, as if they were one thing, so that there is little need to distinguish *noêmata* from the *phantasmata* they are in.

Initially, then, the *aisthêmata* control practical perception, and—in the shape of *phantasmata*—understanding. Later on, the story is more complex. Now the way things appear to us is a product not of perception alone, but of the various factors that, shaped by habituation and socialization, make up our character:

> Someone may say that everyone aims at the apparent good, but is not in control of the appearance in question, on the contrary, his character controls how the end appears to him. Well, if [as is in fact the case] each person is in some way responsible for his own state [of character], he will also in some way be responsible for the appearance in question. (*NE* III 5 1114ᵃ31–ᵇ3)

In someone with a virtuous character, these factors work together in such harmony that their separate contributions are all but invisible. In pathological cases, such as continence, the various factors come apart. Bird meat isn't salty enough or fatty enough to be consonant with the ratio definitive of *a*'s sense of taste, since that ratio has been skewed by inadequate habituation to be consonant only with things too salty or fatty to be healthy. To *a*, therefore, bird meat will appear displeasing. Yet when he has discovered as a result of deliberation that bird meat is what will best further his happiness, the bird meat will be consonant with the mean definitive of his wish. For wish is a desire susceptible to deliberation's outcomes—that is, to things presented, as they are in the decree expressed by the minor premise of a practical syllogism or demonstration, under the guise of happiness or the unconditional good.

How, then, will the bird meat seem to *a*'s understanding? How will it seem or be represented in the desire—the resultant of appetite and wish—that finally causes *a*'s action? Not as appetite presents it, not as wish presents it, but as a resultant of the two. Since *a* is continent, the bird meat will seem more pleasing than displeasing, but it will not—as in the case of the virtuous—seem simply pleasing. It is because it seems mixed in this way to understanding, indeed, that continent people take less pleasure in doing virtuous acts than virtuous people do. It is also why we often detect in their action something akin to ambivalence or hesitation. They eat the bird meat, but without enthusiasm, chewing but not really savoring, forcing it down, rather than eating it with gusto.

The greater strength of an incontinent's wish isn't simply a matter of greater oomph or muscle. We desire something because it seems pleasant or good, not the other way around. Hence just how much we desire it—how strong our desire is—is itself to be explained by how pleasant or good the thing seems. That is why Aristotle can so readily speak of vice as producing "distortion and false views about the starting-points of action" (*NE* VI 12 1144ᵃ34–36). Vice doesn't push the true views or better desires out of the way, as a stronger person might elbow aside a weaker one, it distorts how the starting-point of action—the end it aims at—appears to us, much as "distorting" the shape of the eyeball makes one thing look like two (*EE* VIII 1 1246ᵃ28–29). What we must do to our feelings, therefore, to establish a mean in them is correct their distortions, as we do when we correct the distortions in pieces of wood in order to straighten them out (*NE* II 9 1109ᵇ6).

Since *phantasmata* encode *noêmata*, they have an intelligible structure. So it makes sense to say of the virtue of character controlling them that it "teaches *correct belief* about the starting-point" (*NE* VII 8 1151ᵃ18–19) or that it is the constituent of practical wisdom ensuring "true *supposition*" about the practical good (*NE* VI 9 1142ᵇ33). Put the other way around, since the relevant intelligible structure is in someone's *phantasmata* because he was brought up under practical wisdom's adult tutelage, its presence there is what the desiring part's listening to the rational one consists in. When a *noêma* approved by reason is the intelligible content of a *phantasma* approved, so to speak, by desire, the two are in perfect harmony and agree in everything.

When no deliberation is involved, as for example in [9], it isn't entirely clear whether the true supposition that virtue of character teaches is always a case of belief (*doxa*), as Aristotle understands this notion. For his belief seems to require as its object a *phantasma* or *noêma* reached by deliberation, with the result that animals do not seem to have *doxa*, because "they do not have the sort [of appearance] that results from syllogism (*ek sullogismou*)" (*DA* III 11 434ᵃ10–11). That is why the part of the soul responsible for belief (*doxastikon*) is the same as the part that calculates or deliberates (*NE* VI 5 1140ᵇ25–26, 13 1144ᵇ14–15). Unlike calculation and deliberation, which are types of inquiry, what is believed is "already determined," since belief is "not inquiry, but already a sort of assertion" (*NE* VI 9 1142ᵇ11–15). But when the *phantasma* or *noêma* is indeed the result of deliberation, like a practical syllogism's minor premise, it is an object of belief, and—if we are virtuous—it is in accord with it that our effective desire is formed: "having discerned through deliberation [what best furthers happiness], we desire (*oregometha*) in accord with our deliberation" (*NE* III 3 1113ᵃ11–12). Nonetheless, the *noêma* in question is not an entirely cognitive object devoid of normative or evaluative content. Given its genealogy, which includes pleasant or painful content stemming from appetite and feeling, how could it be?

What the developmental story reveals, is that even in its earliest stages, desire is consequent on perception of—or appearances of—pleasure and goodness, not the other way around.[9] It's just that in those early stages, the difference between the contributions of perception and desire is harder to detect, since the two occur simultaneously. In other words, perceptibles and appearances play as important a role in the latest stages of development as in the earliest ones, even if these are now much more complex in their mode of generation and subject to different masters, and different conditions of correctness. In the case of pleasant or painful proper perceptibles, such as this pleasing shade of red, perception controls truth as effectively as it does in the case of red itself. That is the message of [3]. This does not mean that our native or untutored perception of either of them is always correct. Senses work properly only in certain conditions and when unimpeded in their operations. Bad light, distance, muddy hues can affect the accuracy of color discernment, as can myopia or cataracts. What the account of practical perception reveals is that other things, such as appetites not in a mean, can affect it also. The mean definitive of sight, is naturally tilted in pleasure's favor, so that its range of maximum consonance is incorrect (*NE* II 9 1109[b]8–9). As people with an illness are poor discerners of bitter and sweet (*NE* III 4 1113[a]27–29), so children and poorly habituated adults are more pleased than they should be by bright garish colors or very sweet tastes. The task of habituation is to properly compensate for the tilt, relocating the range of maximum consonance in the proper place, or as close to it as practically possible. Habituation's task is no different when the mean in question is one involved in detecting the complex multi-sense appearance presented by a substance. The scope of practical perception, then, is large. Our perceptions and beliefs do not present us with a neutral or value-free world, some parts of which acquire value in our eyes because we already desire them; rather, the things they present to us already include constitu-

---

9. In part because he fails to register the transformations in [4–5], David Charles, "Aristotle's Desire," in *Mind and Modality: Studies in the History of Philosophy in Honour of Simo Knuuttila*, ed. V. Hirvonen et al. (Leiden: Brill, 2006), pp. 19–40, sees desire and perception not as separate states but as a single fused state of a distinctive kind.

ents that perforce instill desire, because they are already either pleasant or painful, good or bad.[10]

Understanding

Understanding is like "the visual perception of intelligible things" (*Protr.* B24), and it is on vision in particular that Aristotle's account of understanding is modeled.[11] As the eye-jelly must take on the perceptible forms of visible objects without the associated matter in order for seeing to occur, so some constituent of the understanding must take on the intelligible forms of intelligible objects without their matter if active understanding is to occur: "as that which is capable of perceiving is to perceptible objects, so must the understanding be to intelligible ones" (*DA* III 4 429^{a}17–18); "understanding is a potentiality for being such things [intelligible objects] without their matter" (*DA* III 4 430^{a}7–8). This receptive constituent is "passive understanding" (*pathêtikos nous*) (*DA* III 5 430^{a}24–25), which "serves as matter for each kind of thing" (*DA* III 5 430^{a}10–11) and has a role analogous to that of eye-jelly in the case of visual perception. In addition, there is a productive constituent in understanding, which is "its cause and is productive in that it produces it" and is related to passive understanding "in the way,

10. Compare David Charles, "Aristotle and Modern Realism," pp. 135–172, John McDowell, "Eudaimonism and Realism in Aristotle's Ethics," pp. 201–218, both in *Aristotle and Moral Realism*, ed. R. Heinaman (Boulder, Colo.: Westview, 1995), "Deliberation and Moral Development in Aristotle's Ethics," in *Aristotle, Kant, and the Stoics: Rethinking Happiness and Duty*, ed. S. Engstrom and J. Whiting (Cambridge: Cambridge University Press, 1996), pp. 19–35.

11. In the broad sense of the term, someone with *nous* is someone with sound commonsense and the cognate verb *noein*, simply means "to think" (*Mete.* I 3 340^{b}14, *Ph.* IV 1 208^{b}25). In the narrow sense, which is the one relevant for us, *nous* is what makes possible a type of theoretical or contemplative knowledge of universal scientific starting-points which, unlike scientific knowledge in the strict or unconditional sense, is not derived from or justified by anything further. This *nous* is a divine substance (*NE* I 6 1096^{a}24–25, X 7 1177^{b}19–1178^{a}8)—or anyway the most divine one in us (*NE* X 7 1177^{a}16)—and, among sublunary animals, is fully possessed only by human beings (*PA* II 10 656^{a}7–8, *NE* X 8 1178^{b}24–25). No English term is a precise equivalent for this sense of *nous*. "Intellect," which is in many ways the best choice, lacks a cognate verb. "Understanding" is better in this respect, but shares with "intellect," "intelligence," "intuitive reason," "apprehension," and other common translations the defect of not being—as *nous* clearly is—factive or truth entailing.

for example, a craft is to its matter" (*DA* III 5 430ᵃ12–13). This is productive understanding (*nous poiêtikos*) (*DA* III 5 430ᵃ15).

The relationship between productive and passive understanding is explained by analogy with the role of light in color perception: "To the [passive] understanding . . . that becomes all things there corresponds the understanding that makes all of them, as some kind of state, like light, does; for in a way light too makes colors in potentiality into colors in actuality" (*DA* III 5 430ᵃ14–17). For, first, just as light, which is itself a color, is a visible object, so productive understanding is an intelligible one, since "it can understand itself"[12] (*DA* III 4 429ᵇ9). Second, just as no color is in actuality a color without light, so without productive understanding, passive understanding "understands nothing" (*DA* III 5 430ᵃ25). Third, just as light, since it is the actualization of "the transparent qua transparent" (*DA* II 7 418ᵇ9–10), is never a color merely in potentiality, needing to be made actual by something else, so productive understanding is in "substance or essence an actuality or activity" (*DA* III 5 430ᵃ18).

In the following passage, Aristotle expands on this picture:

[Understanding], since [1] it understands all things, must be unmixed . . . and hence [2] it must have no other nature than this, namely, that it is in potentiality [something]. That part of the soul, then, called understanding (and I mean by understanding that by which the soul understands and grasps [things]) is in actuality none of the beings [that is, none of the intelligible forms] before it is understanding [one of them]. Hence too, [3] it is reasonable that it should not be mixed with the body; for in that case it would become of a certain kind, either hot or cold, or it would have an organ as perception does; but as things stand it has none. Those who say, then, that [4] the soul is a place of forms speak well, except that it is not the whole soul, but that which can understand, and it is not the forms in actuality, but in potentiality. . . . [5] Given, then, that the understanding is something pure [that is, unmixed] and unaffected, and that it has nothing in common with anything else, as Anaxagoras says, someone might raise these problems: [6] how will it understand, if understanding is being affected in some way (for it is insofar as two things have something in common that the one is held to affect and the other to be affected)? And [7] can it itself also be understood? . . . [8] Being affected in virtue of something common has been discussed before—to the effect that the understanding is somehow the intelligible objects in potentiality, although it is nothing in actuality before it understands; in potentiality in the same way as there is writing

12. Reading δὲ αὐτὸν with the mss.

on a wax tablet on which there is nothing written in actuality; that is precisely how it is in the case of the understanding. [9] And it is an intelligible object in just the way its [other] objects are. For, [10] in the case of those things that have no matter, what understands and what is understood are the same, since [11] theoretical scientific knowledge and what is known in that way are the same. . . . [12] In those that have matter each of the intelligible objects is present in potentiality. (DA III 4 429ª18–430ª7)

Because the understanding can [1] understand each intelligible form, making it [4] the place of intelligible forms, it must be each of them in potentiality. As a result, [2] the only nature its passive component can have is that very potentiality, since if it had an intelligible form of its own, it would be unable to take on any other form distinct from it. This is similar to the argument that the eye-jelly must be transparent. For essentially the same reason, [3] understanding cannot be mixed with (sublunary) body: if it were already earthy, for example, it couldn't take on the form of fire. That it has no bodily organ, and so is not mixed with matter in that way, seems to be based on observation.

One difficulty with a featureless passive understanding is that it seems to violate the requirement that what is affected must [6] have something in common with what affects it, since "it is through a certain similarity and kinship" with its objects that a part of the soul has knowledge of them (NE VI 1 1139ª10–11). [8] responds that while passive understanding has nothing in common with an intelligible object *before* being affected by it, *at the moment* that it is affected and becomes active, the two do have something in common, since they then share the same intelligible form. Similarly, in the case of seeing, the eye-jelly has nothing in common with the visible object until, through being affected by it, it comes to share its visible form.

A second difficulty now comes into play concerning how passive understanding can [9] itself be understood if it lacks any determinate nature of its own. Again the case of seeing provides the putative solution. Just as a transparent object is visible because of "the color of something else" (DA II 7 418ᵇ5–6), so passive understanding is intelligible because it can take on the intelligible forms of other things:

> Understanding understands itself in partaking of the intelligible object; for it becomes an intelligible object in touching and understanding its objects. . . . For that which can receive the intelligible object—that is, the substance—is the understanding. And it is an activity when it possesses it. (Met. XII 7 1072ᵇ20–23)

This raises the further difficulty—addressed in [10–11]—of how taking on the forms of *other* things can possibly amount to *self*-understanding. Generally speaking, it cannot, but in some cases [10] the productive understanding of an intelligible form F is identical to F, so that understanding F is at the same time self-understanding. Since these are cases in which the sort of understanding involved is [11] theoretical scientific knowledge, F must be a universal form or essence that does not involve sublunary matter. That is why [12] contrasts it with "those that have matter."

The reason [11] is true only of forms or essences that do not involve sublunary matter emerges from consideration of an essence G that does involve a sublunary material constituent *m*, such as flesh and bones. As present in passive understanding, G is a second potentiality, a universal, but when it is grasped by productive understanding, it is an actualization of that universal—a particular:

> Scientific knowledge, like knowing scientifically, is of two kinds, one potentiality, one actuality. The potentiality—being (as matter) universal and indefinite—is of what is universal and indefinite, but the actuality, being a this, is of a this. It is only [coincidentally] that sight sees universal color, because this color which it sees is *a* color, and this A, which is the object the grammarian has theoretical knowledge of, is *an* A. (*Met.* XIII 10 1087ᵃ15–21)

Because G involves *m*, its actualization by productive understanding would have to contain an actualization of *m*—that is, some flesh and bones. Since that is impossible, the productive understanding of G is not identical to G itself. As essentially an activity, productive understanding can be identical only to an intelligible object that is itself an activity. An activity, however, is just what *m* can never be, since it is essentially a mere potentiality: matter is potentiality, form, activity, or actuality (*Met.* IX 6 1048ᵃ35–ᵇ6). By parity of reasoning, when a form or essence F contains no material constituent, the productive understanding of F is F itself.

What is true and cannot be false when we perceive a special perceptible is *that it exists*: perception "does not make errors about whether there is color or whether there is sound" (*DA* II 6 418ᵃ15) or "whether there is white" (*DA* III 3 428ᵇ21). Similarly, what is true and cannot be false when we understand a form or essence F is that F exists, so that if "the thing in fact is [exists], it is in that sense [true]" (*Met.* IX 10 1051ᵇ35). This holds, however, only when F's being understood guarantees F's existence, and this holds, in turn, only in the case in which F is a form or essence that involves no sublunary matter, since it is only then that F is identical to the productive understanding of itself: "with regard to those items that are just what it is for something to be and actualities it is not possible to err, but only to understand, or not" (*Met.* IX 10 1051^{b}30–32). In the case of forms involving no sublunary matter, therefore, the understanding's control of truth is as absolute as perception's is in the case of proper perceptibles (*NE* VI 2 1139^{a}17–18). If F does involve sublunary matter, understanding's control slackens, since what it grasps in grasping that F exists holds for the most part: "every syllogism proceeds either through necessary premises or through premises that hold for the most part. If the premises are necessary, the conclusion is also necessary, but if they hold for the most part, the conclusion does also" (*APo.* I 30 87^{b}22–25).

In explaining why human beings have a better functioning understanding than other animals, Aristotle appeals not to understanding itself but to material processes in the body:

> Instead of having forelegs and forefeet, a human being has arms and so-called hands. For a human being is the only animal that stands upright, and this is because its nature, that is, its substance is divine. Now the function of that which is most divine is understanding and thinking; and this would not be easy if there were a great deal of the body at the top weighing it down, for weight hampers the movement of understanding and of the common sense. Thus when the weight and the body-like quality becomes too great, the body itself must lurch forward toward the ground; and then, for preservation's sake, nature provides forefeet instead of arms and hands—as has happened in quadrupeds . . . because their soul could not sustain the weight bearing it down. . . . In fact, compared with man, all other animals are dwarf-like [that is, topheavy]. . . . That is why all animals are less wise than man. Even among human beings, indeed, children, . . . though possessing some other exceptional potentiality, are inferior in the possession of understanding as compared to adults. The reason . . . is that in many of them the starting-point of the soul is movement-hampered and body-like in quality. (*PA* IV 10 686^{a}25–687^{a}2)

To see more concretely what is going on in the account of understanding, it is useful partly to follow Aristotle's example by looking at material processes, but also at the scientific knowledge they make possible.

What codes for understanding in all animals that have it is the forward circular movement of ether. When it is present in an adult human being, equipped with a functioning perceptual system, inductive processes lead to the transmission of forms from perceptible objects to memory, where they are stored, not as actual movements but—as in the case of menses—as potential ones. When, as a result of the development of scientific knowledge, these forms become accessible to understanding, memory is transformed into passive understanding. That is why Aristotle can distinguish between perception and understanding in the following way:

> Active perceiving is spoken of in the same way as active contemplating, but with a difference. In the case of perceiving, what produces the activity—that is, the thing that is seen, or heard, or perceived in some other way—is external. The reason for this is that active perceiving is of particulars, whereas scientific knowledge [of which contemplation is a sort] is of universals, and these are somehow in the soul itself. Because of this it is up to us to understand when we wish, but perceiving is not up to us, since the perceptible object must be present. (DA II 5 $417^{b}19$–26)

In animals without understanding, or in those, such as children, in which its operations are hampered by processes in the body, this transformation of memory doesn't take place. Hence they have accesses to stored appearances, but not to their intelligible contents.

What happens when these forms are actively understood is that they touch or come into contact with ether, which starts them moving, vitalizing them much as *pneuma* does their originals in the natural world outside the soul— but with this crucial difference: because what passive understanding takes on is form without matter, what get actualized are just those potentialities for movements that realize constituents of the form, not those that realize constituents of the matter. That is why when we understand the form of an elephant, no elephant comes to be in our understanding. On the other hand, when what is present in our passive understanding is a form or essence that involves no sublunary matter, understanding it is identical to the form itself, since it just is a complex pattern of movements. But that all this should be experienced as something like having the light go on in one's mind is no easier to explain than the fact that creatures in whose brain C-fibers fire feel pain or see red, or that the actualization of the transparent is experienced as light.

Practical Understanding

What controls deliberately chosen action, and so practical truth, is a variety of understanding Aristotle calls practical understanding:

> Understanding and desire . . . can both produce movement with respect to place, understanding, however, that is of the practical sort, which calculates for the sake of something, and differs from the theoretical sort in respect of the end. Every desire, too, is for the sake of something—indeed, the thing desired is the starting-point of practical understanding, and the last thing [reached by calculation] is the starting-point of the action. Hence it is reasonable to regard these two things—desire and practical thought—as producing movement. For the desired thing moves us and practical thought moves us in that its starting-point is the desired thing. . . . As things stand, then, understanding evidently does not move anything without desire—for wish is a desire, and when movement is in accord with calculation, it is in accord with wish. . . . Hence what moves us is in every case the desired object, which is either the good or the apparent good—not every variety of it, however, but the good done in action, and what is done in action is what admits of being otherwise. (*DA* III 10 433ᵃ13–30)

But though practical understanding does have this special sort of control, it is not some new part of the soul distinct from theoretical understanding. Instead—as the passage to some extent suggests—it is more like a combination of theoretical understanding and wish. In this regard, it is analogous to practical perception.

Aristotle is sometimes insistent that theoretical understanding "never contemplates what is done in action, and says nothing about what is to be avoided or pursued" (*DA* III 9 432ᵇ27–29). That is to say, it never contemplates practical matters as such, or qua practical. Nonetheless, this does not prevent what it does think about from being coincidentally relevant to action, pursuit, and avoidance in precisely the way scientific knowledge of other sorts can be:

> Even when it [theoretical understanding] does contemplate something of the kind [that is, something practical], it does not at once command avoidance or pursuit; for example, it often thinks of something fearful or pleasant, but does not command fear. . . . Besides, even when understanding does issue a command and tells us to avoid or pursue something, we are sometimes not moved, but act in accord with our appetite, like the incontinent person. (*DA* III 9 432ᵇ29–433ᵃ3)

To be sure, theoretical understanding whose objects are the starting-points of the strictly theoretical sciences, and whose virtue or excellence is theoretical wisdom (*sophia*), does not have even this sort of coincidental practical relevance. Nonetheless, it does have practical relevance of a yet more important sort.

The verb *theôrein*, which often means "look at" with the eyes, also means "contemplate" with the mind or "have theoretical knowledge" of it. The cognate adjective *theôrêtikos* presents related problems. When applied to a type of life (*NE* I 5 1095ᵇ19) or activity (*NE* X 7 1177ᵃ18), it is usually translated as "contemplative." When applied to a type of scientific knowledge or thought, on the other hand, it is usually translated as "theoretical," as opposed to "practical" (*praktikos*). While in many ways apt, this opposition is also somewhat misleading. For what makes something *praktikos* for Aristotle is that it is appropriately related to *praxis* or action, considered as an end choiceworthy because of itself, and not—as with "practical"—that it is opposed to what is theoretical, speculative, or ideal. Hence *theôrêtikos* activities are more *praktikos* than those that are widely considered to be most so:

> It is not necessary, as some suppose, for a *praktikos* life to involve relations with other people, nor are those thoughts alone *praktikos* that we engage in for the sake of the consequences that come from *praxeis*, on the contrary, much more so are the *theôrêtikos* activities and thoughts that are their own ends and are engaged in for their own sake. For *eupraxia* (doing well in action) is the end, so that *praxis* of a sort is too. (*Pol.* VII 3 1325ᵇ16–21)

If some things are *praktikos*, because, like practical ones, they are useful, effective, or feasible means to some end, others are yet more *praktikos* because they further an end by constituting it or being identical to it: "we term both health and wealth as *prakton*, as well as the actions we do for their sake, the ones that further health or the making of money, so it is clear that happiness should be set down as the best for human beings of things *prakton*" (*EE* I 7 1217ᵃ37–40). Though the term used here is *prakton* rather than *praktikos*, the point remains the same: means to ends are practical, as—preeminently—are the ends themselves. So even though theoretical wisdom does not "contemplate any of the things from which a human being will come to be happy (since it is not concerned with anything coming-to-be)" (*NE* VI 12 1143ᵇ19–20), since it is itself what complete happiness consists in, it is much more practical even than the practical wisdom that does contemplate them.

3

THEORETICAL WISDOM

Theoretical wisdom (*sophia*) is the virtue of the the scientific part, which is the part of the human soul responsible for scientific knowledge (*epistêmê*). As such, it is one of five states "in which the soul grasps the truth by way of assertion and denial" (*NE* VI 3 1139^{b}15–16). As "the most rigorous of the sciences" (*NE* VI 7 1141^{a}16), it involves not just knowledge of what follows from scientific starting-points but knowledge of the starting-points themselves. Since understanding is what provides such knowledge (*NE* VI 6 1141^{a}7–8), "theoretical wisdom must be understanding plus scientific knowledge; scientific knowledge, having a head as it were, of the most estimable things" (*NE* VI 7 1141^{a}18–20). The various constituents of this definition are our next topics.

Starting-Points

The notion of an *archê* (starting-point, first principle, origin, source) is a protean one in Aristotle. *Archai* include substance, nature, the elements (earth, water, air, fire, ether) the various types of causal factors (formal, final, efficient, material), as well as practical thought and deliberate choice (*Met.* V 1 1013^{a}16–23). In the case of the sciences, however, starting-points are of two kinds (*APo.* I 10 76^{a}37–^{b}22). Those *special* to a science are definitions of the real (as opposed to nominal) essences of the beings with which the science deals (*APo.* II 10 93^{b}29–94^{a}19, *DA* I 1 402^{b}25–26). Because these are definitions by genus and differentiae, a single science must deal with a single genus (*APo.* I 7 75^{b}10–11, 28 87^{a}38–39). The other starting-points (so-called axioms) are common to all or many sciences. A third sort of starting-point posits the existence of the genus with which the science deals, but this may often be left implicit if the existence of the genus is clear (*APo.* I 10 76^{b}17–18).

The route by which understanding comes to grasp starting-points is *induction* (*epagôgê*). This begins with [1] perception of particulars, which leads to [2] retention of perceptual contents in memory, and, when many such contents have been retained, to [3] an experience, so that for the first time "there is a universal in the soul" (*APo.* II 19 100ª3–16). Finally, [4] from experience come craft knowledge and scientific knowledge, when "from many intelligible objects arising from experience one universal supposition about similar objects is produced" (*Met.* I 1 981ª5–7). The universal reached at stage [3] is "indeterminate" and "better known by perception" (*Ph.* I 1 184ª22–25). It is the sort of universal, often quite complex, that constitutes a nominal essence picked out by the nominal definition or meaning of a general term. Thus the nominal definition of the general term "gold" might pick out the universal *heavy, yellow, ductile metal found in rivers and streams*, so that anything instantiating this universal may be correctly designated as gold. When science investigates the class of things so designated, it may find that they constitute a genuine natural kind, one whose members all share a nature in terms of which their other features can be scientifically explained. Such a nature is the real universal essence of the kind.[1] Analyzed into its "constituents (*stoicheia*) and starting-points" (*Ph.* I 1 184ª23), this real essence makes intrinsically clear what the nominal essence made clear only to us. As a result, the kind itself becomes better known not just to us, but unconditionally (*NE* I 4 1095ᵇ2–8). These analyzed universals, which are the sort reached at stage [4], are the ones suited to serve as starting-points of the systematically teachable sciences and crafts: "People with experience know the facts, but not the reason why, whereas [those with craft knowledge] know the reason why, that is, the explanation. . . . That is why we think craft knowledge is closer to scientific knowledge than experience is; for those with craft knowledge can teach and those with experience cannot teach" (*Met.* I 1 981ª28–ᵇ10).

Induction includes two rather different sorts of transitions from particulars to universals, then, the broadly perceptual and noninferential process by which we reach [3] unanalyzed universals from the perception of particulars and the other, obviously more intellectual and discursive one by which we proceed from unanalyzed universals to [4] analyzed ones and their defi-

---

1. In distinguishing the stage at which a nominal essence or definition is reached from the one at which a corresponding real essence is discovered, I have been influenced by the discussion in David Charles, *Aristotle on Meaning and Essence* (Oxford: Clarendon Press, 2000).

nitions. It is at this second stage that a back and forth between candidate starting-points and perceptual data or evidence appropriately occurs:

> It seems that the knowledge of the what-it-is [that is, the essence] isn't only useful for gaining theoretical knowledge of the causes of the coincidental attributes connected to the essences[2] . . . but also, conversely, knowing these coincidental attributes contributes in great part to knowing the what-it-is. For when we can give an account of how either all or most of these coincidental attributes appear to be, we will then be able to speak best about the essence. For the starting-point of all demonstration is [the definition of] the what-it-is, so that insofar as definitions do not lead us to know the coincidental attributes, or fail even to facilitate a likely conjecture about [how to demonstrate] them, it is clear that they have all been stated in a dialectical and empty way. (*DA* I 1 402[b]16–403[a]2)

Hence in trying to frame scientific definitions of essences that can serve as starting-points of demonstrations or causal explanations, we usually need a rich and detailed knowledge of the coincidental attributes that are connected to those essences by putatively following from them. Any definition from which coincidental attributes of this sort fail to follow—or that is of no help in finding a definition from which they do follow—is empty of the appropriate empirical content, and so is irrelevant to science. As immune to falsification by the perceptual evidence, such definitions are dialectical in nature, and as such are to be handled not by science but—in a way we are about to explore—by aporematic philosophy.

Because of its origins in perception, scientific knowledge of any sort is dependent on perceptual data: "Most of the starting-points of each science are special to it. That is why it is the role of experience to provide the starting-points of each. I mean, for example, that experience in astronomy does so in the case of astronomical science (since it is only when the appearances were adequately grasped that astronomical demonstrations were discovered), and the same is true of ever other craft or science whatsoever" (*APr.* I 30 46[a]17–22). Hence "it is necessary to discern some types of starting-points from their consequences, above all, from the ultimate one. And the ultimate one in the case of a productive science is the product, whereas in the case of natural science it is the perceptual appearances that always have the controlling vote" (*Cael.* III 7 306[a]14–17). To favor abstract argument

---

2. "Coincidental attributes connected to the essences" are the intrinsic coincidental attributes (per se accidents) discussed below.

over perception, therefore, is a serious error: "What causes our inability to take a comprehensive view of the agreed-upon facts is lack of experience. That is why those who dwell in more intimate association with the facts of nature are better able to lay down starting-points which can bring together a good many of these, whereas those whom many arguments have made unobservant of the facts come too readily to their conclusions after looking at only a few facts" (*GC* I 2 316ᵃ5–10).[3]

Nonetheless, when the perceptual data are scarce, it is still possible to make some headway, although the science or nascent science that results will be reasonable or sensible (*eulogon, logikôs, kata logon,* or *katholou*) rather than demonstrative (*APo.* II 8 93ᵃ14–15) or strictly scientific (*analutikôs*) (*APo.* I 22 84ᵃ7–9). Astronomy is a case in point. Our theoretical knowledge of the heavenly bodies is relatively slight, "since as regards both those things on the basis of which one would investigate them and those things about them that we long to know, the perceptual appearances are altogether few" (*PA* I 5 644ᵇ25–28). There are many puzzles in astronomy, therefore, about which we can do little but conjecture, since "where things not apparent to perception are concerned, we think we have adequately proven our case to be in accord with reason if we have brought things back to what is possible, given the available appearances" (*Mete.* I 7 344ᵃ5–7). To become a "little less puzzled" in areas like these is—until further perceptual data becomes available—the most we can hope for (*Cael.* II 12 291ᵇ24–28).[4]

When a science has identified starting-points from which all its theorems can be demonstrated, it falls to dialectic or—more precisely—to *aporematic philosophy* to defend these against various sorts of attack, since "because it examines, dialectic provides a path to the starting-points of all lines of inquiry" (*Top.* I 2 101ᵇ3–4).[5] The evidence used in this defense are *endoxa,*

---

3. Also *Cael.* II 12 291ᵇ31–292ᵃ3, *DA* I 1 402ᵇ21–403ᵃ2, *GA* II 8 747ᵇ27–748ᵃ14, III 10 760ᵇ27–33.

4. That we should understand matters in this way is argued in Robert Bolton, "Two Standards for Inquiry in Aristotle's *De Caelo,*" in *New Perspectives on Aristotle's De Caelo,* ed. Alan C. Bowen and Christian Wildberg (Leiden: Brill, 2009), pp. 51–82. Nonetheless, the explanatory principles Aristotle uses in *De Caelo,* when, for example, he argues that the heavenly bodies must be celestial animals, are ones that have proven their worth in the sublunary realm. The resulting theory is scientific in aspiration, therefore, not merely dialectical.

5. Dialectic is more systematically discussed in my, "Aristotle's Philosophical Method," in *The Oxford Handbook of Aristotle,* ed. Christopher Shields (Oxford: Oxford University Press, 2012).

which are opinions accepted by "everyone or by the majority or by the wise, either by all of them or by most or by the most notable and reputable" (*Top.* I 1 100^{b}21–23). And the defense itself consists in going through the puzzles (*aporiai*) "on both sides" (*Top.* I 2 101^{a}35) until they or the majority of them are solved. For "if the puzzles are solved and the *endoxa* are left, it will be an adequate proof" (*NE* VII 1 1145^{b}6–7).

In a merely dialectical argument, the opponent may refuse to accept a proposition a philosopher would accept:

> The premises of the philosopher's syllogisms or those of the one investigating by himself, though true and known, may be refused by . . . [an opponent] because they lie too near to his starting-points, and so he sees what will happen if he grants them. But the philosopher is unconcerned about this. Indeed, he will presumably be eager that his axioms should be as known and as near to the question at hand as possible, since it is from premises of this sort that scientific syllogisms proceed. (*Top.* VIII 1 155^{b}10–16)

Since the truth may well hinge on propositions whose status is like that of these premises, there is no guarantee that a dialectician and a philosopher will reach the same conclusion on a given puzzle. *Endoxa* must not be confused with truths. Something is *endoxon* if the right people *believe* it, but what they believe is not guaranteed to be true. For the purposes of philosophy, however, we "must treat matters according to their truth, though for dialectic only in relation to belief" (*Top.* I 14 105^{b}30–31).

What enables the philosopher to meet this requirement, despite his reliance on *endoxa*, is that he is well educated in the various sciences, and so can determine what constitutes genuine scientific knowledge. When he learns from scientific psychology that happiness, which is a starting-point of ethics, is rational activity in accord with complete virtue, he knows that this is what he must defend.[6] When puzzles arise about it, therefore, resulting from arguments based on *endoxa*, his goal will be to solve these puzzles by undermining the arguments: "We must not only state the true view, but also give the reason why of the false one, since that furthers confidence. For when we have a clear and good account of why a false view appears true, that makes us more confident of the true view" (*NE* VII 14 1154^{a}22–25). If he is successful, he will have shown that the definition is in accord with most

---

6. Contrast Robert Bolton, "The Epistemological Basis of Aristotelian Dialectic," in *From Puzzles to Principles? Essays on Aristotle's Dialectic*, ed. May Sim (Lanham, Md.: Lexington Books, 1999), pp. 57–105.

of the most compelling *endoxa*, with the preponderance of unproblematic beliefs. Only at this point will he have an adequate proof of it and have grasped the starting-point in the way requisite for genuine understanding: "If we are to have scientific knowledge through demonstration . . . , we must know the starting-points better and be better convinced of them than of what is being proved, but we must also not find anything more convincing or better known among things opposed to the starting-points, from which a contrary mistaken conclusion may be deduced, since someone who has unconditional scientific knowledge must be incapable of being convinced [out of it]" (*APo.* I 2 72^{a}37–^{b}4).[7]

In defending some starting-points against dialectical objection, we provide a sort of demonstration of them, namely, a "demonstration by refutation" (*Met.* IV 4 1006^{a}11–12). Included among these are such very secure or fundamental starting-points as the principle of noncontradiction, which we must know in order to know anything. This may also be true more generally: "a disputant's refutation of what is opposed to his accounts is a demonstration of them" (*EE* I 3 1215^{a}6–7). But even if philosophy doesn't always offer us this sort of demonstration of starting-points, what it does offer is no puzzling knots—no impediments to clear and strict understanding (*NE* VII 2 1146^{a}24–27).

The empirical evidence that supports a science, then, also supports its starting-points. These are as made true by the facts as are the theorems that perception itself more directly validates. It is as such truths that aporematic philosophy takes them on board. Our epistemic grasp of them remains defective, however, so long as we cannot see clearly how they can be true in the face of the *endoxa*-based puzzles to which they give rise. Once we are able to solve these puzzles in the requisite way, this defect in our grasp is remedied, and the clear-sighted understanding of them required for unconditional scientific-knowledge is achieved.

---

7. Also *Top.* V 5 134^{a}34–35. Compare Plato, *Republic* VII 534b–d: "Unless someone can give an account of the form of the good, distinguishing it from everything else, and can survive all examination as if in a battle, striving to examine things not in accordance with belief, but in accordance with being, and can journey through all that with his account still intact, you will say that he does not know the good itself or any other good whatsoever. And if he does manage to grasp some image of it, you will say that it is through belief not knowledge that he grasps it, that he is dreaming and asleep throughout his present life, and that, before he wakes up here, he will arrive in Hades and go to sleep forever."

Truth and Understanding

One sort of truth (falsehood)[8] Aristotle recognizes is *objectual* truth (falsehood), which is a feature of objects, whether particulars, universals, or combinations of them. A second is the more familiar *nonobjectual* truth (falsehood), which is a feature of propositions, statements, or thoughts:

> As for what is, in the sense of being [objectually] true, and what is not, in the sense of being [objectually] false, they depend on[9] composition and division, which together are concerned with apportioning a contradictory pair . . . (how understanding [things] together or separate comes about is another story, but I mean together and separate in such a way that what results is not a succession of things but a single thing), for [nonobjectual] falsehood and truth are not in objects, as if good things were true and bad ones immediately false, but in thought (and in the case of simple things and the what-it-is of things not even in thought)—what needs to be considered about what is and what is not in this [objectually true] sense, then, must be considered later, but when the connection and the division are in thought, not in objects, what is in this sense [nonobjectually true] is different from what is unconditionally (for thought joins or subtracts[10] either the what-it-is or quality, or quantity, or something else, whatever it may be). (*Met.* VI 4 1027^b18–33)

Both objectual truth and falsity are present in objects, unless the objects are either simple (noncomposite) or essences of a certain sort, in which case—as the subsequent discussion will make clear—only objectual truth can be present, since no combination or separation is involved. Nonobjectual truth (falsity), by contrast, is in thought, not in objects, and what *is*—in the sense of what is nonobjectually true—is not what unconditionally is, since only primary substances have that status.

It is in terms of objectual truth that nonobjectual truth is defined:

> What is and what is not are spoken of, in some cases with reference to the types of predication [or categories], in some, with reference to the potentiality or actuality of these or their opposites, in others by reference to what is in the fullest sense true or false—this, in the case of objects, is being combined or being divided,[11] so that someone has hold of the truth who thinks of what is divided

---

8. My account of truth owes much to Paolo Crivelli, *Aristotle on Truth* (Cambridge: Cambridge University Press, 2004).

9. Reading παρὰ.

10. Reading ἀφαιρεῖ.

11. Reading τοῦτο δ' ἐπὶ τῶν πραγμάτων ἐστὶ τὸ συγκεῖσθαι ἢ διῃρῆσθαι with Crivelli, *Aristotle on Truth*, p. 238.

that it is divided and of what is combined that it is combined, and someone has hold of the false who is in a condition contrary to the objects. (*Met.* IX 10 1051ᵃ34–ᵇ5)

In a briefer and better-known formulation: "to say that what is, is and that what is not, is not, is true" (*Met.* IV 7 1011ᵇ26–28). About propositional truth, as about scientific knowledge, Aristotle is a realist: "It is not because of our truly thinking you to be pale that you are pale, on the contrary, it is because of you being pale that we who say this have hold of the truth" (*Met.* IX 10 1051ᵇ6–9).

The truth-making relationship between assertions and objects, which articulates the way the latter cause the former to be true (false), is of two varieties, depending on whether the objects constitute composites or non-composites (*Met.* IX 10 1051ᵇ17–1052ᵃ4). In the case of composites, two intrinsic beings, *a* and *b*, are combined or separated in a variety of ways corresponding to the assertion or denial of the four types of subject-predicate propositions—*a* belongs to all *b* (A*ab*), *a* belongs to no *b* (E*ab*), *a* belongs to some *b* (I*ab*), *a* does not belong to all *b* (O*ab*) (*Int.* 6 17ᵃ25–26, 17ᵇ16–20). To take just one example, when *a* and *b* are both universals, they can be combined or separated in two ways—either universally or particularly. If they are universally combined, they are the ontological correlate or truth-maker for A*ab*; if particularly combined, for I*ab*; if universally separated, for E*ab*; if particularly separated, for O*ab*.

When objects constitute composites, nonobjectual truth mirrors objectual truth, and the structure of assertions mirrors that of the composites. When they constitute noncomposites, things are different:

As regards noncomposite items, what is being or not-being and what is truth and falsehood? For it is not composition, so that they would be if combined and not be if divided, like the log being white and the diagonal being incommensurable, nor will truth and falsehood still hold in the same way in their case. Or rather just as truth is not the same in their case, neither is being. Instead, truth or falsity consists in this—to touch and to announce is true (for assertion [*kataphasis*] and annunciation [*phasis*] are not the same), but to be ignorant is not to touch, since it is not possible to be in error about the what-it-is, except by coincidence. The same holds, too, with regard to noncomposite substances, for it is not possible to be in error about them. And they are all in actuality,[12] not in potentiality. . . . Thus with regard to those things that are just what something is and actualities, it is not possible to be in error, but

12. Reading ἐνέργειαι.

either to understand or not understand, but where they are concerned, their what-it-is *is* inquired into, whether it is such-and-such or not. With what is, in the sense of what is true, and what is not, in the sense of what is false, one kind is true, if it is in fact combined, while it is false if it is not combined, the other if the thing in fact is, it *is* in that sense, and, if it is not in that sense, it *is not*. But truth consists in understanding these things, while falsehood does not exist and neither does any error, but ignorance does exist, though it is not like blindness. For blindness would be like wholly lacking the part that understands. (*Met.* IX 10 1051^{b}17–1052^{a}4)

At work in this complicated passage are three different doctrines and ideas. The first, which we may set aside as already familiar, is about what objectual truth is in the case of composites, and why it fails to carry over to noncomposites. The second is about understanding (thought) and its relationship to different sorts of objects. The third concerns the difference between annunciation and assertion.

When we understand something, what we understand is generally distinct from our understanding of it. If the thing in question is a form or essence involving no matter, however, this is not so: "In the case of those things that have no matter, what understands and what is understood are the same, since theoretical scientific knowledge and what is known in that way are the same" (*DA* III 4 430^{a}3–5). The being of such objects, then, and their objectual and nonobjectual truth all come to the same thing. That is why, in their case, nonobjectual truth can serve as a direct guide to objectual truth and being.

The way understanding engages with forms or essences, and so with starting-points, is touching or announcing, which is contrasted with assertion or denial and analogized to seeing a special object of sight:

An assertion (*phasis*)[13] is something about something (*ti kata tinos*), as too is a denial, and each one is either true or false. By contrast, not all understanding is such, but that of the what-it-is in the sense of the essence is true, and is not something about something. However, just as the seeing of a special object is true, but seeing that the pale thing is man or not is not always true, so also with what is without matter. (*DA* III 6 430^{b}26–30)

13. *Phasis* is distinguished from *kataphasis* at *Met.* IX 10 1051^{b}24–25 and used elsewhere in that distinct sense (*Int.* 4 16^{b}27–28, 5 17^{a}17, *DA* III 7 431^{a}8), but it is also—as here—used as its equivalent (*Int.* 12 21^{b}21–22, *APr.* I 17 37^{a}12, 46 51^{b}20, *Top.* V 6 136^{a}5, VIII 13 163^{a}15, *Met.* IV 4 1008^{a}9, V 7 1012^{a}14).

The relevant sense of touching, therefore, is that of perceiving the perceptible that is proper to the sense of touch.[14] Now what is true and cannot be false when we perceive such a proper perceptible is *that it exists*, so what is true and cannot be false when we understand a form or essence is also *that it exists.*

If what was understood, when the object of understanding is a form or essence involving no matter, was something about something, it would be that a predicate (*ti*) holds of a subject (*tinos*)—since that is just what *ti kata tinos* means (*Int.* 6 17ª25). Because a predicate cannot signify anything except a universal, this cannot be the case, since being or existence—which is what the predicate in question would have to signify—is not a universal. It must be, indeed, that *nothing at all* is being combined with the form or essence by the understanding when it is touched or announced, since only then is falsehood, and so error, precluded: "falsehood always involves combination, since even if it [understands] the white thing not to be white, it combines not-white [with it]" (*DA* III 6 430ᵇ1–3). What ignorance of a form or essence would have to amount to, therefore, is a sort of failure to make contact that is unlike blindness in only this respect—the person failing to make contact does have a functioning understanding, unlike the blind person, who does not have functioning eyes.[15] In other respects, understanding and the lack of it are very much like sight and blindness, which is probably why Aristotle feels the need explicitly to distinguish them in this one (compare *NE* VI 12 1144ª29–30, 13 1144ᵇ8–13).

In the case of special objects of perception, what we can be in error about is whether some predicate holds of them, for example, whether man holds of this particular existent instance of pale. In the analogous case of existent forms or essences, therefore, what we can be in error about is whether some predicate holds of *them*. This is characterized as erring "by coincidence" (*Met.* IX 10 1051ᵇ26), because in such cases we are thinking of the predicate as coincident with the form or essence (*Met.* I 1 981ª18–20, VII 5 1030ᵇ20–21). Where falsehood is possible, combination exists in the understanding. So in these cases what is understood *is* something about (or predicated of) something. Included among these are definitions of essences or forms. For definitions of essences, since they must serve as starting-points of scientific demonstrations, are universal affirmative assertions (*APo.* I 14 79ª24–29, II

14. The proper perceptibles of touch include dry, wet, cold, hot (*DA* II 11 422ᵇ25–27, 423ᵇ27–29).

15. See Crivelli, *Aristotle on Truth*, p. 106 n. 16.

3 90^{b}3–4), in which the *definiens* is predicated of the *definiendum* as subject (*Top.* I 4 101^{b}11–25, VII 5 154^{a}36–^{b}2). Within the *definiens* itself, however, one thing is "not predicated of another, for example, animal of biped or the latter of animal" (*APo.* II 3 90^{b}34–36; also *Met.* VII 12 1037^{b}18–21)— unless, that is to say, what is being defined contains a universal material constituent, since in that case the formal constituent of the definition *is* predicated of the material one:

> Some substances do have a definition and an account, namely, composite ones, but their primary constituents do not, since, in fact, a definitional account must signify one thing predicated of another, the second of these playing the part of matter and the other that of form. (*Met.* VIII 3 1043^{b}28–32)[16]

Hence understanding a form or essence that involves no matter, and so knowing—without the least possibility of error—that it exists, is no guarantee of having a true definition of it. That is why we do not inquire whether such things exist or not, but "their what-it-is *is* inquired into, whether it is such-and-such or not" (*Met.* IX 10 1051^{b}32–33). When this inquiry meets with success, the result is a definition structurally isomorphic to the essence it signifies: "the definition is an account, and every account has parts, and as the account is to the thing, so the part of the account is to the part of the thing" (*Met.* VII 9 1034^{b}20–22). Here too, then, nonobjectual truth mirrors objectual truth.

Unconditional Scientific Knowledge

An assertion is the true (or false) predication of a single predicate term *a* of a single subject term *b*, either as an affirmation (*a* holds of *b*) or a denial (*a* does not hold of *b*) (*Int.* 8). What makes a term a single subject term, however, is not that it is grammatically singular or serves as a grammatical subject but that it designates a substantial particular—a canonical example of which is a perceptible hylomorphic compound, such as Socrates. Similarly, what makes a term a predicate is that it designates a universal (man, pale)— something that can have many particular instances. When the role of predicate is restricted to universals, therefore, while that of subject is left open to both particulars and universals, it is more on ontological or metaphysical

---

16. Contrast Crivelli, *Aristotle on Truth*, p. 116.

grounds than on what we would consider strictly logical ones. Subjects and predicates are thus ontological items, types of beings, rather than linguistic or conceptual ones, and logical principles, such as the principle of noncontradiction, are very general ontological principles, truths about all beings as such or qua being.

Particular assertions (Socrates is a man) and general assertions (Men are mortal) have the same subject-predicate form, but when the subject is a universal, the assertion may itself be either universal (All men are mortal) or particular (Some men are mortal)—that is to say, the predicate may be asserted (denied) of the subject either universally (*katholou*) or in part (*kata meros*) or, if the quantifier is omitted (Men are mortal), indefinitely (*adihoristos*). Assertions, as a result, are of the four types we encountered in the previous section: *a* belongs to all *b* (A*ab*), *a* belongs to no *b* (E*ab*), *a* belongs to some *b* (I*ab*), *a* does not belong to all *b* (O*ab*).

A syllogism is "an argument in which, certain things having been supposed, something different from those supposed things necessarily results because of their being so" (*APr.* I 2 24ᵇ18–20). The things supposed are the argument's premises; the necessitated result is its conclusion. In Aristotle's view, such arguments consist of a major premise, a minor premise, and a conclusion, where the premises have exactly one "middle" term in common, and the conclusion contains only the other two "extreme" terms. The conclusion's predicate term is the *major term*, contributed by the major premise; its subject is the *minor term*, contributed by the minor premise. The middle term must be either subject of both premises, predicate of both, or subject of one and predicate of the other. The resulting possible combinations of terms yield the so-called figures of the syllogism:

	First figure		Second figure		Third figure	
	Predicate	Subject	Predicate	Subject	Predicate	Subject
Premise	*a*	*b*	*a*	*b*	*a*	*c*
Premise	*b*	*c*	*a*	*c*	*b*	*c*
Conclusion	*a*	*c*	*b*	*c*	*a*	*b*

Systematic investigation of the possible combinations of premises in each of these figures results in the identification of the *moods* or modes that constitute valid deductions. In the first figure, these are as follows:

Form	Mnemonic	Proof
Aab, Abc | Aac	Barbara	Perfect
Eab, Abc | Eac	Celarent	Perfect
Aab, Ibc | Iac	Darii	Perfect (or from Camestres)
Eab, Ibc | Oac	Ferio	Perfect (or from Cesare)

A mood is perfect when there is a proof of its validity that is *direct*, in that it does not rely on the validity of any other mood. Only first figure syllogisms have perfect moods.

Besides their logical interest as admitting of direct proof, perfect syllogisms in Barbara are also of particular importance to science. For, first, "syllogisms that give the reason why, which hold either universally or for the most part, in most cases are carried out through this figure. That is why it is the most scientific of all; for theoretical knowledge of the reason why is most important for [scientific] knowledge" (*APo.* I 14 79^{a}20–24). Second, "only through this figure can you hunt for scientific-knowledge of something's essence" (*APo.* I 14 79^{a}24–25): essences hold universally, only perfect syllogisms in *Barbara* have universal conclusions, and definitions of essences, which are scientific starting-points, must hold universally. Finally, this figure "has no need of others, but they must be thickened and increased through it, if they are going to reach the immediates" (*APo.* I 14 79^{a}29–31). Barbara can be used by itself to hunt for scientific starting-points, but each of the other figures must use it to find a middle term c, such that Yac, Zcb \| Xab (where X, Y, Z are variables taking A, E, I, O as values). When this process continues until an assertion Wij is reached that is immediate or unmediated, in that no further term k can be found to mediate between i and j as c does between a and b, the thickening of Xab terminates, and a starting-point is reached.

To have "unconditional scientific knowledge (*epistasthai haplôs*) of something (as opposed to the sophistical or coincidental sort)" and so to be convinced of it in the appropriate way, we must "know (*gignôskein*) the explanation because of which the thing holds, know that this is its explanation, and know that the thing does not admit of being otherwise" (*APo.* I 2 71^{b}9–12). What provides such knowledge is a *science* consisting of two components: a set of indemonstrable starting-points and a set of explanations or theorems in the mood Barbara, which are the results of applying the syllogistic logic we just looked at to starting-points or theorems.

To constitute a demonstration from starting-points, a syllogism's premises must meet a number of conditions. First, they must be immediate or in-demonstrable, and so must be reached through induction. Second, as sources of *unconditional* scientific knowledge, our confidence in them must be un-surpassed. Finally, they must be necessary (and so, of course, true) in a spe-cial sense: the predicates in them must belong to the subjects in every case, intrinsically or *per se* (*kath' hauto*), and universally (*APo.* I 4 73^{a}24–27).

In every case: A predicate *a* belongs to every subject *b* if and only if there is no *b* to which it fails to belong and no time at which it fails to belong to a *b*: "for example, if animal belongs to every man, then if it is true to say that this thing is a man, it is also true to say that it is an animal, and if the former is the case now, the latter is also the case now" (*APo.* I 4 73^{a}29–31).

Intrinsically: A predicate *a* belongs intrinsically to a subject *b* just in case it is related to *b* in one of four ways: [1] *a* is in the account or definition of what *b* is or of *b*'s essence (*APo.* I 4 73^{a}34–37); [2] *b* is a complex subject φb_1—for example, odd number or male animal—and *a* is in the definition of φb_1's essence;[17] [3] *a* just is *b*'s essence; [4] *a* is not a part of *b*'s essence or identical to it but stems causally from it, so that being *b* is an intrinsic cause of being *a* (*APo.* I 4 73^{a}34–^{b}24).

Universally: A predicate *a* belongs to a subject *b* universally just in case "it belongs to it in every case and intrinsically, that is, insofar as it is itself" (*APo.* I 4 73^{b}26–27). The effect of this requirement, then, is mostly to eluci-date further what an intrinsic predicate (or predication) is. It must apply to a subject *b* just because that subject is a *b*, so that for any arbitrary *b*, *a* will belong to it, and for any arbitrary *x*, if *a* belongs to it, it will be because *x* is a *b* of some sort:

> For example, containing two right angles is not universal to figures; for though you can prove that some figure contains two right angles, you cannot prove it of an arbitrary figure, nor do you use an arbitrary figure in proving it, since a quadrilateral is a figure but does not contain angles equal to two right angles. Moreover, although an arbitrary isosceles triangle does have angles equal to two right angles, it is not the primary case, since triangle is prior. Thus if an arbitrary primary case is proved to have two right angles (or whatever), then

17. *APo.* I 4 73^{b}16–24 implies that φ must be one of a pair of opposites (straight and bent, odd and even). But acute, right, and obtuse as applied to angles, and perfect as applied to numbers, yield complex per se beings yet are not pairs of opposites. Similarly, while some instances of φ are differentiae, not all are: male animal is an intrinsic being, but male is not a differentia of animal (*Met.* VII 5 1030^{b}25–26). The interpretation of [2] is controversial, in any case.

this belongs intrinsically and universally to this primary case, and the demonstration holds of this case intrinsically and universally. Of the other cases it holds in a way, but not intrinsically—even to the isosceles triangle it does not apply universally, but more widely. (*APo.* I 4 73^{b}33–74^{a}3)

Because intrinsic predicates stem in various ways from essences, the subjects to which they belong must have essences. Hence they must be *intrinsic beings*, since—stemming as they do from essences—intrinsic predicates identify or reveal them: "the kinds of intrinsic beings are precisely those that are signified by the types of predication" (*Met.* V 7 1017^{a}22–23).

These types of predication are the so-called categories:

Anything that is predicated of something must either be . . . a definition . . . if it signifies the essence . . . or, if it does not, a special attribute . . . or one of the terms in the definition, or not; and if it is one of the terms in the definition, it must [signify] the genus or the differentiae, since the definition is composed of genus and differentiae. If, however, it is not one of the terms in the definition, plainly it must be a coincidental attribute; for a coincidental attribute was said to be that which a thing has, but is neither a definition nor a genus nor a special attribute. Next we must determine the different kinds of predication in which one will find the four kinds [of predication] mentioned above. These are ten in number: what-it-is, quantity, quality, relative, when, where, position, having, affecting, and being affected. For the coincidental attributes, the genus, the special attributes, and the definition will always be in one of these categories. For all the premises that involve these four things signify either what-it-is, or quantity, or quality, or one of the other categories. (*Top.* I 8–9 103^{b}7–27)

The entire complex apparatus of definition, essence, genus, differentiae, special attribute,[18] and coincidental attribute can thus be brought to bear on any intrinsic being, whatever category it is in:

The what-it-is, taken in one way, signifies the substance and the this, but taken in another, it signifies each of the other things predicated—quantity, quality, and the like. For just as being too belongs to all (not in the same way, however, but rather to one primarily and to the others derivatively), so too the

---

18. "A special attribute (*idion*) is one that does not reveal the essence of a thing yet belongs to that thing alone and is predicated convertibly of it. Thus it is a special attribute of human beings to be capable of learning grammar, since if someone is a human being he is capable of learning grammar, and if he is capable of learning grammar he is a human being" (*Top.* I 5 102^{a}18–22).

what-it-is belongs unconditionally to substance, and to the others in a derivative way: we may ask what-it-is even of a quality, so that quality too is what-something-is. (*Met.* VII 4 1030ª18–24)

While accounts of intrinsic beings in any category are, in a sense, definitions of essences, only accounts of substances are definitions in the strict sense of the term:

> If there are definitions of these things too [for example, odd, even, male, female], either they have them in another way, or . . . definition and essence must be spoken of in many ways, so that in one way only substances have definitions and essences but in another way nonsubstances also have them. Clearly, then, a definition is the account of the essence, and the essence is either of substances alone or of them most of all and primarily and unconditionally. (*Met.* VII 5 1031ª7–14)

This is a reflection at the level of essences of the more familiar doctrine of the ontological dependence of nonsubstantial intrinsic beings (attributes, universals) on substantial ones. A consequence for epistemology is that only sciences dealing with substances can provide unconditional scientific knowledge: sciences dealing with nonsubstantial beings depend epistemologically on those dealing with the substantial beings on which the nonsubstantial ones ontologically depend.

Two things follow directly from the account of demonstration. The first is that unconditional scientific knowledge, since it is of essences and their intrinsic relations to attributes, is exclusively of universal necessities. The second is that no Aristotelian science providing such knowledge can deal with cases in which *a* belongs to *b* coincidentally or contingently: "no science—practical, productive, or theoretical—supervises the coincidental" (*Met.* VI 2 1026ᵇ4–5). When *a* belongs to *b* intrinsically because *a* is related to *b* in way [4], however, *a* is an intrinsic coincidental attribute (or *per se* accident) of *b*. Hence some coincidental attributes—the intrinsic ones—*are* objects of scientific knowledge. For example, if a triangle is defined as essentially a plane figure bounded by three straight lines, the fact that it has internal angles equaling two right angles is an intrinsic coincidence, since this follows from its definition, but is not identical to or a part of its essence (*PA* I 3 643ª27–31). Much of geometry is devoted to establishing such intrinsic coincidences: "every demonstrative science provides theoretical knowledge of the intrinsic coincidental attributes of some subject" (*Met.* III 2 997ª19–20).

Four Types of Scientific Explanation

While every demonstration constitutes an explanation of the sort required for scientific knowledge, not every such explanation is of the same type:

> We think we have scientific knowledge when we know the explanation (*tên aitian*), and there are four types of explanation: one, what it is to be something; another, that if certain things are the case, it is necessary for this to be the case; another, what initiated the movement; fourth, what is for the sake of something. All of them are demonstrated through the middle term. (*APo*. II 11 94ᵃ20–26; also *Ph*. II 3 194ᵇ23–195ᵃ3, *Met*. V 2 1013ᵃ24–1014ᵃ25)

Although these types of explanation are usually referred to as the formal (what it is to be something), material (if something is to be the case, this must be the case), efficient (what initiated the movement), and final (the for the sake of which) *causes*, we need to distinguish between the type of explanation (*aitia*) embodied in a demonstration and the type of cause (*aition*) expressed by its middle term, since these may be different.[19]

Aristotle's discussion of [4] final or teleological explanation is a case in point:

> Regarding cases in which what serves as a cause is that for the sake of which. For example, what is the reason why he walks? In order to be healthy. What is the explanation of why there is a house? In order to keep possessions safe. In the one case, it is for the sake of being healthy (*tou hugiainein*), in the other, for the sake of safekeeping. The reason why it is necessary to walk about after dinner and that for the sake of which it is necessary do not differ. Walking about after dinner: *c*. Food not floating on the surface: *b*. Being healthy: *a*. Suppose then that *making food not float on the surface at the mouth of the stomach* belongs to *walking about after dinner*, and suppose that the former is *healthy*. For it seems that *b* (food not floating on the surface) belongs to *c* (walking about after dinner), and that *a* (being healthy) belongs to *b*. What then is the cause for *c* of *a*—the for the sake of which—belonging to it? It is *b* (the not floating). This is like a definition of *a*, since *a* will be explained here in this way. And what is the

19. My account is indebted to Mariska Leunissen, *Explanation and Teleology in Aristotle's Science of Nature* (Cambridge: Cambridge University Press, 2010), pp. 176–207. The significance of distinction between *hê aitia* (feminine) and *to aition* (neuter) is discussed in Michael Frede, "The Original Notion of Cause," in *Doubt and Dogmatism: Studies in Hellenistic Epistemology*, ed. M. Schofield, M. Burnyeat, and J. Barnes (Oxford: Clarendon Press, 1980), pp. 217–249. Although Aristotle does not systematically observe the distinction, it is *hê aitia* that figures in his definitions of scientific knowledge.

reason why *b* belongs to *c*? Because this—being in such condition—is what being healthy is. One must substitute the definitions (*metalambanein tous logous*), and in this way each of these will become more evident. Here the events occur in the opposite order from cases where the causes are in accord with movement. For there the middle term must occur first, while here it is *c*—the last thing—and finally the for the sake of which. (*APo.* II 11 94ᵇ11–26)

What is to be explained in the case of walking about after dinner is why it promotes being healthy, or why someone whose end is to be healthy should do it. In the demonstration that constitutes the explanation, the explanatory burden falls on the middle term, *b* (food not floating on the surface at the mouth of the stomach): walking after dinner is healthy (*being healthy* belongs to *walking after dinner*) because of *the food not floating*. The causal relation holding between the food not floating (*b*) and being healthy (*a*) is not itself teleological, but rather material: in order for *being healthy* to be present, something else must be present, namely, food not floating on the surface at the mouth of the stomach.

What makes the food not float is walking about after dinner, and it is neither a final (teleological) nor material cause, but an efficient one:

> That the end serves as a cause is clear from teaching. For having defined the end, teachers demonstrate that each of the other things is a good, since what is for the sake of something is the cause. For example, since being healthy (*to hugiainein*) is such and such, then this must be beneficial [that is, good] in furthering it. And what is healthy will be the efficient cause of health (*tēs hugieias*), but an efficient cause of health's existence, not of its being a good. (*EE* I 8 1218ᵇ16–22)

The definitions that one must "substitute" to make more evident the way in which *a* is related to *b* and *b* to *c* are most probably those of "healthy" and "health" adverted to here.[20] Thus health is a certain bodily condition. Since what its definition specifies is *what it is to be* health, the definiendum is the formal cause of health. Something is heal*thy* in the relevant sense when it furthers that condition, for example, by being its efficient cause. Walking is healthy, then, because it causes a certain bodily condition, namely, having food not be floating on the surface at the mouth of the stomach, which, in the context of having just eaten dinner, is what health (partly) consists in. In

20. See *Top.* VI 4 142ᵃ34–ᵇ6, 9 147ᵇ12–14. Other interpretations are possible, however, and the precise connotation of the phrase *metalambanein tous logous* has caused much controversy.

the order of final or teleological causes, health—the end to be aimed at—comes first, and walking about after dinner comes last, since it is "the last thing" arrived at in deliberation about what to do to promote health. In the order of efficient causes, walking about comes first, since is the first thing in the chain of efficient causes that leads to the final thing—being healthy (compare *NE* III 3 1112ᵇ11–24).

For the formal cause to operate, it typically needs appropriate matter to operate on:

> Why is a saw such as it is? So that this may be—that is, for the sake of this. It is impossible, however, that the thing it is for the sake of should come-to-be unless the saw is made of iron. It is necessary, then, that it should be made of iron, if there is to be a saw and the function belonging to it. The necessity here, then, is necessity proceeding from a hypothesis, and not as an end: the necessity is in the matter, the for the sake of which is in the definition [of the form]. (*Ph.* II 9 200ᵃ10–15)

It is the formal and material causes working together that produce a hylomorphic compound capable of performing its function and achieving its end: "What is only in potentiality flesh or bone, before it acquires the form with which the account accords that defines the essence of flesh and bone, does not yet have its proper nature, and does not yet exist by nature" (*Ph.* II 1 193ᵃ36–ᵇ3). Moreover, for form to do its shaping work, something also has to serve as its efficient causal correlate. In the case of human beings, the complex *pneuma*-based movements in a male's blood and semen, within which his form is encoded, plays this role, so that when transmitted to female menses of a suitably receptive sort, it results in a new creature that shares that form (*GA* I 22 730ᵇ12–23). Thus the various causes involved in the four types of explanation typically work closely together: "what something is and what it is for the sake of are one, while what the motion first originates from is the same as them in form, since a human being generates a human being" (*Ph.* II 7 198ᵃ25–27).

Scientific Knowledge of Other Sorts

Unconditional scientific knowledge is exclusively of unconditional necessities, but not all scientific knowledge is unconditional: "There is neither [unconditional] demonstration nor unconditional scientific knowledge of what is perishable, but only the coincidental sort, because it does not hold of this universally, but at some time (*pote*) and in some way (*pôs*)" (*APo.* I 8 75ᵇ24–26). Crabs, for example, are perishable things, which come-to-be, pass-away, and undergo change and alteration. Nonetheless, "All crabs have the right claw bigger and stronger than the left," is a theorem of biology, demonstrable from the essential definition of crabs. Yet, because it holds only *in some way*—namely, *hôs epi to polu* or "for the most part" (*HA* IV 3 527ᵇ6–7)—exceptions to it can occur: "nothing can happen contrary to nature considered as eternal and necessary, but only where things for the most part happen in a certain way, but may also happen in another way" (*GA* IV 4 770ᵇ11–13). If a perceptible particular, *a*, is known to be a crab, therefore, we cannot infer from the theorem that its right claw is bigger. For even though "the contrary of what happens for the most part is always comparatively rare" (*Top.* II 6 112ᵇ10–11), *a* may be the rare exception. At t_1, we may discover that *a* is not an exception. As a result, we have coincidental scientific knowledge that *a*'s right claw is bigger *at that time*. At t_2, when *a* isn't under observation, we no longer have that knowledge, since *a* may have changed in the meantime: it may no longer exist, its right claw may have been lost in a fight, its left claw may have grown, and so on.

The fact that scientific knowledge, even of this coincidental sort, is available in the case of perceptible particulars has an important consequence, all the same, since it gives scientific knowledge a practical or action-determining application it would otherwise lack, so that it can be "coincidentally useful to us where many of the necessities of life are concerned" (*EE* I 5 1216ᵇ15–16). A theorem of avian biology tells us that all bird meats are low in fat and high in protein. A theorem of human medicine or dietetics tells us that all such meats are light on the stomach, nutritious, and healthy. At t_1, perception tells us that *a* is a bird. Knowing the relevant biology and medicine, we infer that *a*'s meat is healthy for us to eat at t_1. Since we are hungry at t_1, and *a* is available for eating, we decide to eat it. Coincidental though it may be, because subject to the vicissitudes of time and change, such knowledge is clearly crucial to our success as practical agents, striving to live well and achieve happiness.

What makes an intrinsic being the ontological correlate or truth-maker of a theorem is its essence. What explains why the theorems applying to some such beings (namely, the sublunary or natural ones) hold for the most part is the fact that their essences can be realized only in sublunary matter—in some mixture of earth, water, air, and fire:

> Since not all beings come-to-be by necessity and always, but the majority of things hold for the most part, there must be coincidental being. A white man,

for example, is not always or for the most part musical, but since this sometimes happens, it must be coincidental (if not, everything will be the result of necessity). The matter, therefore, which is capable of being otherwise than it for the most part is, is the cause of the coincidental. (*Met.* VI 2 1027ª8–15)

Animal reproduction provides a vivid illustration of this. In embryogenesis, the male (M) provides "the form and the source of movement" while the female (F) provides "the body—that is, the matter" (*GA* I 20 729ª9–11). The reason M can play this role is that his own form (or essence) can be transmitted as movements to his seed, and these movements, in turn, can be transmitted to F's menses (*GA* II 3 737ª20–22). Were F's menses perfectly receptive of the movements in M's seed, the resulting offspring would have M's form and would perfectly resemble M, just as two bronze statues from the same mold have exactly the same shape. But this is not the case. For even though F's menses doesn't contain any formative movements, it does contain *potentialities* for movements analogous to those in M and activated by them (*GA* IV 3 768ª11–14). When the two meet up with one another, therefore, various outcomes are possible. If the movements in M's seed "stand fast" (*GA* IV 3 768ª32), the offspring will perfectly resemble M. If instead they "slacken," the resulting offspring may not resemble M to the same degree. If the two types of movements sufficiently "run together," the offspring may not "resemble any of its own or kin" (*GA* IV 3 768ᵇ5–12). Similarly, any form that must be realized in matter can be so deformed by that matter's resistant potentialities that exceptions can occur to universal theorems concerning it.

Because theorems that hold for the most part admit of exception, they also, in a sense, admit of being otherwise. This prevents them from being unconditionally necessary. But since holding for the most part also distinguishes them from what is coincidental or contingent, it still leaves them squarely within the sphere of a type of necessity:

What admits of being otherwise is spoken of in two ways: in one, it means what holds for the most part and falls short of [unconditional] necessity, for example, a man's turning grey or growing or decaying, or, in general, what belongs [to something] by nature (for this does not belong by continuous necessity, since a man does not exist forever, although if a man does exist it belongs either necessarily or for the most part); in the other, it means what is indeterminate (*to aphoriston*), which is what is capable of being thus or not thus—for example, an animal's walking or an earthquake's taking place while it is walking, or, in general, what is the result of luck (for it is not more natural for it to be that way rather than the opposite). (*APr.* I 13 32ᵇ4–13)

That is why there *is* scientific knowledge of what holds for the most part:

> Scientific knowledge and demonstrative syllogism of indeterminate things is not possible, because the middle term lacks order, but of natural things it is possible, and arguments and inquiry are pretty much concerned with what is possible in this sense—about the former a syllogism might come about, but it isn't usual, at any rate, to inquire about them. (*APr.* I 13 32^{b}18–22; also *Met.* VI 2 1027^{a}19–21)

We can no more change what happens by this sort of natural necessity, therefore, than we can change what happens by the unconditional necessity found in geometry, astronomy, or theology.

Like the natural sciences, and for the same sorts of reasons, political science and ethics, in common with other practical and productive sciences, deal with "what holds for the most part" and so reach "conclusions that are also of the same sort" (*NE* I 3 1094^{b}21–22). Thus many action-guiding ethical principles allow for the possibility of exceptions: "we should for the most part return favors rather than do favors for our companions, just as we should for the most part return a loan to a creditor rather than make one to a companion" (*NE* IX 2 1164^{b}31–33). In drafting universal laws, too, we have to acknowledge—as we do in the case of the zoological study of crabs and other animals constituted of sublunary matter—that some of them will also hold for the most part:

> All law is universal, yet there are some cases about which it is impossible to make correct universal pronouncements. In those cases, then, where it is necessary to make a universal pronouncement, but impossible to do so correctly, the law adopts what holds for the most part, knowing full well the error that is being made. And it is no less correct on this account. For the source of the error is not in the law or in the legislator, but in the nature of the case, since the matter (*hulê*) of things done in action is like that to start with. (*NE* V 10 1137^{b}13–19)

Still, as is clearly implied here, some universal practical laws do not involve an "error" of this sort, and so do hold universally, rather than for the most part. This point aside, holding for the most part clearly puts the practical and productive sciences somewhat in the same camp as the natural ones, not in some nonscientific alternative.[21]

21. Compare T. H. Irwin, "Ethics as an Inexact Science: Aristotle's Ambitions for Moral Theory," in *Moral Particularism*, ed. B. Hooker and M. Little (Oxford: Oxford University Press, 2001), pp. 100–129.

For the Most Part

Aristotle associates what holds by necessity with what holds always—"*necessary* and *always* go together (since what is necessary cannot not be)" (*GC* II 11 337^{b}35–36)—and what holds *hôs epi to polu* with what rarely fails to happen (*Top.* II 6 112^{b}10–11). It might seem, then, that *hôs epi to polu* is to be understood in terms of relative frequency, so that, at a first pass, to say that "for the most part all (*hôs d' epi to polu pantes*) crabs have the right claw bigger and stronger than the left" (*HA* IV 3 527^{b}6–7) is to say that *most* crabs do. One obvious problem with this proposal is that *hôs d'epi to polu pantes* becomes a combination of two potentially inconsistent quantifiers—"all" and "most." The same problem arises if we interpret the relevant claim to be that not having a bigger and stronger right claw is rare relative to being a crab.[22]

A second problem pertains to validity. On Aristotle's view, syllogisms with universal premises and conclusions remain valid even when these hold *hôs epi to polu*: "What follows from a thing *hôs epi to polu* and what it follows from must also be taken; for in the case of problems about what holds *hôs epi to polu*, syllogisms depend on propositions that, either all or some of them, hold *hôs epi to polu*, since the conclusion of each is similar to its starting-points [premises]" (*APr.* I 27 43^{b}32–36). The corresponding syllogisms with Most (M) in place of All (A), on the other hand, are not always valid. For example, all syllogisms of the form

A*ab*, A*bc* | A*ac*

are valid. But this is not true of all syllogisms of the form

M*ab*, M*bc* | M*ac*.

Most centenarians are women; most women are under seventy; but no centenarians are under seventy. Similarly, if something is a centenarian, it is rare that it is not a woman; if it is a woman, it is rare that it is not under

---

22. *Hôs epi to polu* is discussed somewhat inconclusively in Jonathan Barnes, *Aristotle: Posterior Analytics*, 2nd ed. (Oxford: Clarendon Press. 1994), pp. 192–193, and Lindsay Judson, "Chance and 'Always or For the Most Part' in Aristotle," in *Aristotle's Physics: A Collection of Essays*, ed. L. Judson (Oxford: Clarendon Press, 1991), pp. 73–100. The most philosophically astute discussion is Michael Thompson, *Life and Action: Elementary Structure of Practice and Practical Thought* (Cambridge, Mass.: Harvard University Press, 2008), pp. 63–82.

seventy; but it does not follow that, on the condition that something is a centenarian, it is merely rare that it is not under seventy. Thus if scientific laws or theorems that hold *hôs epi to polu* are of the form M*ab* or the like, the logic Aristotle provides for them is inconsistent.

Besides associating what holds *hôs epi to polu* with a notion of relative frequency, Aristotle also associates it with what holds "provided there is no impediment" (*Ph.* II 8 199^{b}18). It might seem, then, that theorems that hold *hôs epi to polu* might be transformed into theorems that hold necessarily and always by incorporating an explicit reference to the conditions under which the impediments are missing. M*ab* would then be analyzed as A*ab* on condition C. The problem with this suggestion is that the conditions under which A*ab* holds need not be the same as those under which A*bc* does. When they aren't, the validity of *hôs epi to polu* syllogisms is compromised, since

$$\text{A}ab \text{ on condition } C_1, \text{ A}bc \text{ on condition } C_2 \mid \text{A}ac \text{ on condition } C_x$$

is not generally valid.

Since what holds *hôs epi to polu* rarely fails to occur, it seems that the impediments that prevent something that does hold *hôs epi to polu* from holding always must themselves occur rarely. Yet this Aristotle seems to deny: "Nature tends, then, to measure the coming-to-be and passing-away of animals by the regular movements of these bodies [the sun and moon], but nature cannot bring this about rigorously because of the indeterminateness of matter, and because many starting-points exist which impede coming-to-be and passing-away from being according to nature, and often cause things to occur contrary to nature" (*GA* IV 10 778^{a}4–9). Since the "indeterminateness of matter" seems to be a standing condition, while the "many causes that hinder" are not, we should presumably divide things up as follows. The indeterminateness of matter explains why laws or theorems of natural science hold *hôs epi to polu*, and so have contraries that are rarely true, while impediments explain why what otherwise would occur rarely may occur quite often. All human beings are quadrupeds, and this would remain true even if some freak accident or genetic disorder resulted in all or most human beings having only one leg. Nonetheless, it would still hold *hôs epi to polu*, since even under normal conditions a human offspring may be born with only one leg, simply due to facts about his father's sperm (form) and his mother's menses (matter).

The moral of this investigation, then, is that when we want to explain what it is for scientific theorems to hold *hôs epi to polu*, we should begin not with the theorems themselves but with their ontological correlates or (objectively true) truth-makers—with $a{\wedge}b$ rather than Aab. Whenever we have a true scientific theorem Aab, whether holding always or *hôs epi to polu*, the fact that a and b are related by the invariant and necessary relation $\wedge$ is what makes it true. Because $\wedge$ is transitive, so that $a{\wedge}b$ and $b{\wedge}c$ cannot exist unless $a{\wedge}c$ does, the corresponding syllogism Aab, Abc | Aac is valid. That's step one. The second step brings in the indefiniteness of matter. This is a standing and ineliminable condition. It is also one that cannot be captured in universal terms, which might then be used to make the laws or theorems more rigorous by turning what holds *hôs epi to polu* into something holding universally. To think so would be the equivalent of thinking that political-ethical laws could be so transformed if only they were long and complex enough; but this is not true:

> Not everything is regulated by [universal] law, for there are some things about which a law cannot be established, so that decrees are needed instead. For the standard applying to what is indefinite is itself indefinite, like the lead ruler used in Lesbian building: the ruler adapts itself to the shape of the stone, and does not stay fixed, and the decree to actual circumstances. (*NE* V 10 1137^{b}27–32)

The effect of introducing the indefiniteness of matter is not to threaten the existence of $a{\wedge}b$, the transitivity of $\wedge$, or the validity of the corresponding syllogism. Instead, it explains why, even though the indefiniteness of matter doesn't threaten them, the law or theorem Aab nonetheless admits of exceptions because of it.

Universal ethical-political universal laws, just like natural ones, are made true by a necessary and invariant relation between universals, but they too, because of the indefiniteness of matter, hold *hôs epi to polu*. For "the noble and just things," which are the "matter" that political science investigates,[23] "admit of so much variation and irregularity that they come to seem noble and just by law alone, and not by nature" (*NE* I 3 1094^{b}14–16; compare V 10 1137^{b}19). To the well-educated person, however, who understands the degree of rigor to be expected in a given science, noble and just things are expected to hold *hôs epi to* polu, and so are rightly seen to hold by nature (*NE* I 3 1094^{b}19–27, V 7 1134^{b}24–1135^{a}5). In the case of ethics, the result of lack of education is ethical relativism and skepticism about the value of vir-

---

23. Compare *NE* V 10 1137^{b}19: "the matter (*hulê*) of what is done in action."

tue (*NE* I 3 1094^{b}16–18). In the case of natural science or medicine (say), it might be vice of a different sort, such as mistrust of reputable authorities or gullible attention to those who promise a specious certainty.

Sometimes, when Aristotle gives a sketch (*tupos*) of something, it means that a more rigorous account may be forthcoming later, so that the sketchiness is merely provisional: "At the moment we are speaking sketchily and in summary, contenting ourselves with just that; later we shall distinguish these things more rigorously" (*NE* II 7 1107^{b}14–16). But when things in a given area hold for the most part, it seems that the truth about them *must* be stated sketchily, rather than rigorously or *akribós* (*NE* II 2 1104^{a}1–5). In this case, sketchiness seems to be a function of the degree of rigor that the subject matter imposes on the science dealing with it, so that it is because "we are discussing things that hold for the most part" in ethics and political science that these sciences are sketchy or nonrigorous (*NE* I 3 1094^{b}11–22). This sort of endemic sketchiness, far from being a correctable flaw in a science, seems to be a sign of its intellectual probity—of its understanding that its degree of rigor *should* match that of its subject matter. That is why it is a mark of lack of education to expect greater rigor in a science than its subject matter permits.

Since rigor goes along with demonstration from starting-points, we might expect sketchiness to be a negative measure, so to speak, of demonstration's reach. So if a demonstration holds for the most part, its reach will to some extent be measured by the exceptions—by the variety of particular cases in which what holds for the most part fails to hold. In a brief discussion of the impact of the fortunes of our descendants and friends on our happiness, this is the connection Aristotle seems to be drawing on:

> The idea that the luck of a person's descendants and friends have not the slightest effect on him seems too devoid of friendly feeling and contrary to opinion. But since the things that happen are many and admit of all sorts of variation, some of which affect us more, some less, it would seem to be a long—even endless—task to distinguish all the particular cases, and it would perhaps be adequate to speak about the matter in general or universal terms and sketchily. (*NE* I 11 1101^{a}22–28)

It is the degree of variability especially in particulars, and the fact that they or the universals they instantiate come in degrees of more or less that explains why the universal account of them, though perhaps adequate, will inevitably be sketchy. The greater the degree of that variability, the more degrees the relevant universals exhibit, the less rigorous, and so more sketchy, the universal account of them inevitably is. The error, to call it that, is not in the science, therefore, but in its subject matter itself (*NE* V 10 1137^{b}13–19). Transmitted from there to the science, it then reemerges, when the science is practical or productive, as a measure of the level of guidance the science provides in particular cases. The more various the particular cases, the less rigorous or more sketchy the laws applying to them, the less guidance they provide, and the greater need for deliberation about what to do in those cases (*NE* II 2 1104^{a}5–10).

Natural, Mathematical, and Theoretical Sciences

The distinction between essences that involve sublunary matter and those that do not is the ontological basis for the distinction between natural and theoretical sciences, and so for the distinction between unconditional scientific knowledge and scientific knowledge of other sorts:

> If all thought were either practical or productive or theoretical, natural science would be a theoretical science, although it would provide theoretical knowledge only about such being as can undergo a process of change, and only about substance that according to its account holds for the most part, not being separate [that is, separate from perceptible or sublunary matter]. We must not fail to notice, then, the way the essence is and its account, since, without this, inquiry achieves nothing. Of things defined—that is, essences—some are like snub, some like concave. These differ because snub is bound up with matter (for snubness is concavity in a nose), while concavity is without perceptible matter. If then all natural things are like snub (for example, nose, eye, face, flesh, bone and, in general, animal, or leaf, root, bark and, in general, plant; for none of these can be defined without reference to change, but always have matter), it is clear how we must seek and define the essence of a natural thing. It is also clear that it belongs to the natural scientist in a way to provide theoretical knowledge even of the soul, that is, of so much of it as is not without matter. That natural science is theoretical, then, follows clearly from these considerations. On the other hand, mathematics is theoretical, too, but whether its objects are unchangeable and separate is unclear at present—although it is clear that there are some mathematical objects that it contemplates qua unchangeable and separate. If, however, there is something eternal and unchanging and separate, clearly the knowledge of it belongs to a theoretical science, but certainly not to natural science (for natural science deals with certain changeable things), nor to mathematics, but to a science prior to both. For natural science deals with things that are not sepa-

rate and not unchangeable; some parts of mathematics, deal with things that are unchangeable but perhaps not separate but in matter; while the primary science deals with things both separate and unchangeable. (*Met.* VI 1 1025^{b}25–1026^{a}16)

The essence of a natural being has a certain structure, which is illustrated by the example of snubness: it is a form (concavity) in sublunary matter (a nose) (*Met.* VII 8 1033^{b}24–26, XI 7 1064^{a}19–28). By having such a structure, it reflects the fact that natural beings are essentially changeable things, which come-to-be and pass-away (*Met.* VII 11 1036^{b}21–32). Similarly, the essences of eternal beings, by lacking universal sublunary matter, reflect the fact that such beings are unchangeable and immortal (*Met.* VII 11 1037^{a}29–^{b}5, XII 8 1074^{a}33–36).

For the same reason, psychology, the science of soul, is a divided science. For most affections of the soul are affections of the hylomorphic compound that is the ensouled body, so that their definitions are "enmattered definitions" (*DA* I 1 403^{a}25), whose structure is akin to that of snub. Anger, for example, should be defined as "a particular movement of a body of such and such a kind (or part or potentiality of it) as a result of this thing and for the sake of that" (*DA* I 1 403^{a}26–27). That is why anger, which is "boiling of the blood around the heart" (*DA* I 1 403^{a}31–^{b}1) for the sake of revenge, can cause *pneuma* to expand, which can, in turn, cause the appropriate movement of the limbs by the relevant sort of pushing and pulling. Understanding, since it does not involve any sublunary matter, is not like this. Hence, provided it does not depend for its existence on such an embodied affection as imagination, it is studied not by a natural science but, like astronomy or theology, by a strictly theoretical one (*DA* I 1 403^{a}8–10).

Mathematical objects (lines, numbers, and so on) also have a distinctive material constituent, namely, intelligible matter: "Some matter is perceptible, such as bronze, wood, and all changeable matter, whereas other matter is intelligible—that is, what is present in perceptible objects but not *qua* perceptible, such as the matter of mathematical objects" (*Met.* VII 10 1036^{a}9–12). Such matter is not something besides earth, water, air, and fire, but an abstraction from them:

Mathematicians produce theoretical knowledge that deals with abstractions. For in their theorizing they eliminate all perceptible attributes—such as weight and lightness, hardness and its contrary, heat and cold, and all the other perceptible contraries—and leave only the quantitative and the continuous, sometimes in one, sometimes in two, sometimes in three dimensions, and the attributes of things *qua* quantitative and *qua* continuous, and do not theorize about any of their other aspects. (*Met.* XI 3 1061ª28–35)

Because they are constituted of intelligible matter, mathematical objects are essentially spatial, numbers being conceived of as "sections and divisions of lines" (*Met.* XI 2 1060ᵇ15), while their intrinsic attributes are those that belong to them "qua lengths or qua planes" (*Met.* XIII 3 1078ª8–9). Hence their essences, as mathematical starting-points, must reveal their essential spatiality by also containing a material constituent: "Some matter is intelligible, and some perceptible, and of the account [that is, the essence] always one part is the matter and the other the actuality [that is, the form]—circle, for example, is plane figure" (*Met.* VIII 6 1045ª33–35). Like natural essences, therefore, mathematical ones are "a sort of compound of this account [form] and this matter taken universally" (*Met.* VII 10 1035ᵇ29–30)—that is to say, they are the result of abstracting from both the material and formal constituents of particular mathematical objects. In the case of a circle's essence, these are *plane* (matter) and *figure* (form). Since intelligible matter is an abstraction, there is no question of it offering any resistance to, or anywise deforming, the formal constituent of a mathematical essence. Hence it poses no obstacle to a mathematical theorem's holding universally and with unconditional necessity.

Astronomical objects (heavenly bodies) are similar in structure to natural and mathematical ones, except that their material constituent is ether. Because ether is not, like intelligible matter, an abstraction, astronomical objects are perceptible substances. Because it is invariantly homogenous throughout, different bits of it are not differently resistance to form.[24] It is these facts that explain why astronomy provides "theoretical knowledge of substance that is perceptible but eternal, whereas the others, namely, arithmetic and geometry, do not deal with substance at all" (*Met.* XII 8 1073ᵇ5–8). As in the other cases, this fact about astronomy must derive from the structure of the essences of the heavenly bodies, since these are its starting-points. By parity of reasoning, therefore (since no text explicitly says as much), these essences, too, must have a material constituent, which must be ether taken universally.

24. Although variation of some sort occurs as we approach the sublunary realm: "We say that the upper region as far down as the moon (*mechri selênês*) is occupied by a body [ether] different from air or fire, but varying in purity and freedom from admixture, and admitting of variation (*diaphoras echein*), especially toward its limit on the side of the air, and the heavens surrounding the earth" (*Mete.* I 3 340ᵇ6–10).

God, the subject of theology, is "eternal and a substance and an activity" (*Met.* XII 7 1072ª25–26), and so is entirely without matter (*Met.* XII 6 1071ᵇ20–21). For matter is "what is in potentiality [something]" (*Met.* VIII 2 1042ᵇ9–10), and God is not in potentiality anything, since he is in essence an activity or actuality (*Met.* XII 6 1071ᵇ17–20). Since form is both activity and substance (*Met.* IX 8 1050ᵇ2–3), it follows that God is a pure form. As a result, he stands in a different relation to his essence from those beings whose essences involve a universal material component stand to theirs:

> The [primary] substance is the form present in the thing, and the compound substance is said to be composed of it and the matter. Concavity is an example [of such a form], for a snub nose and snubness are composed of it and nose. . . . And in the compound substance (for example snub nose and Callias) matter will also be present. . . . But in some cases, a thing and its essence are the same, that is, in the case of primary substances (for example, curvature is the same as the essence of curvature, if curvature is a primary substance). By primary substance I mean one that does not imply the presence of something in something else—that is, in a subject which is its matter. But if a thing is a substance by being matter or composed of matter, it is not the same as its essence. (*Met.* VII 11 1037ª29–ᵇ5)

These different relations in which beings stand to their essences, explained by the different structures of those essences, explain why theology is the most rigorous of the theoretical sciences.

Rigor and Esteem

What determines a craft's or science's degree of rigor (*akribeia*) is measured along three different dimensions:

> One science is more rigorous than another, and prior to it, if [1] it is both of the fact and the reason why, and not of the fact separately from giving the scientific knowledge of the reason why; or if [2] if it is not said of an underlying subject and the other is said of an underlying subject (as, for example, arithmetic is more rigorous than harmonics); or if [3] it proceeds from fewer things and the other from some additional posit (as, for example, arithmetic is more rigorous than geometry). By from an additional posit I mean, for example, that a unit is a substance without position and a point is a substance with position—the latter proceeds from an additional posit. (*APo.* I 27 87ª31–37)

Differences between [1] scientific knowledge of a fact and of its explanation are divided into two classes: [1a] those that occur within a single science, and [1b] those that occur between two different sciences. [1a], in turn, is divided into [1a*] cases in which "the syllogism does not proceed through immediates (that is, where the primitive explanation is not employed, but scientific knowledge of the reason why is in accord with the primitive explanation)," and [1a**] cases in which "the syllogism does proceed through immediates, although not through the explanation, but through the more familiar of the converting terms" (*APo.* I 13 78ᵃ22–28).

A purported "demonstration that the planets are near through their not twinkling" (*APo.* I 13 78ᵃ30), for example, belongs to [1a*]. For while it is a fact that the planets do not twinkle and a fact (established by perception or induction) that what does not twinkle is near, a syllogism from them showing that the planets are near "is of the fact, but does not give the reason why; for it is not because the planets do not twinkle that they are near—rather, because they are near they do not twinkle" (*APo.* I 13 78ᵃ36–38). A second example—which deduces that the moon is spherical from the fact that whatever waxes in a certain way is spherical, and the moon so waxes— belongs to [1a**]. Here the syllogism is supposedly from immediates, since "if the middle term is reversed, the syllogism does give the reason why" (*APo.* I 13 78ᵇ7–8). Instead of using the correct middle term "waxes," however, it uses the more familiar "spherical," thus preventing the syllogism from giving the explanation: "for it is not because of its waxing that the moon is spherical—rather, because it is spherical it waxes in this way" (*APo.* I 13 78ᵇ8–10). The version of astronomy that demonstrates that the moon waxes from its being spherical is thus more rigorous than the one that deduces its sphericity from the fact that it waxes.

As examples of [1b], Aristotle cites cases in which a science that is of the facts falls under another science that gives their explanation:

> The reason why differs from the fact in another fashion, when each is considered by means of a different science. These are sciences that are related to one another in such way that the one is under the other, as, for example, optics is under geometry, mechanics under solid geometry, harmonics under arithmetic, and stargazing under astronomy. . . . For here it is for the scientists who deal with perceptibles to know the facts and for the mathematical scientists to know the reasons why. For the latter possess demonstrations that give the explanations, and often they do not know the facts, just as people who have theoretical knowledge of universals often do not know some of the particulars through lack of observation. (*APo.* I 13 78ᵇ34–79ᵃ6)

In some cases, however, the less rigorous science need not fall under the more rigorous one. Thus medicine does not fall under geometry, yet it belongs to medicine to know the fact that curved wounds heal more slowly, and to geometry to explain why this is so (circles have the largest area to periphery ratio).

[2] is a further explication of [1b], and so, in effect, of [1]. For one science may be more rigorous than another because they deal with the same universal essences or forms, but in an importantly different way: "These are [sciences] which, being somewhat different in essence, make use of [the same] forms. For mathematics is concerned with forms, since its objects are not said of any subject, since even if geometrical objects *are* said of some subject, still it is not insofar as they are said of a subject that they are known" (*APo.* I 13 79ᵃ6–10). Thus optics, for example, provides knowledge of lines, insofar as these are visible—that is, insofar as they are said of some perceptible sublunary matter that serves as their underlying subject. Geometry, on the other hand, because it deals with lines and points in abstraction from matter, can achieve far greater *akribeia*: "There will be difficulties in natural science that are not present in mathematics, for mathematical objects are spoken of in abstraction [from matter], physical ones, with an additional posit" (*Cael.* III 1 299ᵃ13–17). That is why "mathematically rigorous arguments are not to be demanded in all cases, but only in the case of things that have no matter" (*Met.* II 3 995ᵃ14–16). Since positing is the inverse of abstraction, [3] is related to [2]. The reason sciences "involving fewer posits are more rigorous than those involving additional ones" (*Met.* I 2 982ᵃ25–27) is that each further posit is a further undemonstrated fact, which a different science will be needed to explain.

The upshot of [1–3] is thus twofold. First, the most rigorous version or formulation of a science is the most explanatory one—the one consisting of demonstrations from starting-points. Second, of two sciences, formulated in the most rigorous way, one is more rigorous than the other if it demonstrates facts that the other deals with but does not demonstrate. Since strictly theoretical sciences, such as theology, astronomy, or mathematics, have essences that involve no sublunary matter as starting-points, they will be more rigorous than any natural science, because a natural science has to posit sublunary matter in addition to such starting-points. It is among the strictly theoretical sciences, therefore, that the most rigorous one will be found; and it will be the one that explains what the others treat as a fact or undemonstrated posit.

According to *Top.* II 4 111ᵃ8–9, "illuminating" (*saphês*) and "rigorous" (*akribês*) are equivalent in meaning: "it is well to replace a word with a better known equivalent, for example, instead of 'rigorous' in describing a supposition, 'illuminating.' " Rendering a truth illuminating, however, consists in giving an explanation of it by demonstrating it from the starting-points of a science: "Beginning with things that are truly stated, but not illuminatingly, we proceed to make them illuminating as well. . . . That is precisely why even political scientists shouldn't regard as irrelevant to their work the sort of theoretical knowledge that makes evident (*phaneron*) not only the fact, but also the reason why" (*EE* I 6 1216ᵇ32–39). Hence the notion of illumination is also related to explanatoriness, and so—in Aristotle's mind at least—to demonstration from starting-points.

Esteem, too, has similar connotations and connections. To say that something is estimable (*timios*) is to ascribe a distinct sort of goodness or value to it: "By what is estimable I mean such things as what is divine, what is superior (for example, soul, understanding), what is more time-honored, what is a starting-point, and so on" (*MM* I 2 1183ᵇ21–23). Thus happiness is "something estimable and complete . . . since it is a starting-point . . . and the starting-point and the cause of goods is something we take to be estimable and divine" (*NE* I 12 1102ᵃ1–4). Similarly, architectonic craftsmen are more estimable than handicraftsmen "because they know the explanations of their products"(*Met.* I 1 981ᵃ30–ᵇ1). The core sense of *timios*, however, is perhaps best captured in the remark that ordinary people "commonly say of those they find especially estimable and especially love that they 'come first' " (*Cat.* 12 14ᵇ5–7). Something is thus objectively *timios* when—like starting-points and causes—it "comes first by nature" (*Cat.* 12 14ᵇ3–5). Since sciences inherit their level of esteem from the kinds of beings they deal with (*Met.* XI 7 1064ᵇ4–5), the "most estimable science must deal with the most estimable genus of beings" (*Met.* VI 1 1026ᵃ21–22).[25] Because the most rigorous science provides scientific knowledge of ultimate starting-points and causes, it follows that the most rigorous science must also be the most estimable. That is why theoretical wisdom, as "the most rigorous of the sciences," must deal with "the most estimable things" (*NE* VI 7 1141ᵃ16–20).

Human beings are certainly the best—in the sense of most estimable or most divine—of the *sublunary* animals, since they alone have divine understanding full blown. But they are not the best or most divine of animals

---

25. For parallel reasons, "expenditures for the gods—votive offerings, ritual paraphernalia, and sacrifices, and so on for everything having to do with the divine" are particularly *timios* (*NE* IV 2 1122ᵇ19–21).

unconditionally speaking. For the heavenly bodies are also animals or living beings, possessed of divine understanding and wish, and they, as fundamental starting-points of movement, whose own movement is immortal and unchangeable, are more estimable than human beings (*Cael.* II 12 292ᵃ18–21, *Met.* XII 8 1073ᵃ23–ᵇ1). As "the most evident" of divine beings (*NE* VI 7 1141ᵇ1), because clearly visible in the night sky for all to see, they are the "most divine of things evident [to the senses]" (*Ph.* II 4 196ᵃ33–34), and the ones that make it "clear that if the divine is present anywhere," it is in the subject matter of astronomy and theology (*Met.* VI 1 1026ᵃ19–21). It is among these sciences, then, that theoretical wisdom is to be found.

To explain why there is movement in the universe, including in the heavens studied by astronomy, there must be a mover that actualizes the potentiality that things have to move without itself being in movement. If this mover were not a substance, it would depend ontologically on something that was a substance, and so would not itself be a starting-point of movement. If it were a substantial hylomorphic compound, it would be a potentiality (matter) actualized (form), and so its actualization would need explanation by something whose own actualization needed no further such explanation. Finally, if it were subject to coming-to-be and passing-away, if it were not eternal, if its existence were not essential to it, the fact that it existed would require further explanation. It follows that there must be a mover "the substance or essence of which is activity," and so is "without matter" (*Met.* XII 6 1071ᵇ20–21), and it must "move without being moved, since it is eternal, a substance, and an activity" (*Met.* XII 7 1072ᵃ25–26). This unmoved *prime mover*, which is the explanatory starting-point of all movement or change, is, as we saw, God.

God himself, however, is self-explanatory. For as an active understanding of active understanding (*Met.* XII 9 1074ᵇ15–35), he is his own efficient cause, eternally actualized by himself as the object of his own understanding. As a pure form, he is his own formal cause, and needs no material one. As the best good, he is his own final or teleological cause. For just as the final cause for a human being is the human good or happiness, which is activity in accord with theoretical wisdom, so God's final cause is also that activity. The crucial difference is that God *is* that activity, while we are not (*EE* VII 12 1245ᵇ18–19, *Met.* XII 9 1075ᵃ5–10). In actively understanding his form or essence, then, God is understanding both himself and his own starting-points and causes:

> Of some things the cause of their necessity is something else, of others nothing [else], but rather it is because of them that other things are necessary. It

follows that what is necessary in the primary and full sense is what is simple [namely, God], since it does not admit of more than one state, so that it does not admit even of one after the other, since it would thereby admit of more than one. (*Met.* V 5 1015^{b}9–14)

Apparently, then, theology—the science of God—meets all three of the conditions for being the primary and most rigorous science. In particular, it does not posit or presuppose the fact of God's existence in demonstrating things about him, since in his unique case, the fact that he exists and the reasons why he does are the same. Since theoretical wisdom is the most rigorous scientific knowledge of the most estimable things, it must just be theology.

4

VIRTUE OF CHARACTER

While theoretical wisdom ensures the well-functioning of the scientific part of the soul, shown by its correct grasp of plain truth about the most estimable things, practical wisdom does the same for the calculative or deliberative part, ensuring its correct grasp of the practical truth about human actions, ends, and goods. Without the existence of virtue of character in the soul's desiring part, however, practical wisdom cannot exist in the calculative or deliberative one. It is with virtue of character, therefore, that an account of practical wisdom must begin.

The Doctrine of the Mean

Virtue of character (*NE* II 1–6) is a starting-point of political science (*politikê*), the science of which ethics or ethical science (*êthikê*) is a part (*NE* I 2 1094^{b}10–11). To meet the requirements of scientific explanation, its definition must determine virtue's real essence by specifying its genus and differentia (*NE* II 5–6 1106^{a}12–15) and so must be based on the appropriate sort of evidence. In the case of ethics, such evidence consists of "what is known to us" about noble and just things, because we have been brought up with the right sort of habits (*NE* I 4 1095^{b}4–6). Beginning with this, we proceed—as in all sciences—to try to explain it by giving a demonstration of it from starting-points whose definitions we have articulated and aporematically defended. When this task is complete, what was known to us on the basis of things with which we were already familiar becomes known unconditionally (*NE* I 4 1095^{b}2–8).

Noble and just things, however, admit of "much variation and irregularity," and so we should be content "to demonstrate the truth [about them] roughly and in outline, and, because we are discussing things that hold for the most part, and starting from them, to draw conclusions of the same sort" (*NE* I 3 1094^{b}11–22). It is with an elaboration of this warning about the aim of ethics and the quality of evidence available in it that Aristotle begins his attempt to define virtue.

Ethics is a practical science, whose purpose is not knowledge merely but ethical improvement: "It is not to know what virtue is that we are inquiring into it, but to become good people, otherwise there would be no benefit in it, and so we must inquire into matters relating to actions, that is, how we should do them, since it is they, indeed, that determine what sorts of states [of character] we come to have" (*NE* II 2 1103^{b}27–31). It is generally agreed, moreover, that we should "act in accord with the correct reason" (*NE* II 2 1103^{b}31–34). Hence a fuller characterization of the relevant actions must await an explanation of what that reason is, and how the virtues of character relate to it (*NE* VI 1 1138^{b}18–20).

Even with this explanation in hand, the account of the universal class of these actions "must be stated in outline, not rigorously," since "matters of action and what things are advantageous, just like matters of health, have nothing fixed about them" (*NE* II 2 1104^{a}1–5). And if the account of the universal is like that, the one dealing with particulars will be "even less rigorous, since they do not fall under any craft or set of instructions, and agents must consider in each case what is opportune in the prevailing circumstances, as also happens in the cases of medicine and navigation" (*NE* II 2 1104^{a}5–10). For more than one reason, then, we should not expect an account of the universal class of actions that produce virtue to provide much in the way of guidance about what to do in particular cases.

The first component of the account of the actions productive of virtue consists of evidence derived from everyday experience of training athletes and bringing up children:

> We should observe first that states of this sort are by nature destroyed by deficiency and excess, just as we see happen—since we must use clear cases to testify on behalf of unclear ones—in the case of strength and health. For both excessive and deficient exercise destroy physical strength and likewise too much or too little food and drink destroys our health, whereas the proportionate amount produces, increases, and preserves it. The same goes in fact for temperance, courage, and the other virtues: the one who runs away from and fears everything and stands up to nothing becomes cowardly, while the one who fears nothing at all but faces up to everything becomes rash. Similarly, too, someone who indulges in every pleasure and refrains from none becomes intemperate, while someone who runs away from every pleasure, as boors do,

becomes somehow insensitive. Temperance and courage are destroyed by excess and deficiency, then, and preserved by the mean. (*NE* II 2 1104ª11–27)

What this evidence suggests is that virtue, like strength and health, is some sort of mean state or condition, which in turn helps explain why it is preserved and destroyed in the way it is.

With a foothold established for a mean in actions that further the acquisition of the virtues, a second is found in those stemming from virtues already acquired. When someone possesses physical strength as a result of "taking much nourishment and withstanding much exertion," these are also things that he becomes most capable of doing (*NE* II 2 1104ª31–33). Similarly, when we have become temperate through abstaining from pleasures, we are "most capable of abstaining from them," and when we have become courageous "though being habituated to disdain frightening situations," we are most capable of standing firm in the face of them (*NE* II 2 1104ᵇ1–3). This, too, is a broadly empirical claim—albeit one Aristotle thinks particularly uncontroversial (*NE* III 5 1114ª9–10). For there is no conceptual guarantee that the actions productive of virtue of character must themselves be virtuous: temperance might be produced by doing actions of one sort, while manifesting itself in actions of a quite different sort.

It is hardly an accident that he finds these particular (putative) facts to be of potential relevance to defining and explaining what virtue is.[1] For mean conditions of various sorts play fundamental explanatory roles in his other sciences: (*physics*) "It is due to a mean that the dry and the moist and the other elements produce flesh and bone and the remaining compounds" (*GC* II 7 334ᵇ28–30); (*physiology*) "The blood in the middle cavity of the heart is a mean both in quantity and in heat, though it is the purest; for the starting-point should remain as calm as possible, which it is when the blood is pure and in a mean in quantity and heat" (*PA* III 4 667ª3–6); (*embryology*) "If the hot is too powerful it dries up wet things, if it is too deficient, it fails to make them set, what it must have in relation to the thing being produced is the proportionate mean" (*GA* IV 2 767ª17–19). Moreover, because "nature, like the understanding, always does what it does for the sake of something, which something is its end" (*DA* II 4 415ᵇ16–17), these mean conditions have a normative status. Their role in the theory of perception shows this

1. Noticed by Rosalind Hursthouse, "The Central Doctrine of the Mean," in *The Blackwell Guide to Aristotle's Nicomachean Ethics*, ed. R. Kraut (Oxford: Blackwell, 2006), pp. 96–115.

clearly: "We do not perceive anything as dry or wet, or as hard or soft, but only the excesses in either direction, because the sense is a sort of mean between the contraries in objects of perception" (*DA* II 11 424ª2–5). To function well, therefore, and discern sounds or textures accurately, a sense organ must be in a certain sort of mean state. Hence if the virtues can be shown to be mean states, they too will emerge as accurate discerners, valuable and choiceworthy as such.

Next comes an important set of—again broadly empirical—claims about the involvement of pleasure and pain in virtue-producing actions.

[1] "Pleasure causes us to do ignoble actions, and pain, to abstain from noble ones" (*NE* II 3 1104ᵇ9–11).

[2] "Every feeling and every action involves pleasure or pain"—for actions are caused by feelings (desires), which they either painfully frustrate or pleasurably satisfy (*NE* II 5 1105ᵇ21–23).

[3] Correction (like other forms of medical treatment) operates through the contraries of punishment (pain) and reward (pleasure) (*NE* II 3 1104ᵇ16–18).

[4] "It is because of pleasures and pains that people become ignoble—by pursuing or avoiding the ones they shouldn't, or at the time they shouldn't, or in a manner they shouldn't, or in however many other ways should be distinguished in one's account" (*NE* II 3 1104ᵇ21–24).

[5] There are three objects of choice and three of avoidance—noble, useful, pleasant, and their contraries, ignoble, harmful, painful. Concerning all of these, the good man "is correct and the bad one in error, but especially where pleasure is concerned. For pleasure is shared with animals and accompanies every object of choice, since the noble and the useful seem pleasant as well" (*NE* II 3 1104ᵇ30–1105ª1).

[6] Pleasure is something "we have all grown up with since infancy, which is why this feeling is difficult to rub out, dyed as it is into the fabric of our lives. To a greater or lesser extent, indeed, what we use as the standard of our actions is pleasure and pain. That is why, then, our whole enterprise must be about them, since whether we feel pleasure or pain well or badly has no small effect on our actions" (*NE* II 3 1105ª1–7).

[7] Pleasure is "more difficult to fight against than spirit . . . and it is with what is more difficult that both craft and virtue are always concerned, since to do well in such a case is also better. So for this reason, too, the entire enterprise of virtue and political science must be concerned

with pleasures and pains. For the man who experiences them well will be good, and the one who does so badly, will be bad" (*NE* II 3 1105ª7–13).

Because the virtues of character are "concerned with actions and feelings" (*NE* II 3 1104ᵇ13–14), these claims about pleasure and pain also have consequences for them.

The first—derived from [1] but probably with at least [2] and [5] in view—is *Conclusion 1*: "We should take as an indication of people's states of character the pleasure or pain that supervenes on their deeds. For someone who abstains from bodily pleasures and enjoys doing simply this is temperate, while someone distressed by it is intemperate, and someone who faces up to frightening situations and enjoys doing so—or at least isn't pained by it—is courageous, while the one who is pained is cowardly" (*NE* II 3 1104ᵇ3–8). What is puzzling about this conclusion is a result of the binary opposition it employs between enjoying and being distressed, which excludes from view two intermediate cases, namely, continence and incontinence. The continent person does what virtue requires, and thus gets the pleasure of satisfying his wish, but at the cost of the distress associated with frustrating his opposing appetites or feelings (*NE* I 13 1102ᵇ13–25, IX 1166ᵇ18–25). The incontinent person, on the other hand, in acting against virtue, gets the pleasure of satisfying his appetites and feelings, but at the cost of the distress associated with frustrating his opposing wish (*DA* III 9 433ª1–8). Someone who felt *only* distress in doing what temperance or courage required would indeed be intemperate or cowardly, therefore, although the person who felt some distress need not be. By excluding these intermediate cases, *Conclusion 1* may avoid complexity, but it does so at some cost to the point it is making. For it is because the differences between a continent or virtuous person and an incontinent or vicious one lie not in their actions but in their desires and feelings that pleasure and pain, and not action alone, should be taken as the sign of someone's state of character.

A second consequence, also drawn from [1]—but surely with [3], [6], and [7] in view—is *Conclusion 2*: "We need to have been brought up in a certain way from childhood onward, as Plato says [*Laws* II 653a-c], in order to take pleasure in and be pained by the things we should, since this is what correct education is" (*NE* II 3 1104ᵇ11–13). Bodily pleasures and pains are there from the beginning of our lives shaping our desires and aversions, which—in their initial forms, at least—just are natural motivating sensitivities to perceived pleasures and pains, of the sort also present in animals. Hence it isn't just our desires that pleasures and pains affect but our practical perception and thought, and how things in the practical sphere look to us. That is why early education is necessary, and why correction can even at that stage take the form of reward and punishment, carrot and stick. Hence political science, concerned as it is with the public education of citizens in virtue, must also be concerned with pleasure and pain (*NE* X 9).

The final consequence, drawn from [1–4]—but with [5] and [6] clearly in view—is *Conclusion 3*: "Virtue is the sort of state that acts in the best ways as regards pleasures and pains, and vice, the contrary one" (*NE* II 3 1104^{b}27–28). This is the most obviously proleptic conclusion of the three. For pleasure and pain could play all the roles described in [1–4] without playing any in an agent's deliberation about what to do, and so without having any direct relevance to virtue and vice, considered as states involving deliberate choice (*NE* II 5 1106^{a}3–4). The further fact, therefore, that all objects of choice involve pleasure and pain, which are themselves employed to some extent as standards for deciding what to do, is needed to reach *Conclusion 3*, which, in turn, supports [7].

Summing up this evidence, Aristotle concludes that virtue "is involved with pleasures and pains; that the things that produce it are also the ones that increase it or—if they are not done in the correlative way—destroy it; and that the things that produce it are also the ones its activity involves" (*NE* II 3 1105^{a}13–16). The puzzle he immediately raises for this conclusion shows again that the virtues and their acquisition, not virtuous actions per se, are his primary concern: "Someone might be puzzled, however, about what we mean when we say that we become just by doing just actions, and temperate by doing temperate ones, because if we are doing just and temperate actions, we are already just and temperate, in the same way as we are grammatical or musical if we are doing grammatical or musical ones" (*NE* II 4 1105^{a}17–21). The first mistake the puzzle-raiser makes, therefore, is to mischaracterize craft production: producing a grammatical sentence not simply by luck or under another's instruction involves doing it "in a grammatical way, that is, in accord with the knowledge of grammar that is in oneself" (*NE* II 4 1105^{a}22–26).

Second, the puzzle-raiser relies on a false analogy between virtues and crafts. The products of a craft "have in themselves the mark of being done well," so that good products are generally the measure of good craftsmanship (*Cael.* III 7 306^{a}14–17). But an agent's actions are not the measure of his state of character (continence also results in actions in accord with virtue). In addition, the agent must do them in a certain way: "first, he must do them knowingly; second, he must deliberately choose to do them, and deliberately choose to do them because of themselves; third, he must do them from a firm and unchanging state of character" (*NE* II 4 1105ᵃ31–33). Besides, a craft is an entirely cognitive potentiality. A musician is someone who knows, for example, how and when to play a B-natural. If his aim is to sabotage the performance, he may play a C-sharp instead, without in any way compromising his status as a skilled musician (*NE* VI 5 1140ᵇ21–24). Where virtue is concerned, bare knowledge of what action virtue requires and how to do it "counts for nothing, or rather for only a little" (*NE* II 4 1105ᵇ2–3), since it is what one reliably chooses to do that determines whether one is virtuous (*NE* VII 10 1152ᵃ8–9). Choice depends not simply on what one knows, however, but on the appetites and desires involved in one's choices. For if these are to be as virtue requires, so that we *feel* them "when we should, about the things we should, toward the people we should, for the end we should, and in the way we should," we must repeatedly do virtuous actions from childhood on (*NE* II 6 1106ᵇ21–22).

The difference between crafts and virtues isn't that virtue is acquired through doing virtuous acts while crafts are not acquired in an analogous way. Aristotle is quite explicit that they are entirely on a par in this regard: "We acquire the virtues through having first engaged in the activities, as also happens in all the crafts, since the way we learn the things we should do is by doing them" (*NE* II 1 1103ᵃ31–33). His point is that repetition has an entirely cognitive role in the acquisition of craft knowledge, but not of virtue. A craft's starting-points are acquired through induction from experience (*APo.* II 19 100ᵃ3–9), as befits a cognitive state best exemplified by the architectonic practitioner who knows the theory behind his products, not the one who knows how to make them (*Met.* I 1 981ᵃ30–ᵇ1). Virtue of character is quite different. It is acquired through habituation (*ethismos*), not induction (*NE* I 7 1098ᵇ4, II 1 1103ᵃ17), and is best exemplified by the person whose deliberate choices and actions involve it.

Having characterized, however vaguely, the universal class of virtue-producing actions, Aristotle turns to the focal question of virtue's definition—its genus and differentia. As a sort of virtue, virtue of character is a quality (*Cat.* 8 8ᵇ29, *NE* I 6 1096ᵃ25). As specifically virtue of character, it belongs to the desiring part of the soul, comprising appetites or emotions (*NE* I 13 1103ᵃ1–10), and "generally, whatever is accompanied by pleasure or pain," and so must be some quality relating to these (*NE* II 5 1105ᵇ21–23). That is why the list of things it might turn out to be is restricted to *pathê*, *dunameis*, and *hexeis*—affections, dispositions or potentialities, and states

(*NE* II 5 1105^{b}19–21). Through possessing a desiring part in an appropriate condition, we may have the quality of actually feeling (or being affected by) an appetite or emotion, or of being capable of feeling it, or of "being well or badly disposed in relation" to it—as we are badly disposed in relation to anger if we are disposed to feel it violently or sluggishly, well disposed if we are disposed to feel it to an intermediate degree (*NE* II 5 1105^{b}21–28).

That virtues are not feelings is clear from the fact that we are not called good because we have feelings but because we have virtues, and are not praised or blamed simply for having feelings but because of feeling them in a certain way (too much, say, or too little). Moreover, we feel things without deliberate choice being involved, whereas the virtues are "kinds of deliberate choice, or at least don't exist without deliberate choice" (*NE* II 5 1106^{a}3–4). Finally, when we feel something, we are moved, but when we are virtuous we are not moved, but in a certain state. The same considerations show that virtues are not dispositions—as does the further fact that we have our dispositions by nature, but not our virtues of character (*NE* II 1 1103^{a}18–^{b}2). By process of elimination, virtue of character is assigned to the genus of states (*NE* II 5 1106^{a}10–12).

Since "every virtue completes the good condition of the thing whose function it is and makes it perform its function well," virtue of character must do this for the soul's desiring part (*NE* II 6 1106^{a}15–17). Hence it must ensure that we desire and feel, and so—since appetites and feelings affect action— act as we should. It is in this regard that the mean *in relation to us* is introduced, and it is what serves as one of virtue of character's differentiae. The discussion begins with an existence claim, which might seem to be conceptually based: "In everything continuous and divisible it is possible to take more, less, and an equal amount, and these either with respect to the object itself or in relation to us; and the equal is a sort of mean between excess and deficiency" (*NE* II 6 1106^{a}26–29).[2] If the disjunction has conjunctive force, however, the claim is not a truth of any sort, let alone a conceptual one. Any segment of the number line has a mid or mean point, but there need be nothing excessive or deficient in the segment, considered in isolation. Similarly, there may be no amount of food that is in an arithmetic mean between an amount excessive for someone and one that is deficient, since food is not indefinitely divisible. If, on the other hand, the disjunction has disjunctive force,

---

2. Christof Rapp, "What Use Is Aristotle's Doctrine of the Mean?," in *The Virtuous Life in Greek Ethics*, ed. B. Reis (Cambridge: Cambridge University Press, 2006), pp. 99–126, argues that the claim is conceptually based.

the claim—while perhaps true—is not a *conceptual* truth. For even if a mean in relation to us existed in feelings and action (which is hardly a conceptual matter), it doesn't follow that this mean is necessarily good or choiceworthy. If nothing really did succeed like excess, it would presumably be neither.

In any event, Aristotle does not treat the existence of a *choiceworthy* mean in feelings and actions as following from the existence claim alone but bases it in part on an argument appealing to empirical facts about crafts and sciences:

> By the mean with respect to the object itself I mean what is equidistant from each of its extremes, this being one single thing and the same for everyone, whereas in relation to us the mean is what is neither excessive nor deficient— and this is not one single thing and is not the same for everyone. So, for example, if ten are many and two are few, six is what people take as the mean with respect to the object, because it exceeds and is exceeded by the same amount. This is the mean with respect to numerical proportion. But that is not how the mean in relation to us should be taken. For if ten pounds is a large amount for someone to eat and two a small one, the trainer will not prescribe six [the arithmetic mean], since this might either be a large amount for the person taking it, or a small one—small for Milo, large for the person just beginning his training; and the same holds in running and wrestling. It is in this way, then, that every expert in a science avoids excess and deficiency, and seeks and chooses the mean—the mean not in the object, then, but the one in relation to us. (*NE* II 6 1106^{a}29–^{b}7)

Implicit in this portrayal of physical training and other crafts and sciences is a conception of them as naturally or essentially good seeking. Because health is medicine's end or the good it seeks, a doctor does not "deliberate about whether he will cure," since insofar as he is simply practicing medicine, he necessarily aims to cure (*NE* III 3 1112^{b}12–13). In the same way, oratory necessarily aims to persuade, household management to acquire wealth, and other crafts and practical sciences to achieve their defining ends (*NE* I 1 1094^{a}6–9, III 3 1112^{b}12–15). This does not mean that crafts or sciences cannot be used for ends other than their natural ones, only that when they are, they are being controlled by something else, which uses them for its purposes, as a vicious person might use his knowledge of medicine to cause someone pain or injury (*EE* VIII 1 1246^{a}26–35).

Since crafts and sciences have this feature, they are suitable for inclusion in *telic hierarchies*, where they are under the control of the maximally architectonic craft of political science, which prescribes and coordinates all their activities, with the aim of furthering happiness. That is why practical wisdom, of which political science is a branch, is a starting-point not just of the practical science of ethics, but of all the productive crafts as well (*NE* VI 2 1139^{b}1–4): we build houses, make shoes, amass wealth, practice medicine, persuade audiences—in fact, do everything we do or do wisely—to achieve the happiness that is practical wisdom's defining end (*NE* I 12 1102^{a}1–4). The supposed fact that all crafts and practical sciences seek and choose the mean in relation to us, therefore, *is* evidence of its relevance to happiness, and so of its choiceworthiness.

The next step in the argument is a complex conditional whose first antecedent has this supposed fact as a conjunct: "If, then, every science completes its function well in this way, by looking to the mean and guiding what it produces by reference to it . . . and if virtue . . . is more rigorous and better than any craft, it will also be the sort of thing that is able to hit the mean" (*NE* II 6 1106^{b}8–16). Crucial to the antecedent's second conjunct is the notion of rigor. The ultimate end of a craft is happiness, but the craft cannot achieve it unaided. For happiness is a starting-point, and about it practical wisdom is "true supposition" (*NE* VI 9 1142^{b}33). Only when controlled by practical wisdom, therefore, can a craft achieve its ultimate end. What makes practical wisdom's supposition true, in turn, is virtue of character, since it is "natural or habituated" virtue of character "that teaches correct belief about the starting-point" (*NE* VII 8 1151^{a}18–19). Just as a science S that provides scientific knowledge of the starting-points of S* is more rigorous than S*, so virtue, in providing correct belief about the ultimate starting-point of the crafts, is more rigorous than any of them.

With the choiceworthiness of the mean in feelings and actions partly justified, two further considerations are adduced in support of it. The first concerns praise and blame: "Virtue of character is concerned with feelings and actions, in which excess and deficiency are errors and are blamed,[3] while the mean is correct and is praised—and both of these are features of virtue. Virtue, then, is a sort of mean insofar as it is able to hit the mean" (*NE* II 6 1106^{b}24–28). The argument here trades on three claims:

[1] Virtue and vice are concerned with feelings and actions.
[2] Virtue is what is praised (praiseworthy), vice what is blamed (blameworthy) (*NE* I 12 1101^{b}31–32, II 9 1109^{a}29–30).

3. Reading ἡ μὲν ὑπερβολὴ ἁμαρτάνεται καὶ ψέγεται, καὶ ἡ ἔλλειψις with C. C. W. Taylor, *Aristotle: Nicomachean Ethics Books II–IV* (Oxford: Clarendon Press, 2006).

[3] Feelings and actions in a mean are praised as correct; excessive or deficient ones are blamed as errors.

Since praise and blame are attracted first by actions, this suggests that [1] and [3] are what explain [2]. The praiseworthy feature of virtue, then, is that it is able to hit the mean. It seems, indeed, that it is itself a *sort of* mean largely because it has this feature, so that, in one way at least, the mean in action precedes the mean in states of character. The second consideration concerns correctness and error: "There are many ways to be in error . . . but only one way to be correct (which is why, indeed, one is easy and the other difficult—easy to miss the target, difficult to hit it). For these reasons too, then, excess and deficiency are characteristic of vice, the mean, of virtue" (*NE* II 6 1106^{b}28–34). For while the mean is one thing, there are many ways of exceeding it or falling short of it. Apparently, then, the mean is the target virtue is able to aim at and hit.

From all these arguments and considerations, Aristotle concludes that in terms of its genus and differentiae, virtue of character "is a state concerned with deliberately choosing, in a mean in relation to us, defined by a reason, that is, the one by which the practically wise man would define it" (*NE* II 6 1106^{b}36–1107^{a}2). He then explains the sense in which it follows that as far as "its essence and the account that says what-it-is are concerned, virtue is a mean" (*NE* II 6 1107^{a}6–7). First, it is "a mean between two vices, one of excess, the other of deficiency" (*NE* II 6 1107^{a}2–3). Second, some vices "are deficient others excessive in relation to what feelings and actions should be, while virtue both finds and chooses the mean" (*NE* II 6 1107^{a}3–6). As before, the clear implication is that what makes virtue of character a sort of mean is that something else that it finds and deliberately chooses is unconditionally in a mean, namely, the feelings and actions with which it is concerned.

Though the mean is located in both actions and feelings, the two locations are interdependent. In the context of acquiring the virtues, the mean in actions has priority, since the state of our appetites and feelings results from the actions we do (*NE* II 2 1104^{a}11–27). In the context of possessing the virtues, the mean in appetites and feelings has priority, since it is partly out of our appetites and feelings that we act, so that if, for example, we are excessively angry at an insult, our retaliation is also likely to be excessive. One puzzle based on these asymmetrical priorities has already been discussed: we can do virtuous actions without already being virtuous, because there is a difference between virtuous actions and actions done virtuously or from virtue (*NE* II 4 1105^{a}18–^{b}12). A second more radical puzzle remains.

"Actions are called 'just' or 'temperate' when they are such as the just or temperate person would do" (*NE* II 4 1105^{b}5–7). It seems to take an already virtuous person, therefore, to identify the actions someone must do to become virtuous. Since we are not virtuous by nature, it seems virtue cannot get started in a nonvirtuous world (*NE* II 1 1103^{a}18–19).

The Politics of the Mean

Like bees, ants, and wasps, human beings are by nature political animals (*NE* I 7 1097^{b}11, *Pol.* I 2 1253^{a}7–9), which "have as their function some single thing they all do together" (*HA* I 1 488^{a}7–8). But unlike these other animals, human beings do not complete or perfect their natures *by nature*. Instead, craft is needed "to complete the task nature is unable to complete" (*Ph.* II 8 199^{a}15–16). Moreover, once someone has acquired virtue, he needs to live as a citizen governed by laws that support his virtue, provide for its exercise, and regulate the various crafts related to it (*NE* I 2 1094^{a}26–^{b}11, X 9 1180^{a}1–5).

The political nature of human beings finds initial expression in their need to reproduce, since this leads them to form a household community: "The friendship of man and woman also seems to be natural. For human beings naturally tend to form couples more than to be political, because the household is prior to the city, and more necessary, and childbearing is shared more widely among the animals" (*NE* VIII 12 1162^{a}16–19). From the outset, therefore, a child is leading a communal life and (at any rate, in a good enough household) acquiring some sort of virtue of character, such as "household justice" (*NE* V 6 1134^{b}17). That is why the household contains "the first starting-points and springs of friendship, constitution, and justice" (*EE* VII 10 1242^{a}40–^{b}1). Since virtue completes or perfects nature, all members of a household will therefore have a (partially) completed nature—a second nature, so to speak—identifying them as household members and suiting them to being so.

Needs unsatisfied in the household lead to the emergence of villages, which are "constituted from several households for the sake of satisfying needs other than everyday ones" (*Pol.* I 2 1252^{b}15–16). Finally, from a community of several villages, the *polis* or city itself comes into existence:

> A complete community, constituted out of several villages, once it reaches the limit of total self-sufficiency, practically speaking, is a city. It comes-to-be for the sake of living, but it remains in existence for the sake of living well. That is

why every city exists by nature, since the first communities do. For the city is their end, and nature is an end; for we say that each thing's nature—for example, that of a human being, a horse, or a household—is the character it has when its coming-to-be has been completed. Moreover, that for the sake of which something is—that is to say, its end—is best, and self-sufficiency is both end and best. It is evident from these considerations, then, that a city is among the things that exist by nature, that a human being is by nature a political animal, and that anyone who is without a city, not by luck but by nature, is either a poor specimen or else more than human. (*Pol.* I 2 1252^{b}27–1253^{a}4)

Household, village, and city are not so much distinct communities with distinct natures, therefore, as different stages in the development of a single nature completed to a different degree in each of them, much like child, teenager, and mature adult. For the impulse to form a city is natural (*Pol.* I 2 1253^{a}29–30), as, too, are the needs that, by preserving its unity, sustain its existence (*NE* V 5 1133^{b}6–8). Nests, hives, and human communities belong in the class of extended phenotypes, as we would put it, and are natural for that reason. The difference between human communities and these others is that socialization, education, and crafts generally are needed to adapt their members to life within them by modifying their nature, and the virtue which completes it, in a way characteristic of the communities themselves. In essence, this is the solution to the puzzle about the radical origins of virtue of character, which emerges, not *ex nihilo*, but from nascent forms of virtue, which are the natural endowments of human political animals.

While one sort of modification resulting in types or gradations of virtue is due to types of communities of different developmental levels, a second is due to the various types of constitution a city can have. On the traditional Greek view, there are just three of these: a monarchy, an oligarchy, or a democracy, depending on whether the city is controlled by "the one, the few, or the many" (*Pol.* III 7 1279^{a}27–28). Aristotle accepts this view to some extent but introduces some important modifications. First, he argues that differences in wealth are of greater theoretical importance than differences in numbers. Oligarchy is really control by the wealthy; democracy is control by the poor. It just so happens that while many people are poor, usually only a few are wealthy (*Pol.* III 8 1279^{b}20–1280^{a}6, IV 4 1290^{b}17–20). This allows him to see the importance of the middle classes, who are neither very rich nor very poor, but somewhere in between (*Pol.* IV 11 1295^{b}1–3), and to recognize the theoretical significance of a constitution—a so-called polity or republic—in which they play a decisive part (*Pol.* IV 7 1293^{a}39–^{b}1). A second way Aristotle modifies the traditional view is in thinking that each of the three traditional constitutions comes in both a correct and a deviant version (*NE* VIII 10 1160ª31–ᵇ22). Rule by "the one" is either a kingship (correct) or a tyranny (deviant); rule by "the few" is either an aristocracy (correct) or an oligarchy (deviant); rule by "the many" is either a polity (correct) or a democracy (deviant). Correct constitutions aim at the common advantage; deviant ones at the advantage of the rulers (*Pol.* III 7 1279ª28–31).

An important difference between these constitutions, whether correct or deviant, is that they have different conceptions of what advantage consists in—different conceptions of happiness:

> Since happiness is the best thing, however, and it is some sort of activity or complete use of virtue, and since, as it happens, some people are able to share in happiness, whereas others are able to do so only to a small degree or not at all, it is clear that this is why there are several kinds and varieties of city and a plurality of constitutions. For it is by seeking happiness in different ways and by different means that individual groups of people create different ways of life and different constitutions. (*Pol.* VII 8 1328ª37–ᵇ2)

In the best constitution, whether a kingship or aristocracy (*Pol.* IV 2 1289ª30–33), happiness is correctly conceived as activity in accord with complete virtue (*Pol.* VII 13 1332ª3–10). A polity also conceives happiness this way but aims at a level of virtue—and so of happiness—that many people and cities can hope to attain (*Pol.* IV 11 1295ª25–ᵇ13). Oligarchy conceives happiness as consisting in wealth or property, or in living rather than living well (*Pol.* I 9 1257ᵇ38–1258ª14, III 9 1280ª25–32). Democracy conceives it as consisting in freedom to do whatever one likes, or as gratifying whatever appetites or desires one has or favors (*Pol.* V 9 1310ª25–34, VI 2 1317ª40–ᵇ2). It is to further happiness as it conceives it that a constitution drafts laws, habituates and educates it citizens, rewards and punishes, since "correct habituation is what distinguishes a good constitution from bad ones" (*NE* II 1 1103ᵇ3–6). A democracy suits its citizens to a democratic way of life by using public education to inculcate democratic virtues, an oligarchy does the same with oligarchic virtue, and so on (*Pol.* V 9 1310ª12–36, VIII 1 1337ª10–18).

Even though oligarchic and democratic virtues are not virtues of the best sort, they are virtues as a democracy or oligarchy conceives of them, since they promote what each of these constitutions takes happiness to be. Provided the democracy or oligarchy in question isn't too deviant, moreover, these types of virtue are extremely worthwhile acquisitions: "It is possible for an oligarchy or a democracy to be adequate (*hikanôs*) in quality, even though it has diverged from the best organization.[4] But if someone tightens either of them more, he will first make the constitution worse, and in the end it will not be a constitution at all" (*Pol.* V 9 1309^{b}31–35). The importance of this fact is no doubt obvious. Neither Aristotle nor his audience were brought up in the unconditionally best constitution, nor, in many cases, even in a polity, yet this did not prevent them from acquiring the "noble habits" that all "adequate (*hikanôs*) students of noble and just things"—of ethics and political science—must have (*NE* I 4 1095^{b}2–8). The virtues acquired in such constitutions make not just a little difference, then, but all the difference. For what is *hikanon* is what is enough to achieve the desired result: a discussion is *hikanon* if its degree of clarity is in accord with its subject matter (*NE* I 3 1094^{b}12); a supply of goods is *hikanon* if it just what is needed for a happy life (*NE* I 10 1101^{a}15); a general outline is *hikanon*, when a more detailed account is made impossible by the endless variety of particular circumstances (*NE* I 11 1101^{a}28); money is *hikanon* to make otherwise incommensurable goods as commensurable as we need them to be (*NE* V 5 1133^{b}20).

Because the virtues of character are implicated in practical wisdom, determining the target at which it aims (*NE* VI 12 1144^{a}8–9), the fact of their relativity to a constitution has obvious consequences for it as well. A household is not entirely self-sufficient, since it produces a surplus of some needed items, not enough of others (*Pol.* I 9 1257^{a}19–28). Household practical wisdom, which corresponds in level of development to household justice, eventually solves this problem by initiating an exchange of goods with other households. Once initiated, exchange then leads to the creation of money, new communal roles (that of merchant, for example), and new areas of expertise, such as commerce (*to kapêlikon*), which was a simple affair at first, but then became "more of a craft as experience taught people how and from

---

4. As David Keyt, *Aristotle: Politics Books V and VI* (Oxford: Clarendon Press, 1999), p. 137, notices, the "best organization" could be an aristocracy of virtue, which is *unconditionally* best, and from which oligarchy is a deviation, or it could be a polity, which is the best more accessible constitution, from which democracy is a deviation, and from which oligarchy also deviates: "Democracy is the least bad (*mochthêron*)" of the deviant constitutions, since it "deviates only slightly from the form of a polity" (*NE* VIII 10 1160^{b}19–21). When Aristotle says such things as "in the deviations, however, there is little in the way of justice" (*NE* VIII 11 1161^{a}30–31), he is presumably generalizing: on average, oligarchies and democracies and (of course) tyrannies have little in the way of justice because there are many extreme or tightened versions of each of them.

what sources the greatest profit could be made through exchange" (*Pol.* I 9 1257ᵇ2–5). In turn, this led to new forms of communal regulation (laws governing commerce) and new opportunities for the exercise of (a further developed) practical wisdom. It is by engaging in this bootstrapping process that practical wisdom developed from the vestigial forms of it found in the household to the unconditional form found in an aristocracy of the fully virtuous.

Among the sciences that practical wisdom comprises, political science is the most architectonic, since it controls all the other crafts and sciences, determining which ones a city should contain, and "which ones each class in the city should learn, and up to what point" (*NE* I 2 1094ᵃ27–ᵇ7). The level of practical wisdom's development in a given constitution has immediate repercussions for all the other crafts and sciences under its control:

> Some people believe that . . . they should maintain their store of money or increase it without limit. The reason they are thus disposed, however, is that they are preoccupied with living, not living well. And since their appetite for life is unlimited, they also want an unlimited amount of what sustains it. Even those who do aim at living well seek what furthers physical gratification. So, since this too seems to depend on having property, they spend all their time acquiring wealth. . . . Since their gratification lies in excess, they seek the craft that produces the excess needed for gratification. If they cannot get it through the craft of wealth-acquisition, they try to do so by means of something else that causes it, using each of their potentialities in an unnatural way. For the end of courage is not to produce wealth but to produce confidence in the face of danger; nor is it the end of generalship or medicine to do so, but rather victory and health. Nonetheless, these people make all of these into forms of wealth-acquisition, in the belief that acquiring wealth is the end, and that everything ought to further the end. (*Pol.* I 9 1257ᵇ38–1258ᵃ14)

In the same way as the homegrown varieties of virtue of character, practical wisdom, and political science, the crafts too have different levels of development and somewhat different aims in different constitutions.[5]

A second relevant factor is that within each such community and constitution, there are people with different natures, and so different roles and different types of virtue:

5. This does not mean, of course, that someone with fully developed practical wisdom and political science cannot serve as an advisor to a city in which it hasn't fully developed, or take up residence there.

Those who talk in universal terms, saying that virtue is a good condition of the soul, or correct action, or something of that sort, are deceiving themselves. It is far better to enumerate the virtues . . . than to define them in this general way. Consequently, we must take what the poet says about a woman as our guide in every case—"To a woman silence is a crowning glory"[6]—whereas this does not apply to a man. Since a child is incompletely developed, it is clear that his virtue too does not belong to him in relation to himself but in relation to his end and his guide. The same holds of a slave in relation to his master. But we said that a slave is useful for providing the necessities, so he clearly needs only a small amount of virtue—just so much as will prevent him from inadequately performing his tasks through intemperance or cowardice. (*Pol.* I 13 1260ᵃ24–36)

All these naturally different types of virtue also vary with the constitution of the city:

As for man and woman, father and children, the virtue relevant to each of them, what is good in their relationship with one another and what is not good, and how to achieve the good and avoid the bad—it will be necessary to go through all these in connection with the constitutions. For every household is part of a city, these are parts of a household, and the virtue of a part must be determined by looking to the virtue of the whole. Hence both women and children must be educated with an eye to the constitution, if indeed it makes any difference to the virtue of a city that its children be virtuous, and its women too. And it must make a difference, since half the free population are women, and from children come those who participate in the constitution. (*Pol.* I 13 1260ᵇ8–20)

A doctor in an adequate democracy treating the wife of a male citizen has his end or goal a type of health that is relative, first, to that democracy and, second, to the role its constitution prescribes for citizen women. It may also be relative to the woman's age group, and—where relevant—to her wealth and social class (*Rh.* II 12–17). It may also be relative, as we shall see, to facts about the woman herself.

In distinguishing the two virtues of thought, theoretical wisdom and practical wisdom, Aristotle says that theoretical wisdom is the same "for everyone" but practical wisdom is not the same, because the good at which it aims varies from species to species, just as health does, being one thing in human beings, another in fish (*NE* VI 7 1141ᵃ22–33). Since full virtue of character

---

6. Sophocles, *Ajax* 293. See also *Pol.* III 4 1277ᵇ22–24, Thucydides II 45.

involves practical wisdom (*NE* VI 13 1144^{b}31–32), the same will be true of it. At one level, therefore, the ethical mean will be in relation to our specifically human nature. It is when we try to fill out what human nature is that we realize how various are the coins in which it is relevantly minted.

Human nature is fully completed or perfected only in those who, like self-ruling citizens of a city with an aristocratic constitution, possess *unconditional* virtue of character:

> The only constitution that is rightly called an aristocracy is the one that consists of the those who are unconditionally best as regards virtue, and not of those who are good men only given a certain assumption.[7] For only here is it unconditionally the case that the same person is a good man and a good citizen. But those who are good in others are so relative to their constitutions. (*Pol.* IV 7 1293^{b}1–7)

The mean embodied in and aimed at by their virtue is what we might call the *absolute mean* in relation to us, since it is in relation to completed or perfected human nature. That only free adult *males* can have such a nature is a reflection of the further view that only they are naturally suited for this sort of self-rule:

> The soul by nature contains a part that rules and a part that is ruled, and we say that each of them has a different virtue, that is to say, one [virtue of thought] belongs to the part that has reason and one [virtue of character] to the nonrational part. It is clear, then, that the same holds in the other cases as well, so that most instances of ruling and being ruled are natural. For free rule slaves, male rules female, and a grown man rules a child in different ways, because, while the parts of the soul are present in all these people, they are present in different ways. The deliberative part of the soul is entirely missing from a slave; a woman has it but it lacks control (*akuron*);[8] a child has it but it is incompletely developed. We must suppose, therefore, that the same necessarily

7. Someone with oligarchic virtue is good on the assumption that the oligarchic virtue in question is sufficiently like genuine virtue.

8. Part of what this implies may be that a woman, having arrived through deliberation at what she judges is the best thing to do in particular circumstances, may sometimes decide to do something else, because she tends to be less able to control her appetites and emotions than a man (*NE* VII 7 1150^{b}1–16). On the other hand, the fact that it is women's lack of fitness to command that is at issue (*Pol.* I 13 1259^{b}1–3) makes it more likely that what women lack control over is not so much themselves as *other people*, since females have less spirit than males (*HA* IX 1 608^{a}33–^{b}16, *PA* III 1 661^{b}33–34), and spirit is responsible for the ability to command (*Pol.* VII 7 1328^{a}6–7).

holds of the virtues of character too: all must share in them, but not in the same way; rather, each must have a sufficient share to enable him to perform his own function. Hence a ruler must have virtue of character complete, since his function is unconditionally that of an architectonic craftsman, and reason is an architectonic craftsman, but each of the others must have as much as pertains to him. It is evident, then, that all those mentioned have virtue of character, and that the temperance, courage, and justice of a man are not the same as those of a woman, as Socrates supposed [*Meno* 73a-c], on the contrary, men have the courage and similarly the other virtues appropriate in a ruler, whereas women have those appropriate in an assistant. (*Pol.* I 13 1260ª5–24)

It follows that the absolute mean is doubly limited in its practical application. First, it is seldom the mean aimed at in the case of actual males, since few men find themselves citizens in an aristocracy of virtue. Second, it is never the mean aimed at in the case of nonmales no matter what sort of city they live in.

In an aristocracy of the completely virtuous, as in constitutions of other types, one sort of physical training will be provided to male citizens, and different sorts to males with other social roles. The sort suited to professional athletes, for example, will "maim the shape and development" of bodies, in comparison to those suitable for the body of a citizen, just as a professional musical education would their souls (*Pol.* VIII 4 1338ᵇ9–11, 6 1341ª5–ᵇ18). The fact that Aristotle selects a famous professional wrestler—Milo of Croton (*NE* II 6 1106ᵇ3)—as his initial illustration of a mean in relation to us is important, therefore, since the mean relevant to Milo is categorically not one generally applicable to human beings. In any case, even though a craft, such as physical training or medicine, is unlike experience-based know-how in including knowledge of universals and causal explanations, it is still the particular case that it must deal with: "it is not *human being* that medical treatment makes healthy (except coincidentally), but Callias or Socrates or someone else spoken of in this way who is coincidentally a human being" (*Met.* I 1 981ª18–20; also *NE* I 6 1097ª8–13, X 9 1180ᵇ7–23). By referring to Milo by name, therefore, rather than using the general term "athlete," Aristotle is most naturally taken as making a cognate point: the mean is relative to us by being relative not to the species *human being* but to particular instances of it: "the mean that each sort of person can actually achieve must be best" (*Pol.* IV 11 1295ª35–39).[9]

Finally, while the mean initially relevant to Milo may be the one—or

9. Contrast Lesley Brown, "What Is 'The Mean Relative to Us' in Aristotle's *Ethics*?," *Phronesis* 48 (1997): 77–93.

ones (*NE* X 9 1180^{b}10–11)—physical training aims at when treating already fully trained athletes or wrestlers, this may surely change. For this mean may be at some point no longer within reach for Milo, given his actual physical condition. Perhaps it is a matter of bringing him as close to that condition as possible. Perhaps it is time for him to retire, so that the right mean for physical training to aim at is an entirely different one: "it isn't the function of medicine to produce health, but to do so as far as possible, and as far as possible further it; for it is still possible to give good treatment even to those who cannot acquire health" (*Rh.* I 1 1355^{b}12–14). Something similar is also true of political science:

> It clearly belongs to the same [political] science to acquire theoretical knowledge of the best constitution, and what it must be like if it is to be most ideal of all, with no external obstacles to stand in its way. Also which constitution is appropriate for which cities. For achieving the best constitution is perhaps impossible for many, so that neither the unconditionally best constitution nor the one that is best in the circumstances should be neglected by the good legislator and true political scientist (*politikos*).[10] Further, which constitution is best given certain assumptions, since a political scientist must be able to understand how any given constitution might initially come into existence, and how, once in existence, it might be preserved for the longest time. I mean, for example, when some city happens to be governed neither by the best constitution (but does not even have the necessary resources) nor by the best one possible in the existing circumstances, but by a worse one. Besides all these things, a political scientist should know which constitution is most appropriate for all cities. . . . What should be done, then, is to describe the sort of organization that people will be easily persuaded to accept and participate in,[11] given what they already have, as it is no less a task to reform a constitution than to establish one initially, just as it is no less a task to correct what we have learned than to learn it in the first place. That is why, in addition to what has just been mentioned, a political scientist should also be able to help existing constitutions. . . . And it is with this same practical wisdom that one should try to see both which laws are best and which are appropriate for each of the constitutions. (*Pol.* IV 1 1288^{b}21–1289^{a}13)

For this sort of reason too, what craft, practical wisdom, or political science aims at in actual circumstances is typically not the absolute mean but the

10. A *politikos* is someone who stands to *politikê* (political science) as a *phronimos* (man of practical wisdom) stands to *phronêsis*.

11. Reading κοινωνεῖν with Alois Dreizehnter, *Aristoteles Politica* (Munich: Wilhelm Fink, 1970).

mean achievable in those circumstances, taking into account not only the types and aims of the people involved but also what they can be persuaded to do. Political advice a city cannot or will not follow is as impractical as a medical prescription a patient cannot afford or will not take.

As a way of bringing the various strands of the mean together, instead of the somewhat complex ethical mean, consider the relatively simpler mean that enables the eye to discern visible objects. 20/20 vision is what someone has when at twenty feet his eye can resolve lines with a spacing of about 1.75 millimeters. 20/40 vision is half that acuity for distance vision, and 20/10 vision would be twice normal acuity. The 20/n number does not directly relate to the prescription required to correct vision, since it doesn't specify the nature of the problem with the eye's natural lens, only the resulting performance. In the case of the male human eye, the absolute mean, we may suppose, is what achieves 20/10 vision. That mean may be accessible to both a and b, but the correction in their lenses needed to achieve it may not be the same. The condition that in a's visual system constitutes its being in a mean is different—perhaps very different—from the one in b's visual system, therefore, although both result in eyesight with the same acuity. For c, another male, 20/10 vision, though also the absolute mean for him, is simply inaccessible. The closest achievable approximation is 20/20 or whatever. The condition in his visual system that gives him 20/20 vision is the mean relative to him. Obviously, there is nothing arbitrary about it, nor need it be easy to achieve. For d, who is a woman, 20/10 vision may not even be what to aim at in the ideal case. Perhaps the female eye is naturally adapted for the close work of gathering rather than, as the male eye might be, for the distance work of hunting. The mean relative to d as a citizen of a certain city and constitution may be something else altogether. The same is true, mutatis mutandis, for a, b, and c.

Continuity and Divisibility

For a mean to exist in something it must be "continuous and divisible" (NE II 6 1106^{a}26). So a crucial reason for thinking that virtue of character is some sort of mean is that it is concerned with feelings and actions, since they do seem to have this characteristic. When the mean condition is specified in feelings, however, a variety of dimensions are mentioned. They are in a mean just in case we feel them "when we should, about the things we should, toward the people we should, for the end we should, and in the way we should" (NE II 6 1106^{b}21–22). In the case of time (when) and intensity (way), the notions of continuity and divisibility have clear enough application (too late, too early, too strongly, too weakly), but in the case of the other dimensions, this is not so. Anger at an offense leads a man to want revenge. His revenge should be proportionate to the offense, which it is more likely to be if the anger itself is proportionate to it. But that *a* should be the object of his revenge is due simply to the fact that *a* was the one who committed the offense, not that *a* is in any sort of mean. Similarly, penicillin may be prescribed as part of a treatment for infection quite independently of any considerations of excess and deficiency, though how much to give and how often may not be.

One way to proceed in the face of these fairly uncontentious facts is to try to redescribe the recalcitrant dimensions of virtue's target so that they too begin to look more like mean-points in a continuum. Even if this can be done, it is unlikely to prove illuminating, since what makes the redescribed dimension correct is unlikely to be that it is a mean: *a* may be a mean point in some continuum, but that isn't why he is the correct object of anger and revenge. A second way is more modest. Virtue's target is a mean, it suggests, just in case some of its dimensions are means. The problem is to explain why these dimensions are the ones figuring in virtue's essential definition, since this gives them a significance they seem not to merit. What we want is some sort of explanatory connection between the dimensions of virtue's target that are continua, and so do admit of a mean condition, and those others that do not.

At this point the second distinctive feature of the ethical mean comes into play: it must be "defined by a reason, that is, the one by which the practically wise man would define it" (*NE* II 6 1107ᵃ1–2). Working under the surface of this feature is the familiar account of the human soul. One part, comprising the scientific and calculative or deliberative subparts, has "reason fully, by having it within itself" (*NE* I 13 1103ᵃ2). It can engage in scientific reasoning and explanation in the way that a mathematician can reason out proofs, can evaluate the different ends proposed by different desires, using a single standard to determine which of them best furthers happiness, and can calculate the most effective means of achieving the one selected (*DA* III 11 434ᵃ5–11). Another part, the desiring one, cannot reason in this full-blooded sense, but is susceptible to reason "in a way, insofar as it both listens to reason and obeys it, which is the way we are said to have the reason of our father or our friends, not in the way we have the reason, for example, in mathematics" (*NE* I 13 1102ᵇ30–33). Thus the correct reason that defines the ethical mean is supplied by the calculative or deliberative part of the soul, whose virtue is practical wisdom, while the part that listens to and obeys that reason is the desiring part, whose virtue is virtue of character.

A second aspect of appetites and feelings—namely, their different degrees of strength—is most clearly exemplified in the phenomena of continence and incontinence. For "even when understanding commands us and thought tells us to avoid or pursue something, we are sometimes not moved, but we act in accord with our appetites, as the incontinent person does" (DA III 9 433ª1–3). In this case, appetite "overcomes and moves" the wish that is always on the side of understanding and thought, in part by corrupting it, or distorting its content (DA III 11 434ª12–14). Sometimes, wish does something similar to appetite, as in the case of a continent person (NE VII 1 1145ᵇ13–14).

Intentional content is what individuates feelings, so that, although we can speak of anger quite generally, types of anger with different intentional contents are different and may have quite different roles in an individual's psychology. One person may be prone to feel too much anger where harms to self-esteem or vanity are concerned, too little when what is at issue is harm to health. In his case, one sort or species of anger, with one sort of intentional content, is too strong, while another, with a different sort of intentional content, is too weak. A second person may be appropriately sensitive to moral harms or injustices, whether the victim is himself or another, while being entirely insensitive to insult. In his case, one type of anger is functioning properly, while another type, with a different content, is either missing or not functioning at all. A third person may have a mix of these problems. In thinking about excess, deficiency, and the mean in feelings, therefore, we need to be careful to individuate those feelings correctly.

What operates on both the propositional and nonpropositional components of appetites and feelings to produce virtuous, continent, or incontinent people is habituation (NE I 4 1095ᵇ2–8), which has both a cognitive component and a noncognitive one that is more like a sort of conditioning (Pol. VII 17–VIII 7). It is when such training is successful that virtue or continence, with its attendant obedience to reason and wish, results:

Least to be indulged is the part that desires ignoble things and tends to grow large—and most like this are appetites and children, for it is in accord with appetite that children indeed live, and desire for what is pleasant is found most of all in them. If, then, whatever desires ignoble things is not obedient and subordinate to the ruling constituent, it will grow and grow. For the desire for what is pleasant is insatiable and indiscriminate in someone who lacks understanding, and the activity of appetite makes his natural tendency grow, and if his appetites are big and strong, they actually drive out calculation. That is why appetites must be moderate and few, and never contrary to reason—this is the condition we call obedient and not self-indulgent. For just as a child[12] should live in accord with his tutor's instructions, so too the appetitive part should be in accord with reason. Hence the temperate person's appetitive part should be consonant with reason; for the target of both is what is noble, and the temperate person has an appetite for the things one should, in the ways one should, at the times one should, which is just what reason also prescribes. (NE III 12 1119^{b}3–18)

Listening and obedience to reason is the result of long prior habituation to reason, produced by being brought up under its control: it is to those who "form their desires and act in accord with reason" that knowledge of ethics and political science is alone "of great benefit" (NE I 3 1095^{a}10–11).[13] It is this fact that gives a special significance to pain and pleasure.

Especially when young, people tend to measure (kanonizein) actions and feelings by the pleasure and pain they involve, and tend to choose what is pleasant as something good, and avoid what is painful as something bad (NE II 3 1105^{a}3–5, III 4 1113^{b}1–2). Since pleasure appears to be a good thing when it is not, and pain a bad one, the result is that such people are frequently mistaken (NE III 4 1113^{a}33–^{b}2). Nonetheless, pleasure and pain are the first manifestations of value in the young soul. When a child tastes something sweet, he finds it naturally pleasant and good, and so desires it. Seeing where his eating habits are headed, a wise parent tries to steer them in a healthier direction. In doing so, he might apply to the child the sorts of procedures Aristotle recommends he apply to himself: "In all cases, we should especially be on our guard against pleasant things—pleasure, that is—because we are not impartial discerners in its case. So we should feel precisely the same way about it as elders felt toward Helen, and repeat on every occasion what they said.[14] For by dismissing pleasure in this way, we shall be less in error" (NE II 9 1109^{b}7–12). Because we discern pleasure and pain through our feelings, all of which "involve pleasure or pain" (NE II 3 1104^{b}14–15), for us to be nonim-

---

12. Reading ὥσπερ γὰρ.

13. Compare Hendrik Lorenz, The Brute Within (Oxford: Clarendon Press, 2006), pp. 186–201.

14. What they said was that she should be sent away lest her too pleasing beauty lead to Troy's destruction (Homer, Iliad III 156–160).

partial discerners of them is in the first instance for *our feelings* to be such. Yet, like the beam in a biased laboratory balance, our feelings are naturally tipped in pleasure's favor and pain's disfavor. Since pleasure and pain are involved in every object of choice and every action, it follows that their natural bias, if uncorrected, has a capacity to derail any choice. That is one basis for the claim that when the natural virtues, which are separate states, are possessed together with the practical wisdom required for deliberate choice, they become inseparable (*NE* VI 13 1144^{b}32–1145^{a}2).

An obvious way to cash out this bias in our feelings where pain and pleasure are concerned is in terms of strength: whatever the pleasure, our natural tendency is to desire it more strongly than we should; whatever the pain, our natural tendency is to be more averse to it than we should. Strength or intensity of desire or feeling seems to be a continuum, however, within which the notions of more, less, and a mean amount do have relatively uncontroversial application. Consequently, a dimension of the ethical mean that is a continuum does play the sort of explanatory role we were seeking in relation to the other dimensions that are not (or not obviously) continua. For any dimension whatsoever can be affected by feelings or desires that are too strong or too weak. *A* may be the correct object of *b*'s revenge, but if *a* is a tough customer, likely to inflict great pain and suffering on an attacker, *b*'s aversion to pain may lead him to punish someone less threatening instead, as happens in displacement behavior.

That there are direct correlates in action of degrees of intensity in desire is ensured, Aristotle thinks, by the fact that movement "is continuous, and action is movement" (*EE* II 3 1220^{b}26–27). In some cases, therefore, it will be possible to effect changes in the intensity of desire by adjusting it to a level in movement already judged to be in a mean, so that such movement can, over time, result in feelings in mean. *B*'s punishing *a* as severely as he does may be a case in point: his blows may have to be just the right number and just hard enough. But that they are correctly delivered to *a* is not—and need not be—something directly reflected in any degree of movement. Hence we may need to see how propensities to feel pleasure and pain can deflect desires from their correct objects in ways that themselves can be corrected through being habituated by movements in a mean.

When habituation is effective in correcting the natural bias in our feelings, it turns them into good or impartial discerners of pleasures and pains. It does what we do to a biased laboratory balance when we restore its beam to equilibrium, so that it now weighs things correctly. Equilibrium in the case of feelings, however, is that mean condition of strength or intensity, between too much and too little, that enables them to discern pleasures and pains in agreement with correct reason, and so to function as reliable measures of them. That is why, having used the verb *kanonizein* to characterize the role of pleasure in pain in evaluation, Aristotle uses its nominal form *kanôn* to characterize the good or virtuous person, whose feelings are in this condition: "Each state of character has its own particular conception of what is noble and what is pleasant, and perhaps what most distinguishes the good man is his ability to see what is true in each case, being himself like a standard (*kanôn*) and measure (*metron*) of these" (*NE* III 4 1113ᵃ31–33). Later, by reusing the noun *metron*, he makes explicit that when ignoble things appear pleasant, it is due to the sort of defect in the desiring part of the soul, which at once shows its possessor to lack virtue of character and to be a poor measure of pleasure and pain:

> In all such cases, it seems that what *is* so is what appears so to the good man. And if this is right, as it seems to be, and virtue—and the good man insofar as he is such—is the measure (*metron*) in each of them, then pleasures, too, will be what appear so to him, and pleasant things will be what he enjoys. If the things that disgust him appear pleasant to someone, there is nothing surprising in that, since there are many ways for human beings to be corrupted and ruined. Pleasant, however, such things are not, except to people like that in such condition. Clearly, then, we should say that the pleasures that everyone agrees to be ignoble are not pleasures at all, except to corrupt people. (*NE* X 5 1176ᵃ15–24)

Accurate discernment even of what is noble thus depends on pleasure and pain, since "what is noble and what is advantageous also appear pleasant" (*NE* II 3 1105ᵃ1), and so can fail to appear so to someone whose feelings are not in a mean.

Partly for this reason, being able to find the ethical mean in a reliable manner is not easy:

> Being virtuous is a difficult task, since in each case it is a difficult task to find the mean. Thus it isn't anyone who can find the center of a circle, for example, but the one with knowledge. So, too, whereas getting angry or giving or spending money is easy, and anyone can do it, doing it to the person one should, to the extent one should, when one should, for the end one should, and in the way one should—this is no longer easy and not everyone can do it, which is why doing it well is something rare, praiseworthy, and noble. (*NE* II 9 1109ᵃ24–30)

The difficulty here is sufficiently great, indeed, that we are "not blamed if we deviate a little, whether in excess or deficiency, from doing well, but only if we deviate more widely" (NE II 9 1109^{b}18–20; compare IX 11 1170^{b}32–33). Though in part a consequence of the fact that praise and blame track difficulty, the failure of small deviations to attract blame also has an epistemic source: large deviations are easily noticed, while small ones are not. And this is due not simply to their size but to inherent vagueness in the definition of excess and deficiency, and so in the mean itself: "But how far and to what extent someone must deviate in order to be blameworthy is not easy to define by a reason, any more than any other perceptible things—such things are particulars and their discernment depends on perception" (NE II 9 1109^{b}20–23). That is why "We should not search for the same rigor or accuracy in reasons as in what comes though perception" (Pol. VII 7 1328^{a}19–21).

In some cases, however, there seems to be little or no need for perception, since the feelings or actions at issue, because they do not admit of a mean, are always wrong:

> Not every action admits of the mean, nor does every feeling, since some have names connected with baseness right from the start, such as spite, shameless-ness, envy, and—in the case of actions—adultery, theft, homicide. For all of these, and others like them, are so called because they themselves, and not their excesses and deficiencies, are ignoble. In their case, then, we can never be correct, but are always in error. Nor can we do them well or not well—committing adultery, say, with the woman one should, and when and how one should. On the contrary, simply to do any of them is to be in error. (NE II 6 1107^{a}8–17)

What is going on in such cases is that the role of practical wisdom and practical perception in them is simply disguised. When these have established that we should never under any circumstances have sex with another's spouse, it becomes a fixed point in determining the mean in sexual feelings and actions. Any desire for adulterous sex is then excessive and wrong, as is the sex itself should it take place. The same is true of feelings, such as spite or being pained by the good fortune of others, that are already excesses relative to a fixed point of feeling that practical wisdom determines as a mean. In effect, then, these cases involve an analogue of the absurd thought that having reached an extreme by finding the mean once, we can then look for the mean of that extreme, so that there would be "a mean of excess, a mean of deficiency, an excess of excess and a deficiency" (NE II 6 1107^{a}20–21).

Justice and External Goods

Goods of the soul, goods of the body, and external goods constitute the three (not necessarily mutually exclusive) classes of goods Aristotle recognizes as relevant to virtue of character (*NE* I 8 1098^{b}12–16, *MM* I 3 1184^{b}1–6). This virtue and activity in accord with it are goods of the soul, whereas external goods and goods of the body are things "the good man has the potentiality to use well and the ignoble one to use badly" (*MM* I 2 1183^{b}28–30). Of these, some are necessary, some choiceworthy for their own sake: "The necessary ones are the bodily ones (I mean those concerned with food, sexual intercourse, and the sorts we took to be the concern of intemperance and temperance), whereas others are not necessary, but are choiceworthy by themselves (I mean victory, for example, and honor, wealth, and similar good and pleasant things)" (*NE* VII 4 1147^{b}23–31). In addition, some are so-called goods of competition, such as money, honors, and bodily pleasures, for which people compete with one another (*NE* IX 8 1168^{b}15–19).

Initially, external goods of these different varieties seem to play as many as six different roles in regard to virtue and happiness:

[1] In many actions, we "use friends, wealth, and political power, just as we use instruments (*organôn*)."

[2] Deprivation of certain external goods, such as good birth, good children, and beauty, "mar our blessed happiness" (*NE* I 8 1099^{a}31–^{b}6).

[3] Some external goods are "necessary (*anagkaion*) conditions" of happiness).

[4] Others are "naturally useful and cooperative as instruments (*organikôs*)" (*NE* I 9 1099^{b}27–28).

[5] Wise people and just people need "the good things necessary (*anagkaiôn*) for life."

[6] When the goods in [5] are adequately supplied, a just person still need other people "as partners and recipients of his just actions, and the same is true of the temperate person, the courageous person, and each of the others" (*NE* X 7 1177^{a}28–32).

The use of *organôn* in [1] and *organikôs* in [4] suggests that these roles—and so those with which they are contrasted in [2] and [3]—are identical. The use of *anagkaion* and of friends as examples in both [1–2] and [3–4] similarly suggests that the same contrast is being drawn in each. It seems, then, that the six roles reduce to that between external goods required *by the activity itself*, regardless of the nature of the agent engaging in it, and external goods required *by certain agents* to engage in an activity but not by others. Thus external goods are not required by the activity of contemplation, in the way that, for example, private property is required by generous activity. Nonetheless, a human being, unlike a god, does need external goods if he is to be in a condition to contemplate.

Now the actions that produce virtue of character in citizens are those "the laws prescribe regarding education relating to the common good" (*NE* V 2 1130^b25–26), and it is with the equal distribution of external goods that these laws—and the justice they embody—are largely concerned:

> What is just exists among those whose relations are also governed by law; and law, where there can be injustice between people, since the judicial process discerns what is just and what unjust. But where there is injustice between people, there is also unjust action (although where there is unjust action there isn't always injustice), and this consists in assigning to oneself too many of the things that are unconditionally good [that is, external goods [(*NE* V 1 1129^a34–^b6)]] and too few of the things that are unconditionally bad. That is why we do not allow a human being to be the ruler, but rather reason, because a human being always acts in his own interest and becomes a tyrant. The ruler, however, is a guardian of what is just, and if of what is just, of what is equal, too. (*NE* V 6 1134^a30–^b2)

It is when external goods are distributed equally that the needs that hold the city together are reliably satisfied throughout life, and the common good or general happiness is achieved (*NE* V 5 1133^a26–27, VIII 9 1160^a22–23). But what it is for external goods to be distributed equally depends on how equality is understood.

Aristocratic, oligarchic, and democratic constitutions agree that a distribution of goods in which x is given to a, and y to b, is equal, if the ratio between the values of x and y is the same as the ratio between the merit of a and the merit of b. They agree, too, about the conditions under which x and y are of equal value, but they disagree about those under which a and b are of equal merit. Aristocratic constitutions claim that merit is proportional to virtue, oligarchic ones that it is proportional to wealth, democratic ones that all free citizens are equal in merit (*NE* V 3 1131^a25–29). In making such claims, these constitutions are implicitly locating the ethical mean in different places. For justice is some sort of mean—some sort of equality—in the apportioning of goods (*NE* V 3 1131^a10–24).

When means are first introduced, as we saw, they are divided into two kinds: arithmetic and in relation to us (*NE* II 6 1106ª26–ᵇ7). Equality is similarly divided into proportionate and arithmetic (*NE* V 6 1134ª27–28). Since equality is a sort of mean, the mean in relation to us should be—or be intimately related to—proportionate equality (*NE* V 3 1131ª14). If it weren't, there would be three kinds of means, not two. Proportionate equality, however, is equality that is proportionate to a merit differently measured or understood in different constitutions. The mean in relation to us, then, must be the mean in relation to us considered as possessors of a sort of virtue that varies in different sorts of constitutions. This is just the conclusion we reached earlier by looking at the ethical mean without considering its relationship to equality and justice.

Nobility and Self-Interest

The adjective *kalon* (adverb: *kalôn*) is often a term of vague or general commendation ("fine," "beautiful," "good"), with different connotations in different contexts: "as applied to a living thing, *kalon* has *aischron* ["ugly," "deformed"] as its contrary, as applied to a house, *mochthêron* ["humble," "wretched"], so that *kalon* is a homonym" (*Top.* I 15 106ª20–22). All the same, it has a distinctive evaluative coloration, suggestive of "order (*taxis*), symmetry (*summetria*), and definability (*hôrismenon*)," which Aristotle singles out as the chief forms of *to kalon* (*Met.* XIII 3 1078ª36–ᵇ1).

In ethical or political contexts, *kalon* is restricted in its application to what is intrinsically choiceworthy and intrinsically praiseworthy: "Of all goods, the ends are those choiceworthy for their own sake. Of these, in turn, the *kalon* ones are all those praiseworthy because of themselves" (*EE* VIII 3 1248ᵇ18–20; also *NE* I 13 1103ª9–10). But whereas many things—including "honor, pleasure, and understanding" (*NE* I 7 1097ᵇ2)—have the first of these features, only "the virtues and the deeds resulting from virtue" have the second (*EE* VIII 3 1248ᵇ36–37, *NE* I 12 1101ᵇ12–16). Hence wealth, good birth, power, and other external goods, though also *kalon*, inherit their status from that of the good and *kalon* man, who does "many *kalon* actions because of them" (*EE* VIII 3 1249ª13–14). It is in this restricted sense of *kalon*, which is roughly equivalent in meaning to "noble," that the sphere of political science and practical wisdom consists of "*kalon* and just things" (*NE* I 3 1094ᵇ14) and that a virtuous person acts for the sake of *to kalon,* and desires and loves it (*NE* III 7 1115ᵇ13, X 9 1179ᵇ9). Since the specific constituent of virtue and virtuous action that attracts praise is their being in a mean (*NE* II 7 1108ª14–16), and a mean is a kind of symmetry (*MM* I 5 1185ᵇ20) and order (*NE* X 9 1180ª18), the ethical *kalon*, too, is connected to the broader, more general sort.

Some things Aristotle says encourage the thought that in being motivated to pursue what is noble, virtuous agents are being motivated to pursue what benefits others as an intrinsically choiceworthy end: "those who wish goods to their friend for the friend's own sake are friends most of all" (NE VIII 3 1156^{b}9–10); "it is noble to do good to someone, without meaning to be repaid" (NE VIII 13 1162^{b}36–1163^{a}1); "the fair-minded person is thought to act because of what is noble, all the more the better he is, and for the sake of a friend, disregarding his own interests" (NE IX 8 1168^{a}33–35); "the good person does many things for the sake of friends and fatherland, and will die for them if he has to" (NE IX 8 1169^{a}18–20). At the same time, he also says things that point in a quite opposite direction: "each person wishes good things most of all to himself" (NE VIII 7 1159^{a}12); the virtuous person "awards the noblest things and the ones that are most good to himself" (NE IX 8 1168^{b}29–30).

What allows Aristotle to have it both ways, so to speak, is a contrast he draws between two kinds of self-love or self-interest:

> Those who make self-love a matter for reproach call those people "self-lovers" who award themselves the larger share in money, honors, and bodily pleasures; for these are the things that the masses desire and eagerly pursue as if they were the greatest goods, and that is why they are objects of competition. . . . And since the masses are like that, the term has taken its meaning from the most common sort, which is bad. This sort of self-love, then, *is* justly reproached. And it is pretty clearly someone who awards himself things of this sort that the masses call a "self-lover." After all, if someone is always eager that he most of all should do what is just, or temperate, or whatever else is in accord with the virtues, and generally always gains what is noble for himself, no one will call *him* a "self-lover" or blame him for it. This sort of person, however, would seem actually to be more of a self-lover. At any rate, he awards the noblest things, and the ones that are most good, to himself. (NE IX 8 1168^{b}15–30)

The masses think exclusively in terms of money, honors, bodily pleasures, and other external goods of competition. If we measure sacrifice in their terms, the virtuous agent *is* self-sacrificing, since he will "sacrifice, money, honors, and goods of competition generally in procuring what is noble for himself" (NE IX 8 1169^{a}20–22). If we measure sacrifice in terms of the greatest goods, on the other hand, the virtuous agent is entirely egoistic, and not self-sacrificing at all. True, he will sacrifice doing noble actions to a friend, but only because "it may be nobler to be responsible for his friend's action than to do it himself," so that he awards "more of what is noble to himself" (NE IX 8 1169^{a}33–^{b}1).

Because virtue seems like self-sacrifice to those who value only external goods, they praise it in others because it benefits themselves:

> The noble, in fact, is that which, being choiceworthy because of itself, is praiseworthy as such, or that which is good and pleasing because good. If that is what the noble is, however, virtue must be noble, since it is praiseworthy because good. Now virtue is thought to be a potentiality to provide and preserve good things, or a potentiality to do many great good things to all people in all circumstances. . . . [Hence] the greatest virtues must be those that are *most useful to others*, and because of this just people and courageous ones are honored most of all; for courage is useful to others in war, justice both in war and peace. (*Rh.* I 9 1366ᵃ33–ᵇ7)

Since the goods such people value are precisely goods of competition, moreover, they see a conflict between doing what is good for another and doing what is good for oneself. Once virtues are seen as being themselves great goods, this conflict disappears. Virtuous action benefits everybody, including those who do it: "when everyone is contending to do what is noble and strains to do the noblest things, the community will gain everything it should, and each individual will gain the greatest of goods, since that is what virtue is like" (*NE* IX 8 1169ᵃ8–11). More precisely, that is what generally just action is like:

> [General] justice is also above all complete virtue, because it is the complete use of complete virtue. And it is the complete use because the person who possesses it is able to use his virtue in relation to another, not only as regards himself; for many are able to use virtue in their own affairs, but unable to do so in relation to another. That is why Bias seems to have been correct in saying that ruling reveals the man; for being a ruler immediately implies a relationship to another in a community. That is also why [general] justice is the only virtue that seems to be another's good, in that it is virtue in relation to another; for it does what is advantageous to another, whether ruler or member of the community. (*NE* V 1 1129ᵇ30–1130ᵃ5)

In deliberately choosing the complete use of complete virtue for its own sake, a virtuous person is deliberately choosing what benefits others for its own sake too. Once it is agreed that actions manifesting general justice benefit both the agent who does them and all the others in the community, a question still seems naturally to arise about the virtuous person's motives for doing them—a question that is sharpened, if anything, by the account of self-interest's two varieties. The question is this: Does the virtuous person choose to do generally just actions *because* they benefit others, or does he choose to do them *because* they benefit himself?

What is distinctive of *to kalon* is that it is intrinsically choiceworthy and praiseworthy. But what people praise as *kalon* depends on the habits they have acquired in the process of being socialized and educated, since what they see as *kalon*—like what they see as generally just—is what their constitution has educated them to see and do as such. Later on, if they receive the appropriate further education, and the constitution they live in is an adequate one, they learn that doing what is *kalon* furthers the happiness of those who do it, as well as that of all the others in the community. What they learn at this stage is not that what is *kalon* isn't intrinsically choiceworthy and praiseworthy at all, but that it is so only as a means to happiness. To suppose otherwise would be to confuse the fact with the reason why—the stage at which they see that something is *kalon* and become motivated to do it as something intrinsically choiceworthy and praiseworthy with the stage at which they learn (if they do) the explanation of why it is they should see it and do it as such (*NE* I 4 1095^{b}2–8).

Since what makes a constitution correct rather than deviant is that its conception of happiness—and so of virtue and what is *kalon*—is correct, what is genuinely *kalon* is not independent of what happiness is. Nonetheless, it is independent of happiness in another sense: it is because what is *kalon* is intrinsically choiceworthy and praiseworthy that it bears on happiness in the way it does. So the answer to the question with which we began is this: The virtuous person is motivated to do what is *kalon* neither because it benefits himself nor because it benefits others, but because it is *intrinsically* choiceworthy and praiseworthy. When he learns, if he does, that it benefits everyone in the community, he doesn't gain a new motive, rather he comes to understand why he has the motive he had all along.[15]

Natural Virtue and Cleverness

The souls of children contain "traces and seeds" of the states they will have later (*HA* VIII 1 588^{a}33), as well as natural conditions of the affections or feelings that tend toward virtues, which, because they have this natural source, are themselves natural:

15. My thinking about *to kalon* has been partly shaped by T. H. Irwin, "Aristotle's Conception of Morality," *Boston Area Colloquium in Ancient Philosophy* 1 (1985): 115–143.

> All the [natural] mean states are praiseworthy, but they are not virtues, nor are their opposites vices—for they do not involve deliberate choice. All of them belong in the class of affections, since an affection is what each of them is. But because they are natural they tend toward virtues that are natural; for . . . each virtue is in some way both natural and otherwise (namely, when it involves practical wisdom). Envy, then, tends toward injustice (for the actions that stem from it are in relation to another), righteous indignation to justice, shame to temperance. (EE III 7 1234ª23–32)

The natural virtues are the ones stemming directly from these seeds and mean precursor emotional conditions. Hence what is distinctive of those motivated by natural virtue is that they act because of their feelings, not "because of what is noble or as [correct] reason [prescribes]" (NE III 8 1117ª8–9). These natural virtues are the basis for the universal belief that the virtues themselves are "in some way natural" and present in us from birth (NE VI 11 1143ᵇ6–14).

For his own part, Aristotle somewhat downplays the importance of these virtues: "natural virtue itself, which lacks reason, is of little account when separated from reason, and falls short of being praiseworthy" (MM I 34 1198ª3–5). This is because habituation can so easily alter it:

> Surely people become virtuous or good because of three things: nature, habit, and reason. For first one must possess a certain nature from birth, namely, that of a human, and not that of some other animal. Similarly, one's body and soul must be of a certain sort. In the case of some of these qualities, however, there is no benefit in just being born with them, because they are altered by our habits. For some qualities are naturally capable of being developed by habit either in a better direction or in a worse one. The other animals mostly live under the guidance of nature alone, although some are guided a little by habit. But human beings live under the guidance of reason as well, since they alone have reason. Consequently, all three of these factors need to be harmonized with one another. For people often act contrary to their habits and their nature because of reason, if they happen to be persuaded that some other course of action is better. (Pol. VII 13 1332ª38–ᵇ8)

Nature may dispose us to virtue, but if that disposition is to develop appropriately, it needs habituation's helping hand: "The virtues develop in us neither by nature nor contrary to nature. Rather we are by nature capable of acquiring them, and completion comes through habituation" (NE II 1 1103ª23–26). Nonetheless, when it is adequately habituated or not spoiled by bad habituation, natural virtue remains immensely important, since it is virtue "whether natural or habituated, that teaches correct belief about the starting-point" (*NE* VII 8 1151ª18–19).

In the following passage, this aspect of natural or habituated virtue is given a narrower focus:

> The state, the one pertaining to this eye of the soul, does not come about without virtue,[16] as we have said and is clear. For practical syllogisms have a starting-point, "since the end—that is, the best good—is such and such," whatever it may be (let it be any chance thing for the sake of argument); this, however, is not evident, except to the good man; for vice produces distortion and false views about the starting-points of action. So it is evident that it is impossible to be practically wise without being good. (*NE* VI 12 1144ª29–ᵇ1)

The end or best good—happiness—is what is defined by the major premise of a practical-syllogism of the sort that, as the focus of a piece of practical deliberation, is the quintessential ethically correct reason. Like all starting-points, it is grasped by understanding. That is why it is precisely understanding that needs to be added to natural virtue to produce full virtue:

> For to both children and beasts these natural qualities also belong; but without understanding they are evidently harmful. At any rate, this much we can surely see, that just as a heavy body moving around without sight suffers a heavy fall because it has no sight, so it happens in this case too. But if someone should acquire understanding, it makes a difference in his action; and his state, though similar to the one he had, will then be full virtue. (*NE* VI 13 1144ᵇ8–14)

Understanding, therefore, is "the eye of the soul" mentioned in the earlier passage, and its lack is what is analogized to lack of sight in the later one: "as sight is to the body, so understanding is to the soul" (*NE* I 6 1096ᵇ28–29; compare *Protr.* B70, *Met.* IX 10 1052ª3–4). It is to understanding, therefore, that natural virtue teaches correct belief about happiness, confirming that the understanding in question is practical or wish-involving. For the object of wish is what appears to be happiness or the good, and it is to the virtuous person that genuine happiness appears as such (*NE* III 4). At the same time, understanding is also involved in the deliberative perception that grasps the minor premise of the syllogism in question, which is the one stating the correct prescriptive reason with which full virtue, in contrast with natural

---

16. That this is natural virtue is made clear by what follows (*NE* VI 13 1144ᵇ1–17).

virtue, must be in accord. Since this reason is or is provided by practical wisdom, the circle is complete. Add understanding to natural virtue and it becomes full virtue, while its possessor becomes both good and practically wise.

It is when we subtract natural virtue from practical wisdom that the other constituent—cleverness (*deinotês*)—comes into clear view:

> There is, then, a potentiality called cleverness; and this is the sort of thing which, when it comes to the things that further [hitting] a proposed target, is able to do these and to discover them.[17] If, then, the target is a noble one, this potentiality is praiseworthy, but if it is a bad one, it is unscrupulousness; and that is why both practically wise people and unscrupulous ones are said to be clever. Practical wisdom, however, is not cleverness, but does not exist without this potentiality. (*NE* VI 12 1144ᵃ23–29)

Thus the constituent of practical wisdom ensuring its true supposition about the unconditional end of action is natural virtue together with understanding, while the constituent that, as a result of correct deliberation, ensures that it optimally furthers this end is cleverness. This clear and precise account of practical wisdom's relationship to virtue of character, the need for which Aristotle recognizes (*NE* VI 12 1144ᵃ22–23), is the one foreshadowed in the less precise accounts: "Good deliberation will be the sort of correctness that is in accord with what is advantageous in furthering the end about which practical wisdom is true supposition" (*NE* VI 9 1142ᵇ32–33): that is to say, what makes practical wisdom's supposition about the end true is natural virtue; what makes it good at calculating what furthers that end is cleverness. "Virtue makes the target correct, and practical wisdom what furthers it" (*NE* VI 12 1144ᵃ8–9): that is to say, natural virtue makes the target correct, and so practical wisdom minus natural virtue (= cleverness) is what correctly calculates the means to it.

If the target someone aims at is noble, his character must be virtuous, and so praiseworthy, since virtue of character is what ensures the correct delib-

---

17. Reading τυγχάνειν αὐτῶν with the mss. Alternatively: τυγχάνειν αὐτοῦ (and discover or hit it), I. Bywater, *Aristotelis Ethica Nicomachea* (Oxford: Clarendon Press, 1894). On the plausible assumption that the potentiality referred to is cleverness, the following passage favors the transmitted text over the alternative: "it belongs to another potentiality to discover all that must be done to further the end; but that the deliberate choice's end is correct—of this virtue [of character] is the cause" (*EE* II 11 1227ᵇ39–1228ᵃ2).

erate choice of noble and praiseworthy ends. An unscrupulous person, by contrast, is someone who "greedily takes anything from anywhere" (*EE* II 3 1221ᵃ36–37; compare *Pr.* XVI 4 917ᵃ1–2). In other words, he takes as much as he can of money, honors, bodily pleasures, and other goods of competition, which are greed's particular targets (*NE* IX 8 1168ᵇ15–21), regardless of to whom they belong. If cleverness is unscrupulousness in someone whose end is bad, therefore, the end in question must be the bad equivalent, so to speak, of the unconditionally good end that practical wisdom furthers. This might explain why practical wisdom appears in a list of virtues and vices as the virtuous mean between the too much of unscrupulousness and the too little of unworldliness (*euêtheia*) (*EE* II 3 1221ᵃ12). Although the doctrine of the mean is not applied directly to the virtues of thought in the *Nicomachean Ethics*, practical wisdom does seem to be a sort of mean state, in that the virtues of character involved in it are mean states.

5

PRACTICAL WISDOM

The correct reason relevant to the virtues of character is the reason by which a practically wise man defines the mean with which actions and feelings *should*—since practical wisdom is a prescriptive virtue (*epitaktikê*)—be in accord (*NE* II 6 1106^{b}36–1107^{a}2, VI 10 1143^{a}8). Indeed, practical wisdom is sometimes simply identified with the correct reason (*NE* VI 13 1144^{b}27–28), just as the craft of medicine is sometimes identified with "the reason of health" (*Met.* XII 3 1070^{a}29–30). Practical wisdom's prescriptive reasons are as internal to it, in other words, as medical reasons are to medicine or mathematical reasons to mathematics (*NE* II 9 1109^{a}24–30). Hence we shouldn't expect these reasons to be any more accessible or intelligible to those who lack practical wisdom or the adequate habituation it presupposes than these others are to people ignorant of the relevant crafts or sciences:

> Argument and teaching surely do not prevail on everyone—on the contrary, the soul of the listener has to have been prepared beforehand in its habits, with a view to enjoying and hating in a noble way, like soil that is to nourish seed. For someone who lives in accord with his feelings would not listen to *or even understand* a contrary argument. And, in that condition, how could he be persuaded to change? Feelings generally seem to yield not to argument, indeed, but to force. Someone must, then, have a preexisting character that is somehow akin to virtue, one that is fond of what is noble and disgusted by what is ignoble. (*NE* X 9 1179^{b}23–31)

On parallel grounds, we should not expect any general characterization of correct reasons—that they all aim at mathematical truth, for example, or at health or happiness—to have the action-guiding or epistemic significance of the reasons themselves. Knowing that a geometrical construction must accord with mathematical truth doesn't tell us how to perform it, any more than knowing that we should make people healthy tells us how to treat a particular patient. Among the things a general characterization can do, though, is contribute to well-educatedness, by explaining how, for example, the *type* of correct reason provided by practical wisdom differs from the types provided by other things, whether craft knowledge, scientific knowledge, theoretical wisdom, or understanding (*NE* VI 3 1139^{b}16–17). This can help determine whether the reasons are of the sort they purport to be.

At one level, the nature of these reasons, and of the correctness appropriate to them, seems relatively straightforward. Practical reason is the virtue of the part of the soul that forms beliefs, which is the same as the calculative or deliberative part, since both deal with what admits of being otherwise (*NE* VI 5 1140^{b}25–28). But practical wisdom is not itself a type of belief. For a belief is a state "involving reason alone" (*NE* VI 5 1140^{b}28), since it is a type of assertion based on calculation or deliberation (*NE* VI 9 1142^{b}11–15), whereas practical wisdom is not such a state. This is because its existence in the part that forms beliefs presupposes the existence of natural or habituated virtue in the desiring part (*NE* VI 12 1144^{a}29–30), since it is natural or habituated virtue of character, as we know, that teaches "correct belief about the starting-point" (*NE* VII 8 1151^{a}18–19). A sign of this is that a state, such as belief, that involves reason alone can be forgotten, whereas practical wisdom cannot (*NE* VI 5 1140^{b}28–30). We might expect, then, that the correctness of practical wisdom's reasons will involve just three things: first, correctness of the appetites and desires in the desiring part; second, correctness of what is asserted by the believing part of the soul; and, third, correctness of the calculation or deliberation on which that assertion relies.

Target

A *skopos* in archery is a target, and so, by extension, anything aimed at, especially by deliberate choice, is a *skopos* (*NE* I 1 1094^{a}22–24, *EE* I 2 1214^{b}6–9). In the case of medicine, the target is health, which is a certain mean or balance between hot and cold elements (*Top.* VI 2 139^{b}20–21), and the possessor of the medically correct reason is the doctor. In the case of ethics, the target is a certain mean in feelings and actions, or the happiness that such actions done from such feelings constitute, and the possessor of the ethically correct reason is the practically wise man (*NE* II 6 1107^{a}1–2).

While keeping his eye on the target, the possessor of the correct reason "tightens or loosens" (*NE* VI 1 1138^{b}22–23), as a musician tightens or loosens his instrument's strings until a certain target note is struck (*Pol.* IV 3

1290ᵃ22–29; compare Plato, *Lysis* 209b). The notion of tightening and loosening is then extended to vocal cords, sinews, and other string-like things (*GA* V 7 787ᵇ10–24). Eventually, it is employed wherever a certain tripartite structure is thought to exist, consisting of a continuous underlying subject, often referred to as "the more and the less" (*to mallon kai to hêtton*), a pair of opposed attributes that can vary in degree, and a target, typically a mean condition of some sort, that can be achieved by increasing (tightening) or decreasing (loosening) the underlying subject to change the degree of the attributes. Hence Aristotle speaks of tightening and loosening in characterizing a wide range of phenomena, from the parts of animals to political constitutions:

> One thing must not be overlooked, which is in fact overlooked by the deviant constitutions: the mean. For many of the features that are held to be democratic destroy democracies, and many that are held to be oligarchic destroy oligarchies. But those who think that this [democratic virtue] is the only kind of virtue push the constitution to an extreme. They do not know that constitutions are just like parts of the body [*HA* I 1 486ᵃ25–ᵇ17]. A straight nose is the most beautiful, but one that deviates from being straight and tends toward being hooked or snub can nevertheless still be beautiful to look at. Yet if it is tightened still more toward the extreme, the part will first be thrown out of due proportion, and in the end it will cease to look like a nose at all, because it has too much of one and too little of the other of these opposites. The same holds of the other parts as well, but it can also happen in constitutions. (*Pol.* V 9 1309ᵇ18–31; also *Rh.* I 4 1360ᵃ23–30)

In the case of noses and other such parts, the continuous underlying subject is flesh and bone (or its shape), the pair of opposite attributes is hooked and snub, and the target—which lies somewhere in between the two, and so (as in political constitutions) in a mean of some sort—is being a straight nose, or at the very least a nose of some sort. In the case of political constitutions, the target is the mean condition that preserves them, and the continuous underlying subject may be, for example, the amount of money or wealth that qualifies someone to be a citizen, which may be either too small or too large:

> [To prevent an oligarchy from becoming a polity] it is beneficial to discover what the total communal assessment is compared with that of the past. . . . If the total is many times greater or many times less than it was when the rates qualifying someone to participate in the constitution were established, it is

advantageous to have a law that tightens or loosens the assessment; tightening it in proportion to the increase if the total has increased, loosening it or making it less if the total has decreased. (*Pol.* V 8 1308ᵃ35–ᵇ6)

The case of health is similar. For though health has a definition, the same "balance does not exist in every healthy person, nor does the same one always exist in the same person, but it may be loosened to a certain point and still remain present, so differing in terms of the more and the less" (*NE* X 3 1173ᵃ23–28). In the case of colors, too, while many are constituted out of white and black in some definite ratio, others are constituted in "some incommensurable ratio of excess or deficiency," and so are apt for tightening and loosening (*Sens.* 3 439ᵇ30).

No explicit example of tightening and loosening is provided for the focal case of ethics and practical wisdom, but the following surely comes close:

> We should also consider the things that we ourselves are more easily drawn toward, since different people have different natural tendencies toward different things, and we can find out what they are from the pleasure and the pain that the things cause in us. And we should drag ourselves off in the opposite direction, for if we pull far away from error we shall reach the mean, in precisely the way people do when they are correcting the distortions (*diestrammena*)[1] in pieces of wood. (*NE* II 9 1109ᵇ1–7)

Presumably, then, practical wisdom also follows the model we have been exploring. The target is the mean in feelings and actions, specified by the correct reason, while tightening and loosing is an adjustment made in some continuous underlying subject of these, which increases or diminishes the degree of a pair of opposite or contrary attributes. Since "every feeling and every action involves pleasure or pain," and "pleasure causes us to do ignoble actions, and pain, to abstain from noble ones," the underlying subject in question is almost certainly that of the pleasure-pain continuum (*NE* II 3 1104ᵇ9–11). If so, the target is the mean in feelings, and so in states of character, and the adjustment is one made to produce virtue by overcoming our natural bias in favor of pleasure and against pain.

When Aristotle says that we pardon bad actions done "because of conditions that over-tighten or overstrain human nature" (*NE* III 1 1110ᵃ23–26),

---

1. *Diestrammena* is a participle of the verb *diastrephomai*, used in related contexts at *NE* VI 5 1140ᵇ13, 12 1144ᵃ34.

then, he is speaking literally. Our feelings, like our senses, discern things lying between two extreme points on a continuum by being in a mean between them. Things that exceed those extremes overstrain the sense, as weights that are too heavy for a given scale ruin its mechanism, so that it can no longer make accurate discriminations: "A sense is a proportion; excessive objects dissolve or destroy it" (*DA* III 2 426^{b}7). Similarly, when excruciating pain or terrifying fear overstrains our feelings, it disables our practical perception, and so may excuse what we end up doing.

Defining-Mark

In addition to the target on which the possessor of the correct reason keeps his eye, which is the relevant mean state or condition, and the tightening and loosening he employs to hit it, there is also "some sort of *horos* of the mean [states], which we say are between excess and deficiency, being as they are in accord with the correct reason" (*NE* VI 1 1138^{b}23–25). A common meaning of *horos*—and the most common one in the *Nicomachean Ethics*—is "term," in the logical sense, in which a syllogism has three terms (for example *NE* V 3 1131^{b}5, 16). At *NE* I 7 1097^{b}11–13, however, it is used in a related but somewhat different sense. The context is a worry about happiness. Since a human being is a political animal his happiness is bound up with that of others, but how extensive is the relevant class? We must impose some *horos* on it, since otherwise the class "will go on indefinitely." Here, then, as often elsewhere, a *horos* is what gives definition to what would otherwise lack it, in the way that a stone marker (also called a *horos*) defines the boundary of a territory or piece of land in a perceptible way. Similarly, the ethical or medical *horos* seems to be something that brings the target itself within reach of perception. Hence the doctor's *horos* is the thing "*by reference to which he discerns* what is healthy for a body from what isn't" (*EE* VIII 3 1249^{a}21–22)—the thing that must be "looked to in saying what the correct reason is" (*EE* II 5 1222^{b}7–8). Similarly, the political scientist must have "certain *horoi*, derived from nature and from the truth itself, by reference to which he will discern what is just, what is noble, and what is advantageous" (*Protr.* B47). Since the noun *horos* is etymologically related to the verb *horizein*,[2] which means "define," and what the man of practical wisdom does to the ethical mean is provide the correct reason that "defines"

---

2. Pierre Chantraine, *Dictionnaire Étymologique de la Langue Grecque* (Paris: Éditions Klincksieck, 1968), pp. 825–826.

(*hôrismenê[i]*) it (*NE* II 6 1106^b36–1107^a2), the ethical *horos* must be the defining-mark of the target that he looks to in determining what that reason is. Hence, by a sort of transitivity, the practically wise man is himself sometimes said to *be* the *horos*, since others can use him as an effective way to determine the correct reason (*Protr.* B39).

The order of progression, then, is this: the practically wise man knows what the target is, discovers an appropriate defining-mark of it, looks to that mark in defining the correct-reason, and uses the correct reason to define the mean. The following example from medicine illustrates the point:

> The healthy thing comes to be [when the doctor reasons] as follows: Since health is this, necessarily if the thing is to be healthy this must be present—for example, a uniform state—and if the latter is to be present, there must be heat, and he goes on, always understanding like this, until he is led to a final "this" that he is able to make himself. Then the process from this point onward, toward health, is called production. (*Met.* VII 7 1032^b6–10)

The doctor can tell by touch whether the muscle is in a uniform state, which is a mean between being too tense and too limp, so it becomes his *horos*. He then has to find something he can do directly, and can tell by perception that he is doing "when actually doing" it (*EE* II 10 1226^a37), that will produce the requisite uniform state (*Pol.* VII 13 1331^b36), such as making the muscle hot by rubbing it. Health itself, by contrast, which is his target, need not be defined in a way that makes it accessible to perception.

The defining-mark the practically wise man employs is characterized succinctly in the *Eudemian Ethics*:

> [1] For the good man (*spoudaios*), too, where actions and deliberate choices of things naturally good but not praiseworthy are concerned, there should be some defining-mark both for their possession and their choice, pertaining to the avoidance of excess and deficiency of wealth and good luck. Now in what we said earlier it [the defining-mark] was *as the [correct] reason prescribes.* That, however, is like saying, where nutrition is concerned, as medicine and its reason prescribes, which, though true, is not illuminating. [2] One should, of course, just as in the other cases, live by reference to the ruling constituent (*to archon*), that is, by reference to the state and[3] activity of the ruling constituent, like a slave by reference to its master, and each thing by reference to its proper ruling constituent. Since, then, a human being, too, is by nature composed of a

---

3. Reading καὶ for ms. κατὰ.

ruling constituent and one that is ruled, each of them should also live by reference to its ruling constituent. [3] But this is of two sorts, for medicine is one sort and health another. And that is how it is with the contemplative constituent. For the god (*ho theos*) is not a prescriptive ruler, but the one for whose sake practical wisdom prescribes. But that for the sake of which is of two sorts (they have been distinguished elsewhere), since the god, at least, is in need of nothing. [4] So if some choice and possession of natural goods—either goods of the body or money or of friends or the other goods—will most of all produce the contemplation of the divine constituent (*tên tou theou theôrian*), that is the best, and that is the noblest defining-mark. But whatever, through deficiency or excess, hinders the service and contemplation of the divine constituent (*ton theon therapeuein kai theôrein*) is bad. So much, then, for noble-goodness's defining-mark, and what the target is of things unconditionally good. (VIII 3 1249ᵃ24–ᵇ25)[4]

Here the target is the contemplative activity of the soul's divine constituent, and the *horos*, which is obviously a different thing, is the choice and possession of natural goods that will best further that activity. Although no comparable account is given in the *Nicomachean Ethics*, markedly similar—not to say identical—doctrines are expressed there piecemeal.

The good man in [1] is the one who possesses the virtues of character, each of which determines a mean in accord with correct reason for a specific range of external or natural goods and the feelings involved with them. In the case of luck, which controls such goods, the *Nicomachean Ethics* is specific about how the *horos* that defines it is related to happiness: "when luck is excessive, it is actually an impediment to happiness—and presumably then it is no longer rightly called *good* luck, since its defining-mark is determined by reference to happiness" (*NE* VII 13 1153ᵇ21–25; also I 7 1097ᵇ5–13). That is why happiness is described as "the starting-point and the cause of goods" quite generally (*NE* I 12 1102ᵃ3–4), and why "the political philosopher"—that is, the political scientist insofar as he focuses especially on starting-points—is referred to as the "architectonic craftsman of the end we look to in calling something unconditionally bad or good" (*NE* VII 11 1152ᵇ1–3).

Happiness, however, at any rate of the complete sort, just is contemplation (*NE* X 7 1177ᵃ16–17). Hence the *horos* described as "noblest" in [4], by which

4. Some of the textual difficulties presented by this passage are explored in Michael Woods, *Aristotle: Eudemian Ethics, Books I, II, and VIII*, 2nd ed. (Oxford: Clarendon Press, 1992), pp. 199–200.

the man of practical wisdom defines the ethical mean, is determined by reference to what in the *Nicomachean Ethics* is complete happiness. This, too, is *Eudemian* doctrine. For happiness, which is the "target" on which a person should keep his eye "in all his actions" (*EE* I 2 1214^{b}6–9), is intimately related to God: "God is in a state of well-being . . . by being too good to contemplate anything besides himself. And the explanation for this is that while our well-being is in accord with something different, he is himself his own well-being" (*EE* VII 12 1245^{b}16–19). The "something different" is the object our contemplation must accord with—the object that, in the case of God's own contemplation, is God himself. When the object of our contemplation is also God, therefore, our happiness will be as close to his as possible.[5]

The term *to archon* in [2] refers to the soul's contemplative constituent, which is *nous* or understanding. It is used with the same reference in the *Nicomachean Ethics*, where understanding "by nature rules (*archein*) and leads" (X 7 1177^{a}14–15) and is or is part of "the ruling constituent (*to archon*)" (III 12 1119^{b}7–10) of the soul. The soul's other constituent, referred to as "the one that is ruled," is the desiring part (as it is, for example, in *NE* I 13), within which reside the appetites and desires for the external goods, such as money and friends, referred to in [4]. That one should live "by reference to the state and activity" of the understanding is also the view of the *Nicomachean Ethics*, where we are told that we should live in accord with our understanding, since it is the divine constituent in us, the one with which we are most identified, the one whose activity makes us happiest (X 7 1177^{b}33–1178^{a}8).

Since a slave is "an assistant in the class of things having to do with action" (*Pol.* I 5 1254^{a}8), what he should do is determined by reference to his master's actions and activities, so that such virtue as he has "does not belong to him by reference to himself" but "by reference to his master" (*Pol.* I 13 1260^{a}32–33). Similarly, the desiring part of the soul is "by nature a follower of the part that has reason" and possesses the virtues of character insofar as it is in harmony with reason's prescriptions (*EE* II 1 1220^{a}8–11). All the same, understanding rules desire not—as the soul does the body—with the rule of a master but with "political or kingly rule" (*Pol.* I 5 1254^{b}5–6). For the desiring part of the soul can have the sort of share in virtue of character that analogizes it to free male citizens and distinguishes it from slaves (*Pol.* I 13 1260^{a}31–39, III 4 1277^{b}25–30).

---

5. The comment about illumination in [1] is repeated almost verbatim at *NE* VI 1 1138^{b}25–26.

Like *to archon* in [2], the term *ho theos* in [3] refers to the (human) understanding, which is so-called because it is [4] "the divine constituent" (*to theion*) or the "divine thing" (*theion ti*) in the human soul (*NE* X 7 1177^{b}28). This is also the reference of the term in the following passage:

> No one praises happiness as one does justice, but calls it blessed, as being more divine and better [than justice]. It seems, in fact, that Eudoxus put it well in pressing the claims of pleasure to supremacy [among goods]. By not praising pleasure, though it is a good, we indicated, he thought, that it is superior to everything praiseworthy—but [only] the god and the good (*ton theon kai tagathon*) have this superiority since the other [goods] are praised by reference to them. (*NE* I 12 1101^{b}25–31)

Eudoxus thought that pleasure is "the good" (*tagathon*; *NE* X 2 1172^{b}9) but not that it is "the god." Hence the final clause ("but only . . .") is Aristotle's own thought. "The god and the good" are superior to other goods, which is why we do not praise them as we do justice and the other virtues. At the same time, what no one praises is happiness, which is the human good.[6] It consists in contemplation, which, as an activity of the divine constituent, is itself more divine than justice and the other virtues of character (*NE* X 8 1178^{a}9–23). The god, in other words, is not God, but human understanding, so that only one thing—namely, active understanding—is beyond praise. That is why other goods are praised by reference to it. For as "the starting-point and the cause of goods," it is something "estimable and divine" (*NE* I 12 1102^{a}3–4). Similarly when "*ho theos kai ho nous*" is cited as an example of a good that is a substance, the import of the phrase is almost certainly "the god, that is, the understanding," making our understanding again the reference of *ho theos* (*NE* I 6 1096^{a}24–25).[7] That our understanding "is in need of nothing," that is, of no external goods, and can even—as in [4]—be impeded or hindered by them, is repeated and amplified at *NE* X 8 1178^{b}3–5: "someone who is contemplating needs none of these external goods—at least, for the activity; indeed, for contemplating itself at least, they are even impeding factors."

Practical wisdom, which prescribes for the sake of the understanding in [3], is a prescriptive virtue at *NE* VI 10 1143^{a}8 and is characterized as prescribing for the sake of the contemplative or philosophical activity of the

---

6. The good at *NE* I 2 1094^{a}22 = the human good at 1094^{b}7 = happiness at I 3 1095^{a}14–20.

7. A more controversial case is *NE* IX 4 1166^{a}22–23.

understanding, as medicine does for the sake of health (*NE* VI 13 1145ª6–11). As a *hou heneka* or a for-the-sake-of-which, such activity is of two sorts, since it could be either "the end (*hou*) or the beneficiary (*hô[i]*)" (*DA* II 4 415ᵇ2–3). The activity of understanding needs nothing, however, and so cannot be a beneficiary of practical wisdom, any more than health can be a beneficiary of medicine. Hence it must be the end for which practical wisdom prescribes. It is in this sense that the understanding is a ruling constituent: it determines practical wisdom's prescriptions by being the end or target that determines their correctness. For although he issues no prescriptions and makes no choices, God too is analogized to prescriptive rulers, such as the general of an army and the ruler of a city (*Met.* XII 10 1075ª11–25, 1075ᵇ37–1076ª4). Similarly, the understanding is characterized as the constituent in the soul that has "most control," the one a virtuous person always "obeys" or "obeys as his ruler," and the one that always "chooses what is best for itself" (*NE* IX 8 1168ᵇ28–1169ª18).

The phrases *tên tou theou theôrian* and *ton theon therapeuein kai theôrein* in [4] could refer to the human understanding and its contemplation of any appropriate object. As we saw, however, it is doctrine common to both *Ethics* that if the contemplation in question is to constitute complete happiness, it must have God as its object—as it must, indeed, if it is be in accord with theoretical wisdom. It is also common doctrine that practical wisdom must issue its prescriptions with the ultimate aim of furthering such contemplation. In the *Eudemian Ethics*, the defining-mark for these prescriptions is the "choice and possession of natural goods—either goods of the body or money or of friends or the other goods—[that] will most of all produce the contemplation of the divine constituent." The *Nicomachean Ethics* settles for saying that we should "do everything" to live in accord with our understanding (X 7 1177ᵇ33). In the end, though, its message is less extreme than it may sound. For the *Nicomachean Ethics* also assures us that insofar as "someone is human, and so lives together with a number of other human beings, he chooses to do the actions that are in accord with virtue [of character]" (*NE* X 8 1178ᵇ5–7). This brings its message into harmony with that of [4]. For full virtue of character is particularly involved with external goods, and—since practical wisdom is implicated in it (*NE* VI 13 1144ᵇ16–17)—aims to further contemplation to the fullest extent possible (*NE* X 8 1178ᵇ29–31).

Although we now know what practical wisdom's *horos* is, we are not any closer to being able to use it to guide our actions in particular circumstances. Target, defining-mark, correct-reason, and mean are constituents of practical reasons whose interrelations allow us to see the *structure* of such reasons; they are not an algorithm for constructing the reasons themselves. To construct them, we need to be practically wise. There is no substitute for that, just as there is no substitute for being a doctor in being able to construct medically correct reasons.[8]

End or Goal

The noun *praxis* (verb: *prattein*) is used in a broad sense to refer to any intentional action (*NE* III 1 1111[a]25–26, 2 1111[b]8–9), including those performed by children and beasts, and in a narrower one to refer exclusively to what results from deliberation (*bouleusis*) and deliberate choice (*prohairesis*), of which neither beasts nor children are capable (*Ph.* II 6 197[b]6–8, *NE* I 9 1099[b]32–1100[a]5). As the virtue or excellence of the calculative or deliberative part of the soul, practical-wisdom's unconditional end is thus *eupraxia* or excellent *praxis* of the deliberately chosen sort: "Thought by itself moves nothing; but the one that is for the sake of something and is practical does. Indeed, it even rules productive thought. For every producer produces for the sake of something, and the end unconditionally (as opposed to in relation to something and for something [else]) is not what is produced but what is done in a *praxis*. For *eupraxia* is an end, and the desire [namely, wish] is for it" (*NE* VI 2 1139[a]35–[b]4). *Eupraxia* is the same as *eudaimonia* (happiness) (*NE* VI 12 1143[b]19–21), therefore, and the same as *to eu zên holôs* (living well as a whole) (*NE* VI 5 1140[a]28). What suits *praxis* (plural: *praxeis*) to play this distinctive teleological role is revealed in the focal contrast of a *praxis* with a *poiêsis* (plural: *poiêseis*) or production: a *poiêsis* is for the sake of something else, namely, the product in which it results; a *praxis*, by contrast, isn't for the sake of something else. Consequently, a *praxis* is suited to be an unconditional end; a *poiêsis* isn't (*NE* X 4 1174[a]19–21).

The distinction between *praxeis* and *poiêseis* is a special case of a more general distinction Aristotle draws between *energeiai* (singular: *energeia*) and *kinêseis* (singular: *kinêsis*):

> Of the *praxeis* that have a [temporal] limit none is an end, but all are in relation to an end—as for example, slimming is. For the things themselves, when one is slimming them, are *en kinêsei*, since what the *kinêsis* is for the sake of [namely, its end] does not yet belong to them. Hence these are not cases

8. Contrast Sandra Peterson, "*Horos* (Limit) in Aristotle's *Nicomachean Ethics*," *Phronesis* 33 (1988): 233–250.

of *praxis,* at least not of complete *praxis,* since none is an end. But the sort in which the end belongs *is a praxis.* For example, at the same time one is seeing [a thing] and has seen [it], is being practically wise and has been practically wise (*phronei kai pephronêke*), is understanding [something] and has understood [it], whereas it is not the case that [at the same time] one is learning [something] and has learned [it], nor that one is being cured and has been cured. Someone who is living well, however, at the same time has lived well and is happy and has been happy [at the same time]. If this were not so, these would have to come to an end at some time, as when one is slimming [something]. But as things stand there is no such time, but one is living and has lived. Of these, then, one group should be called *kinêseis* and the other *energeiai.* For every *kinêsis* is incomplete, for example, slimming, learning, walking, building. These are *kinêseis* and are certainly incomplete. For it is not the case that at the same time one is walking and has taken a walk, nor that one is building [something] and has built [it], or is coming-to-be [something] and has come-to-be [it], or is being changed [in some way] and has been changed [in that way], but they are different, as are one's changing and having changed [something]. By contrast one has seen and is seeing the same thing at the same time, or is understanding and has understood. The latter sort, then, I call an *energeia,* the former a *kinêsis.* (*Met.* IX 6 1048ᵇ18–35)

Expressed linguistically, the contrast is one of aspect rather than tense. Roughly speaking, a verb whose present tense has imperfective meaning designates a *kinêsis,* while one whose present tense has perfective meaning designates an *energeia.*[9] The distinction itself is ontological, however, not linguistic: *energeiai* and *kinêseis* are types of beings, not types of verbs. A *poiêsis* or *kinêsis* is something that takes time to complete and, like the time it takes, is infinitely divisible (*Ph.* III 7 207ᵇ21–25, *Met.* V 13 1020ᵃ26–32). It has a definite termination point or limit, before which it is incomplete and after which it cannot continue (*NE* X 4 1174ᵃ21–23). A *praxis,* by contrast, does not take time to complete, and so does not really occur "in time" (*Ph.* VIII 8 262ᵇ20–21) but is temporally point-like (*NE* X 4 1174ᵇ12–13). Having no definite termination, while it may stop, it need never finish (*Met.* IX 6 1048ᵇ25–27).

As an *energeia,* then, a *praxis* is an end, and so is complete at every moment. As the result of deliberate choice, it presupposes a state of character, such as virtue or vice (*NE* VI 2 1139ᵃ33–34). Indeed, the *praxis* is what results when that state is actualized:

9. On this point, and on various points of translation, I follow M. F. Burnyeat, "*Kinêsis* vs. *Energeia*: A Much-Read Passage in (but Not of) Aristotle's *Metaphysics,*" *Oxford Studies in Ancient Philosophy* 34 (2008): 219–292, especially pp. 245–253.

The result is the end (*to gar ergon telos*), the *energeia* is the result (*hê de energeia to ergon*), and this is why the term *energeia* is called what it is in accord with the result (*dio kai tounoma energeia legetai kata to ergon*) and extends to the actualization [of the state] (*kai sunteinei pros tên entelecheian*). (*Met.* IX 8 1050ᵃ21–23)[10]

The potentiality that *a* has to sing a B-flat, for example, is a state acquired through learning and practice. When actualized, it results in a B-flat being sung. This—the sung B-flat—is an activity in the primary or nonextended sense of the term. The actualization of the state, by contrast, is an activity only in a secondary or extended sense, because what *a* is doing would not be singing a B-flat if it did not result in a sung B-flat. That result, in other words, is a logically necessary or *internal* end of the actualization of the correlative state. Similarly a *praxis* is the internal end of a state of character's being actualized. Hence the *tel*—from *telos*—in *entelecheia*.[11]

The paradigm cases of intentional *actions*, as we understand them, are temporally extended bodily movements appropriately related to (perhaps by being caused by) beliefs, desires, and intentions. Hence "action" is clearly a potentially misleading translation of *praxis*. Nonetheless, there is one type of action that *praxeis* seem to resemble quite closely, namely, so-called *basic actions*. This is especially true, if, as Aristotle himself seems to believe, these are thought to be mental acts of willing, deciding, or trying: "even in the case of external *praxeis*, the one who above all does them in the full sense is the architectonic craftsman who directs them by his thoughts" (*Pol.* VII 3 1325ᵇ21–23). Like *praxeis*, in any case, these sorts of mental acts are not bodily movements and do not seem to take time to perform. Moreover, just as we do not perform basic actions by doing something else first, the same seems true of *praxeis*, so that a human being "is a starting-point and

10. This standard reading treats *dio* ("and this is why") as governing the rest of the sentence. An alternative, proposed by Sarah Broadie, "Where Is the Activity? (An Aristotelian Worry about the Telic Status of *Energeia*)," in *Being, Nature, and Life in Aristotle,* ed. James G. Lennox and Robert Bolton (Cambridge: Cambridge University Press, 2010), pp. 198–211), treats *dio* as beginning a parenthetical comment ending with *to ergon,* so that *sunteinei pros tên entelecheian* is predicated of *energeia*, making the activity itself, not its name, the thing that extends to or strains toward the actualization of the state. *Met.* IX 3 1047ᵃ30–32—"the term *energeia*, which is put together with a view to *entelecheia*, has been extended to other things most of all from movements. For an *eneregia* seems most of all to be a movement"—favor the standard reading.

11. My thoughts here have been influenced by David Charles, "Aristotle: Ontology and Moral Reasoning," *Oxford Studies in Ancient Philosophy* 4 (1986): 119–144.

begetter of *praxeis* just as he is of children" (*NE* III 5 1113^{b}18–19; also VI 2 1139^{b}5). As in the case of productions, where the form in a craftsman's soul is transmitted to the matter via the movements of his hands and instruments (*GA* I 22 730^{b}12–23), so the results of such *praxeis* may be transmitted via bodily movements to other things that, because they admit of being otherwise, are capable of being changed by them. These results, and the bodily movements involved in bringing them about, are what we think of as paradigm actions.

When a group of dramatic actions have a plot-structure (*mythos*) of the sort a good tragedy possesses, Aristotle says they constitute a single action that is "one, whole, and complete" (*Po.* 23 1459^{a}19). By being enactments of the real-life equivalent of the right sort of plot or plan, therefore, the same should also be true of a group of nondramatic actions. As a group of actors can set out to perform *Oedipus Tyrannus*, so a single agent can set out to enact a unified plan of action, which involves doing many different things in some sort of sequence. This complex action may be what practical wisdom prescribes as constituting *eupraxia*. What organizes this plan, in turn, is the practical demonstration that serves as the focus of the agent's deliberation. For his deliberation as a whole is a search, as we shall see, for a minor premise in the shape of a decree that will bring *eupraxia* or *eudaimonia*, as defined in the practical demonstration's major premise, within his effective grasp by having a minor term that is the defining-mark of *eupraxia* or *eudaimonia* as so defined. The unity of this demonstration is thus transferred to the complex action resulting from it.

To understand why the agent is doing any of the things specified by the plan, we will typically need to see it in relation to the plan as a whole. For many of these, taken individually, might not be ends or goods choiceworthy for their own sakes: some might be otherwise valueless means to ends, some might be productions of needed equipment, some might be actions whose status as intrinsically choiceworthy nonetheless depends on their role in the plan. As parts of the whole complex action they help constitute, however, all *are* intrinsically choiceworthy, since the complex action is itself so. Hence the unified plan itself might be likened to the form of health in the soul of the doctor, which dictates the bodily movements that constitute, for example, producing the uniform state in a tense muscle, which is the relevant defining-mark of health (*Met.* VII 7 1032^{b}6–10). The actualization of the plan, the setting of it in motion, is an action, as is the carrying out of the subsequent steps. In performing each of them, the agent is achieving the goal of acting well. For acting well, since it isn't an external end, is not something achieved only when the plan is fully executed, as health is produced only when its plan or form is embodied in the appropriate matter (the tense muscle). At the same time, it does not seem to be an entirely internal end, either, since the plan may fail to be completely carried out.

Unlike actions that are basic, complex ones are in a way hostage to fortune. We set the associated plan in motion, which is a basic action, but whether we will succeed in carrying it out fully is in part a matter of luck. If we fail through no fault of our own, we have in one way done what virtue requires of us—we have tried, we have done all that we could do. In another way, though, we have failed, and may now have something more to do, such as, try again, or make amends of some sort. The possibility of failure taints complex actions with unleisure, since it means there are usually obstacles or resistances to overcome in order to carry them out. For the same reason it threatens the pleasure that is their supervenient end. Courageous actions suffer from both liabilities:

> The end in accord with courage would seem to be pleasant, but to be obscured by the circumstances, as also happens, for example, in athletic competitions. For to boxers the end is pleasant—the thing for whose sake they do it, the victor's wreath and the honors. Being punched hurts them, however, since they are made of flesh and blood, and is painful, as is all the hard work. And because the painful sides are many, the thing they do it for seems small and to have nothing pleasant about it. And so, if the same is true of courage, death and wounds will be painful to the courageous person, and he will suffer them unwillingly, but he will endure them because doing so is noble or not doing so, ignoble. And the more he possesses all of virtue and the happier he is, the more he will be pained at the prospect of death, since a person of this sort, more than anyone, finds living worthwhile, and will knowingly be depriving himself of the greatest goods, and this is painful. But he is no less courageous because of that, perhaps even more courageous, because he chooses what is noble in war in place of those other goods. It is not true, then, of every virtue that its exercise is pleasant, except insofar as it reaches the end. (NE III 9 1117ª35–ᵇ16)

Many—perhaps most—actions in accord with the practical virtues, or virtues of character, are surely complex. They would be unleisured, therefore, and subject to a sort of incompleteness, even if they had no additional external ends.

As the internal ends of actualizing states in making deliberate choices, actions inherit their defining features from those states, just as productions or processes inherit theirs from the states they actualize: "a process is an activity of what is incomplete, whereas an unconditional activity is something different—it is of what has been completed" (*DA* III 7 431ᵃ6–7; also *Ph.* III 2 201ᵇ31–33). Now one way in which a state or potential can be incomplete is by not yet having been fully achieved or acquired, like one's knowledge of a poem while one is still learning to recite it. But that is not the sense relevant here, since even when a productive state or craft is fully achieved, the result of actualizing it is still a process or production, still an activity that is incomplete. Productive states, no matter how completed or perfected, then, are intrinsically incomplete in a way that comparably perfected practical or action-determining states are not.

The relationship between the end or product of a production and the production itself is usually expressed by the preposition *para* ("in addition to," "over and above") (*NE* I 1 1094ᵃ4). Thus a product, such as a house, is a paradigmatic *para* or additional end, because—as something that comes into existence only when the production resulting in it is complete and does not exist while the production is still going on—it clearly is external to the productive process itself. Nonetheless, not all external ends are the ends of productions, or even of processes more generally, since actions, too, have external ends:

> From the practical virtues we try to a greater or lesser extent to gain something in addition to (*para*) the action [in accord with them]. . . . [These] have their activity in politics or war, and in these areas actions seem to be unleisured, and those in war completely so. . . . But the [action] of the political scientist is unleisured, too, and aims, in addition to (*par'*) engaging in politics itself, at mastership and honors, or at any rate at happiness for himself and for his fellow citizens, which is something different from politics, and is clearly sought as being different. Hence, among actions that are in accord with virtues, those in politics and war are preeminently noble and great, but are unleisured and aim at some [further] end, and are not chosen [solely] because of themselves. (*NE* X 7 1177ᵇ2–18)

The difference between productions and actions is not that productions have external ends but that they supposedly have no internal ones.

In fact, the difference is more complex even than that:

> We say, and we have given this definition in our ethical works (if anything in those discussions is of service), that happiness is a complete activity or use of virtue, and not a conditional use but an unconditional one. By "conditional uses" I mean those that are necessary; by "unconditional" I mean those that are noble. For example, in the case of just actions, just retributions and

punishments spring from virtue, but are necessary uses of it, and are noble only in a necessary way, since it would be more choiceworthy if no individual or city needed such things. On the other hand, just actions that aim at honors and prosperity are unconditionally noblest. The former involve choosing something that is somehow bad, whereas the latter are the opposite: they construct and generate goods. (*Pol.* VII 13 1332ᵃ7–18)

Despite Aristotle's claim to the contrary, nothing in the *Nicomachean Ethics* or the other ethical works prepares us for this somewhat surprising claim.[12] Conditional uses of the virtues of character are actions and activities, but it is less clear that they do possess their end, since they are not unequivocally cases of doing well in action or being happy. Even nobility is something they do not unequivocally possess. Perhaps, then, what we should say is this: productions cannot have internal ends, while actions can and perhaps for the most part do have them. When Aristotle implicitly recognizes a class of incomplete *praxeis* (*Met.* IX 6 1048ᵇ21–22), it may be cases like the necessary uses of the virtues of character that he has in mind.

Besides internal, external, and immanent ends, actions, as types of activity, also have *supervenient* ends, so that when actions are said to be "for the sake of other things" (*NE* III 3 1112ᵇ33), there are a number of candidates to choose from. Supervenient ends are best illustrated by the special case of pleasures. At one point, these seem to be identified with activities. Pleasures are not "processes of coming-to-be, nor do they involve a process of coming-to-be, on the contrary, they are activities and an end," namely, those activities or actualizations of a natural state that are unimpeded (*NE* VII 12 1153ᵃ9–15). Later, this identification is recognized as problematic: "it certainly does not seem that pleasure just is understanding (*dianoia*) or perceiving, since that would be a strange idea" (*NE* X 5 1175ᵇ34–35). As a result, pleasure is now identified not with the activity itself but with an end supervening on it: "pleasure completes the activity not as the state does by being present, but as a sort of supervenient end, like the bloom of manhood on those in their prime" (*NE* X 4 1174ᵇ31–33). At the same time, an explanation is given for the earlier identification:

The pleasures [taken] in activities are more proper to them than are the desires for them, since the latter are distinguished from them both in time and in nature, whereas the pleasures are close to the activities, and so little distin-

---

12. As W. L. Newman, *The Politics of Aristotle*, vol. 1 (Oxford: Clarendon Press, 1887), pp. 575–576, notices.

guished from them that there is room for dispute about whether the activity is the same thing as pleasure . . . [and] because of their not being separated, they appear to some people to be the same. (*NE* X 5 1175^{b}30–35)

Supervenient ends thus seem to solve some puzzles about pleasure in a way that conforms to sound dialectical or aporematic methodology. They are enough like activities that the confusion of one with the other is readily explicable. Yet, because they are in fact distinct, the apparent difference between pleasure and activity is also accounted for. Precisely because activities and supervenient ends are so intimately related, it may sometimes be simpler to treat them as identical, especially when nothing of importance hangs on distinguishing them. This may partly explain why, in the discussion of incontinence in *Nicomachean Ethics* VII, they are left out of the story.

As well as solving a puzzle about pleasure, supervenient ends also resolve another issue, which is arguably much more important—that of the involvement of pleasure in happiness. For if happiness just is activity in accord with the most complete virtue, and pleasure is a supervenient end of such activity, the life of the virtuous "does not need pleasure to be added like some ornament tied on to it," since "it has its pleasure within itself" (*NE* I 8 1099^{a}15–16). This enables Aristotle to preserve the *endoxon* that happiness must involve pleasure (*NE* I 8 1098^{b}25), which is an adequacy condition on his account of it, without embracing the problematic hedonistic view that happiness and pleasure are the same thing.

Particulars and Universals

Practical wisdom must "know particulars (*kath' hekasta*); for it is practical, and action has to do with particulars" (*NE* VI 7 1141^{b}14–15). But particulars are not just of one sort: they are the countable objects—canonically, primary substances—into which the world is carved up by forms, but they are also the forms themselves, which do the carving. Coriscus is a particular *this* (*tode ti*), but so too is his form: "Substance is spoken of in two ways, the ultimate underlying subject, which is no longer said of anything else, and whatever being a this is also separate (such as each thing's shape or form)" (*Met.* V 8 1017^{b}23–26). Similarly, both Coriscus and his species form are particulars:

What is special and particular is always stronger in coming-to-be. For Coriscus is both man and animal, but man is closer to what is special [to him] than animal. In coming-to-be, both what is particular [that is, man] and what is genus [that is, animal] are operative, but more so what is particular, since this is the substance. For indeed[13] the offspring also comes to be a sort of thing [that is, an animal], but at the same time [it comes to be] a this, and the latter is the substance. That is precisely why it is from all these potentialities that the movements in the seed come. (GA IV 3 767^{b}29–36)

Hence in seeing this particular color, we coincidentally see the universal color red of which it is an instance, and in contemplating this particular token A, we are contemplating an A, the type of letter it is (Met. XIII 10 1087^{a}19–21).

What practical wisdom knows in knowing particulars are things of the sort that can figure in the minor or particular premise—"Bird meats are light"— of a syllogism embodying all or part of an agent's deliberation (NE VI 7 1141^{b}20). What it knows, in other words, is how to tell what particular tokens of bird meat are tokens of. It is because practical wisdom must know such things that its acquisition requires experience, and its possession the sort of eye that typically come only with age: "We should attend to the undemonstrated sayings and beliefs of experienced and older people, or practically wise ones, no less than to the demonstrations; in that, because they have an eye formed from experience, they see correctly" (NE VI 11 1143^{b}13–14).

In the inductive process leading from perception of particulars to universals, experience occurs when unanalyzed universals are reached that perception itself can discern. What acquisition of such universals and their interrelations allows someone to grasp, therefore, are empirical generalizations readily applicable in particular situations, precisely because the universals they involve are themselves discernible by perception. What experience alone cannot provide is knowledge of fully universal, demonstrative explanations, since these involve analyzed universals, which are very far removed from experience, and so hard to apply directly to it. Hence a scientist who does know such explanations may "not know some of the particular cases through lack of observation" (APo. I 13 79^{a}2–6).

It is for this reason that knowledge of the particular or minor premises of practical syllogisms is a more important component of practical wisdom than knowledge of universals, that is, of their universal or major premises:

In other areas, too, some people who lack knowledge—especially those with experience—are more practical than others who have knowledge. For if

---

13. Reading καὶ γὰρ with the mss.

someone knows that light meats are digestible and healthy, but does not know which sorts of meat are light, he will not produce health, but the one who knows that bird meats are healthy will produce health more. Practical wisdom is practical, however, so one must possess both [sorts of knowledge]—or this one more. (*NE* VI 7 1141^{b}16–22)

Having made this important point, the passage goes on immediately to remind us that experience isn't enough by itself to constitute practical wisdom: "Here too, though, there will be a sort that is architectonic (*architektonikê*)" (*NE* VI 7 1141^{b}22–23).

What makes a craft or science architectonic—like what makes it estimable or rigorous—is that it provides knowledge of the explanatory or analyzed universals that experience fails to provide by itself:

With a view to action, experience seems no worse than craft—on the contrary, we even see that experienced people are more successful than those who possess the reason but lack experience (the cause of this being that experience is knowledge of particulars, craft of universals, and actions and bringing things about are all concerned with particulars); for it is not *human being* that medical treatment makes healthy (except coincidentally), but Callias or Socrates or someone else spoken of in this way who is coincidentally a *human being*. If, then, someone possesses the reason in question but lacks experience, and knows the universal but not the particular falling under it, he will often give the wrong treatment, since it is the particular that is to be treated. All the same, we certainly attribute knowledge (*eidenai*) and expertise to craft more than to experience, and suppose that craftsmen are wiser than experienced people, on the assumption that it is always knowledge rather than experience that accompanies wisdom. This is because craftsmen know the explanation, but experienced people do not; for experienced people know the facts, but not the reason why, whereas [those with craft knowledge] know the reason why, that is, the explanation. And that is why we acknowledge that the architectonic craftsmen in a given craft are more estimable, know more, and are wiser than the handicraftsmen, because they know the explanations of their products. The handicraftsmen, on the other hand, we think to be like some soulless things that produce—as fire burns—without knowing their products. (*Met.* I 1 981^{a}12–^{b}3)

It would be a serious mistake to suppose, therefore, that knowledge of explanatory universals is not an important part of practical wisdom at all, just because it is a less important one than the particularist part of it crucial in deliberation.

On this point, too, Aristotle is emphatic:

> It seems that medical treatment in particular cases is more rigorously worked out when each person gets special supervision, since each then gets more appropriate treatment. The best at providing individual supervision, however, will be the doctor, the physical trainer, or anyone else who has universal knowledge, knowing what applies to all cases or to cases of such-and-such a type. For sciences are said to be—and indeed are—of what is common [that is, the universal]. All the same, there is nothing to prevent someone without scientific knowledge from supervising a given individual well, if, on the basis of experience, he has made rigorous observations of what happens in each case—just as in fact some people seem to be their own best doctors, though incapable of helping anyone else. Nonetheless, this presumably does not mean that if someone at any rate wishes to become skilled in a craft or in something theoretical, he should not proceed to the universal, and come to know it as well as he can; for, as we have said, it is this the sciences are concerned with. Presumably, too, then, someone who wishes to make people better, whether they are many or few, by exercising supervision over them, should try to acquire legislative science, if it is through laws that we would become good. For the production of a noble disposition in whomever one is presented with is not a task just anyone can perform, but if indeed anyone can do it, it is the one with knowledge, as in the case of medicine and rest, where some sort of supervision and practical wisdom are required. (NE X 9 1180^{b}11–28)

In the case of theoretical and natural sciences, the ideal practitioner is the wise theorist, who may have little ability to apply what he knows. In the case of the practical sciences (or productive ones, for that matter), things are different. Here the ideal practitioner must combine scientific knowledge of the universal with the sort of experienced eye that enables him to apply it effectively in particular cases.

Practical Wisdom's Branches

When a thing considered in one way satisfies one account or definition, and another account or definition when considered in another way, Aristotle says that the thing considered in the first way differs in being (einai) from the same thing considered in the second way (Top. V 4 133^{b}4, Ph. III 3 202^{a}20–^{b}22). Thus virtue of character is the same state of the soul as general justice, but "their being is not the same." Instead, what considered in relation to another is "general justice is, as a certain kind of unconditional state, virtue" (*NE* V 1 1130ᵃ10–13). Similarly, what is practical wisdom, when considered in relation to the happiness of the individual who possesses it, is the very same state of the soul that is political science, when considered in relation to the happiness of a whole city (*NE* I 2 1094ᵇ7–10). Popular thought fails to appreciate this, because it narrows the scope of practical wisdom to that of the individual's own welfare. When an individual's welfare is understood to be that of *a member of a species that by nature lives in households and cities*, so that his "own welfare cannot be achieved without household management or without a political constitution" (*NE* VI 8 1142ᵃ9–10), the scope of practical wisdom is seen to include both political science (comprising legislative science, deliberative science, and judicial science) and household management (*NE* VI 8 1141ᵇ29–33).

Legislative science (*nomothetikê*) is an architectonic subbranch of political science, which drafts universal prescriptive laws to further the happiness of citizens by inculcating the virtues in them and directing their actions (*NE* X 9 1180ᵇ23–28). But because not everything can be rigorously defined, even maximally rigorous laws cannot obviate the need for deliberation altogether (*Pol.* III 16 1287ᵇ22–23, *Rh.* I 13 1374ᵃ18–ᵇ23). Besides its architectonic legislative component, therefore, political science also needs a deliberative one, which, among other things, issues decrees. The science of household management (*oikonomia*) deals with the use of private property, and other aspects of household life. It has three (sometimes four) subbranches: the science of mastership (*despotikê epistêmê*), which deals with the management and acquisition of the slaves Aristotle considers all but essential to a household (*Pol.* I 2 1252ᵃ24–ᵇ12); the science of property acquisition and management (*chrêmatistikê, ktêtikê*), which is sometimes included in mastership (*Pol.* I 12 1259ᵃ37–39); the science of child rearing (*teknopoiêtikê*); and finally marital science (*gamikê*) (*Pol.* I 3 1253ᵇ9–10).

When Aristotle first introduces the household as a topic for political science, he describes his discussion as having both a practical and a theoretical dimension: it should "see how matters stand in relation to our need for necessities" and "have an eye to those that bear on knowledge, to see whether we can acquire something better than the views currently held" (*Pol.* I 3 1253ᵇ15–18). A free person, he says, should have "theoretical knowledge of all these aspects, but should gain experience of them only to meet essential needs" (*Pol.* I 11 1258ᵇ9–11).[14] Moreover, even his theoretical knowledge

---

14. This is an example of the sort of architectonic control political science exercises over the other practical sciences, determining who should study them and to what extent (*NE* I 2 1094ᵇ2–6).

should have quite definite limits. He should know what the various types of wealth acquisition and exchange are, but not much more than that, since "while a rigorous account of each separately might be useful as regards practicing them, it would be vulgar to spend one's time developing it" (*Pol.* I 11 1258ᵇ33–35).

With an eye to the physical health and strength of the city's children, the legislator in the best city and constitution should "supervise the union of the sexes, and determine what sorts of people should have marital relations with one another, and when" (*Pol.* VII 16 1334ᵇ31–32), regulating not just the ages at which people marry but when they have sexual intercourse. At the same time, couples themselves "should gain theoretical knowledge of what doctors and natural scientists say about procreation, since doctors have adequately discussed the times that are right as regards the body, and natural scientists have discussed the winds, favoring northerly over southerly ones" (*Pol.* VII 16 1335ᵃ39–ᵇ2). This is a good example of the role that various sciences—including natural or loosely theoretical ones like meteorology—can play in an individual citizen's deliberation and deliberate choice.

Birth control is also something to which political science attends:

> As to the question of whether to rear offspring or expose them, there should be a law against rearing deformed ones, but where it is because of number of children, if it happens that the way custom is organized prohibits[15] the exposure of offspring once they are born, a limit should be imposed[16] on procreation. And if some people have sex in violation of this regulation and conceive a child, it should be aborted before the onset of sensation and life. For sensation and life distinguish what is pious from what is impious here. (*Pol.* VII 16 1335ᵇ19–26)[17]

15. Reading ἐαν ἡ τάξισ . . . κωλυῇ with Alois Dreizehnter, *Aristoteles Politica* (Munich: Wilhelm Fink, 1970)

16. Reading ὡρίσθαι δεῖ with Richard Kraut, *Aristotle: Politics Books VII and VIII* (Oxford: Clarendon Press, 1997).

17. Exposure or abandonment of infants was a fairly common form of family planning in ancient Greece. Aristotle does not approve of this practice, as his condemnation of the abortion of sentient fetuses shows. Like Plato (*Republic* V 459d–462c), however, he does require that deformed offspring be exposed, and that presentient fetuses conceived in violation of the laws be aborted. Those who later turn out to be incurably bad must, he thinks, be expelled from the city altogether, as beyond the reach of either habituation or punishment (*NE* X 9 1180ᵃ9–10).

Aristotle worries, too, about the effects of intercourse on men "while their bodies[18] are still growing," and so sets their marriage age at thirty-seven, whereas that of women is set at around eighteen (*Pol.* VII 16 1335ª24–29). Sperm is a concocted blood product, after all, which takes a large amount of energy to produce, which is why "male animals that copulate frequently and those who produce copious semen age quickly" (*Long.* 5 466ᵇ7–8). This may explain why adultery, though always wrong (*NE* II 6 1107ª8–17), faces especially serious sanctions when committed by a man "during his period of procreation" for the city (*Pol.* VII 16 1335ᵇ38–1336ª2): a man wasting his energy in adulterous sex will be less likely to produce strong and healthy future citizens. When men and women are no longer in their physical prime, they are "released from procreating for the community," so that any sex they engage in thereafter should be "for the sake of health, or for some other such reason" (*Pol.* VII 16 1335ᵇ37–38).

Marital science undoubtedly deals with other topics besides those pertaining to reproduction, but Aristotle says little about them. Since the relation of "male to female is that of natural superior to natural inferior, and that of ruler to ruled" (*Pol.* I 5 1254ᵇ13–14), there may not be all that much to say. A promised discussion of the supervision of children does not appear in Aristotle's extant works (*Pol.* VII 16 1335ᵇ2–4), but what he does say indicates just how extensive he conceives political science's control ideally to be. Essentially a form of eugenics, marital science ensures that a child is being fitted from conception for life in the particular city of which he will later be a citizen. After his conception, his mother's life, especially in matters of diet and exercise, is also controlled for his benefit, so that her mind should "remain somewhat inactive, since unborn children obviously draw resources from their mothers, just as plants do from the earth" (*Pol.* VII 16 1335ᵇ16–19).

Once the child is born, the science of child rearing takes over as the legislator's source of knowledge. A milky diet, no wine, such exercise as is possible are among the things it prescribes, as are the use of "certain mechanical devices" to prevent curvature of the limbs, and the habituating of "children to the cold right from the time they are small, since this is very useful both from the point of view of health and from that of military affairs" (*Pol.* VII 17 1336ª3–21). Children should not engage in formal

---

18. Reading σώματος with Pierre Pellegrin, *Aristote: Les Politiques* (Paris: Flammarion, 1993). Alternatively: σπέρματος ("seed"), W. D. Ross, *Aristotelis Politica* (Oxford: Clarendon Press, 1957).

learning until after the age of five, since this might interfere with their growth by deflecting resources to the wrong place. But adequate exercise should be provided for them through the sorts of games—"neither strenuous nor undisciplined"—that are suited to the development of free citizens, since, like the stories they are told, these should "pave the way for their later pursuits" and "the serious occupations of later life" (*Pol.* VII 17 1336ᵃ23–34).

Although educated within the household until they are seven years old, children are overseen even there by the office and officers in charge of child supervision (*paidonomos*) (*Pol.* IV 15 1300ᵃ4–8). The focus of their concern, as in the case of games and stories, is to prepare their young charges for citizenship. That is why they do not allow them to spend their leisure time with the household slaves, since it is "reasonable to expect that they will pick up some taint of servility or unfreedom from what they see and hear even at that early age" (*Pol.* VII 17 1336ᵇ1–2). They outlaw ignoble or shameful talk from the entire city in part with the same aim in view, since "by speaking lightly of an ignoble activity, one comes closer to doing it" (*Pol.* VII 17 1336ᵇ3–6). The rationale seems to be that the primarily sexual content of such talk, evidenced by its persistent association with sexually explicit comic drama (*NE* IV 8 1128ᵃ22–24, *Pol.* VII 17 1136ᵇ20), encourages servility by so enflaming a person's sexual desire that he will even make himself subordinate to another to satisfy it:

> If it happens, nonetheless [that is, despite all his early training and habituation], that any free man, who is not yet old enough to have been given a seat at the communal messes,[19] is found saying or doing something forbidden, he should be punished by being dishonored or beaten. But if he is older than this, he should be punished with those dishonors usually reserved for the unfree, because he has acted in a manner characteristic of slaves. (*Pol.* VII 17 1336ᵇ8–12)[20]

Until their "education has rendered them immune," therefore, children should never hear or see anything obscene (*Pol.* VII 17 1336ᵇ6–8).

19. That is, before the age of twenty-one or so (*Pol.* VII 17 1336ᵇ40).

20. The social norms associated with man-boy relationships (*paiderasteia*) in Athens permitted a teenage boy to become a virtual slave to an older male in the name of acquiring virtue (Plato, *Symposium* 184b–e), and to play—within limits—the role of his passive sexual partner. It provided harsh punishments, including loss of citizen rights, for a mature man who continued to play a passive role. K. J. Dover, *Greek Homosexuality* (Cambridge, Mass.: Harvard University Press, 1978) is a classic discussion, James Davidson, *The Greeks and Greek Love* (London: Weidenfeld and Nicolson, 2007), a significant reappraisal.

Life in the best city is thus carefully regulated by practical wisdom—and so by political science—from conception on. The social world a citizen inherits is one designed to develop and strengthen his own emerging practical wisdom and virtue, and to provide the optimal environment for its exercise. Our so-called virtues, when we have them, are typically jury-rigged affairs by comparison, as much the result of chance influences as of design. Aristotelian virtues more closely approximate, both in the training that goes into them and the level of competence it produces, the skills of a committed pianist, ballet dancer, tennis player, or trained soldier. While our virtues may as a result be somewhat fragile,[21] Aristotle's are much more robust. Our social world is filled with occasions of sin, and with traps designed to disable our wisdom and common sense and exploit their foibles. Aristotle's is just the opposite. If we think of Aristotle as a virtue ethicist, it is important to keep these things in mind.

Is Practical Wisdom a Science?

In the *Topics*, which is a treatise not on ethics but on how to construct dialectical arguments, Aristotle divides sciences into theoretical, practical, and productive (*Top.* VI 6 145ª15–16), correlates this division with their degree of rigor and the level of esteem of their subject matter (*Top.* VIII 2 157ª8–11), and categorizes *praktikê* and *theôrêtikê* as two differentiae of the genus *epistêmê* (*Top.* VII 1 152ᵇ2–5). He recognizes *phronêsis* as the distinctive virtue of the calculative part of the soul—"it is special to *phronêsis* to be intrinsically and by nature the virtue of the calculative part" (*Top.* V 7 136ᵇ10–12; also VI 6 145ª30–31)—denying it to young people and granting it to older, more experienced leaders (*Top.* III 2 117ª27–29). He also recognizes something he calls *hê kata philosophian phronêsis* or philosophical wisdom (*Top.* VIII 14 163ᵇ9–10), which is clearly related to the *phronêsis* he attributes to Xenocrates, onetime head of Plato's Academy, which "defines and has theoretical knowledge of the beings" (*Top.* VI 3 141ª7–8). He mentions philosophical sciences (*Top.* I 2 101ª27–28), which are particularly concerned with truth (*Top.* I 14 105ᵇ30–31) and with starting-points of scientific syllogisms (*Top.* VIII 1 155ᵇ10–16), referring at one point to a "demonstrative syllogism" as a "philosopheme" (*Top.* VIII 11 162ª15–16; also *Cael.* I 9 279ª30, II 14 294ª19). The only thing missing from the account of

---

21. See John M. Doris, *Lack of Character: Personality and Moral Behavior* (Cambridge: Cambridge University Press, 2005).

hê kata philosophian phronêsis, then, is the name *sophia*, since theoretical wisdom it clearly is. Hence when the *Topics* speaks of *phronêsis* plain and simple, it is—the case of Xenocrates aside—referring to practical wisdom.

Another thing missing from the *Topics*, which again does not mean that Aristotle does not know about it, is overt acknowledgment of the distinction between virtues of character and those of thought: when he speaks of *aretê*, he often or usually means *aretê êthikê* (virtue of character). Justice, which is such a virtue, he argues, is not a type of scientific knowledge: "If justice (*dikaiosunê*) is scientific knowledge, injustice is ignorance of it, and if justly (*dikaiôs*) is equivalent to in a scientifically knowledgeable and experienced way, unjustly is equivalent to in a scientifically ignorant and inexperienced way, whereas if the latter is not true, neither is the former, as in the case we have just now described—for unjustly seems to be more equivalent to in an experienced way than in an inexperienced one" (*Top.* II 9 114ᵇ9–13). Although we should not put too much weight on it, the change that occurs as we move from *dikaiosunê* (noun) to *dikaiôs* (adverb) is quite striking, suggesting that Aristotle is thinking of justice as involving on the one hand scientific knowledge and on the other the experience needed to apply such knowledge in particular cases.

Leaving that point aside for the moment, let us turn to an argument bearing on the scientific status of practical wisdom itself. The context is one of advice on how to deal with genera and special attributes, since these are constituents of puzzles relating to the definitions and starting-points with which dialectic is often concerned (*Top.* IV 1 120ᵇ11–12):

[1] One should examine, too, whether there is any other genus of the given species which neither includes the given genus nor falls under it. For example, suppose someone were to propose the thesis that scientific knowledge is the genus to which justice belongs, since virtue is also its genus, and neither of these genera includes the other one. Scientific knowledge cannot be the genus of justice, then, since it seems that whenever one species falls under two genera, the one includes the other. [2] In certain cases, however, a puzzle arises in this regard. For some people think that practical wisdom is both a virtue and scientific knowledge, and that neither of its genera includes the other. Although, of course, not everyone would accept that practical wisdom is scientific knowledge, if someone *were* to accept the truth of what has been said, it would at least seem necessary that its genera either be subordinate to one another, or that both be subordinate to the same genus—which is just what happens in the case of virtue and scientific knowledge. Both, in effect, are subordinate to the same genus, since each of them is a state or disposition. [3] One should exam-

ine, therefore, whether neither of these things is true of the given genus, since if the genera are subordinate neither to one another nor both to the same one, what is given could not be the [correct] genus. (*Top.* IV 2 121^{b}24–122^{a}2)

One problem raised by this passage may be quickly set aside. Aristotle acknowledges that the simple rule of genus subordination he gives in [1] may admit of exceptions in certain cases, but that does not mean it cannot be used in dialectical argument, since the topic of the argument may not be one of those cases. That Aristotle continues to use the simple rule, therefore, as indeed he does (*Top.* IV 2 122^{b}1–6), need be no cause for surprise or alarm.[22] Advice on what to look for in examining a dialectical thesis is just that. Look and see if this—the rule in [1] works. If it does, use it. If it doesn't, try the rule in [2], because [3] one of these must apply.

The claim in [2] that practical wisdom belongs in the genus of virtue and in the genus of scientific knowledge seems to be presented as Aristotle's own view of the matter. Since he has just argued in [1] that justice, which includes all the virtues of character, does not belong in the genus of scientific knowledge, he can hardly now be countenancing—in the shape of practical wisdom—a virtue of character that does belong entirely in that genus. Nor is he. For the argument in [2] is precisely to the effect that practical wisdom belongs in two different genera—that of scientific knowledge and that of virtue. If it were *sophia* or *hê kata philosophian phronêsis* he was talking about, one of these genera *would* fall under the other, since *sophia* just is the most rigorous kind of scientific knowledge of the most estimable things. We might suppose, therefore, that in moving from [1] to [2], Aristotle has silently shifted from talking about virtue of character to talking about virtue of thought.[23] But that, besides being very hard to credit, won't really help with anything. For what we will still have to acknowledge is that the reason practical wisdom is included in two genera that are *not* subordinate to one another is that it is not, like *sophia*, simply a type of scientific knowledge, or, like justice, simply a virtue of character. It is the involvement of practical wisdom with virtue of character, after all, is part of what makes it the distinctive virtue of thought it is. So, while Aristotle may already have seen the need to distinguish virtue of thought from virtue of character,

---

22. Contrast Jacques Brunschwig, *Aristote: Topiques (Livres I–IV)* (Paris: Budé, 1967), pp. lxvii n. 1, and Carlo Natali, *The Wisdom of Aristotle* (Albany: State University of New York Press, 2001), pp. 2–6.

23. Alexander of Aphrodisias seems to have proposed something like this, as Natali, *Wisdom of Aristotle*, pp. 4–5, points out.

which is what his recognition of two kinds of practical wisdom suggests, there is no reason to see him making use of that distinction here. Virtue of character is what he needs to make the point in [2], and it is all he needs.

A third passage from the *Topics* also deals with the scientific status of practical wisdom. In this case, the context is one of advice on whether the attribute involved in the thesis proposed for examination is or is not a special attribute (*Top.* V 1 128^{b}14–15):

> Since practical wisdom is related in the same way to the noble and the ignoble, in that it is the scientific knowledge of each of them, and it is not a special attribute of practical wisdom to be scientific knowledge of the noble, it will not be a special attribute of practical wisdom to be scientific knowledge of the ignoble. But if it is a special attribute of practical wisdom to be scientific knowledge of the noble, it will not be a special attribute of it to be scientific knowledge of the ignoble.[24] For it is impossible for an attribute to be special to more than one thing. (*Top.* V 7 137^{a}12–20)

The important lesson lies in the second clause ("in that . . ."), which expresses Aristotle's own view. Practical wisdom, insofar as it is scientific knowledge, is related to the noble and to the ignoble. Insofar as it is also a virtue, however, it is not related to both in the same way, since unlike a craft or science, which can be used for ignoble ends, practical wisdom can be used only for noble and good ones (*NE* VI 5 1140^{b}21–24). Like its two sister texts, then, this one forms part of a coherent account of practical wisdom's scientific status. Justice isn't scientific knowledge alone, since it involves the experience needed to act justly on particular occasions. Hence practical wisdom isn't scientific knowledge alone, either, since it is a virtue that involves justice. Insofar as it is scientific knowledge, therefore, practical wisdom is similarly related to the noble and ignoble, but insofar as it is a virtue, it is related to them in different ways, pursuing the one, avoiding the other.

Also pertaining to the scientific status of practical wisdom is a somewhat difficult passage from the *Eudemian Ethics*. Central to it is the idea, expressed in the *Topics*, that scientific knowledge has two uses, one to achieve a noble end, the other to achieve an ignoble one, as an eye can be used for seeing or—as when one distorts the shape of the eyeball until one thing appears as two—for mis-seeing. Both uses are intrinsic to the things in ques-

---

24. Natali, *Wisdom of Aristotle*, pp. 5–6 defends the transmitted text of this sentence. Difficulties are discussed in Brunschwig, *Aristote: Topiques (Livres V–VIII)* (Paris: Budé, 2007), pp. 187–189.

tion, since scientific knowledge is functioning as such even when used to accomplish something bad or ignoble, just as an eye is functioning as such even when its vision is distorted. Selling or eating an eye, by contrast, is a coincidental use of it (*EE* VIII 1 1246ᵃ26–31), just like selling a shoe (*Pol.* I 9 1257ᵃ5–14). Virtues, such as justice, cannot be forms of scientific knowledge, therefore, since one cannot act unjustly from them. In their case, there is no analogue of distortion of vision (*EE* VIII 1 1246ᵃ35–ᵇ4).

As in the *Topics*, however, practical wisdom seems to be something of a puzzle case:

> If practical wisdom is scientific knowledge, and something true, it will behave in the same way as other sciences, since it would be possible for people to act in a practically unwise way from practical wisdom, and to make precisely the same errors as the practically unwise. Moreover, if each thing had a single intrinsic use, they would also be acting in a practically wise way in doing what they do. Now in the case of the other sciences, what produces the distortion is another science, which controls the first. But what can control that which controls all of them? For it cannot any longer be scientific knowledge, at any rate, or understanding. But it can't be virtue [of character] either. For it is the virtue of the ruling constituent that uses the virtue of the one that is ruled [not the other way around]. What, then, is it? (*EE* VIII 1 1246ᵇ4–12)

At this point various revelatory answers are canvassed:

> Or is it the way it is with incontinence, which is said to be a vice of the nonrational part of the soul, and the way the incontinent person is said to be intemperate, though possessing understanding? But, if when appetite²⁵ is strong, *it* will do the distorting, and so the practical wisdom of the incontinent person will reach opposite conclusions in its calculating, it is clear that if there is virtue in this part, and lack of understanding in the rational part, the other²⁶ will be reversed. So it will be possible to use justice in a not just way, virtue in a bad way, and practical wisdom in a practically unwise way, and also the opposite way around. For it would be strange if when there is virtue in the calculative part, vice in the nonrational one *will* change it, and *will* cause it to lack understanding, yet when there is virtue in the nonrational part and lack of understanding in the calculative one, it *will not* change it and *will not* make it discern things in a practically wise way and as it should. Again, practical wisdom in the calculative part and intemperance in the nonrational part will not

25. Reading ἡ ἐπιθυμία.
26. Reading ἡ ἑτέρα.

result in actions that are done temperately—since that would seem to be precisely a case of *continence* [not virtue]. So it will also be possible to act in a practically wise way from lack of understanding.[27] (*EE* VIII 1 1246ᵇ12–25)

The conclusion reached from an examination of the consequences of these different answers is that virtue of character in the nonrational part and practical wisdom—or understanding or scientific knowledge (the three are treated as equivalent here)—in the rational one must go hand in hand: "Hence it is clear that it is *at the same time* that men become practically wise and the states of the nonrational part become good [or virtuous], and that the view of Socrates, that nothing is stronger than practical wisdom, is correct. But in saying that it is scientific knowledge, he was not correct, since it is a virtue and not scientific knowledge, but knowledge of a different kind" (*EE* VIII 1 1246ᵇ32–36). Practical wisdom cannot be a kind of scientific knowledge, then, because if it were, it could be misused. Moreover, which is a point not explicitly made in the *Topics*, it cannot be a virtue of character, because it uses the virtues of character, in that it supplies the correct reason that they involve. Moreover practical wisdom and virtue of character must be joint and simultaneous achievements, since any attempt to give precedence to one leads to puzzles. In the *Nicomachean Ethics* (VI 13 1145ᵃ1–2), we are told that this is the case, but no comparably detailed examination is provided.

What we should say about practical wisdom, then, is that it is not a science but, as the *Eudemian Ethics* puts it, a different sort of knowledge. All the same, it has many practical sciences as components and, through these, controls the productive ones. Since political science is one of these practical sciences, so too is ethics or ethical science, since it is a sort of political science (*NE* I 2 1094ᵇ10–11). As genuine types of scientific knowledge equipped with starting-points and affording demonstrations from them, these are intrinsically concerned with universals—a point Aristotle makes explicitly about legislative science in what are almost his last words in the *Nicomachean Ethics* (X 9 1180ᵃ29–ᵇ28). There is, therefore, something of an architectonic side to all of them which, because it deals with universals, is theoretical: ethics is a practical science, to be sure, but just as there is *ta phusikês theôrias* (theoretical natural science), there is also *ta êthikês theôrias*—theoretical knowledge of ethics (*APo.* I 33 89ᵇ9). Yet to the extent that each of these sciences, in being *practical*, must deal with particulars,

27. Some of the problems involved in reconstructing the text of this passage are discussed in Woods, *Aristotle: Eudemian Ethics, Books I, II, and VIII*, pp. 196–197.

each also requires experience and a trained eye—each requires practical perception. Their structure, in other words, mimics that of practical wisdom itself. Desire-infused from the beginning, and with correctness conditions determined by the ethical mean, practical perception is our only mode of access to the "noble and just things" that are the starting-points of ethics, the perceptual data from which induction reaches universals, which—when analyzed, defined, and aporematically defended—become the starting-points of the ethical demonstrations that are theory's contents (*NE* I 4 1095^{b}2–8). Even within this perceptual data, therefore, we find the intertwining of what will eventually be recognizable as the two inseparable faces of practical wisdom, its two genera, as the *Topics* calls them: scientific knowledge and virtue.

Practical Luck and Deliberation's Sphere

The sphere of deliberation is delimited by a number of different factors. The first of these derives from deliberation's own nature. Happiness is the unconditional end (*NE* VI 2 1139^{b}2–4) at which practically wise people aim (*NE* VI 9 1142^{b}29–33). As a sort of universal, however, it is something we reach, as we do all universals, not by deliberation but by induction from the understanding-involving practical perception of particulars, which are thus the "starting-points of the end in view" (*NE* VI 11 1143^{b}4)—the starting-points of the inductive grasp of happiness. At the same time, more general scientific theorizing about ourselves and the universe of which we are a part leads us to the conclusion, we may suppose, that happiness consists in rational activity in accord with "the best and most complete virtue" (*NE* I 7 1098^{a}16–18). This theory must then be evaluated from the inside, so to speak, by applying it to what we do and what sorts of lives we live—that is, to the results of our induction. If the two harmonize, we should accept it, but if they conflict, we should reject it (*NE* X 8 1179^{a}18–22). For when arguments conflict with the facts of experience, it is they that must give ground: "Arguments about actions and feelings are less credible than the facts; hence any conflicts between arguments and perceptible facts arouses contempt for the arguments and undermines the truth as well as the arguments" (*NE* X 1 1172^{a}34–^{b}1).

Since we deliberate "not about ends, but about what furthers ends" (*NE* III 3 1112^{b}11–12), it is the conception of happiness emerging from this two-part process that deliberation, and so practical wisdom, insofar as it is a deliberative potentiality (*NE* VI 5 1140^{a}25–31), takes as a starting-point. For the fact that happiness is our end is determined by our nature and function, and so holds with a necessity that puts it outside the range of what is up to us to affect or change. Deliberation about some other ends is excluded for a parallel reason. A doctor, for example, cannot "deliberate about whether he will cure, or an orator about whether he will persuade, or a political scientist about whether he will produce good order, or any other about the end" (NE III 3 1112^{b}12–15). Medicine is a craft partly defined by health, which is its intrinsic end or goal. Hence insofar as that craft dictates someone's actions, he necessarily pursues health. (In the same way, oratory is defined by its intrinsic end, which is persuasion, political science by good order, and other such things by their defining ends.) The point is not that *no one* can deliberate about whether to cure or to persuade or to produce good order, but rather that just as human beings cannot deliberate about their unconditional end, so doctors as such, orators as such, and political scientists as such cannot deliberate about theirs. What we can do, though, is engage—as much of the *Nicomachean Ethics* does—in dialectical or aporematic clarification of what science tells us happiness is. Such clarification may not be strictly speaking deliberative, but it is of considerable deliberative importance all the same, since we are more likely to hit the target if we can command a clear view of it (NE I 1 1094^{a}22–24).

The second factor delimiting deliberation's sphere is perception: "We do not deliberate about particulars either, for example, about whether this is a loaf or whether it has been cooked as it should; for these belong to the sphere of perception. And if we keep on deliberating at each stage, we shall go on indefinitely" (NE III 3 1112^{b}34–1113^{a}2). By the same token, we do not deliberate about whether something is cowardly, intemperate, or noble, when by means of practical perception we can see this straight off. If we do not have natural or habituated virtue of character, of course, our practical perception will not be correct or reliable, any more than our eyesight is if we have cataracts, or the light is poor. Once we do have this sort of virtue, though, much of the world of pleasures, pains, and values more generally will be as immediately accessible to us as that of colors, sounds, or perceptible substances, such as loaves of bread. Since happiness involves pleasure, the inductive process that leads to our grasp of it must begin with values directly accessible in this way. It is an easy inference that natural or habituated virtue is as much a correctness condition of that induction as it is of its first perceptual steps.

A third factor delimiting deliberation's scope stems from the natural and theoretical sciences. The desiring part of the soul, whose virtues are those of character (EE II 1 1220^{a}10), is not fully rational, because, unlike the rational part, it cannot give reasons or construct explanatory demonstrations or syllogisms: "desire does not possess a deliberative part" (*DA* III 11 434ᵃ11–12). Yet it can listen to the deliberative part, whose virtue is practical wisdom, and obey it, as a child does its father, so that it shares in reason in a way (*NE* I 13 1102ᵇ14–1103ᵃ3). It is because the calculative part can also listen to the scientific one on matters to which it has no autonomous access, indeed, that the division between the scientific and calculative part is made "in the same way" as that between the rational part they comprise and the desiring one (*NE* VI 1 1139ᵃ5–6). What it hears are universal necessary truths, such as that all "light meats are healthy" (*NE* VI 7 1141ᵇ18–19), which are "coincidentally useful to us where many of the necessities of life are concerned" (*EE* I 5 1216ᵇ15–16).

The sphere of action and production is the sphere of the practical and productive sciences. Once they are factored into the equation, the scope of deliberation within the sphere is delimited in a fourth way. Leave medicine out of the equation, and it may be a matter of luck whether you survive a disease; include it, and it may no longer be so: "experience made craft . . . inexperience luck" (*Met.* I 1 981ᵃ3–5).[28] That, presumably, is why luck and craft are concerned with the same things only "in a certain way" (*tropon tina*) (*NE* VI 4 1140ᵃ18). As the scope of craft expands, the sphere of luck contracts, and with it the scope of deliberation:

> In relation to the sciences that are rigorous and self-contained, there is no deliberation—for example, in relation to the craft of writing the letters of the alphabet (for we are in no two minds about how to write them). But those things that come about through us, but not in the same way on every occasion, in relation to *them* we do deliberate—for example, in relation to things in the sphere of medicine or of moneymaking, and in relation to navigation more than in relation to physical training, to the extent that the latter has been less rigorously worked out, and similarly again where the rest are concerned, but more in relation to crafts than to sciences, since we are more in two minds about them. Deliberation occurs, then, in the case of things that hold for the most part, but where outcomes are unclear, that is, in the case of those where there is something indeterminate. (*NE* III 3 1112ᵃ34–ᵇ9)

As Aristotle succinctly puts it at one point: "Craft does not deliberate" (*Ph.* II 8 199ᵇ28). He means that a craft, insofar as it is rigorous and self-contained, does not do so.

28. Compare Plato, *Euthydemus* 280b.

Even when the productive sciences are less rigorous or developed, as is true, for example, of medicine and wealth-acquisition, their universal prescriptive laws should generally be followed:

> Those who think it advantageous to be ruled by a king hold that laws speak only of the universal, and do not prescribe with a view to actual circumstances. Consequently, it is foolish to rule in accord with written rules in any craft, and doctors in Egypt are rightly allowed to abandon the treatment prescribed by the manuals after the fourth day (although, if they do so earlier, it is at their own risk). It is evident, for the same reason, therefore, that the best constitution is not one that follows written rules and laws. All the same, the rulers should possess the universal reason as well. And something to which the passionate constituent is entirely unattached is better than something in which it is innate. This constituent does not belong to the law, whereas every human soul necessarily possesses it. But perhaps, to balance this, it ought be said that a human being will deliberate better about particular cases. In that case, it is clear he must be a legislator, and laws established, although they must not be in control insofar as they deviate from what is best, since they should certainly be in control everywhere else. (*Pol.* III 15 1286ª9–25; also 16 1287ª33–1287ᵇ5)

It is when the universal laws fail us, as the Egyptian doctors imagine them doing by the fourth day of a patient's unresponsiveness to the prescribed treatment, that deliberation comes into play: we "speak of people as practically wise in some area, when they calculate well about what furthers some good end, concerning which no craft [prescription] exists" (*NE* VI 5 1140ª28–30).

Under the architectonic direction and control of political science, medicine, physical training, and all the other crafts and sciences are coordinated and harmonized to best further the human good. This delimits the scope of deliberation in a fifth way, since political science's aim is to leave little to "human wish, which is not a safe standard" (*Pol.* II 10 1272ᵇ6–7). At the same time, the social world, whether human or the product of craft, will itself have been standardized by the ongoing work of political science, further reducing the scope of deliberation. If the meals available in the communal messes that well-organized cities provide for their citizens (*Pol.* VII 10 1330ª3–8) are all healthy, for example, a good diet will not be something it takes much deliberation to achieve, even if one has to balance one entree against another to decide which one likes best.

Between cases where a law of a craft or science (including legislative science) tells us exactly what to do and those where no craft or scientific prescription exists lie cases of two other sorts. The first are those in which the relevant universal laws, though they may be quite precise, hold for the most part, and so with less than unconditional necessity. The law that all adult males have hair on their chins is like that (*APo.* II 12 96ª10–11). Second are cases in which the laws are imprecise "owing to the endless possible cases presented, such as the kinds and sizes of weapons that may be used to inflict wounds—a lifetime would be too short to make out a complete list of these" (*Rh.* I 13 1374ª26–ᵇ1). Hence, if having a beard is used as a legal test for adulthood, we will face disputable cases. Similarly, it may be unclear whether a ring or a professional boxer's fist is a deadly weapon, given the necessarily incomplete specification contained in the law. When an assault involves such things, it may be unclear how the law applies to them. If it is unclear, deliberation will be needed to settle the question.

Besides these broadly epistemic limits on deliberation's scope, there are also ontological ones. Some things "do not *at all* admit of being otherwise," because, as eternal or unchanging, they are unconditionally necessary (*NE* VI 3 1139ᵇ20–24). The subject matter of mathematics, astronomy, or theology is not within deliberation's sphere. About it, no one with any understanding would deliberate, although a fool or a madman might (*NE* III 3 1112ª19–26). Similarly, no sensible person deliberates about what happens "in different ways at different times—droughts and rains, for example" (*NE* III 3 1112ª26–27). For these, too, are things that come about by nature and necessity, even though they do so for the most part rather than always: "All things due to nature come about always or for the most part, but nothing which is the outcome of luck or chance does that. For we do not think it is luck or coincidence when there is a lot of rain in winter, but when there is a lot in summer, nor when there are heat waves in summer, but when there are in winter" (*Ph.* II 7 198ᵇ34–199ª3). In both cases, what explains our not deliberating is the same: "No one deliberates about things that cannot be otherwise, or about things that do not admit of being done in action by himself" (*NE* VI 5 1140ª31–33). Thus some things *a* can deliberate about, *b* cannot: "no Spartan would deliberate, for example, about how Scythians might best govern themselves politically. . . . Rather each group of human beings deliberates about the things done in action that are up to it" (*NE* III 3 1112ª28–34).

Finally, no sensible person deliberates about what is in the past: "Nothing that happened in the past is deliberately chosen—for example, nobody deliberately chooses to have sacked Troy; for nobody deliberates about the past, but about the future, and what admits of being otherwise, but what is past does not admit of not having happened" (*NE* VI 2 1139^{b}5–9). Before Troy was sacked, suitably situated agents could have deliberated about whether to sack it; but not any longer. Even things that are in the future and that do admit of being otherwise may be too immanent to allow adequate time for deliberation. That is why unconditionally excellent deliberation is "correctness with regard to the beneficial thing [to do], the way in which, *and time*" (*NE* VI 9 1142^{b}27–28). One can fail to be a good deliberator, in other words, because one fails to deliberate at or in the opportune time, even though in other respects one's deliberation is *nonpareil*. By making the opportune time unavailable, therefore, the world can exclude even things that are otherwise up to us from being in deliberation's sphere.

The sphere delimited by all these factors is that of *practical luck* (*tuchê*), which Aristotle often but not always distinguishes from that of broad luck (also *tuchê*) or chance (*to automaton*). What happens by *broad luck* happens as the result of a coincidental cause. Thus "a builder is an intrinsic cause of a house, but that which is pale or knows music is a coincidental cause," even when what is pale and knows music is the builder (*Ph.* II 5 196^{b}26–27). For the fact about the builder that explains his building a house is not his being pale but his knowing the craft of building. Since "the coincidental is indeterminate in number" (*Ph.* II 5 196^{b}28), so that any old coincidental fact about the builder can play the role of his being pale, such causes are clearly not of any scientific interest. What happens by practical luck, on the other hand, must have a certain kind of coincidental final cause. If a tree's being by the door is the sort of thing that might be "an outcome of [deliberative] thought" (*Ph.* II 5 196^{b}21–22), it is a candidate final cause of action. If *a*'s wish, which is the desire involved in such thought, is the intrinsic efficient cause of the tree's being by the door, its being by the door is a genuine final cause of *a*'s action of planting it there. If no one's wish plays that role, the tree's being by the door has only a coincidental final cause, and so is the result of practical luck. (How lucky for *a*, the thought is, that the tree was just where he would have planted it.) That is why the defining-mark of practical luck is determined by reference to happiness, which is the proper object of correct wish (*NE* VII 13 1153^{b}17–25).

When "the causes of things" are specified as "nature, necessity, and luck, and understanding, too, and everything that comes about through human agency" (*NE* III 3 1112^{a}31–33), the sort of luck involved is broad luck, since it covers the entire sphere of the coincidental or contingent. When it is denied a few lines earlier that anyone deliberates about "things that are the result of luck (*apo tuchês*), such as finding a treasure" (*NE* III 3 1112^{a}27), therefore, it is again broad luck that is in view. The luck that is restricted to the sphere of deliberately chosen action, on the other hand, is clearly practical luck: "Luck and the results of luck are found in things that are capable of being lucky, and, generally, of action. That is why, indeed, luck is concerned with things done in action. . . . Hence nothing done by an inanimate object, beast, or child is the result of luck, since things of that sort are incapable of deliberate choice" (*Ph.* II 6 197ª36–ᵇ8). It is the sphere of practical luck, therefore, that is deliberation's sphere.

Decrees as Deliberation's Outcomes

Because *eupraxia* or doing well in action is practical wisdom's end and practical wisdom exerts architectonic control over all the crafts, the end "unconditionally (as opposed to in relation to something and for something else) is not what is produced, but what is *prakton*" (*NE* VI 2 1139ᵇ2–3).[29] Looked back at, what is *prakton* is what is already done, already actualized. Looked forward at, as it is when we are deliberating, what is *prakton* is what is doable—something possible, but not yet actualized. We might expect, therefore, that *prakton* will sometimes refer to an action considered as a possibility and sometimes to one considered as an actualization of a possibility.

Verbals ending in *–ton*, of which *prakton* and *poiêton* are both examples, are tailor made to serve both purposes, since they sometimes [1] have the meaning of a perfect passive participle and sometimes [2] express possibility.[30] A decree (*psêphisma*), for example, seems to be *prakton* in sense [2], since it is a prescription specific enough to be acted on. What it specifies, therefore, is a possibility (a type of action), which many different particular (token) actions might actualize. The "things done in action" that are particular objects of perception (*NE* VI 11 1143ª32–33), on the other hand, seem to be *prakton* in sense [1]. Within the class of things that are *prakton* in sense [2], Aristotle draws a further distinction, which we noted earlier in a different context: "Things are spoken of as *prakton* in two ways, for both the things for the sake of which we act and the things we do for their sake have a share in action" (*EE* I 7 1217ª35–37). For ends, of course, are typically pro-

---

29. My understanding of *prakton* was deepened by Pavlos Kontos, "A Key Term, Its Misuse and Rehabilitation: 'τό γὰρ ψήφισμα πρακτόν' (*EN.* 1141ᵇ7)," *Elenchos* 1 (2009): 99–115.

30. H. W. Smyth, *Greek Grammar* (Cambridge Mass.: Harvard University Press, 1920), sec. 472.

spective, as, therefore, are the actions that will further them (*DA* III 10 433^{b}5–13). Since *prakta* are *kath' hekasta* or particulars (*NE* VI 11 1143^{a}32–33), the type-token ambiguity of *prakton* matches that of *kath' hekaston,* which can also refer to a type or a token.

Unlike a universal law, a decree is so adapted to actual circumstances as to render any further deliberation unnecessary (*NE* V 10 1137^{b}27–32).[31] That is what makes a decree a last thing, and so something *prakton*:

> The thing desired is the starting-point of practical understanding, and the last thing is the starting-point of the action. Hence it is reasonable to regard these two things—desire and practical thought—as producing movement.... Hence what moves us in every case is the desired object, which is either the good or the apparent good—not every variety of it, however, but the good done in action, and what is done in action is what admits of being otherwise. (*DA* III 10 433^{a}15–30)

Practical thought, calculation, or deliberation begins with an end an agent desires or wishes for, and concludes with a specification of what he can do to achieve that end. In his case, this specification is not technically a decree, since it is not something stemming from the legislative body of a city, but it is the personal analogue of one. For as Aristotle conceives of them, agents and cities are both telic systems with similar structures: "Just as a city and every other system seems to be most of all the constituent in it with most control, the same is true of a human being" (*NE* IX 8 1168^{b}31–33). Hence a human being is a natural thing identified above all with its understanding (*NE* X 7 1178^{a}2–3); a city is a natural one (*Pol.* I 2 1252^{b}30) identified with its governing body: "A constitution is an organization both of a city's other offices, but especially of the office that has control over everything. For the governing body (*politeuma*) has control in every city, and the governing body is the constitution" (*Pol.* III 6 1278^{b}8–11). A decree stemming from a governing body is thus analogous to one stemming from a human agent's practical understanding, in that both produce the actions of the very telic systems of which they are parts. That is why a city *a* must honor a treaty made by a city *b* just in case *a* and *b* have the same constitution (*Pol.* III 3 1276^{a}7–^{b}15)—that is to say, just in case they have the same governing part.

31. Actual *psephismata* issued by the Athenian Assembly and Council are analyzed and discussed in P. J. Rhodes, *The Athenian Boule* (Oxford: Clarendon Press, 1972), pp. 52–87.

Deliberation's Logical Form

Like reasoning in the broadly theoretical sciences, deliberation is "a type of syllogizing" (*Mem.* 2 453ª13–14), but whereas theoretical syllogisms have a propositional conclusion, practical ones conclude in an action:

> One belief [that is, believed proposition] is universal; the other deals with particulars, which perception already controls. When one [proposition] is generated from them, it is necessary, for the soul to assert what has been concluded, but, in the case of productive ones (*tais poiêtikais*),[32] to act at once. For example, if everything sweet should be tasted, and this (some particular thing) is sweet, it is necessary for someone who is able and is not prevented also at the same time to do this. (*NE* VII 3 1147ª25–31)

In a parallel passage, the point is made again:

> How does it happen that understanding is sometimes followed by action sometimes by inaction, that is, sometimes by moving and sometimes by not moving? What happens seems parallel to the case of understanding and syllogizing about unchanging objects. There, however, the end is a theoretical proposition (for when one has understood the two premises, one has understood—that is, put together—the conclusion), whereas here the conclusion that follows from the two premises [being put together] becomes the action.[33] Some examples: whenever someone understands that every man should take walks, and that he is a man, at once he takes a walk, or if he understands that no man should take a walk now, and that he is a man, he at once stays put. And he does each of these things provided nothing prevents him [from doing it] or compels him [to do something else]. (*MA* 7 701ª7–16)

The conclusion is an action, but the last thing reached in deliberation is not an action but a decree: "a decree is [to be] done in action, as the last thing" (*NE* VI 8 1141ᵇ27–28). Thus conclusion and last thing—though readily

---

32. As at *NE* VI 12 1144ª3, *poiêtikos* here includes *praktikos*. That is why a *poiêtikos* syllogism concludes in an action done.

33. It isn't the propositional conclusion of a practical syllogism that becomes the action by engaging with active desire in the way the propositional conclusion of a theoretical syllogism engages with "thought and inquiry" (*MA* 7 701ª31–32), as David Charles, *Aristotle's Philosophy of Action* (London: Duckworth 1984), pp. 94–95, argues. Rather what is a propositional conclusion in a theoretical syllogism becomes an action in a practical one.

confused—are not the same. It is "the final *premise*," as a belief about something perceptible, that controls actions (*NE* VII 3 1147ᵇ9–10).

We can see this plainly in the following description of productive deliberation:

> From craft come the things whose form is in the soul of the producer—and by form I mean the essence of each thing and the primary substance. . . . For example, health is the account in the soul, the scientific knowledge [of the form]. So the healthy thing comes to be as follows: Since health is this, necessarily if the thing is to be healthy this must be present—for example, a uniform state— and if the latter is to be present, there must be heat, and he goes on, always understanding like this, until he is led to a last thing that he himself is able to make. Then the process from this point onward, toward health, is called production. . . . Of comings-into-being and processes, one part is called understanding and the other producing—what proceeds from the starting-point and form is understanding, what proceeds from the final stage of understanding is producing. (*Met.* VII 7 1032ᵃ32–ᵇ17)

Since understanding is what grasps starting-points, in the case of crafts it is also called "having theoretical knowledge of how something may come-to-be," while the phase called "producing" is called "crafting" (*NE* VI 4 1140ᵃ11–12).

Just as producing or crafting follows on the grasp by understanding of the last thing, thus serving as the conclusion of the doctor's deliberation, so action follows on the grasp by understanding of the last thing in practical deliberation. For once the relevant decree is reached, nothing remains except to act on it immediately:

> What is deliberated about and what is deliberately chosen are the same, except that what is deliberately chosen is already something definite, since what is deliberately chosen is what is discerned on the basis of deliberation. For each of us stops inquiring about how to act once he brings the starting-point back to himself, and, within himself, to the leading constituent, since this is the constituent that deliberately chooses. This is also clear from the ancient constitutions described by Homer, where the kings would first deliberately choose and then issue a proclamation to the people. (*NE* III 3 1113ᵃ2–9)

As the king's proclamation, which has the status of a decree (*Pol.* IV 4 1292ᵃ6–18), signals the termination of his deliberation, and is followed by its being acted on by the people, so an agent's deliberate choice terminates his deliberation, and is followed (unless something prevents it) by his acting on it. This symmetry between cases of production and those of action is just what we should expect. For practical wisdom, though differing from craft knowledge in the kind of end it has, is otherwise structurally isomorphic to it: a craft "is some sort of state involving true reason concerned with production" (*NE* VI 4 1140^{a}20–21); practical wisdom "is a state, involving true reason,[34] a practical one, concerned with what is good or bad for a human being" (*NE* VI 5 1140^{b}5–6).

The ultimate or unconditional topic for the practical deliberator is: what in these circumstances constitutes happiness—that is, rational activity in accord with the most complete virtue (V)? He will have answered it when he finds a middle term F with the following features: first, doing an action that is F in these circumstances will best further V; second, an F action is one he can do (or begin to do) in these circumstances without doing anything else; third, an F action is one he can tell he is doing on the basis of perception. A syllogism with these major and minor premises need not—and typically will not—embody the entirety of the deliberator's reasoning or inquiry, but it does constitute its *focus*: it tells him what it is he is ultimately looking for, namely, a middle term with the requisite features. Nonetheless, to find such a term he may need to find many other things first. Some of these a science or craft may provide, some may be provided by perception, some he may need to find by further deliberating or syllogizing, some will identify external means to his subordinate ends, others essential components.[35] In the end, though, when he has found them, all will fall under the umbrella of his focal syllogism. So that in being the focus of his deliberation it is also the organizing and unifying principle—the defining-mark or *horos*—of his

---

34. Reading λόγου ἀληθοῦς. There are two reasons to prefer this text, in which "true" (*alêthous*) qualifies reason, to the transmitted one, in which "true" (*alêthê*) qualifies the state itself. First, in the reprise of the definition of practical wisdom at *NE* VI 5 1140^{b}20–21, some manuscripts record *alêthous*. Second, when Aristotle specifies the function of practical wisdom he uses the verb *alêtheuein*, which is used elsewhere in the *Ethics* (I 10 1100^{a}35, IV 7 1127^{a}19, 33, ^{b}4, VI 3 1139^{b}13, 15, 6 1141^{a}3, VII 9 1151^{b}20) with its standard meaning of saying or thinking or grasping true things (sentences, propositions, predications). If we preserve the transmitted text, therefore, we should treat it as a case of hypallage or transferred epithet.

35. L. H. G. Greenwood, *Aristotle: Nicomachean Ethics Book VI* (Cambridge: Cambridge University Press, 1909), pp. 46–48, seems to have been the first to notice the distinction between external and component means and its importance in understanding Aristotle. In the focal syllogism of a piece of deliberation, the minor premise always specifies a component means, just as a decree always specifies what the associated universal law would say, if its maker had envisaged the situation at hand (*NE* V 10 1137^{b}19–24).

plan of action. It is the complex action implementing this entire unified plan, in turn, that constitutes his acting well and being happy.

Because all practical syllogizing—all deliberation—has a syllogism of this kind as its organizing focus, we may take it as our paradigm case and assign it the following schematic form:

Major premise: Definition of happiness
Minor premise: Decree
Conclusion: Action

Deliberation, as a consequence, will consist in a search for a decree connecting the definition of happiness to something that can be acted on directly, using perception. That is why just two errors are possible in practical syllogizing:

> In all cases, doing it well consists in two things: setting up the target and end of action correctly and discovering the actions that further it. These factors can be in harmony with one another or in disharmony. For people sometimes set up the end well but fail to achieve it in action; and sometimes they achieve everything that furthers the end, but the end they set up is a bad one. Sometimes they make both errors. For example, in medicine it sometimes happens that doctors are neither correct in their judgment about what condition a healthy body should be in, nor successful in producing the condition they have set up as their defining-mark. (*Pol.* VII 13 1331^{b}26–37)

The formal invalidity of the syllogism is omitted as a possible error, presumably because it results from an impaired ability to handle syllogisms generally, so that avoiding it is not a peculiarly deliberative matter. Hence, though invalidity contaminates deliberation, it is not a defect that it is part of deliberation's specific virtue or correctness to avoid. Being a good deliberator presupposes but does not include being a competent syllogizer. That is the idea.

The error in setting up the end if you are a doctor consists in getting the definition of health wrong: the condition of the body you think is health is not health. If you are an agent, it consists in getting the definition of happiness wrong: As errors about the essential and necessarily true definitions of universals, which are established inductively and aporematically not deliberatively, these too are scientific errors not specifically deliberative ones. The second error, which consists in being wrong about what best furthers the end you may have set up quite correctly, is a deliberative one. This is described as reaching the correct end by "a false syllogism, that is, reaching the thing that should be done, but not by the means one should, *the middle term being false*" (*NE* VI 9 1142^{b}22–24).[36] The restriction of deliberation to what furthers ends, which we noticed earlier, is of a piece, therefore, with the logical structure of practical demonstrations.

That the conclusions of deliberative syllogisms are actions is also of a piece with something—in this case, with the notion of practical truth. For just as what one believes is what one asserts in the calculative part of one's soul (*NE* VI 9 1142^{b}13–14), so what one believes in a practical or action-determining way is what one both asserts there, effectively desires to do, and so does (*NE* VI 2 1139^{a}21–31). Hence if practical deliberation is to be action determining, it is not enough that the last thing reached in it—the decree—be believed or asserted in thought (as with a theoretical conclusion); in addition it must be acted on: "someone does not have practical wisdom simply by knowing; he must also act on his knowledge" (*NE* VII 10 1152^{a}8–9). It follows that the conclusion cannot be a proposition of any sort but must be an action that makes the (propositional content of the) decree true.

Because what happiness is is determined by our unchangeable nature and function, the definition of it that serves as a practical demonstration's major premise is itself fixed and unchangeable—which is another reason we cannot deliberate about it. Its being so, in fact, is an essential condition of the syllogism itself being practical or action determining. This is so because for something to produce movement it has to have a complex structure:

> What produces movement in an instrumental way is found where a starting-point and an end are the same, as, for example, in a hinge or ball-and-socket joint, since there the convex and concave are respectively the end and the starting-point of movement (that is why the one [the concave socket] remains at rest while the other [the convex ball] moves), the two being different in account, but not spatially separate. For everything is moved by pushing and pulling. Hence just as in the case of a circle or sphere, so here there must be a point that remains fixed, and the movement must have it as starting-point. (*DA* III 10 433^{b}21–27)

When the syllogism is practical, this ball-and-socket structure is reflected in its construction:

> The scientific part is not moved, but remains at rest. Since the one supposition and premise is universal and the other is particular (for the first says that any

36. Compare W. F. R. Hardie, *Aristotle's Ethical Theory* (Oxford: Clarendon Press, 1968), p. 242.

man of kind F should do an action of kind G, and the second that this is an action of kind G, and I a man of kind F), it is the latter belief that produces movement, not the universal one—or, rather, it is both, but the one remains entirely at rest, while the other doesn't. (*DA* III 11 434ª16–21)

The scientific knowledge of the universal premise cannot change, since it is a state whose object is a necessary truth concerning the relations between the universals F and G. So by nature it remains fixed from situation to situation. Which particular action will be G and which particular man will be F, on the other hand, do change from one situation to another. Moreover, beliefs or suppositions, as dealing with things that admit of being otherwise, are not fixed either, since they may be made true or again false by those changeable things, and so must adapt to changing circumstances (*NE* VI 3 1139ᵇ17–18).

In describing what happens in cases of continence and incontinence, Aristotle writes:

> Desire does not possess a deliberative part. Sometimes it defeats wish and causes movement, sometimes wish does this to it, just as with a ball (*hôsper sphaira*),[37] one desire does it to the other, as when incontinence occurs. By nature though the higher one is more architectonic and causes movement. (*DA* III 11 434ª11–15)

The description of wish as defeating and moving desire in this way does not mean that an orectic kinematics is being countenanced, where desires hit one another like billiard balls. Nor, though *sphaira* can also mean "sphere," is Aristotle referring to the heavenly spheres, or the influence of God on deliberate action (*EE* VIII 2 1248ª25–29).[38] Instead, he is returning to the simile of the hinge or ball-and-socket joint. Wish in being for the fixed end of action, grasped by scientific knowledge or understanding, is by nature fixed, like the concave socket. The desire it moves (as in cases of continence) is thus described as a ball or sphere, since it now joins wish in producing the action

---

37. Reading νικᾷ δ' ἐνίοτε καὶ κινεῖ τὴν βούλησιν, ὅτε δ' ἐκείνη ταύτην, ὥσπερ σφαῖρα with the mss.

38. Ancient commentators on Aristotle explored both the kinematic and the celestial options, as R. D. Hicks, *Aristotle De Anima* (Cambridge: Cambridge University Press, 1907), pp. 569–571, points out. Aquinas, too, *Commentary on Aristotle's De Anima* (Notre Dame, Ind.: Dumb Ox Books, 1994), pp. 249–250, detects a reference to heavenly bodies in the passage.

dictated by the ball-like minor premise. In cases of incontinence, wish is moved against nature by appetite, affecting practical understanding's grasp of the major premise. The movement is against nature in just the way that a socket's being moved by an arm held fixed is a nonnatural movement.

Because the action that is the conclusion of a practical demonstration occurs only if nothing prevents it, it is not entailed by the premises but is caused, rationalized, and explained by the fact that the premises are believed or accepted by the agent. Nonetheless, an entailment does lie behind it. Aristotle adverts to this by distinguishing between practical wisdom, which is a prescriptive virtue, from a nonprescriptive constituent in it, comprehension (*sunesis*), which can construct practical syllogisms (or their inert analogues) not with action in view but criticism, so that what is practical wisdom in an agent is comprehension in a discerning critic: "practical wisdom is a prescriptive virtue, since what *should* be done or not is its end, while comprehension is merely discerning" (*NE* VI 10 1143ª8–10). The critic's syllogism terminates not in an action, therefore, but in a proposition.

Looked at psychologically, the difference between an agent's deliberation and a critic's is that the agent's engages with his own wish for happiness in a way that the critic's does not. For "thought by itself moves nothing" (*NE* VI 2 1139ª35–36), but "when we have discerned, as a result of deliberation, [what we should do] our desire to do it is in accord with our wish" (*NE* III 3 1113ª11–12). We might represent an agent's deliberation, therefore, as a syllogism occurring within the scope of an operator Π, which expresses this active engagement:

Π

1. Happiness is action or activity in accord with   (definition)
   complete virtue
2. An action in accord with complete virtue is an   (decree)
   action of type T_1

Since the agent can perform an action of this type directly, guided only by perception, the conclusion of his deliberation is an action of type T_1. For he actively wishes for happiness, and so wishes to do an action of type T_1 once he realizes, as a result of his deliberation, that doing it constitutes happiness. When a critic engages in a similar piece of reasoning, he does so outside the context of Π. Hence he draws the propositional conclusion:

3. An action of type T_1 is (or constitutes) happiness.

This conclusion, unlike the agent's action, *is* entailed by 1 and 2. An agent's deliberation is valid by extension, since it inherits its status from that of the corresponding critical syllogism, which is straightforwardly valid. While it is the validity of the critical syllogism that rationalizes the agent's action, it does so only because, as occurring within the context of ∏ in a suitably modified form, it causes it. It is ∏, then, that gives the assertoric premises in the critic's syllogism their action-determining and prescriptive force.

Although not all practical syllogisms are demonstrations, any more than all theoretical syllogisms, Aristotle characterizes them in a similar way. A practical syllogism must have a premise dealing with the good, and a particular premise, characterized as being "with a view to the possible," because, like a decree, it specifies something the agent can do directly (*MA* 7 701ª20–25). When we look at the examples he gives of practical syllogisms, however, we notice immediately that few of them fit this characterization. His most elaborate example is a case in point: "I need a covering; a cloak is a covering; I need a cloak. What I need I should make; I need a cloak; I should make a cloak. And the conclusion, the 'I should make a cloak' is an action" (*MA* 7 701ª17–20). What explains this apparent mismatch between characterization and illustration is a feature of deliberation we have already noticed in discussing deliberation's sphere. Unlike theoretical reasoning, deliberation is *time sensitive*, and so can fail to be good by taking too long or by occurring at the wrong time, so that the critical moment for action is missed (*NE* VI 9 1142ᵇ26–28). Hence the practically wise man, as a good deliberator, will not waste time on the already obvious:

> As sometimes happens in asking [dialectical] questions, however, so here [in practical deliberation] thought does not stop to consider the other premise, the one that is clear. For example, if taking walks is good for a man, he does not linger over the thought that he is a man. That is why whatever is done without calculation is done quickly. For whenever someone is actually aware of the end, whether by perception, or imagination, or understanding, what he desires, he does at once. (*MA* 7 701ª25–30)

What someone needs, he will—everything else being equal—see as good, or happiness-promoting. So he won't bother making this explicit in his deliberation. Instead of thinking of our wish for happiness as needing to be expressed in a premise, implicit or otherwise, of all deliberative syllogisms, therefore, it is more revealing, for this reason too, to represent it using our operator ∏, within whose scope all such syllogisms occur. The cloak example would then be represented as follows:

Π
What I need I make
I need a cloak
[He makes a cloak]

It will be a valid piece of deliberation just in case the corresponding critical syllogism is valid.

Of course, there may be many kinds of covering besides (or better than) cloaks, and many ways to get cloaks besides (or better than) making them, so even if the agent's deliberation is valid, it seems that it may not be *sound*. In the abstract, this is true enough, but because practical syllogisms culminate in deliberate choice, and what is deliberately chosen is chosen before or in preference to other things (*NE* III 2 1112ᵃ16–17), it is safe to assume that contextual features constrain the premises in deliberation to those the agent takes to represent his best options:

> We set up the end and examine how and by what means it will come about; and if it appears that it will come about by more than one means, we examine by which of them it will happen most easily and most nobly [or best], whereas if it can be attained by only one means, we examine how it will come about by it, and through what [further] means *that one* will come about, until we come to the first cause, which is the last thing to be discovered. (*NE* III 3 1112ᵇ15–20)

There is no reason for an agent to consider other sorts of covering if a cloak is the best one available, and no reason to consider other ways of getting hold of a cloak if making it is the best available one.

Moreover, the context relevant to evaluating the soundness of a piece of deliberation must itself be properly understood, so that the features of it relevant to the soundness of syllogisms are those a practically wise man would recognize. These features constitute not the actual context, obviously, but the context as interpreted by him—making him in that way, too, the relevant "standard and measure" (*NE* III 4 1113ᵃ33). If we represent the context as he interprets it as the result of applying an operator Ψ to the actual or uninterpreted context, a further layer of complexity can be added to the cloak example:

Ψ
Π
What I need I make
I need a cloak
[He makes a cloak]

When, as will sometimes be the case, the agent's own interpretation of his situation differs from that generated by Ψ, the soundness of his deliberation will typically be affected. The defect in him as a deliberating agent may lie not in his strictly deliberative abilities, however, but rather in his appetites and feelings, which, failing to be in a mean, distort his practical perception, causing him to misperceive his situation. Of course, just what the output of Ψ is for a given situation—just what that situation is when represented correctly—may not be something that can be captured in a fully explicit formulation. The evaluation of practical syllogisms cannot generally be reduced to a formula, since it is itself (in part) an exercise of practical wisdom.

The Role of Understanding in Practical Demonstration

The roles of understanding in different sorts of demonstrations are described in the following dense passage:

> Understanding is concerned with things that come last in both directions. For concerning the primary terms (*tôn protôn horôn*) and the things that come last there is understanding but no reason—that is to say, on the one hand, in the case of demonstrations (*tas apodeixeis*), it [understanding] is of the unchanging (*akinêtôn*) and primary terms (*horôn*), on the other hand, in the case of those that are practical (*tais praktikais*), it is of the last thing and the one that admits of being otherwise and the other premise; for these are starting-points of the that for the sake of which, since it is from particulars that universals come. Of these, therefore, we must have perception, and this is understanding. . . . And that is why understanding is both starting-point and end; for demonstrations are from these and concerned with these. (*NE* VI 11 1143ª35–ᵇ11)

Demonstration in the strict sense is found only in theoretical sciences, whose starting-points and theorems hold with unconditional necessity. In them, understanding is of the terms or definitions—a *horos* can be either—that are primary in the science, because they are its starting-points, and are unchanging, because they are "eternal" (*NE* VI 3 1139ᵇ24). The use of *akinêton* to characterize these terms might seem to suggest that they are exclusively the eternal ones, so that the demonstrations at issue must be of the strict and unconditional variety. But the fact that the antecedent of *tais praktikais* ("the ones that are practical") is *tas apodeixeis* ("demonstrations") precludes this interpretation. For practical demonstrations are of the less strict variety applicable to things that hold for the most part.

Since things that hold for the most part also constitute the starting-points and subject matter of the natural sciences, and natural starting-points are (in the relevant sense) *akinêton*, so too are those of the practical sciences:

> Some people think that everything just is like that [that is, merely legal], since what is natural is unchangeable (*akinêton*) and has the same potentiality everywhere, as fire burns both here and in Persia, while they see what is just as changing. But this is not so, although in a way it is. Among the gods, at any rate, there is probably no change at all, but among us, while there is indeed such a thing as what is natural, still everything is changeable; and yet, despite this, some things are so by nature, and some are not. It is clear what sorts of things, among those that admit of being otherwise, are natural, and what sorts are not so, but are legal and conventional—assuming that both sorts are equally changeable. And the same distinction will hold in other cases: for the right hand is naturally superior, and yet it is possible that everyone become ambidextrous. The sorts of things that are just in accord with convention and expedience are like units of measurement. For measures of wine and corn are not the same everywhere, but larger in wholesale markets, smaller in retail ones. Similarly, things that are not just by nature but merely by human enactments are not the same everywhere, since constitutions are not the same either, although only one is by nature the best everywhere. (*NE* V 7 1134ᵇ24–1135ᵃ5)

Thus when comprehension is assigned a role in deliberation, and so in practical demonstration, that is restricted, like the role of consideration (*gnômê*), to last things and particulars, it is characterized as "not concerned with what always is and is *akinêton*" (*NE* VI 10 1143ᵃ4–5), because its focus is the particular (type of) action to be done in the circumstances. The universal premise in such demonstrations, on the other hand, must be unchangeable and unmoving, as we saw, because it is the analogue of the socket in a ball-and-socket joint.

Because the demonstrations in which the role of understanding is to grasp the unchanging primary terms are demonstrations generally, not just strict ones, two things follow. First, the contrast being drawn is not between strict demonstrations and practical ones but between demonstrations generally (including practical ones), in which understanding has one role, and practical demonstrations, in which it also has another role. Second, since both roles are attributed to the same state of the soul, the theoretical understanding involved in theoretical demonstrations is the same state as the practical understanding involved in practical ones (*DA* III 10 433ᵃ13–30). Understanding is one state, we may again infer, with different functions, not two different states.

If a premise in a practical demonstration is (or embodies) a starting-point, it must be the demonstration's major premise, and its major term, while definable, must be indemonstrable from anything else. Hence understanding's second role in such a demonstration must be to grasp the demonstration's "other" or minor premise, which, as the last thing reached in deliberation, is a decree. It "admits of being otherwise" because the particular (type of) action it prescribes varies from situation to situation, and is up to us to do, or not to do. In this premise, the crucial term is the middle one, since it is the one that can be predicated of something on the basis of perception, and so can be acted on directly, without the need for further deliberation. Just as there is no giving a reason for or demonstrating a major term that is a starting-point of any sort, so there is no giving one for a middle term in a practical demonstration. We simply *see* that this meat is bird meat, and so do not need to justify our predicating "bird meat" of it by yet another practical demonstration that would constitute our ground or reason for doing so. The concern of understanding with both universal and particular last things is characterized as being "in both directions," for the same reason that understanding is characterized as "opposed" to practical wisdom (*NE* VI 8 1142^{a}25): universals are opposed to—or lie in the opposite explanatory direction from—particulars (*APo.* I 2 72^{a}4–5).

The major term in a practical demonstration is or designates happiness, which, as a practical starting-point, is an end: "in actions the end for the sake of which [the action is done] is starting-point" (*NE* VII 8 1151^{a}16). Understanding is end, then, because it grasps the end, and so is what in the deliberating agent brings the end within his action-determining ken—similarly, the function of the parts that involve understanding is said to be truth, because they grasp truth (*NE* VI 2 1139^{b}12). In such a demonstration's minor premise, the middle term is or designates a particular (type of) action, which, like every particular, is grasped by perception (*NE* VII 3 1147^{a}25–26). Perception, however, always involves the concurrent grasp of universals: "we perceive particulars, but perception is of universals—for example, of man and not of Callias the man" (*APo.* II 19 100^{a}16–^{b}1). In the case of perception of the action-designating middle term, this grasp is due to understanding grasping the syllogistically arrived-at combination of the major premise and the minor one:

> What happens seems parallel to the case of understanding and syllogizing about unchanging objects. But there the end is a theoretical proposition (for when one has understood the two premises, one has understood—that is, put

together—the conclusion), whereas here the conclusion that follows from the two premises [being put together] becomes the action. (*MA* 7 701ª8–13)

Since perception of the middle term (or the action it designates) must be mediated in this way to be of the relevant deliberative or action-determining kind, it is an exercise both of perception and of understanding. Like deliberate choice, therefore, which is "either understanding involving desire or desire involving thought" (*NE* VI 2 1139ᵇ4–5), deliberative perception is either perception-involving understanding or understanding-involving perception.

When happiness is grasped by an agent, his deliberative task is to find the particular (type of) action that constitutes it in the actual circumstances. Once found, it plays two roles in his practical thought: it serves [1] as the minor premise of the practical syllogism that embodies his deliberation, and [2] as a concrete specification of his end. In [1], the action concludes the downward path from a universal end to its particular instances, and so the understanding embodied in the deliberative perception that grasps it is concerned with the application of a universal (happiness, acting well) to particulars (this action). In [2], the action is the starting-point of an induction that proceeds up to a universal from the understanding-involving perception of particulars. It is "the actions in life," we are reminded, that discussions in ethics and politics are "concerned with and [proceed] from" (*NE* I 3 1095ª3–4), and adequate habituation that ensures that we reach the correct conclusions from these actions, by being pleased or pained by the correct ones. In one way, then, happiness is a starting-point, since it is the ultimate end of all action. In another, the particular actions that instantiate it are starting-points, since it is from them that a filled-out understanding of (the universal) happiness comes.

Deliberative Perception

The *deliberative perception* of the last things involved in practical wisdom is not perception of such proper perceptibles as colors and smells but more like the kind by which we perceive that a triangle is the last thing among mathematical objects:

[1] [Practical wisdom] concerns the last thing, of which there is not scientific knowledge, but rather perception—not the [perception] of special objects, but like the sort by which we perceive that the last thing among mathematical objects is a triangle, since there too will come a stopping-point. [2a] Practical

wisdom, however, is more this perception. [Alternatively, 2b] This [mathematical] perception is more perception than it is practical wisdom. [Alternatively, 2c] This [mathematical perception] is more perception than practical wisdom.[39] But [3] it is a different kind from the other. (*NE* VI 8 1142ᵃ26–30)

An earlier discussion helps explain:

> We deliberate not about ends, but about what furthers ends. . . . We set up the end and examine how and by what means it will come about; and if it appears that it will come about by more than one means, we examine by which of them it will happen most easily and most nobly, whereas if it can be attained by only one means, we examine how it will come about by it, and through what [further] means *that one* will come about, until we come to the first cause, which is the last thing to be discovered. For a deliberator would seem to inquire and analyze in the way stated as though [analyzing] a diagram (for apparently all deliberation is inquiry, but not all inquiry—for example, mathematical—is deliberation), and the last thing in the analysis is the first that comes-to-be. (*NE* III 3 1112ᵇ11–24)

What the mathematician is inquiring into, apparently, is how to construct a diagram using the means he has available—for example, a pencil and set square. He continues inquiring until he has analyzed the diagram into simple figures, such as triangles, which he can draw with such implements using perception alone as his guide (*EE* II 10 1226ᵃ37). These figures are the last things reached in the analysis, but the first ones that come-to-be in the subsequent construction: "the last thing is the starting-point of the action" (*DA* III 10 433ᵃ16–17). At that juncture inquiry reaches a stopping-point (compare *NE* VI 8 1142ᵃ29), just as a practically wise man's deliberation does when he reaches a decree, since perception enables him to act directly on it.

Deliberative perception is a close relative—in that it is the essential precursor—of calculative or deliberative imagination:

> Perceptual imagination the other animals have too . . . , but the deliberative sort exists [only] in those with calculative parts. For when one comes to whether to do this or that one at the same time comes to a task for calculation. And one must measure by a single [standard], since one is pursuing the greater

39. [2a] Reading ἡ φρόνησις with the mss. [2b] Reading ἢ φρόνησις with I. Bywater, *Aristotelis Ethica Nicomachea* (Oxford: Clarendon Press, 1894). [2c] Reading ἢ ἡ φρόνησις with T. H. Irwin, *Aristotle: Nicomachean Ethics* 2nd. ed. (Indianapolis: Hackett, 1999).

[good]. And so one must be able to make out of many appearances a single one . . . the one resulting from a syllogism. (*DA* III 11 434ª5–11)

What makes calculative or deliberative perception *calculative* or *deliberative* is that it results from calculation or deliberation, and inherits conditions of correctness therefrom. What makes it a sort of *perception* is that the one appearance it makes out of many—that is, the universal figuring in it (for example, *triangle* in the case of mathematical calculation or inquiry)— is one whose particular instances are perceptible. Though calculative or deliberative perception cannot, for these reasons, occur in a creature whose soul lacks a calculative part, an act of deliberative perception is nonetheless a fully perceptual act, since it is the discernment of a perceptible particular by the perceptual part of the soul.[40] If the particular in question is a proper perceptible (as it might be, for example, if we were deliberating about what color clothing best protects us from the sun), this act is more narrowly that of a proper sense (sight). If it is a common perceptible (such triangular shape), it is an act of the common sense.

While the simple perception of white is always correct or minimally prone to error, the deliberative perception of it can be mistaken if, for example, the deliberation that leads to it is false or invalid. That is why practical wisdom can be at once a type of perception and most of all deliberative (*NE* VI 7 1141ᵇ9–10). The point of contrasting deliberative perception with perception of special objects in particular is presumably to highlight this fact. For the correct perception of common perceptibles does often depend on calculation and in this regard is somewhat similar to deliberative perception.

Although deliberation and calculation are commonly identified (*NE* VI 1 1139ª12–13), a narrower sort of practical or action-determining deliberation is also recognized, whose distinctive target is "the best for a human being of things done in action" (*NE* VI 7 1141ᵇ13–14). The deliberative perception central to practical wisdom is thus the precursor not of calculative imagination generally but of deliberative imagination. It follows that deliberative perception is a special case of practical perception, so that its correctness conditions depend also on those of practical perception generally, which involve having appetites and feelings that are in a mean. For what makes perception practical is that its object involves pleasure or pain, which

---

40. Contrast Troels Engberg-Pedersen, *Aristotle's Theory of Moral Insight* (Oxford: Clarendon Press, 1983), pp. 206–207.

the object of deliberative perception, as a case of wished for happiness, clearly does.

The text of [2] is somewhat unsettled. If we adopt [2a], the first clause is about practical wisdom and identifies it more with *deliberative* perception ("this perception") than something else. If we accept either of the alternative texts, the clause is about mathematical perception, saying that it is [2b] more perception than it is practical wisdom, or [2c] more perception than practical wisdom is. Whether we look at acts of mathematical perception and deliberative perception themselves, however, or at the calculative processes from which they result, both seem to be equally cases of perception, and equally cases of calculation. This gives us good reason to reject [2c].

When Aristotle says that *a* is *mallon* (more) F, there is always an implied or implicit *b* it is more F than, and two ways in which it can be so:

> We do not [Way 1] only call something [*a*] *mallon* [F than *b*] in accord with excess, when [F] is one in account, but also [Way 2] in accord with priority and posteriority. For example, we call health *mallon* good than healthy things, and what is by its own intrinsic nature choiceworthy *mallon* choiceworthy than the things that produce it. Yet we see that at any rate there isn't a single account predicated of both, when we say both of useful things and of virtue that each is good. (*Protr.* B85)

When *a* is *mallon* F than *b* in *Way 1*, *b* must also be F, since *a* has an excessive amount or degree of F compared to the amount or degree of it that *b* has.[41] Thus even if the Platonic good itself is eternally good, it is not thereby *mallon* good than something that is good for a short time, since "a white thing is no whiter if it lasts a long time than if it lasts a single day" (*NE* I 6 1096^{b}3–5). Here goodness, like whiteness, is treated as having a single account, and the excessive amount of time the good itself possesses goodness is considered inadequate grounds for thinking that it possesses it to a higher degree or in greater quantity than other things.

If *a* is *mallon* F than *b* in *Way 2*, F must again apply to both *a* and *b*, but this time the account of F as it applies to *a* is different from the account of F as it applies to *b*. Nonetheless, as the examples of health and goodness and the reference to priority and posteriority suggest, F cannot simply be a chance homonym. For example, we cannot say that a line is *mallon* straight

---

41. The vacuous case in which *a* is more F because *b* is not F at all is not one Aristotle considers.

than a straight (heterosexual) person. Rather the possession of F by *a* must be the focal case in terms of which its possession (in a slightly altered sense) by *b* is explained, so that *a*'s possession of it is logically or metaphysically prior to *b*'s. Hence health is *mallon* good than healthy things, because "everything healthy is related to health, some by preserving, some by producing, and others by being indicative of health, or receptive of it" (*Met.* IV 1 1003^{a}34–^{b}1). Like being and goodness (*NE* I 6 1096^{a}23–24), therefore, health is "spoken of in many ways," but "always with reference to one thing—that is, to one nature—and not homonymously" (*Met.* IV 1 1003^{a}33–34). God's happiness is *mallon* happiness than ours (*Met.* XII 7 1072^{b}24–26), not just because "he is always in that good condition, in which we sometimes are" but because it is by reference to his happiness that ours is so called (*NE* X 8 1178^{b}21–23).

According to [2b], mathematical perception is *mallon* perception than it is practical wisdom. Since there is no question of priority and posteriority in this case, or of any of the items involved being spoken of only in relation to one thing or nature, the way mathematical perception is *mallon* perception must be *Way 1* (although the same conclusion would follow if it were *Way 2*). This means that mathematical perception's perceptual quality or aspect must be excessive in relation to that of *its own* practically wise quality or aspect. But mathematical perception does not have any practically wise quality or aspect at all, since mathematical inquiry or calculation is entirely different, as we saw, from the practical deliberation involved in practical wisdom. Hence [2b] should also be rejected.

Our passage should be taken to be [2a] about practical wisdom, then, saying that it is more deliberative perception than something else. About the identity of this something else the text is silent, but the most likely candidate in context is surely the architectonic component of practical wisdom, which has been serving as the salient point of contrast with the perceptual component since *NE* VI 7 1141^{b}14. [3] goes on to say of this perceptual component that it is a different sort of perception than some other unspecified sort. One possibility is that [3a] this is mathematical perception (*NE* VI 8 1142^{a}28). For deliberative perception involves a universal reachable only through practical deliberation, and so inherits its reliability conditions from those of practical deliberation. Among these conditions is the possession of desires and feelings in a mean, since if these are excessively weak or strong, they constitute the vice that produces "distortion and false views about the starting-points of action" (*NE* VI 12 1144^{a}34–36), although not about those of mathematics (*NE* VI 5 1140^{b}12–16). It is this that distinguishes practical deliberation and inquiry from mathematical inquiry and calculation (*NE* III 3 1112^{b}21–23). Another possibility is that [3b] the unspecified kind of perception is perception of proper perceptibles, which was declared different from deliberative perception a few lines earlier (*NE* VI 8 1142^{a}27). Between [3a] and [3b] there is little to choose, but [3a] has the advantage of making a new point rather than one already made.

Correct Reason and Practical Truth

It is clear from his discussion of it that Aristotle is thinking of theoretical wisdom not as a *nascent* science that is in the process of being developed or perfected but as an already completed science, in need neither of addition nor correction. A virtue, after all, is a perfection of a sort, a completion (*Ph.* VII 3 246^{b}2), which ensures that its possessor achieves his end. This applies equally well to practical wisdom (*NE* VI 1 1139^{a}16–17, 2 1139^{b}12–13). As with any starting-point, Aristotle warns us at the outset, we "must not overlook the difference between arguments *from* starting-points and arguments *toward* starting-points" (*NE* I 4 1095^{a}30–32). Much of the *Nicomachean Ethics* is an argument toward such starting-points as happiness. Someone who already possesses these starting-points argues from them, not to them.

When deliberation is part of already complete practical wisdom, then, it is not providing content for or filling out the agent's conception of what happiness is. Instead, a fully worked out conception is presumed to be already available to him. The reason he needs to deliberate is that even with such a conception to hand, even with all the practical and productive sciences to aid him, there will still be circumstances in which he has to work out for himself what to do. It isn't the case that each new occasion for deliberation results, as it were, in a refinement of the laws, an enrichment of the principles of the practical or productive sciences, or a better implicit universal definition of happiness that they further—these are already presumed to be as rich or as good as can be. Yet deliberation is sometimes needed anyway. What does get enriched, what does become more discerning, is the agent's eye, his powers of practical and deliberative perception. This makes him better at deliberating, certainly, but only by making him better able to discover what best fits the laws and the conception of happiness he brings to the deliberative situation, not by modifying the content of what he brings. If we think in nascent terms, the conception of happiness the agent brings to the deliberative situation may seen too vague, too lacking in content, to serve as an action-guiding "grand end" for practical wisdom. If we think in terms of completed sciences and laws, the grand-end picture is more plausible—although the inelim-inable need for deliberation reveals some of its limitations.[42]

In the *Eudemian Ethics*, Aristotle embraces a grand-end view, but in a form that reveals his awareness of the difference between these two ways of thinking of it:

[1] To be happy, to live blessedly and nobly, would seem to reside most of all in three things, the ones that seem to be most choiceworthy. For some say that practical wisdom is the greatest good, others virtue, and others pleasure. And some dispute about the importance of these as regards happiness, claiming that one contributes more than another to it—some holding that practical wisdom is a greater good than virtue, others that virtue is a greater good than it, others that pleasure is greater good than either. Moreover, some think that living happily consists in some of these, some of two of them, others that it consists in a certain one. [2] Knowing, then, these things, everyone able to live in accord with his own deliberate choice should adopt some target of the noble life, whether honor, reputation, wealth, or education, one on which he will keep his eye in all his actions—at any rate, not to have ordered one's life in relation to some end is the sign of great folly. [3] Most of all, though, and be-fore everything else, he should define for himself in which of our possessions living well consists, and [4] what those things are without which it cannot belong to human beings. For being healthy is not the same as the things with-out which it is not possible to be healthy, and this holds likewise in many other cases too, so that living nobly is not the same as the things without which it is not possible to live nobly. (*EE* I 1–2 1214ᵃ30–ᵇ17)

[1] reminds us that happiness is a contested notion, because it is not clear in what good thing or things it consists—practical wisdom, virtue, pleasure,

42. John McDowell, "Virtue and Reason," *Monist* 62 (1979): 331–350, and Sarah Broadie, *Ethics with Aristotle* (Oxford: Oxford University Press, 1991), pp. 198–202, think Aristotle is not a grand-end theorist. Richard Kraut, "In Defense of the Grand End," *Ethics* 103 (1993): 361–374, and Alasdair MacIntyre, "Rival Aristotles: Aristotle against Some Modern Aristotelians," in his *Ethics and Politics: Selected Essays,* vol. 2 (Cambridge: Cambridge University Press, 2006), pp. 22–40, think Aristotle is a grand-end theorist. J. L. Ackrill, "Aristotle on *Eudaimonia*," *Proceedings of the British Acad-emy* 60 (1974): 339–359, and Daniel Devereux, "Aristotle on the Essence of Happiness," in *Studies in Aristotle,* ed. J. O' Meara (Washington, D.C.: Catholic University of Amer-ica Press, 1981), pp. 247–260, think Aristotle's grand end is inclusive of some or all intrin-sic goods. John M. Cooper, "Contemplation and Happiness: A Reconsideration," *Synthese* 72 (1987): 187–216, Richard Kraut, *Aristotle on the Human Good* (Princeton: Princeton University Press, 1989), and Anthony Kenny, *Aristotle on the Perfect Life* (Ox-ford: Clarendon Press, 1992), pp. 1–42, think the grand end is a single dominant end.

or education and cultivation of one's character and thought. Because of this, [2] any wise (or nonfoolish) person who can live as he chooses should set up one of these as the target or grand end of his life—virtue if he makes his target honor or reputation, wealth if he makes it pleasure, education or cultivation if he makes it practical wisdom—and look to it in all his actions to determine whether or not they further it. But he should [3] do this only after defining or determining for himself what that grand end consists in, being careful to distinguish its constituents from [4] its enabling conditions. The grand end, in other words, is not something we start with a fully developed conception or definition of, so that even nascent deliberation already has it in view. Instead, it is something we must first define for ourselves using the scientific and aporematic methods employed in the *Nicomachean* as in the *Eudemian Ethics*—something we are not in a position to do until, at the age of forty or so, our good early upbringing and subsequent education has been complemented by substantial life experience.

Because complete practical wisdom has both an architectonic side and a deliberative side, the true or correct reasons it is its function to provide come in two quite different varieties. The first are those universal reasons that obviate the need for deliberation altogether. The second are those reasons provided by the decrees that constitute the minor premises of the practical demonstrations that serve as the focus of a practically wise agent's deliberation. Because these are specific to particular situations, they are precisely not universal in scope. We might well wonder, then, why Aristotle requires all virtuously done actions to be chosen on the basis of deliberation and deliberate choice (*NE* II 4 1105ᵃ31–33), since this seems to narrow practical wisdom's correct reasons to nonuniversal deliberative ones.

In part the answer has to do with codification, in part with delegation. Why does an agent need to be practically wise himself (*NE* VI 12 1143ᵇ28–33)? Why can't he just consult the universal laws in the ethical-political handbook—the practical equivalent of the complete biology or physics textbook? Answer: because even if that handbook were as complete or close to perfection as possible, it wouldn't be enough. Problem cases will always arise, which deliberation is required to solve. That is why correct practical reasons are not the same as correct reasons in the natural or theoretical sciences, which because they deal exclusively with universals *are* codifiable (at any rate, in the ideal case). Why, then, can't the agent simply consult someone else who is practically wise—why, to repeat, does he need to be practically wise himself? In a craft, too, the cases that best reveal the practitioner's wisdom are the problem cases, where the craft manual is insufficient and deliberation is required: "we speak of people as practically wise in some [area], when they calculate well about what furthers some good end, concerning which no craft [prescription] exists" (*NE* VI 5 1140ª28–30). There, however, delegation is an open possibility. For it doesn't matter who solves productive problems, since the only important thing is that the resulting product be good (*Cael.* III 7 306ª14–17). In the case of practical problems, it is a different story: an agent who delegated the problem would commit the Victorian error of letting his servants do his living well for him. For to enjoy doing virtuous actions—to achieve the happiness they can constitute—we must do them virtuously, out of appetites, desires, and wishes that are in a mean. We must do them, as Aristotle puts it, not only *kata ton orthon logon* but *meta tou orthou logou* (*NE* VI 13 1144ᵇ26–28)—that is to say, we must do them from the correct reason that we ourselves generate and possess. Correct practical reasons as a whole, then, cannot be codified, a feature they do not share with correct reasons in the natural or theoretical sciences but do share with productive ones, and cannot be delegated, a feature they do not share with productive ones.

Since it is the deliberative reasons, in particular, that exhibit both these distinctive features, they are the quintessential practical reasons—the ones that best reveal what a correct practical reason is. Hence actions in accord with them are the ones that best exhibit practical wisdom and the virtues of character whose possession it presupposes. They are the ones in which practical wisdom shines forth. Someone who has internalized the complete ethical-political handbook, to put it in another way, acts on the equivalent of autopilot. What shows him not to be virtuous or practically wise, therefore, are not the situations the handbook is designed to deal with but the problem cases, where, as Aristotle puts it, the agent must consider "what is opportune in the prevailing circumstances, as also happens in the cases of medicine and navigation" (*NE* II 2 1104ª8–10).

Because deliberative reasons are the quintessentially practical ones for Aristotle, it is their characteristic type of correctness that he employs in defining *practical truth* as "truth in agreement with correct desire" (*NE* VI 2 1139ª29–31). The truth that does the agreeing here or *a-truth* does not arise from the deliberative reason adapting itself to the desire, as a nonobjectual plain truth adapts to its truth-maker, but from the desire listening to and obeying the reason (*NE* I 13 1102ᵇ14–1103ª3). The correct desire isn't the *a-truth*-maker for the reason, then, rather the *a-true* reason is the correctness maker for the desire.[43] Hence the agreement between the two must

---

43. A point parallel to one famously made by G. E. M. Anscombe, "Thought and Action in Aristotle," in *New Essays on Plato and Aristotle*, ed. Renford Bambrough (London: Routledge, 1965), pp. 143–158.

be a matter of sameness of intentional content, appropriately caused, so that it exists when the *a-true* reason prescribes φ-ing and, because of that, the desire is to φ—or Rφ^Dφ. If no more were required for practical truth than such agreement, a proposition asserting Rφ^Dφ would be a practical truth just in case Rφ^Dφ obtained. But practical truth also requires that the desire be effective in causing φ to occur: "the very things the one [R] asserts the other [D] must pursue" (*NE* VI 2 1139ᵃ25–26). Hence it isn't Rφ^Dφ alone that is relevant to practical truth but a state-of-affairs involving the actual existence of the action φ itself, as brought about by Rφ^Dφ. In other words, (Rφ^Dφ)^φ.

By turning from *a-truth* to the corresponding state-of-affairs, which is its truth-maker or objectually true correlate, then, we can see why Aristotle recognizes practical truth of this sort as a distinct type of *truth*. For because propositions are all true in precisely the same way, namely, by corresponding in some sense (whether freighted or not) to their truth-makers, there is really only one type of nonobjectual truth. So if we treat nonobjectual truth as primary or fundamental, practical truth will differ from other sorts (geographical truth, anthropological truth, theoretical truth) simply in its subject matter, not, so to speak, in its nature or structure. When, like Aristotle, we treat objectual truth as primary, however, we will treat states-of-affairs with different types of constituents, explained by appeal to different starting-points, as different in nature or structure.

Starting-points themselves, for example, when they are forms or essences that involve no matter, are objectually true in a distinctive way that involves no combination. Similarly, states-of-affairs with the structure (Rφ^Dφ)^φ are also objectually true in a distinctive way, since they have as constituents both a correct desire and the action it causes. That is why, when we try to explain their existence, we must appeal to different starting-points from in the case of objectual scientific truths, namely, human beings and their deliberate choices (*NE* VI 2 1139ᵇ5), and why, when we try to explain our grasp of them, we must appeal not to scientific knowledge but to practical wisdom. As Aristotle puts it: "the truth and falsity that involve no action are the same in kind as good and bad [that is, the truth and falsehood that do involve action]; but they differ in that the first is unconditional and the second relative to someone" (*DA* III 7 431ᵇ10–12). For here the assertion that something is good (bad) by understanding is a practical truth, since it takes the form of pursuit or avoidance, and is relative to someone, because it has a starting-point in a particular agent's deliberate choice (*DA* III 7 431ᵇ6–10).

This account of the general structure of correct or practically true reasons will not, of course, do the work of practical wisdom itself, any more than a similar account of medically correct reasons will do the work of medicine:

> People think that to know what things are just and what unjust one does not need to be at all wise, because it is not difficult to comprehend the things the laws speak about (although it isn't these that are the just ones except coincidentally). But knowing how actions are to be done, and distributions made if they are to be just—*that* is a bigger task than knowing what things are healthy, since even in that case while knowing it is things such as honey, wine, hellebore, cautery, and surgery may be easy, knowing how to administer them to produce health, and to whom and when, is no less a task than being a doctor. (*NE* V 9 1137^{a}9–17)

If we have been well brought up with noble habits, so that we have natural or habituated virtue of character, we have what it takes to be adequate students of the noble and just things that are the starting-points of ethics (*NE* I 4 1095^{b}2–8). What we will not yet have, simply by having such habits, is a clear understanding of the target—happiness. We will know the facts that experience teaches, and may possess the cleverness required for calculating effective means to ends, but we will not have the explanation of those facts that a science, whether practical, productive, or theoretical, can alone provide (*Met.* I 1 981^{a}28–^{b}10).

As a work of political or ethical philosophy (*Pol.* III 12 1282^{b}19–20), or "the philosophy of human affairs" (*NE* X 9 1181^{b}15), the *Nicomachean Ethics* is a practical not a theoretical work, whose aim is not knowledge but to help people become good (*NE* II 2 1103^{b}27–31). That is why its central task is to determine what happiness is, so that we can the better achieve it: "Regarding our life, too, won't knowing it [the good] have great weight and, like archers with a target won't we be better able to hit what we should? If so, then we should try to grasp in outline at least what it is" (*NE* I 2 1094^{a}22–25). For once our understanding does grasp the target, so that instead of being blind to the goal of our life we see what it is, our natural or habituated virtue is transformed into full virtue, and we really do thereby become fully good (*NE* VI 12 1144^{a}29–^{b}1, 13 1144^{b}1–17). At the same time, the natural virtues, which can be possessed separately, become collectively integrated into a single state, since all are required by practical wisdom, as it is by them (*NE* VI 13 1144^{b}32–1145^{a}2). The courage that in isolation destroys some people is thus revealed to be not full courage but natural courage (*NE* I 3 1094^{b}18–19).

Generalism or Particularism?

Ethical *generalism* accords normative priority to general or universal rules or principles, so that particular ethical or moral judgments are true or correct because they accord with them. It need not deny that a trained eye or properly habituated appetites and feelings will typically be required to apply the principles in particular cases. Ethical *particularism*, on the other hand, accords normative authority to particular judgments, and pride of place to the virtuous agent who makes them, so that ethical rules or principles are correct because they accord with these judgments. It need not deny that such rules or principles exist or even that they are important in practice. The issue is the source of their normative authority, not their existence.[44]

One common form of ethical particularism holds that virtues, not general principles, are what enable us to make correct judgments in particular cases. When Aristotle claims that the fully virtuous practically wise man is the standard and measure of what is noble or pleasant (*NE* III 4 1113ª31–33), or that actions are "called 'just' or 'temperate' when they are such as the just or temperate person would do" (*NE* II 4 1105ᵇ5–7), he seems to be embracing such a view. His many comments about the lack of rigor in ethics, about how ethical premises and conclusions hold for the most part, and how agents must decide for themselves what to do seem to tend in the same particularist direction, suggesting that rules and principles are flawed guides at best.

When a universal law or principle of one of the practical or productive sciences, such as house-building or political science, tells us precisely what to do, so that there is no need to deliberate, normative authority seems to stem directly from it. As in the case of the natural and theoretical sciences, however, these practical ones begin with the perception of particulars, proceed by induction from these to perceptible universals, and from these, via dialectic or aporematic philosophy, to the analyzed universals that serve as their starting-points. Even in their case, therefore, one sort of normative priority belongs to particulars, since these are the ultimate sources of universals, the ultimate truth-makers for their definitions, and so the ultimate truth-makers, too, for the explanatory principles deriving from them. There is no question, as there is for example in the case of Immanuel Kant's cate-

---

44. In seeing the issue in this way, I follow T. H. Irwin, "Ethics as an Inexact Science: Aristotle's Ambitions for Moral Theory," in *Moral Particularism*, ed. Brad Hooker and Margaret Little (Oxford: Oxford University Press, 2001), pp. 100–129, especially pp. 100–104.

gorical imperative, of a source for practical principles lying in reason alone, independently of experience. But from the point of view of explanation, and so of justification, normative priority belongs to universals. Why will this bird meat further happiness? Because it is light and all light meats are healthy. Practical reasons that guide action directly, without the need for deliberation, fit this general profile. Hence they are appropriately thought of as generalist rather than particularist in nature. Induction uncovers universal real essences, after all, not just true universal generalizations. It goes beyond the particulars, therefore, to universals and relations between them that are every bit as much a part of reality as the particulars themselves. Aristotle is not an *ante rem* theorist of universals, like Plato, but he is an *in re* theorist of them, not a nominalist or some other sort of antirealist.

If we have recently been reading Ludwig Wittgenstein on rule following, we will raise a question about what is involved in knowing how correctly to apply such universal principles in particular circumstances.[45] That is to say, we will question the very possibility of direct guidance by them. Aristotle is unperturbed by such questions. In some cases, a practical science can tell us unproblematically what to do, decisively settling all questions of application and interpretation. But the reason he is unperturbed should do much to quiet Wittgensteinian worries. For Aristotle is always presupposing the existence in agents of some ethical formation or other, some shared form of life—indeed, of political life. He is not imagining, in other words, that universal principles can guide just anyone, or anyone minimally rational, or what have you. A good upbringing is required.

In cases where the practically wise man does have to deliberate, the practical reason he acts on is embodied in a decree. It tells him directly what to do, without the need for anything besides perception on his part. It is a particular practical reason, not a universal one, since unlike a universal law, it applies—and is intended to apply—only in these particular circumstances. On the other hand, it is a practical *reason*, because its middle term, which is a universal, albeit one that can be applied to particulars on the basis of perception, is related by necessity to the universal definition of happiness, which is its major premise. Its normative authority, therefore, stems from that relation.

Since a given practical reason, whether embodied in a universal law or a decree, cannot be correct unless universals are necessarily related in the

---

45. Ludwig Wittgenstein, *Philosophical Investigations* (Oxford: Blackwell, 1953), sec. 258 and following.

appropriate way in reality, its correctness cannot consist simply in the fact that it is or would be the practically wise man's reason. What is rather the case is that the practically wise man is the epistemically most reliable provider of such reasons—the measure, in that sense, of which actions we should call just, temperate, or otherwise virtuous. The actions he would do are the ones we call just or virtuous, because we have no better epistemic standard available to us in applying those terms than he. Nonetheless, he is the standard because he reliably tracks the relevant way the world is, not because his judgment makes something true of that world.

In according normative authority to particular judgments and giving pride of place to the virtuous agent who makes them, ethical particularism is in one way Aristotelian and in another not. It is Aristotelian in that Aristotle, too, gives pride of place to the virtuous agent—that is, epistemological pride of place. He is the best detector of correct practical reasons. Nonetheless, these reasons gain their normative authority—as correct scientific reasons gain their explanatory authority—from universals and universal principles. And this is true even when, as in the case of decree-based reasons, they are intended to apply only in a particular case.

6

IMMORTALIZING BEINGS

Previous chapters discuss things human beings can do, such as contemplate, deliberately act, and so on, because they have souls of a certain sort, and can do well because they can acquire various virtues, whether of thought or character. This chapter marks a change of direction, focusing instead on what sorts of beings human beings are, and what their place is among beings more generally.

Substance and Attribute

Being is "spoken of in many ways," so that there are many different distinct kinds of being—substantial being, qualitative being, quantitative being, and so on for each so-called *category* of being, as well as intrinsic and coincidental being, being in potentiality or in actuality, and true or false being (*Met.* VI 2 1026ᵃ33–ᵇ2). Nonetheless, all these kinds have something important in common:

> Being is indeed spoken of in many ways, but all in relation to a single starting-point—some are spoken of as beings in that they *are* substances, some in that they are attributes of substances, some in that each is a way toward substance—either destructions, privations, or qualities of substance, or productive or generative of substance—some because they are said in relation to substance, or negations of some of these or of substance. That is why we say that even nonbeing *is* nonbeing. (*Met.* IV 2 1003ᵇ5–10)

Unconditionally speaking, only substances or substantial beings are beings (*Met.* VII 1 1028ᵃ30–31), while, in a weaker sense, anything that *is* or *is* something is one: "being and being one are predicated of simply everything" (*Top.* IV 6 127ᵃ33–34); "being is common to all things" (*Met.* IV 2 1004ᵇ20).

What gives substances their peculiar status is that they alone are *separate* (*chôriston*): "If one does not suppose the substances to be separate, and in the way that among the beings the particulars are said to be, one will destroy substance as we wish to speak of it" (*Met.* XIII 10 1086^{b}16–19). What makes the other beings not separate is that all of them "are *said of* substance as of a subject" (*Ph.* I 2 185^{a}31–32; also *Met.* V 8 1017^{b}13–14). Being predicated of a substance, then, or being an *attribute*, is a sufficient condition of not being separate, and so of being ontologically dependent: "All the other things are either *said of* the primary substances as subjects or *in* them as subjects. So if the primary substances did not exist, it would be impossible for any of the other things to be anything" (*Cat.* 5 2^{b}3–6). Since all beings besides substances are attributes, the separation of substances involves at least three things: being separate from attributes; not being predicated of them; and being ontologically independent of them.[1] That is why Aristotle usually characterizes substances as separate *tout court* rather than separate *from something*: by being separate from attributes, substances are separate from everything else. An attribute is something predicated of a substance, whereas a substance is an ultimate subject of predication: "A substance—that which is called a substance most strictly, primarily, and most of all—is that which is neither said of a subject nor in a subject" (*Cat.* 5 2^{a}11–13). Since an "examination of cases" (*Cat.* 5 2^{a}35–36) reveals such subjects to be particulars of some sort, being a substance is regularly associated with being a *this*—a particular (*GA* IV 3 767^{b}34–35, *Met.* XI 2 1060^{b}1–2).

Form, Matter, Change

What seems most distinctive of such substances is that they can remain numerically one and the same and yet be able to "receive contraries" (*Cat.* 5 4^{a}10–11). In other words, they can undergo change: they can be F at one time and not-F at another. To explain how this is possible, Aristotle thinks they must be analyzed into two components, namely, matter and form. This immediately raises the question of what now is the substantial constituent

---

1. Just what such ontological independence amounts to is controversial. A plausible view is that substances can exist separate from attributes, not because they can exist when stripped of attributes altogether, a possibility Aristotle rejects (*GC* I 3 317^{b}23–33), but because they can exist whether or not attributes exist through being instantiated by such nonsubstances as Platonic Forms (*Long.* 3 465^{b}12–14).

in them. Is it the material component, or the formal component, or the compound of matter and form (*Met.* VII 3 1028^{b}33–1029^{a}7)? Change is thus the point of entry into matter, form, and the hylomorphic analysis of substance.

In order for a *canonical change* to occur, the very same thing has to be one way at one time and the contrary way at another time. That is,

Fa at t$_1$ & Gb at t$_2$ & ($a = b$) & Contraries (F, G).

The prime example of such change is attribute change, which occurs when a or b is a substance, such as Socrates, and F and G are two of his contrary coincidental attributes, such as, being pale and being tan. Substantial or existence changes, on the other hand, which occur when a substance comes-to-be or passes-away, seem not to be canonical. If we substitute does-not-exist (not-E) for F, and does-exist (E) for G, we get:

Not-Ea at t$_1$ & Eb at t$_2$ & ($a = b$).

Since "a" has no referent at t$_1$, the entire proposition of which it is a part cannot be true (*Cat.* 10 13^{b}18–19) and so cannot report a canonical change, or anything else.

When a undergoes a substantial change by coming-to-be at t$_1$, we cannot simply suppose that *nothing* was a prior to t$_1$ and *something* was a after t$_1$. For if something can come-to-be from nothing, it seems that anything can come-to-be from anything, and that would leave substantial changes ungrounded in being or reality, and so preclude their scientific explanation. That is why "our first point must be that nothing whatever is by nature such as to affect or be affected by any chance thing, nor does anything come-to-be from just anything, unless you take a case of coincidental causation" (*Ph.* I 5 188^{a}31–34; also *Met.* XII 7 1072^{a}19–21). Since the scientific demand that change be grounded in being or reality is what in the end must guide an analysis of it, there is good reason for Aristotle to try to model substantial changes on canonical ones, which are grounded in the substances that persist through them:

Whatever comes-to-be is always compound: there is something that comes-to-be and another that comes-to-be it. The latter is of two sorts: either the subject or the opposite. By the opposite I mean in one case [attribute change] the unmusical and by the subject the man, and in the other [substantial change] the absence of shape or form or order [are the opposites], and the bronze, stone, or gold is the subject. (*Ph.* I 7 190^{b}11–17)

The subject that underlies the coming-into-being of Socrates is his *matter (m)*, and the other factor (the analogue of the attribute in attribute change) is his form (S). Omitting the redundant identity clause, the canonical or *hylomorphic analysis* of such change will thus be: Not-Sm at t_1 & Sm at t_2.

One problem this analysis faces is readily seen in the case of artifacts. If m is a quantity of bronze and S a statue of Socrates, why does the hylomorphic analysis report S's undergoing a substantial change rather than m's undergoing a change in its coincidental attributes? Aristotle's answer is that when we state things accurately we see that m does not really become S at all:

> As for that out of which as matter things come-to-be, some, after they have come-to-be, are said to be not that, but made of that—for example, the statue is not stone but *of stone*, and the man (that is, the healthy man) is not said to be that out of which he came-to-be. The reason is that he comes-to-be out of both the privation and the subject, which we call the matter (for example, it is both the man and the sick thing that come to be healthy), but he is more correctly said to come-to-be out of the privation—for example, out of what is sick, what is healthy comes, rather than out of what is a man. Hence what is healthy is not called sick, but is called a man, and the man is called healthy. (*Met.* VII 7 1033ª5–13)

What comes-to-be S is non-S-formed m—usually referred to as the *privation (sterêsis)*. But it does not persist through the change that takes place in m, any more than something sick persists when a man changes from being sick to being healthy. Indeed, no quantity of bronze could play the role in relation to S that Socrates plays in attribute change, since none shares S's existence and identity conditions. For S can—for example, through a series of repairs—change its matter over time, so that distinct quantities of bronze, m and m^*, constitute it at different times. As a result, S cannot be an attribute of m. For attributes are ontologically dependent on their subjects and cannot float free of them as S—by coming-to-be constituted by m^*—can float free of m. The arrival of a new substantial artifact in the world is the arrival of something that employs already existing matter for ends of its own, and that does not usually depend for its existence or identity on any particular quantity of matter. It can gain new matter or lose old matter, much as Socrates can change from being pale to being tan, without threat of passing-away.

Particulars, Universals, and Quasi-Universal Forms

With the hylomorphic analysis of substance legitimated by its role in analyzing substantial change, three contenders emerge for being primary substance—form, matter, and the compound of the two. Matter and the compound are quickly excluded: matter because it is neither separate nor a particular this; the compound because it is "posterior to the other two" (*Met.* VII 3 1029ᵃ30–32). The formal component thus seems to win, as it were, by default, so that it is Socrates' form, not Socrates himself, that is a primary substance. But when Aristotle tries to fit this conclusion together with his views about the structure of scientific knowledge in the way that his realism about truth demands a puzzle immediately arises. The starting-points of scientific knowledge are *universal* essences. Primary substances are *particular* thises, primary subjects of predication. Yet realism requires that what comes first in being or reality must come first in knowledge, too, so that whatever a primary substance is, it must be primary in knowledge and definition (*Met.* VII 1 1028ᵃ32–33). It is this that creates the puzzle: "If the starting-points of scientific knowledge are universals, they will not be substances, since nothing common signifies a this but rather a such, but substance is a this. . . . If they are not universals, however, but in the nature of particulars, they will not be knowable. For the scientific knowledge of all things is universal" (*Met.* III 6 1003ᵃ7–15). This *primacy puzzle* is the "greatest puzzle" that the investigation of substance faces (*Met.* XIII 10 1087ᵃ10–13).

The first step toward resolving this puzzle consists in uncovering a concealed complexity in the apparently exclusive distinction between particulars and universals:

> That of which [something is said], that is, the subject, is differentiated in this way: either [1] in being a this or [2] in not being a this; for example, the subject for attributes is a man, that is, a body and a soul, whereas musical or pale is the attribute. . . . Whenever this is so, the ultimate subject is a substance; but whenever this is not so, but the predicate is a form and a this, the ultimate subject is matter and substance that involves matter. (*Met.* IX 7 1049ᵃ27–36)

In [1] the subject is Socrates (or the like) and what is predicated of him is a universal. In [2], the subject is Socrates' matter (or the like), and what is predicated of it is a form or essence. Thus, while [1] involves universal attributes, [2] involves *quasi-universal* forms.

Universals are wholly present in many particulars: "what is said universally is by nature such as to belong to many things" (*Met.* VII 13 1038ᵇ11–12). Particulars are severally *one* and jointly many: "this is just what we mean by a particular: what is numerically one" (*Met.* III 4 999ᵇ34–1000ᵃ1). Matter and form, as a result, seem to belong in neither camp. For form is what particularizes matter, and matter is what, prior to being formed, is not a particular this: "We speak of one kind of being as substance, but of this one thing, the one that is not intrinsically a this, we speak of as matter, another, that in virtue of which it is then said to be a this, we speak of as form or shape" (*DA* II 1 412ª6–9). Just as we can think of matter as preparticular, then, we can think of form as preuniversal. Forms carve up or individuate the world into particular subjects of predication, whereas universals are instantiated by bits of the world that are already individuated.

Matter is excluded from being a primary substance, then, because, as preparticular, it is neither a subject of universal attributes nor a particular this (*Met.* IX 7 1049ª27–36). Moreover, because it is not intrinsically anything, it cannot exist separate from the quasi-universal forms that particularize it, and is intrinsically undefinable and unknowable (*Met.* VII 3 1029ª20–28, VII 10 1036ª8–9). Hence it lacks all the features a primary substance must possess. When we turn to the compound of matter and form, things are less clear. On the negative side, the compound inherits some of matter's failings: as a hylomorphic particular, it is not identical to its essence, and so cannot be epistemologically primary (*Met.* VII 6 1031ª28–b14); as a compound of matter and form, it seems to be posterior to these more primitive constituents. On the positive side, the compound is a subject of universal attributes, and so is both unconditionally separate and a particular (*Met.* VIII 1 1042ª29–31).

This story about forms as quasi-universals goes some way toward legitimating the distinction between forms and universals. But it does not by itself resolve the primacy puzzle in form's favor, since quasi-universals still seem not to be particulars. Primary in scientific knowledge they may be, but if primary substances must be particulars, they cannot, it seems, be the primary beings.

Actuality and Potentiality

The next steps in Aristotle's analysis of primary substance are taken in *Metaphysics* VIII and IX, where matter is identified with potentiality, form with activity or actuality. These represent definitional bedrock—the place where explicit definition gives out, and analogy takes its place:

> What we mean to say will be clear by induction from particular cases: we must not seek a definition of everything, but must get a view of some of them by analogy. In this case: as what is building is to what can build, and as what is awake is to what is asleep, as what is seeing is to what has its eyes shut but

has sight, and as what has been shaped out of matter is to the matter, and as the finished work is to what is unworked—let actuality be distinguished by the first part of the contrast, potentiality by the second. (*Met*. IX 6 1048^{a}35–^{b}6)

Leaving aside the details of the analogy and how best to elaborate them, we should notice that once the bedrock identification is made, we have on the one hand the possibility of *prime matter* (that is, matter whose only intrinsic attribute is to be in potentiality something) and on the other that of *pure form* (that is, form that is simply actuality or activity, since it involves no matter, and so no potentiality).

The elements earth, water, air, and fire are by definition the most primitive of sublunary bodies. Yet they can change into one another (*Cael*. III 6 305^{a}31–32). What determine these changes are the ultimate differentiae—hot, cold, wet, dry—by which the elements are distinguished from one another, once duplications (hot and hot) and impossible combinations (hot and cold) are eliminated. Thus earth is cold and dry; water cold and wet; air hot and wet; fire hot and dry (*GC* II 3 330^{a}30–^{b}7). If elements are adjacent, so that like earth and water, they share a differentia, transformation occurs when one of the differentia masters its contrary (*GC* II 4 331^{a}27–30). If a differentia in each element is destroyed, because "either the same or opposite ones are left, in neither case does a body result, as happens, for example, if the dry of the fire and the wet of the air are destroyed, since the hot in both is left" (*GC* II 4 331^{b}26–32). Elemental transformation and animal reproduction thus involve the same explanatory mechanisms.

Suppose that earth (E) is first transformed into water (W), then into air (A), then into fire (F), so that

$$Em \text{ at } t_1 \ \& \ Wm \text{ at } t_2 \ \& \ Am \text{ at } t_3 \ \& \ Fm \text{ at } t_4$$

Since *m* underlies elemental transformation, it cannot have any of the ultimate differentiae essentially: if it did, it would not be able to lose it. Because these differentiae are the ultimate ones, there are no others *m* can possibly have (*GC* II 1 329^{a}10–13). Hence it must have these differentiae, but not in the same way as the elements themselves (*GC* II 1 329^{a}24–35). Thus while fire is essentially or intrinsically hot, *m*, while it may in fact be hot, must also be in potentiality cold, and so must be hot only coincidentally. For matter is "that which, primarily and intrinsically, is *in potentiality*" hot, cold, and the rest, without being any of them intrinsically, essentially, or in actualty (*Met*. XII 4 1070^{b}12–13). In other words, *m* must be prime matter.

If *m* is to underlie elemental transformation, a numerically identical quantity of it must persist through that transformation: "the thing, whatever it is, that underlies [the transformation of the elements into one another] is the same, although it is not the same in being" (*GC* I 3 319ᵇ3–4). But as apparently possessing none of the ultimate contrary differentiae intrinsically, such a quantity of prime matter would seem to impose *no constraints whatsoever* on element transformation, so that, at the elemental level (and so on up), anything could come from anything. Since elemental transformation is not in fact indiscriminate but is constrained by the causal relations holding between the ultimate differentiae, this cannot be the case. It must be, then, that *m*'s defining potentialities are themselves constrained by these causal relations. That is why Aristotle can simultaneously think that the elements come-to-be from prime matter, and that they come-to-be from one another: "Since the elements cannot come-to-be either from what is bodiless [such as, a mathematical object] or from some other sort of body, the remaining possibility is that they come-to-be from one another" (*Cael.* III 6 305ᵃ31–32).[2] What an element comes from is another element, but what underlies the transformation of one into the other is prime matter, which is not a body separate from the elements, and has no essential or intrinsic attributes besides the potentialities determined by the causal relations between the ultimate differentiae. (That it does have the higher-order attribute of having essential attributes that are so determined is neither here nor there.)

Normally, of course, a thing's potentialities or dispositional properties are based in its actual or categorical properties, as table salt's solubility in

---

2. The implication of this passage, that *m* cannot be bodiless, constitutes an apparent stumbling-block to the otherwise interesting suggestion in David Charles, "Simple Genesis and Prime Matter," in *Aristotle's On Generation and Corruption*, ed. Frans de Haas and Jaap Mansfeld (Oxford: Clarendon Press, 2004), pp. 151–169, that *m* should be understood as a logical or abstract entity. Aristotle does claim that *m* is imperceptible, which might seem to offer some support for the suggestion. The context makes it clear, however, that he means *difficult to perceive*, not *impossible to perceive because abstract*: "When no same thing persists as underlying subject, and the thing changes as a whole (when, for example, the seed as a whole is converted into blood, or water into air, or air as a whole into water) such an occurrence is the coming-to-be of one substance and the passing-away of another—especially if the change proceeds from *an imperceptible something to something perceptible* (either to touch or to all the senses), as when water comes-to-be out of, or passes-away into, air, since air is *fairly imperceptible (epieikôs anaisthêton)*" (*GC* I 4 319ᵇ14–21). Were *m* abstract, indeed, and imperceptible for that reason, prime matter would be indistinguishable from the intelligible matter of abstract mathematical objects.

water is based in its molecular structure. But when we get down to ultimate constituents, there may be no base of this sort, as may be true, for example, in the case of mass or gravitational attraction. At that point, what we confront are dispositions or potentialities that are, so to speak, simply brute. All we can say is that *m* is something that [1] when coincidentally cold and dry (earth) has the potentiality to become cold and wet (water), and [2] when coincidentally cold and wet (water) has the potentiality to become hot and wet (air), and [3] when coincidentally hot and wet (air) has the potentiality to become hot and dry (fire), and [4] when coincidentally hot and dry (fire) has the potentiality to become cold and dry (earth). The different potentialities *m* possesses at each of these four stages—which are themselves explained by the different coincidental attributes it possesses at each stage—explain why *m*'s being is not always the same, while the causal continuities exhibited across the stages explain why *m* is nonetheless the same thing throughout them.

A thing's form is the same as its essence: "by the form I mean the essence of each thing and the primary substance" (*Met.* VII 7 1032^{b}1–2). Consequently, pure forms are essences that involve no matter of any sort. It is these (or their definitions) that are the starting-points of the theoretical sciences, which alone constitute unconditional scientific knowledge. Like all scientific starting-points, they are grasped by understanding. But in contrast to essences involving matter, they are identical to the active or productive understanding of them. Since the latter is a particular, so too is the essence that it grasps:

> Scientific knowledge, like knowing scientifically, is of two kinds, one potentiality, one actuality or activity. The potentiality—being (as matter) universal and indefinite—is of what is universal and indefinite, but the actuality or activity, being a particular this, is of a particular this. But coincidentally sight sees the universal color, because this particular color that it sees is *a* color, and this A, which is the object the grammarian has actual theoretical knowledge of, is *an* A. (*Met.* XIII 10 1087^{a}15–21)

In one case, moreover, we know that what is grasped in this way is in fact a substance. For Aristotle's God is an intelligible substance (*Met.* XII 7 1072^{a}25–26), whose "very substance" (*Met.* XII 6 1071^{b}20) is "the active understanding of active understanding" (*Met.* XII 9 1074^{b}34–35). Hence he is at once a substantial understanding subject and the substantial object he understands.

We seem to have come a long way from *Categories*, with its almost commonsense ontology of perceptible particulars as ontologically primary, and their various attributes as dependent on them. Yet even in the *Organon*—

to which *Categories* belongs—a few texts suggest that nonperceptible (or intelligible) substantial particulars are already part of the picture: primary substances are "actualities without potentiality" (*Int.* 13 23ª23–24); God is "an intelligible living being" (*Top.* V 6 136ᵇ7). In the *Nicomachean Ethics*, too, particular human beings, such as Socrates, who serve as examples of primary substances in *Categories*, have their status as strictly perceptible substances put in question. For though Socrates is indeed a human being, he has a divine and intelligible understanding, and it is with it, as we shall see, that he is most of all to be identified. This has important consequences, obviously, for what the human good consists in, since it provides a metaphysical foundation, so to speak, for identifying that good with the contemplative activity of understanding in accord with theoretical wisdom. In addition, it harmonizes Aristotle's metaphysics, not just—as his realism requires—with his epistemological views on scientific knowledge, and the psychology that goes along with them, but with his ethical views as well.

This grand synthesis, to be sure, leaves the status of perceptible hylomorphic compounds, such as Bellerophon and other animals—including ourselves, to the degree that we are less than fully divine and intelligible—somewhat unsettled. Are they (we) primary substances, or something else? The claim to primacy of sublunary hylomorphic substances is hostage, Aristotle thinks, to the question of whether there are substances not constituted by sublunary nature: "If there were no other substances besides those constituted by [sublunary] nature, natural science would be the primary science" (*Met.* VI 1 1026ª27–29). Once the existence of intelligible substances becomes part of the picture, therefore, the status of natural ones remains to be decided. That there are degrees of substantial primacy is the implication of a passage in the *Metaphysics* that we looked at earlier in a different context: "intrinsically intelligible objects are in one of the two columns [of opposites], and in this column substance is primary, and in this [the column of substances] the simple one and an activity [is primary]" (*Met.* XII 7 1072ª30–32). Since God alone is a substance that is simple and an activity (*Met.* V 5 1015ᵇ11–12, *NE* VII 14 1154ᵇ24–26), it follows that he is more primary than other primary substances. In the early *Protrepticus*, we meet a being—clearly God—who "is by nature simple and does not have its substance in relation to something else," and a human being, whose nature, because it is "naturally cocomposed of several potentialities," does have its substance in relation to something else (B64–65). The joint implication of these different texts is that God is a primary substance ontologically dependent only on himself, while we, though also primary substances, are ontologically dependent on him, and so are less primary.[3]

God and Productive Understanding

Although the soul is not generally something separate from the body but more like its form or vital organization, productive understanding seems to have a different status:

> This [productive] understanding is [1] separate, impassive, and unmixed, being in substance an activity. For what makes is always more estimable than what is affected, that is, the starting-point of the matter. . . . And it is not the case that it is sometimes understanding and at other times not. [2] And when separated it is alone just that which it is, and it alone [of the parts of the human soul] is immortal and eternal. [3] We do not remember, because this [productive understanding] is unaffected, whereas the passive understanding passes-away, and without this understands nothing. (DA III 5 430ª17–25)

It is convenient to begin with [3] and work backward. Like understanding, memory functions in a similar way to perception:

> We might be puzzled about how, when the affection is present but the thing producing it is absent, what is not present is ever remembered. For it is clear that one must understand the affection, which is produced by means of perception in the soul, and in that part of the body in which it is, as being like a sort of picture, the having of which we say is memory. For the change that occurs stamps a sort of imprint, as it were, of the perceptible object, as people do who seal things with a signet ring. That is also why memory does not occur in those who undergo many changes, because of some affection or because of their age, since it is just as if the change, that is, the imprint of the seal, were falling on running water. In others, it is because of wearing down, as in the old parts of buildings, and because of the hardness of what is receiving the affection, the imprint is not produced. (Mem. 1 450ª25–ᵇ5)

Thus passive *memory* is stamped with the perceptible form, but not the matter, and as a result the soul acquires a potential to remember the thing

3. André Laks, "Metaphysics Λ 7," in *Aristotle's Metaphysics Lambda*, ed. Michael Frede and David Charles (Oxford: Clarendon Press, 2000), pp. 207–243, p. 225 n. 50, notes that *Met.* XII 6 1071ᵇ20–22 also implies that there are a number of types of primary substances. Human beings are one type, the heavenly bodies another.

responsible for the stamping. As a psychological potentiality, however, a passive memory must be based in sublunary matter akin to eye-jelly, if memory is to malfunction in the way [3] describes, since it is features of the material on which a form is imprinted that determine whether and how well it will be remembered.

Of the starting-points of the various psychological potentialities, understanding "alone enters additionally from outside and alone is divine" (GA II 3 736^{b}27–28). Since productive understanding is [2] immortal and eternal, this makes it natural to wonder why we do not remember things that, for example, happened before our understanding in the form of ether entered our body. [3] explains why we don't. Memory is one step in the inductive process leading from perception to understanding's grasp of universal essences. Passive memory, however, like perception, involves sublunary matter, so that before our understanding entered our body, it could not perceive or remember anything. That is why we find Aristotle wondering about whether the understanding "when not separate from a spatial magnitude [that is, from sublunary matter and the body] can understand anything that is separate" (DA III 7 431^{b}17–19). For "when one contemplates, one must at the same time contemplate an appearance" (DA III 8 432^{a}8–9), that is, an image derived from perception and perhaps preserved in memory.

The claim in [1] that productive understanding is not sometimes actively understanding and sometimes not suggests that it is always active. Aristotle's views on sleep show that this suggestion, while true, does not entail that human beings are always understanding:

> Sleep is not every incapacity of the perceptual part, but rather this affection arises from the evaporation that attends eating food. For that which is vaporized must be driven on to a given point and then must turn back and change just like the tide in a narrow strait. In every animal the hot naturally rises, but when it has reached the upper parts, it turns back, and moves downward in a mass. That is why sleepiness mostly occurs after eating food, for then a large watery and earthy mass is carried upward. When this comes to a stop, therefore, it weighs a person down and makes him nod off; but when it has actually sunk downward, and, by its return, has driven back the hot, then sleepiness comes on and the animal falls asleep. (Somn. 3 456^{b}17–28)

Because of its mode of operation, then, sleep could not affect any part of the soul unless, like the perceptual part, it was incarnate, since what causes sleep is the presence of too much vaporized food.

Now sleep does affect the scientific knowledge and practical wisdom of which understanding, by grasping their starting-points, is a component part:

When someone changes from drunkenness, sleep, or disease, we do not say that he has acquired scientific knowledge again—even though he was unable to use his knowledge [while drunk, asleep, or diseased]. . . . For it is due to the soul's stopping its natural restlessness that something becomes practical wisdom or scientific knowledge. . . . In some cases nature itself causes the soul to settle down and come to a state of rest, while in other cases other things do so. But in either case *the result is brought about through the alteration of something in the body*, as we see in the case of the use and activity [of practical wisdom or scientific knowledge], when someone becomes sober or wakes from sleep. (*Ph.* VII 3 247^{b}13–248^{a}6)

Sleep, drunkenness, disease, and the like are thus the sorts of things that explain why "there is not always understanding"—the sorts whose effects Aristotle promises to consider (*DA* III 4 430^{a}5–6). Because such factors can affect only a productive understanding that is incarnate and not separated from the body, one that is discarnate is immune to them. Hence a *discarnate* productive understanding is always active. Since productive understanding is [1] in substance an activity, it follows that [2] it is just what it is only when separated from the body.

Even when *incarnate*, productive understanding remains ever active, just like the eternally moving ether that codes for it. But when we are asleep or drunk or for some other reason unconscious, the state of our body—the presence in it of too much vaporized food or what have you—makes our productive understanding inaccessible to us, just as too much perturbation makes our memory so. When, on returning to consciousness or sobriety, we again actively understand things, active understanding doesn't in some miraculous way start up uncaused, but rather, having always been active, becomes accessible because of changes in the body and in passive understanding. As we are self-movers in the practical realm, since we are starting-points of our actions (*NE* VI 2 1139^{b}5), so in the contemplative one, too, we are starting points of those actions that are contemplative, since the ever active productive understanding is what we most of all are, and it "in a way does all the moving" (*EE* VIII 2 1248^{a}25–29).[4]

If a human being's productive understanding did not preexist its incarnation at conception, the problem about memory in [3] would not arise. That it continues to exist after the death of the body is something Aristotle is explicit about:

4. Compare the brief but perceptive discussion in M. L. Gill, "Aristotle on Self-Motion," in *Aristotle's Physics: A Collection of Essays*, ed. Lindsay Judson (Oxford: Clarendon Press, 1991), pp. 243–265, especially 252–254.

> The understanding seems to be born in us as a sort of substance, and not to pass-away. For it would be destroyed most of all by the feebleness of old age, while as things are what happens is similar to what happens in the case of the organs of perception. For if an old man acquired an eye of a certain kind, he would see even as well as a young man. Hence old age is not due to the soul's being affected in a certain way, but to this happening to what the soul is in, as in the case of drunkenness and disease. Thus understanding and contemplation are extinguished because something else within passes-away, but it itself is unaffected. (*DA* I 4 408^{b}18–25; also *Long.* 2 465^{a}26–32).

Understanding is extinguished *in our bodies* at our death, because something else passes-away at that point, namely, the appropriately organized sublunary matter required for perception and memory, and the appearances they make available to understanding. But productive understanding itself is not affected by this, any more than it is affected by drunkenness, disease, or sleep.

If a human being's productive understanding exists before the birth of his body and after its death, and is in substance an activity, it must be a separate substance even when it is present in the body and affected by it: "Since the virtues of the compound [of body and soul] are [merely] human virtues, so too is the life and happiness in accord with them. The happiness of understanding, however, is separate" (*NE* X 8 1178^{a}20–22). Contemplating is not an activity that ever involves our body in any way: "bodily activity is in no way associated with its activity" (*GA* II 3 736^{b}28–29). That is why God, as a productive understanding, can be outside the realm of body altogether:

> It is clear that neither place nor void nor time exists outside the [outermost] heaven. For in every place body can exist; and void, it is said, is that in which body does not exist, but can exist; and time is a measure of movement, but there is not movement without physical body. But it has been shown that outside the [outermost] heaven no body exists or admits of existing. It is evident, therefore, that neither place nor void nor time exists outside. That is why the things there are of such a nature as not to be in a place, nor does time make them age, nor does anything situated beyond the outermost moving thing undergo change. Instead, unalterable and impassive and possessing the best and most self-sufficient life they are achieving their end for all their timeless eternity. (*Cael.* I 9 279^{a}11–22)

It is when we ask what a discarnate productive understanding understands or contemplates that we run into difficulties.

What keeps productive understanding active is its object: "understanding is moved [activated] by intelligible objects" (*Met.* XII 7 1072^{a}30). If it is always active, therefore, it must always have some object, even when, as discarnate, it is not in vital connection with any perceptual system or memory. Yet because of the way human understanding works, this seems impossible. For understanding requires appearances (*DA* III 8 432ª8–9), and without a perceptual system and memory no appearances seem to be available to it. In the case of one separate and discarnate understanding, Aristotle confronts this issue head on:

> Matters concerning the [divine] understanding involve certain puzzles. . . . For either it understands nothing, in which case . . . it would be just like someone asleep, or it understands something, in which case something else controls it. For, in this case, what it is, its substance, isn't active understanding, but a potentiality to understand [or passive understanding], and it would not be the best substance, for it is due to active understanding that its esteem belongs to it. And furthermore whether it is [passive] understanding or active understanding that is its substance, what does it understand? For it understands either itself or something else. And if something else, always the same thing or sometimes this and sometimes that. Does it, then, make a difference or none at all whether it understands the good or some chance object? Or would it not be absurd for it to be understanding certain kinds of things? It is clear, then, that it understands what is most divine and most estimable, and it does not change [its object], since change would be for the worse, and would at the same time be a sort of movement. Going back to the first alternative, then, if it is not active understanding that is its substance, but a potentiality to understand [passive understanding], it is reasonable to suppose that the continuity of its active understanding is wearisome to it. Next, it is clear that something else would be more estimable than understanding, namely, what is understood by it. And indeed [passive] understanding and active understanding will be possessed by what understands even the worst thing, so that if this is to be avoided (since there are even things that it is simply better not to see than to see), the active understanding would not be the best thing. It is itself, therefore, that it understands, if indeed it is the best thing, and it is an active understanding that is an active understanding of active understanding (*hê noêsis noêseôs noêsis*). (*Met.* XII 9 1074ᵇ15–35)

A strand in this argument bears on esteem: God wouldn't have the exalted status he does if the active understanding he is were dependent on something else—especially on something bad or ignoble ("the worst thing"). Another strand allows as a possibility that an active or productive understanding—at any rate, a divine one—can have itself as the intelligible object activating it. If God can understand himself without a perceptual system or memory, however, surely our discarnate productive understanding, as itself something divine, can do the same.

"In the case of those things that have no matter, what understands and what is understood are the same" (*DA* III 4 430ᵃ3–4). Hence if God's understanding contained all the forms or essences that, since they serve as starting-points of strictly theoretical sciences, involve no matter, he would be identical to them. Consequently, our discarnate productive understanding, in understanding him, would understand them, and so would have access to them without the need for perception, memory, induction, and the rest—something Aristotle repeatedly assures us is impossible. Apparently, then, God, in having himself as what he understands, must have his own otherwise blank self as his understanding's sole activating object. When the following passage is properly decoded, that is its message:

[1] If God is self-sufficient and needs no [friends], it does not follow from this that we need none. For the following sort of argument, too, is expressed about God. [2] Since God, it is said, possesses all good things and is self-sufficient, what will he do, since he will not simply sleep? He will contemplate something, it is replied. For this is the best and most appropriate thing [for him to do]. What, then, will he contemplate? If he contemplates something other than himself, it must be something better than he. But it is absurd that there should be anything better than God. Therefore, he will contemplate himself. But that is absurd. For if a human being scrutinizes himself, we criticize him for lacking common sense. It will be absurd, therefore, it is said, for God to contemplate himself. (*MM* II 15 1212ᵇ35–1213ᵃ7)

If we focus on [2], it might seem that Aristotle is rejecting so-called narcissistic theology.[5] When we see it in the context of [1], a different picture emerges, whose point is that we cannot draw immediate inferences about ourselves from truths about God, or vice versa. God is self-sufficient, and so does not need friends, but it does not follow that a human being has no need of them. To think otherwise would be like arguing [2] that because a human being who spends all his time in self-scrutiny is senselessly narcissistic, so God would have the same absurd defect were he to contemplate only himself. The argument is invalid precisely because Narcissus is not God, not the best thing, and so not a worthy object of eternal scrutiny. God, by contrast, as the best thing, is a worthy object of it. For him to contemplate himself is not absurd at all. Indeed, if it were absurd, the absurdity would carry over

5. As Richard Norman, "Aristotle's Philosopher-God," *Phronesis* 14 (1969): 63–74, argues he is.

to any other supposed object of his contemplation. Suppose, for example, that God contemplated the starting-points of the strictly theoretical sciences. When these involve no matter, the contemplation or understanding of them is identical to them. In contemplating them, therefore, God is again contemplating just himself. Narcissism, in other words, is unavoidable, but entirely proper. For parallel reasons, a *good* human being should love himself and desire to contemplate himself in action (*NE* IX 9 1169[b]30–1170[a]4). When Aristotle demands that whatever God contemplates must be simple and incomposite, he means just what he says (*Met.* XII 7 1072[a]30–32, 9 1075[a]5–6). If he had meant anything else, indeed, if he had imagined the divine active understanding as filled with a vast array of forms or essences, he could hardly have chosen a more misleading thing to call it than *hê noêsis noêseôs noêsis*.[6]

Since what God contemplates is his own otherwise blank self, the question arises of whether we could, when discarnate, have his otherwise blank self as our productive understanding's activating object. The only obstacle, given the divine precedent, is that when we understand we must understand an appearance—a *phantasma*. Now normally a *phantasma*, as an object of imagination, is distinct from the *noêma*—the intelligible object—encoded in it. When the productive understanding is its own object, however, this cannot be the case. For, to repeat: "In the case of those things that have no matter, what understands and what is understood are the same" (*DA* III 4 430[a]3–4). When the productive understanding is its own sole object, therefore, no other appearance can, on pain of disrupting that identity, intrude.

Immortalizing Ourselves

The *Nicomachean Ethics* is largely free of ethical injunctions and rules. It contains no equivalent of the principle of utility or the categorical imperative. But in one famous instance, it does tell us in no uncertain—if not entirely perspicuous—terms how we should and shouldn't live:

> We should not, then, [live] in accord with (*kata*) the makers of proverbs and "Think *anthrôpina*, since you are human." . . . On the contrary, we should as far as possible *athanatizein*, and do everything to live in accord with the constituent in us that has most control (*to zên kata to kratiston tôn en hautô[i]*). (*NE* X 7 1177[b]31–34)

6. Contrast M. F. Burnyeat, *Aristotle's Divine Intellect* (Milwaukee: Marquette University Press, 2008).

What we should not live in accord with is what the makers of proverbs say. What we should live in accord with is the constituent in us that has most control. It must be the case, then, that proverbs and constituent require incompatible things. Since what the proverbs enjoin is a sort of thinking, it follows that living (*zên*) in accord with the constituent in us that has most control must also be or involve a sort of thinking—a sort that Aristotle is urging us to do everything to engage in.

The constituent in us with most control is the divine one, productive understanding, which alone of the things in the human soul is "immortal and eternal" (*DA* III 5 430ª23). *To zên kata to kratiston tôn en hautô(i)*, we may infer, refers to productive understanding, which is itself a sort of life: "the activity of understanding is life (*zôê*)" (*Met.* XII 7 1072ᵇ26–27). The life Aristotle is recommending, therefore, is a life activity, a kind of thinking, but one different from the kind recommended by the makers of proverbs, who recommend thinking *anthrôpina*. What this means we learn from another text, where again proverbs are in focus:

> It might be justly regarded as not human to possess this [free science that investigates the starting-points and causes of everything]; for in many ways human nature is enslaved, so that, according to Simonides, "God alone can have this privilege," and it is unfitting that man should not be content to seek the science that is in accord with (*kath'*) himself. If, then, there is something in what the poets say, and jealousy is natural to the divine, it would probably occur in this case above all, and all who excelled in this science would be unlucky. The divine, however, cannot be jealous [compare Plato, *Timaeus* 29e]—but, as the proverb says, "Bards often lie." Moreover, no science should be thought more estimable than this sort. For the most divine science is also the most estimable. And a science would be most divine in only two ways: if God most of all would have it, or if it were a science of divine things. And this science alone is divine in both of these. (*Met.* I 2 982ᵇ28–983ª8)

Anthrôpina are neither the thoughts humans think about themselves, therefore, nor the thoughts they, as opposed to other beings, think.[7] Instead, they are the contents of a certain science—identified only as the one in accord with man. The thoughts contrasted with them, we see, also constitute a sci-

---

7. W. D. Ross, *Aristotle: The Nicomachean Ethics* (Oxford: Oxford University Press, 1925) translates *anthrôpina phronein* as "think of human things," Sarah Broadie and Christopher Rowe, *Aristotle: Nicomachean Ethics* (Oxford: Oxford University Press, 2002), as "think human thoughts."

ence, namely, the one that has God both as its subject and as its preeminent practitioner—theology. Thus theoretical wisdom, which is theology under another name, is contrasted with practical wisdom and political science, which are "concerned with human things (*anthrôpina*)" (*NE* VI 7 1141ᵇ8–9). The target contrast, in other words, is this: the poets and proverb writers urge us to restrict our thoughts to practical wisdom or political science, while Aristotle urges us to devote them to theology.

Precisely what we will achieve if we do so depends in part on the interpretation of the rare verb *athanatizein*, which is often translated in an anodyne way, suggesting that what we do is strive to be *like* an immortal.[8] Aristotle thinks, however, that we achieve much more than mere godlikeness when we theologize. For even if the following fragment is, as its source suspects, a forgery, its use of *athanatizein*, which is the only other use of it in even a putatively Aristotelian work, remains importantly illuminating:

> Aristotle himself, in his defense against the charge of impiety (*asebeias*)—if the speech is not a forgery—says: "You see, if I had deliberately chosen to sacrifice to Hermias as an immortal, I would not have prepared a memorial to him as a mortal, and if I had wished to *athanatizein* his nature, I would not have adorned his body with burial honors." (*Fr.* 645)

Since there is no inconsistency and slim basis for a charge of impiety in preparing a memorial for someone and adorning his body with burial honors on the one hand and regarding him as *like* an immortal on the other, *athanatizein* must mean something stronger.[9] It must mean to treat as really being immortal.[10] Our task, then, is to make sense of literal immortalizing of ourselves as something we can intelligibly do by theologizing. It is a task made more dif-

---

8. T. H. Irwin, *Aristotle: Nicomachean Ethics,* 2nd ed. (Indianapolis: Hackett, 1999): "we ought to be pro-immortal." Broadie and Rowe, *Aristotle: Nicomachean Ethics*: we should "assimilate to the immortals."

9. A writ of impiety or *graphê asebeias* was brought against Socrates in 399 BC, and supposedly—though K. J. Dover, "The Freedom of the Intellectual in Greek Society," *Talanta* 7 (1976): 24–54, is skeptical—against a number of other "sophists" or intellectuals, including Anaxagoras, Protagoras, and Euripides. Aristotle implies that sophists may often have faced trial (*Rh.* II 23 1397ᵇ24), but it is not clear—*Fr.* 645 notwithstanding—that he himself ever did.

10. Roger Crisp, *Aristotle: Nicomachean Ethics* (Cambridge: Cambridge University Press, 2000), has "take on immortality," which nicely captures the right idea. Compare Herodotus IV 93 2, 94 1, V 4 2.

ficult by particular doctrine. For if our understanding is *already* immortal, how can we immortalize it? And if it *alone* is immortal, how can *we*, whose souls include so much more than our understanding, immortalize ourselves?

Because all the other constituents of a telic system subserve the topmost one and its function, the entire system stands in a special relation to it: "a city and every other system seems to be most of all the constituent in it with most control" (*NE* IX 8 1168ᵇ31–32). In the telic system of the human soul, where lower parts and their functions exist for the sake of higher ones, understanding is the topmost constituent. Hence just as the governing class in a city is the constitution (*Pol.* III 6 1278ᵇ11) because it is the part with most control, so a human being is or is most of all his understanding:

> Each human being seems to be this [his understanding], if indeed he is the constituent of his that has most control and is better. It would be absurd, therefore, if he were to choose not his own life, but something else's. And what we have said before will also apply now. For what is proper to each thing's nature is best and pleasantest for it; for a human being too, then, the life in accord with understanding will be best and pleasantest, if indeed it most of all is the human being. This life, therefore, will also be happiest. (*NE* X 7 1178ᵃ2–8; also *Protr.* B58–70).

This gets us closer to seeing how in actively theologizing we are doing something not just to our understanding but to ourselves.

At the same time, something is happening to the concept of a human being—something Aristotle acknowledges in discussing pleasure:

> What sort of pleasure, or what particular pleasure, should we take to be that of a human being? Or isn't it clear from looking at the relevant activities? For the pleasures accompany these. Whether, then, the activities of the complete and blessedly happy man are one or more than one, it is the pleasures that complete these that will be said to be human pleasures in the full sense, and the rest will be so called in a secondary way, or in a many-times removed way, corresponding to the activities. (*NE* X 5 1176ᵃ24–29)

What is fully human is the understanding, which is responsible for active contemplation. What is human in a secondary way—and so what is happiest "in a secondary way" too—is the life of the hylomorphic compound of calculating part and desiring part, responsible for the practical activities that are in accord with virtue of character and practical wisdom (*NE* X 8 1178ᵃ9–23). The parts of us responsible for other pleasures, not already excluded as ignoble or shameful, are human in ever lesser ways.

Although our productive understanding is always active, we are not always actively understanding. For when, for example, too much vaporized food gets mixed into the sublunary matter with which passive understanding is correlated, so that we fall asleep, we can no longer access our active understanding or understand anything. (Alternatively: we who are our active understanding cannot access what is in our memory.) This gives us the distinction we need. For it is our productive, not our passive, understanding that is the immortal constituent in us: "That which can receive the intelligible object, that is, the substance [or essence], is [passive] understanding, and is active when it possesses it, so that this [active understanding] rather than the former seems to be the divine constituent understanding possesses" (*Met.* XII 7 1072^{b}22–23). Our productive understanding is always active and immortal, but we are actively immortal*izing*—actively living our immortal life—only when accessing our ever active understanding. It is a view we find Plato, too, expressing:

> So if a man has become wholly engaged in his appetites or love of victory and takes great pains to further them, all his beliefs must become merely mortal. And so far as it is at all possible he will become thoroughly mortal, and not fall short of it even to the least degree, seeing that he has strengthened these all along. On the other hand, if someone has seriously devoted himself to the love of learning and to truly wise thoughts, if he has exercised these aspects of himself above all, then there is absolutely no way his thinking can fail to be immortal and divine. And to the degree that human nature can partake of immortality, he can in no way fail to achieve this. (*Timaeus* 90b–c)

When what we are actively contemplating is God, moreover, we are immortalizing ourselves in a yet fuller sense. God is an activity, a form that involves no matter of any kind. When we contemplate him, therefore, our active understanding, to which we are most of all identical, becomes temporarily identical to God (*DA* III 4 430^{a}3–4). But only temporarily. For God is always in the good state of actively contemplating himself, whereas we are in it only sometimes, and he is also in it to "a higher degree," since his contemplation of himself is prior to ours and presupposed by it (*Met.* XII 7 1072^{b}24–26).

Finally comes the advice, addressed, of course, to practical wisdom, which alone has the architectonic status and prescriptive potentiality to act on it: "we should immortalize [ourselves], and *do everything* to live in accord with the constituent in us that has most control." In ideal circumstances, practical wisdom (political science) follows this advice by designing a constitution that will guarantee to its practically wise and so virtuous male citizens as much leisure time as possible within which to philosophize and theologize. What it will do when circumstances are less than ideal is less amenable to brief formulation—a great deal depends on the sort of political community in which it finds itself. Still, we can say this much: it should aim at an adequate constitution, that is, one whose laws inculcate the sorts of good habits needed in an adequate student of the noble and just things that are starting-points in ethics.

Becoming God-Beloved

The benefits of immortalizing oneself, especially when doing so constitutes complete happiness, are no doubt obvious. They are not the only ones made available in the life centered on understanding God:

> [1] The one whose activity is in accord with understanding, and who serves it, and is in the best condition, seems also to be the one most loved by the gods. For if the gods exercise supervision of a sort (*tis epimeleia*) over human affairs, as indeed they are thought to, it would also be reasonable to suppose that they delight in what is best and most akin to themselves, which is the understanding, and benefit in return those who most cherish and esteem it for supervising what they themselves love, and acting correctly and nobly. [2] Clearly, all these attributes belong most of all to the wise man. Therefore, he is most beloved by the gods. But the same person is also likely to be the most happy, so that in this way too, the wise man will be most happy of all. (*NE* X 8 1179ª22–32)

The commitment to the existence of gods (plural), who supervise human affairs in some way and benefit those who cherish and esteem the understanding as the activity most akin to their own, is conditional in [1]—"*if* the gods . . . as they *are thought* to." [2], however, assumes that the antecedent of the conditional is true, since it draws nonconditional conclusions from it.[11] Hence Aristotle must believe in the existence of such gods himself.

Aristotle's God with a capital *G* seems incapable of beneficial supervision, since his sole activity is self-contemplation. Hence the small-*g* gods in [1] might seem to need a wider range of interests and powers if they are be aware of us and our characters and act for our benefit. Yet they, too, seem to live an exclusively contemplative life:

> We assume the gods above all to be blessed and happy. But what sorts of actions should we ascribe to them? Just actions? Won't they look ridiculous

---

11. As Broadie and Rowe, *Aristotle: Nicomachean Ethics*, pp. 448–449, point out.

making contracts, returning deposits, and so on? Brave actions, then, endur-
ing frightening things and facing dangers because it is a noble thing to do? Or
generous ones? To whom will they give? Absurd, too, if they have currency or
anything like that. And their temperate actions—what would they be? Isn't it
vulgar praise to say that they have no bad appetites? If we go through them
all, anything that has to do with actions seems trivial and unworthy of the
gods. And yet everyone assumes that the gods are alive, at least, and therefore
engaged in activity, since we surely do not take them to be asleep like
Endymion. If, then, what is living has doing actions taken away from it, and
producing things even more so, what is left but contemplation? Hence the activity of a god that is superior in blessedness will be a contemplative one. And
so the human activity most akin to this will most have the stamp of happiness.
(*NE* X 8 1178ᵇ8–23)

The problem is thus one of explaining how exclusively contemplative gods—
whether with a small or capital *g*—can supervise and benefit those human
beings who are themselves wise and contemplative.

The various heavenly spheres are substantial living beings, moving eternally in fixed circular orbits. Each has an understanding, which actively contemplates God, and wish, which causes it to move. Including the spheres of
the moon and the sun, there are forty-nine such spheres in all (*Met.* XII 8
1073ᵇ38–1074ᵃ14).[12] To these the stars and the various planets—Aphrodite
(Venus), Hermes (Mercury), Zeus (Saturn), and so on—are attached. Of all
these, Aristotle has this to say:

The ancients of very early times bequeathed a tradition to posterity in the
form of a myth that the heavenly bodies are gods and that the divine circumscribes (*periechei*)[13] the whole of nature. The rest has been added later in the
form of a myth, as a way of convincing the masses, and as useful as regard
the laws and what is beneficial. For these gods, they say, are like men in form,
or like some of the other animals, and have traits that follows from the afore-
mentioned one and are compatible with it. But if we separate the first point
from these additions, and take it by itself (namely, that they thought the
primary substances to be gods), we must acknowledge that it is a god-like
utterance. . . . In any case, the beliefs of our forefathers and of our earliest

12. Reading ἐννέα for ἑπτά at 1074ᵃ13.

13. The use of *periechein*, used here to describe the relationship of the divine to the
whole of nature, should be compared to its use at *NE* I 2 1094ᵇ6, to describe the relationship of the end pursued by political science to that of the ends of all the crafts and
sciences subordinate to it.

predecessors is to this extent alone illuminating to us. (*Met.* XII 8 1074^{a}38–^{b}14; also *Met.* II 2 997^{b}8–12)

In saying that the heavenly bodies are divine, tradition got things right. In saying that they are like human beings or other animals, and all the rest that went along with this, it got them wrong. It should follow that supervision, too, is something we ought not anthropomorphize. What the gods—that is, the divine heavenly bodies—are said to exercise is not supervision plain and simple, after all, but [1] *tis epimeleia*—"supervision *of a sort.*"

Demythologize—deanthropomorphize—supervision, love, and benefit, and what you do *not* get is an eternal human being watching you from Heaven, loving you by benefiting you if you follow his laws, and punishing you if you don't. Instead what you get is an impassive object of understanding in the heavens, whose love consists in the benefit that is intrinsic to the life that, in having him as its object, is happiest, and, by immortalizing the one who lives it, is as much like his immortal life as a human life can be. In the case of the small-g gods, the story is, in one way, the same, since in imitating them, we imitate the God they imitate, and so become their beneficiaries too. Because these gods are the heavenly bodies, they are moving, as God himself is not, and so are starting-points of the various cyclical changes found in the sublunary realm, such as the seasons, and the cycles of fertility and infertility of land and animals (*GA* IV 10 778^{a}4–9). Hence these gods confer benefits of their own on all beings, but especially on those wise people who, through astronomical contemplation of the heavens, learn about these cycles, and adjust their lives accordingly.[14] Because the gods, when demythologized, just are the heavenly bodies, the science that deals with them is astronomy. Theology, on the other hand, deals not with them but with God. For theology deals exclusively with God, since it is both the science of God and God's own science.[15]

Immortalizing Friends

"The features typical of friendship for others," Aristotle argues, "and those by which the types of friendships are defined, seem to derive from friendship toward oneself," particularly, from the self-friendship or self-love of a

14. Compare David Sedley, "The Ideal of Godlikeness," in *Plato 2: Ethics, Politics, Religion, and the Soul*, ed. G. Fine (Oxford: Oxford University Press, 1991), pp. 309–328.

15. *Met.* I 2 983^{a}5–10, VI 1 1025^{b}25–1026^{a}11, VI 1 XI 7 1064^{a}28–^{b}3. Contrast Richard Bodéüs, *Aristotle and the Theology of Living Immortals* (Albany: State University of New York Press, 2000).

good or virtuous person, since he and his virtue constitute "a measure for the remaining types of friendships" (*NE* IX 4 1166ª1–13). In the following passage, these are the features under discussion:

[1] The virtuous person is uniformly considerate of himself and desires the same things with his entire soul. Hence he wishes good things and apparent good things for himself and does them in his actions (since it belongs to the good person to work hard for the good), and [does them] for his own sake (since he does them for the sake of his understanding, and this is precisely what each person seems to be). [2] Moreover, he wishes himself to live (*zēn*) and be preserved—his understanding most of all. For being is a good thing for the good person, and each person wishes for good things for himself, but no one chooses to become someone other than himself in order to have everything when the other comes-to-be.[16] [3] Even as things stand, indeed, *ho theos* has *tagathon*. [4] Rather, one chooses to have it while being whatever it is that one is, and each person would seem to be his active understanding or it most of all. . . . [5] The good person, then, has each of these features in relation to himself, and is related to his friend as he is to himself, since his friend is another himself. (*NE* IX 4 1166ª13–32)

If [3a] *ho theos* refers to God, and *tagathon* to *the* good (that is, happiness), Aristotle's thought is that no one would choose to have happiness or the good, and so be "in need of nothing" (*NE* I 7 1097ᵇ15), if he had to become God to get it.[17] This makes the transition in thought in [1–5] difficult to understand. For [3] is flanked by claims that we are most of all our understanding, which is the divine and immortal constituent in us. But if [3b] *ho theos* is our understanding, as it often is elsewhere (*NE* I 6 1096ª24–25, 12 1101ᵇ30), and *tagathon* is the good under discussion, that is, the ongoing life at issue in [2], then Aristotle's thought is more of a piece. The good person, to whom life is a good, wishes for good things *for himself*, and so wishes for his ongoing life to be preserved, since this is a condition of his having all these other good things. In other words, he wishes to become something at each next moment that, when it comes-to-be, will have those good things. If the something in question were other than himself, *its* having those things would not be a case of *his* having them. For as things stand, there is something in him that already has ongoing life (the good in question), namely, his own productive understanding, since it is an immortal and eternal life

16. Reading ἐκεῖνο τὸ γενόμενον with the ms.

17. [3a] is defended by Michael Pakaluk, *Aristotle: Nicomachean Ethics, Books VIII and IX* (Oxford: Clarendon Press, 1980), pp. 171–172, as by all other commentators.

process. Moreover, active understanding isn't something other than himself, since it is what he is or is most of all.[18]

While [3b] has obvious merits, it may seem difficult to reconcile with a related passage:

> When a great disparity in virtue, vices, or resources, or something else arises . . . people are no longer friends, and do not even expect to be. This is most evident in the case of the gods, since they are maximally superior in all good things. But it is also clear in the case of kings, since people who are much needier do not expect to be their friends, nor do worthless people expect to be friends with the best or the wisest. Now there is no rigorous way of defining in such cases up to what point people can remain friends. For even if one of them loses a lot, the friendship still endures, but if the separation is very wide, as in the case of God (*to theou*), that is no longer possible. [6] Hence the puzzle arises as to whether friends might really not wish their friends to have the greatest goods, to be gods, for example, since they will no longer be friends to them, and so not good things either, since friends are good things. [7] If, then, we were right to say that one friend wishes good things to another for the other's own sake, the other should remain whatever sort of thing he is. It is for a human being, then, that he will wish the greatest goods. [8] But presumably not all of them; for it is to himself most of all that each person wishes good things. (*NE* VIII 7 1158^{b}33–1159^{a}12)

The preamble sets up the puzzle in [6]. If we wished the greatest goods to our friends, we would wish them to become gods. But then, as the preamble has argued, they will [6a] be too distant from us and other human beings to have friends, which will deprive them of "the greatest of external goods," since that is just what friends are (*NE* IX 9 1169^{b}9–10). Alternatively, [6b] in depriving ourselves of their friendship, we will deprive *ourselves* of the greatest external goods. Both interpretations are in some sense possible, but [6b] is perhaps more plausible, since the puzzle is one about whether friends really wish to their friends the greatest goods that they wish to themselves— friendship itself being one of these.[19] The interpretation of [6] is a relatively minor issue in any case.

---

18. On this way of understanding the argument in [1–4], it is structurally similar to part of the argument between Socrates and Diotima in Plato's *Symposium*, the gist of which is this: we desire good things, because we believe that through them we will be happy, so, since we desire to be happy always, we desire those good things to be ours forever, and so desire our own eternally ongoing existence (204d–206a).

19. As Irwin, *Aristotle: Nicomachean Ethics*, p. 280, argues.

As we might expect, the solution to the puzzle concedes something to both sides of it. Thus [7] points out that it is to our friend *as a human being* that we wish the greatest goods, which excludes the possibility of wishing him to become a god. It is this that makes [3a] seem like the correct interpretation of [3]. For [5] the good person is related to himself as he is to his friend, so if he can only wish good things to his friend as a human being, he can only wish them to himself as one. To see this as the end of the story, however, is to omit the other side of the solution expressed in [8]. [8] might seem at first to mean [8a] there are some greatest goods that the good man does not wish to his friend. But that conflicts with [5], since the good man will wish some greatest goods to himself that he will not wish to his friend, and so his friend will not be a second himself after all. What [8] must mean, therefore, is that [8b] there are some greatest goods that the good man does not wish to his friend *as a human being*, but as the thing he most of all is, namely, [1–4] his immortal and divine understanding—this being the way he wishes good things most of all to himself. So the one who raises the puzzle is partly right and partly wrong. He is right in thinking that there are some greatest goods that a good man does not wish to his friend as a human being, but wrong in thinking that there are therefore some greatest goods that he doesn't wish to his friend at all. Hence no violation of the nature of friendship is involved. Since this solution offers no support for [3a], it leaves us free to accept [3b].

"The theoretically wise person is able," Aristotle says, "and more able the wiser he is, to contemplate even by himself," and so is "most self-sufficient"; nonetheless "he will do it better, presumably, if he has collaborators" (*NE* X 7 1177ª32–1177ᵇ1). In following Aristotle's injunction to do everything to immortalize *ourselves* by engaging in contemplation of God, therefore, we find ourselves also required to do everything to immortalize our contemplative philosophical collaborators, or to help them immortalize themselves:

> Whatever it is that for each sort of person constitutes his being, or the end for which he chooses to live (*zên*), that is what he wishes to spend his time doing in company with his friends. Hence some drink together, some play dice, others train together, hunt together, or philosophize together. . . . The friendship of inferior people, therefore, turns out to have bad effects (since, not being possessed of a stable character, they share inferior pursuits and become bad through becoming like one another), but that of good people is good, and increases through their association. And they seem to become even better through being active and correcting one another. For each molds the other in what they approve of—hence the saying, "From excellent people, excellent things come." (*NE* IX 12 1172ª1–14)

The debt we owe to "those who have shared philosophy with us" is so great, indeed, that it is like the one we owe to "gods and parents" (*NE* IX 1 1164^{b}2–6). For of the various activities human beings might share, "what seems to count as [really] living together is sharing in conversations and thoughts" (*NE* IX 9 1170^{b}11–12). It is among contemplative collaborators, therefore, that the very best kind of friendship is found. That is the point of saying that it is the good man, who "awards the noblest things and the ones that are most good to himself, and gratifies the constituent in himself with most control, obeying it in everything," (*NE* IX 8 1168^{b}28–31), that serves as the measure for all the other types of friendship, namely, those based on mutual utility or mutual pleasure (*NE* VIII 3). For he alone of all the types of friends wishes what are really good things to his friend for the sake of what the friend really is, namely, a fully human being—a divine eternal understanding.

7

HAPPINESS

Almost everyone agrees that the "highest of all practical goods" is called *eudaimonia*, and that living well (*to eu zên*) and doing well are the same as being *eudaimôn*, but they disagree about what *eudaimonia* is (*NE* I 4 1095ª14–22). The majority think it is pleasure, and so consider "the life of gratification" to be the best one (*NE* I 5 1095ᵇ16–17). "Sophisticated people and men of action," on the other hand, see honor as *eudaimonia*, hence they think the political life is best, since honor is pretty much its end or goal (*NE* I 5 1095ᵇ22–23). Finally, there is the contemplative life, of which Aristotle says only that it is the one "we shall examine in what follows" (*NE* I 5 1096ª4–5). The other lives, in any case, seem to be quickly rejected by appeal to a few fairly simple considerations. The life of gratification is "fit only for cattle" (*NE* I 5 1095ᵇ20) and merits inclusion on the list of putatively *eudaimôn* lives only because pleasure is at least liked for itself (*NE* I 5 1096ª7). Since money doesn't share this feature, the life of making money is a nonstarter for inclusion (*NE* I 5 1096ª5–7). Similarly, honor, though it is liked for itself, is dismissed as "too superficial" to be *eudaimonia*, because "we divine that the good is something of our own and difficult to take from us" (*NE* I 5 1095ᵇ25–26). Even when virtue rather than honor is conceived as its end, indeed, so that it *is* something of our own and difficult to take away, the political life is still rejected, on the grounds that virtue is "too incomplete to be the good, since it seems possible to possess virtue, yet be asleep or inactive throughout life, and, in addition, to suffer the worst evils and strokes of bad luck" (*NE* I 5 1095ᵇ31–1096ª1; also I 8 1098ᵇ30–1099ª7).

The fact that people generally agree that whatever the best good is, the term *eudaimonia* applies to it, shows that the term has a meaning or nominal definition that is relatively uncontroversial. A plausible candidate is "what all by itself makes a life choiceworthy and in need of nothing" (*NE* I 7 1097ᵇ14–15), since this explains why the three candidate *eudaimôn* lives have different goals or ends, in that each takes a different thing to be what makes a life entirely choiceworthy. Moreover, it also explains why advocates of the different lives disagree: "people, not unreasonably, reach their conception of the good—that is, of *eudaimonia*—from their lives" (*NE* I 5 1095[b]14–16). It is by living in a certain way, after all, that we acquire the habits of being pained and pleased that shape our conception of what makes a life choiceworthy. That is why, indeed, only someone brought up in noble habits has access to the correct starting-points of ethics and political science (*NE* I 4 1095[b]2–8).

Etymologically, the word *eudaimonia* means having a good (*eu*) spirit (*daimôn*), a guardian angel, as we might say.[1] Thus Socrates uses the term *to daimonion* to refer to the voice or sign that restrained him if he was about to do something ill-advised (Plato, *Apology* 40a). Moreover, this voice or sign is clearly something quite distinct from his own reason or conscience, since it gives him advice that is prophetic rather than prudential in nature. When he is about to leave the dressing room at the gymnasium, for example, it holds him back, apparently so that he won't miss the chance to have a conversation with people who show up later (Plato, *Euthydemus* 272e–273a). By the time Plato writes the *Timaeus*, however, a *daimôn* has become the divine rational constituent in the human soul:

> Now concerning the kind of soul found in us that has the most control, we must think the following: God has given it to each of us as a *daimôn*, the thing we say has its home in the topmost part of our body, and raises us up away from the earth toward what is akin to us in the heavens, as though we were a heavenly plant, not an earthly one, as we rightly put it. For it is from the heavens, the place from which our soul was first born that the divine suspends our head, that is, our root, and so keeps our whole body upright. (90a–b)

Aristotle, too, locates divine understanding in the head, and analogizes the roots of a plant to an animal's head, so that the plant itself becomes an upside-down animal (*PA* IV 10 686[a]25–687[a]2, *DA* II 4 416[a]2–5).[2] But our understanding, though divine in origin and loved by the gods, is not prophetic, even if it can help us plan for the future (*DA* III 10 433[b]5–10).

1. A point made by David Bostock, *Aristotle's Ethics* (Oxford: Oxford University Press, 2000), p. 11.

2. David Sedley, *Creationism and Its Critics* (Berkeley: University of California Press, 2007), pp. 167–204, explores the relationship between Aristotle and Plato on this topic and on teleology more generally.

As its nominal definition perhaps suggests, "happiness" is an imperfect translation of *eudaimonia*. For even though our own conception of happiness is unsettled and disputed, being happy seems to be a favorable emotional state or state of feeling. If someone emotionally endorses his life, so that he is cheerful or joyful rather than sad, is engaged in it, so that he is absorbed by it rather than bored or alienated, and is attuned to it, so that he is relaxed rather than anxious or stressed—or is these things more than their opposites—he is arguably happy.[3]

Though those who think that *eudaimonia* is pleasure come close in some ways to thinking of it as we think of happiness, hedonistic theories of happiness are nonetheless controversial. One can be unhappy even if one is regularly experiencing pleasures; an intense pleasure, such as orgasm, need not make one very happy; and being in constant pain is not the same as being unhappy, although it can, of course, be a source of unhappiness. Those who think the *eudaimôn* life is the political life or the contemplative one, because they think that being honored or contemplating God is what *eudaimonia* consists in, seem yet further away from thinking of them as *happy* lives. For nothing about these lives seems to ensure that those who live them or live them well or excellently will necessarily be in a favorable emotional state. An excellent political scientist or philosopher, it seems, can be sad, alienated, or anxious. Worthwhile lives these may be, but a life can be worthwhile without being happy.

Aristotle's own account of *eudaimonia* avoids some of these problems of fit with happiness, in part because it intentionally incorporates elements of other views about it. For these, simply because of their appeal to the many or the wise, count as *endoxa* about *eudaimonia*, which sound dialectical or aporematic methodology must respect. Having developed a sketch of his account, Aristotle adverts to this:

> All the things that people look for in *eudaimonia* appear to have been included in our account. For to some *eudaimonia* seems to be virtue, to others practical wisdom, to others some sort of theoretical wisdom, while to still others it seems to be [a combination of] these, involving pleasure or not without pleasure, while others include external prosperity as well. Some of these views are held by many and are of long standing, while others are held by a few reputable men; and it is reasonable to suppose not that either group is entirely wrong but that they are right on one point at least, or even on most points. (*NE* I 8 1098^b22–29)

3. Daniel M. Haybron, *The Pursuit of Unhappiness: The Elusive Psychology of Well-Being* (Oxford: Oxford University Press, 2008), pp. 79–81.

As a result, he sees it as an important strength of his account of *eudaimonia* as activity in accord with the best and most complete virtue that it makes pleasure intrinsic to the *eudaimôn* life: "The things that are pleasant to most people conflict, because they are not pleasant by nature, whereas to lovers of the noble the things that are pleasant *are* pleasant by nature. That is what actions in accord with the virtues are like, so that they are pleasant both to such people and intrinsically. So their life does not need pleasure to be added like some ornament tied on to it, on the contrary, it has its pleasure within itself" (*NE* I 8 1099ª11–16). Although he is not equally explicit that his account also incorporates such truth as there is in the view of those who make *eudaimonia* reside in honor, the virtue of character that attracts it, and the practical wisdom that goes along with it, or in theoretical wisdom, he is explicit that any adequate account would have to do so. In any case, his own two-tiered conception—consisting of incomplete *eudaimonia* (activity in accord with full virtue of character) for the sake of complete *eudaimonia* (activity in accord with theoretical wisdom)—does seem designed to meet this adequacy condition.

Since the Aristotelian *eudaimôn* life is intrinsically pleasant or enjoyable, it is plausibly seen as cheerful or joyful, especially since, as in accord with correct reason, whether deliberative or architectonic, it would seem to be reflectively endorsed by the agent in a way that these emotions evidence. For the same reason, the *eudaimôn* person seems unlikely to be bored, alienated, or anxious about living the life he has been trained and habituated to live and has chosen as best. Although *eudaimonia* is an activity, not a favorable emotional state, it wouldn't be *eudaimonia* if it did not involve such a state by being the activity of it. In this regard, *eudaimonia* is like the simple pleasures it may at times involve—pleasant and valuable in part because evoking desire. Nonetheless, the activity in which *eudaimonia* consists is relatively more important than the enjoyment of it, since it is better to do the noble things the virtuous person does, even if it makes one sad, bored, and anxious (as might be true of the continent person), than to do something else that inspires the opposite feelings (as might be true of the incontinent one). For Aristotelian *eudaimonia*, the noble activity counts for more than the emotional state it evokes in the agent. That is why Aristotle cites with approval the words of Hesiod: "Best of all is the one who understands everything himself, but decent, too, who listens to the good counsel of other people" (*NE* I 4 1095ᵇ10–11).

Because happiness does consist in a favorable emotional state, what evokes it can vary from person to person, and—arguably—the person himself or herself is the final authority on its existence: if a person feels happy, he is happy. These, too, are important points of difference with Aristotelian *eudaimonia*. A further difference seems more important still. When we say that someone is happy, we describe his life in psychological terms. We don't, in the relevant sense, evaluate it. A happy life needn't be successful or accomplished or admirable. It needn't, as we say, amount to much. The very modest can be very happy, while the driven, the brilliant, the heroic, the creative, and even the saintly may have a much harder time of it. Children can be happy, dogs too, it seems, but neither can be *eudaimôn*. Aristotelian *eudaimonia* includes a large perfectionist element, in other words, that happiness seems to lack. *Eudaimonia* may all by itself make a life *worth* living and in need of nothing; happiness cannot change a sow's ear of a life into a silk purse of one.

In some respects, then, Aristotelian *eudaimonia* might be better translated as "well-being" or "flourishing"—although it would seem strange to worry about whether one should wait to say that someone was flourishing until he was dead (compare *NE* I 10–11). One advantage of "happiness" over these alternatives, in any case, is precisely that it highlights the importance of a favorable emotional state—of endorsement and engagement—to the *eudaimôn* life. What in addition is required is that what evokes that emotional state should *be* the best good for a human being—a kind of active living in accord with virtue in which the state is realized and expressed.

Telic Hierarchies

The discussion leading to the identification of happiness with the end or target aimed at by political science (and so by practical wisdom) begins with a reputable belief or *endoxon* (signaled by *dokein*):

> [1] Every craft and every line of inquiry (*methodos*) and likewise every action and deliberate choice is believed (*dokei*) to seek (*ephiesthai*) some good; that is why [2] people did well to assert that the good is "that which all things seek (*ephietai*)." (*NE* I 1 1094a1–3; also X 2 1172b36–1173a2)

According to [1], four different endeavors seek a good, just as medicine, for example, seeks health (*NE* I 1 1094a8). [2] concludes that the good is what everything—that is, all such endeavors—seek.

> [3] A certain difference, however, appears to exist among ends; for some are activities, while some are results of some sort in addition to the activities

themselves. [4] But wherever there are ends in addition to the activities, in those cases the results are by nature better than the activities. (*NE* I 1 1094ᵃ3–6)

Since for one end to be *better* than another it must be a better good, [4] entails that the ends mentioned in [1] are goods, and [3] entails that the good mentioned in [2] is either an activity or the additional end of one. On the assumption that this good is better than any other good, and so the best one (confirmed at *NE* I 2 1094ᵃ22), [4] entails that it must be a *terminal* activity (that is, one with no additional choiceworthy end) or the additional end of a *nonterminal* activity. But if that additional end were itself a nonterminal activity, it could not be the best good, since [4] its own additional end would be better than it is. Either it must be a terminal activity, therefore, or not an activity of any sort.

An obvious objection to [1–2] is that it does not follow from the fact that every endeavor pursues a good that there is a good every endeavor pursues. The next sentences begin an implicit response:

[5] Since there are many sorts of actions, and of crafts and sciences, their ends turn out to be many as well; for health is the end of medicine, a ship of shipbuilding, victory of generalship, wealth of household management. [6] But some of these fall under some one potentiality (*dunamin*), as bridle making falls under horsemanship, along with all the others that produce equipment for horsemanship, and as it and every action in warfare fall under generalship—and, in the same way, others fall under different ones, and [7] in all such cases the ends of the architectonic ones are more choiceworthy than the ones falling under them, since [8] these are pursued for the sake also of the former. (*NE* I 1 1094ᵃ6–16)

The existence of hierarchies among ends, or *telic hierarchies,* holds out the possibility, then, that [1–2] could be true, even in face of the fact, acknowledged in [5], that different endeavors have different ends (compare *NE* I 7 1097ᵃ15–24).

When [1–2] is reprised, it is stated more simply: "every sort of knowledge (*gnôsis*) and deliberate choice pursues some good" (*NE* I 4 1095ᵃ14–15). This suggests that the endeavors mentioned in [1–8] can all be classed as types of knowledge (sciences) on the one hand or as cases of action or deliberate choice on the other. Since both have in common that they seek the good, that is, the "human good" (*NE* I 2 1094ᵇ7), the actions referred to in [1] seem to be ones that, because they are deliberately chosen by wise or rational agents (*NE* III 3 1112ᵃ19–21), are subject to the norms and principles of the sciences.

These sciences, therefore, must be *choice-relevant*. This could be because they are practical or productive sciences, which are intrinsically relevant to choice, or because they are natural or theoretical sciences, relevant to it in that or some other possible coincidental way. The examples given in [1–8] suggest the former; the description at [17–21] suggests the latter.

A science can be thought of either as an abstract body of knowledge (a structure of propositions) or—on the model of a skill or craft—as a potentiality someone has. Aristotle's use of the term *dunamis* in [6] suggests that he is thinking of them—as he usually does (*NE* VI 3 1139^{b}15–17)—as potentialities, and so as things that can be dormant (as in someone who is not currently exercising his science) or active (as in someone who is exercising it). Since the term usually used to refer to an active potentiality is *energeia* (*NE* I 7 1098^{a}5–6), the contrast drawn in [3] is almost certainly that between the case where the action—considered as the actualization of a potentiality or an activity—is the end (terminal activity) and the case where that action, though perhaps also an end, results in some additional end (nonterminal activity).

If [8] implies that whenever *a* is pursued for the sake of *b*, *b* is more choiceworthy than *a*, it provides no support for [7]: we can listen to Bach's French Suites for the sheer enjoyment of it, and for the sake of the relaxation it causes, although (as we may also believe) the enjoyment is more choiceworthy than the relaxation. So presumably [8] is to be understood in a more restrictive way, as applying only to cases in which the *b* for whose sake we pursue *a* is above *a* in a telic hierarchy. The sort of hierarchy envisaged in [6–7] isn't generated, then, whenever *a* is pursued for the sake of *b*, which can be a chance or circumstantial matter, but is rather something objective—something fixed by the concepts or natures of the constituents of the hierarchy. It is because bridle making is the very craft it is that it is subordinate to horsemanship, with the result that its end (good bridles) is less choiceworthy than the latter's (well-trained horses). This helps explain why [4] speaks of a higher end in such a hierarchy as "by nature" better than any below it.

Although [8] might seem to apply only to cases in which *a* has an additional end, the next sentence extends its scope beyond them:

[9] And it makes no difference whether the activities themselves are the ends of the actions or [10] some other thing in addition to them, just as in the sciences we have mentioned. (*NE* I 1 1094^{a}16–18)

[9–10] reprises [3], distinguishing between cases [9] in which the action, considered as the result of activating a choice-relevant potentiality or science, is the end (terminal activity) and [10] cases in which the action or activity has some additional end (nonterminal activity). But because a terminal activity has no further end, it must be the apex of any hierarchy in which it occurs. Since [3] some ends are terminal activities, it follows that some hierarchies of ends must have terminal activities at their apexes that are better and more choiceworthy goods than anything else below them. But if there is to be a unique good, which is better or more worthy of choice than *absolutely any other*, it isn't enough that choice-relevant sciences and the rest form telic hierarchies. In addition, all of them must form a single such hierarchy, at the apex of which is a unique science whose end or goal is—as [7] asserts—better or more choiceworthy than any of those below it. Since this hierarchy must contain terminal activities, the end or goal in question must be a terminal activity.

A new chapter begins at this juncture,[4] but the argument itself seems to make more sense, as we shall see, if it is treated as continuing:

> [11] If, then, there is some end of things done in action that we wish for because of itself, but the others because of it, and [12] we do not choose everything because of something else—for [13] if *that* is the case, it will go on without limit, so that the desire will be *kenon* and *mataion*—[14] it is clear that this will be the good, that is to say, the best one. (*NE* I 2 1094ª18–23)

A *non*terminating desire—which is a desire for *a* because of *b*, for *b* because of *c*, and so on—will, [13] says, be *kenon* and *mataion*. Like their English counterparts "empty" and "vain," these terms are somewhat vague. The primary meaning of the former is that of being like an empty cup or vessel. In Plato's *Republic*, as elsewhere, it is thus readily applied to desires: "hunger, thirst, and the like are some sort of emptiness related to the state of the body"; "lack of knowledge and lack of wisdom" are "some sort of emptiness related to the state of the soul" (IX 585a–b). Presumably, then, a *kenon* desire is one that, as (always) empty, cannot be satisfied, which is just what a nonterminating desire seems to be like. None of this implies, of course, that a desire cannot be *kenon*, but only that one that is *kenon* comes at a high enough cost to raise a question about the rationality of acting on it. It is this fact that lays the ground for *mataion*, the primary connotation of which is foolish or without reason—vain. Thus it is *mataion* for a young person to study a practical science like ethics or political science, since he tends to fol-

---

4. Chapter divisions, which do not go back to antiquity, reflect the views of editors and interpreters.

low his feelings, not what he will learn by studying it (*NE* I 4 1095ᵃ5). If this is how we are to understand [13], it seems obvious that all it entails is—as [12] seems to say—that there must be some end (though not necessarily only one) we do not desire because of something else but (implicitly) because of itself. If [11–14] is supposed to be an independent argument for the existence of the good, then, it is not a compelling one. The question is, is it any more compelling if we see it as continuing the argument of [1–10]?

Suppose that the sphere mentioned in [11] of things done in action is the one within which some of the choice-relevant sciences operate. The end we [11] wish for or [12] choose or [13] desire *because of itself,* and not (lest our desire be nonterminating) because of anything else, will then be [3] a terminal activity or an additional end of a non-terminal one that is not itself an activity. Suppose that [11] this end is also such that we choose all the others we wish for or desire because of it; then [14] will follow at once. That is what [1–10] adds to [11–14]. What [11–14] adds to [1–10] is a solution to the problem of how to fit terminal activities into telic hierarchies—a solution that, in turn, gives us a tighter grip on the good. If a terminal activity is worthy of choice at all, it must be solely because of itself, since, unlike a nonterminal activity, it is not choiceworthy because of any additional end. While things coming under it in a hierarchy may be choiceworthy because of it, it cannot be choiceworthy because of anything above it. Consequently, as we saw, it must be the apex of any hierarchy in which it occurs. Put the other way around, if anything is the apex of such a hierarchy, it must be a terminal activity. It follows that if, as [11] proposes, the good is such an apex, it must be a terminal activity.

While this is no doubt a significant result, it still presupposes rather than proves that there is such a thing as *the* good, and not rather a variety of goods, each the apex of a distinct telic hierarchy. The next sentences seem to share in that presupposition:

[15] So regarding our life, too, won't knowing it [the good] have great weight and, like archers with a target, won't we be better able to hit what we should? If so, then we should try to grasp in outline at least what it is and to which of the sciences or potentialities it belongs. [16] It would seem to belong to the one with the most control, that is, the most architectonic one. (*NE* I 2 1094ᵃ23–27)

But it is also possible, and perhaps likely, that [15] remains under the umbrella of the "if" in [11]: *if* there is something choiceworthy in the way [11] specifies, it will be the good and will be important to know about. The good's status, in other words, may still be hypothetical. Nonetheless, *if* it exists, it must belong to—or be the proper end of—a choice-relevant science, and so must be subject to the conclusions reached in [1–10].

By identifying the most architectonic choice-relevant science as the one with the most control, [16] paves the way for the good's further specification:

> And [17] political science seems to be like this, since [18] it is the one that prescribes which of the sciences there should be in cities, and which ones each class in the city should learn, and up to what point; indeed, we see that even the most estimable potentialities are under it—for example, generalship, household management, and rhetoric; and since [19] it uses the other practical sciences,[5] and moreover legislates about what [actions] should be done and what avoided, [20] its end will *periechein* those of the others, so that [21] it will be the human good. (*NE* I 2 1094[a]27–[b]7)[6]

The primary connotation of the verb *periechein*, which is a compound of the preposition *peri* ("around") and the verb *echein* ("have," "possess"), is that of containing by surrounding. So if that were its meaning in [20], the human good would have to contain all the other goods subordinate to it.[7] But it is hard to see how this can be its meaning. For what entails that the end of a science S_1 *periechein* the end of a science S_2 is simply that S_2 falls under S_1 in a telic hierarchy—or, equivalently, that S_1 is more architectonic than S_2. Thus, while political science may be the *most* architectonic science, generalship is also architectonic, since [6] it is higher in a telic hierarchy than horsemanship, which is itself higher than bridle making. Yet generalship's end—victory—does not seem to contain either trained horses or their bridles, any more than health, which is medicine's end and a certain bodily condition, contains medical instruments, medical treatment, or drugs.

Just as "contain" can also mean "circumscribe" or "limit," as in the doctrine of containment familiar from the Cold War, so too can *periechein*. [20] could mean, then, that political science's end *limits* or circumscribes the ends of all the choice-relevant sciences, including those of the other

---

5. Reading ταῖς λοιπαῖς πρακτικαῖς.

6. *Met.* I 2 982[b]4–7 uses a parallel argument to show that theoretical wisdom "knows that for the sake of which each thing should be done, and this is the good of each of them, and in general the best good in all of nature."

7. A view defended in J. L. Ackrill, "Aristotle on *Eudaimonia*," *Proceedings of the British Academy* 60 (1974): 339–359, and subsequently adopted by many writers.

practical sciences and of actions.[8] This idea seems to fit nicely with the account given in [18–19] of what political science does. By looking to its own end, it sets limits to which sciences should be in cities, to which groups should practice them and to what degree, and to what actions should be done and what avoided. It is when we try to give [7] the purchase on [20] necessary for [21] to follow from it that we run into a problem, since it is unclear why a limiting end of this sort would have to be [14] the best or [21] human good. Other people's rights, for example, may set absolute limits to our pursuit of happiness, and so be limiting ends, but it isn't obvious that respecting their rights is the *best* good. What is required in addition is that what imposes the limit should itself be—as the human good is—an end that all other ends further, so that it is a better good than they.[9] Apparently, then, [20–21] simply recapitulates what has already been stated by [14] and implied by [7].

When [20–21] is understood in this deflationary fashion, the evidence [17–19] provides for the existence of the good, and so for the antecedent of the conditional [11–14], is somewhat weak, since it presupposes the existence of a unique maximally architectonic science. The *existence* of the good, however, seems to be something Aristotle took to be already conceded, since pretty much everyone agrees, he thinks, about what the good is called (*NE* I 4 1095^{a}14–22). Hence [1–21] is probably intended less to establish the existence of the good than to establish its relationship to political science. The sequel confirms this:

> [22] If indeed for its part the good is the same for an individual human being and for a city, [23] that of a city is apparently a greater and more complete one, at any rate, to acquire and preserve; for while it would certainly be satisfactory enough to do this for an individual human being alone, it is nobler and more godlike to do so for a nation and city. [24] And so our line of inquiry (*methodos*) seeks (*ephietai*) [the good] of these things, being a sort of political science. (*NE* I 2 1094^{b}7–11)

The noun *methodos* and the verb *ephienai* in [24], both used in [1–2], indicate that the argument has come full circle, suggesting that its goal has been to characterize the line of inquiry that the *Nicomachean Ethics* will pursue, and to identify ethics as a choice-relevant science, which, as a sort of political

---

8. An interpretation proposed in Richard Kraut, *Aristotle on the Human Good* (Princeton: Princeton University Press, 1989), pp. 220–227.

9. Compare the use of *periechein* at *Met.* XII 8 1074^{b}3.

science, shares the latter's architectonic status. Nonetheless, the argument also helps us better understand what the good or happiness is. It is a terminal activity that, as the end of the maximally architectonic science of politics, is the apex of the unique telic hierarchy that includes all other choiceworthy ends or goods.

Telic Completeness, Self-Sufficiency, and Choiceworthiness

The notion of the *completeness* of an end or good is introduced as follows:

> [1] Something pursued as an intrinsic end is more complete, we say, than an end pursued because of something else, and [2] an end that is never choiceworthy because of something else is more complete than ends that are choiceworthy both intrinsically and because of this end, while [3] what is unconditionally complete is what is always intrinsically choiceworthy and never choiceworthy because of something else. (*NE* I 7 1097^{a}30–34)

[1] explains the notion of completeness in terms of choiceworthiness or worthiness of pursuit, and so of goodness. If E_1 is choiceworthy for its own sake, while E_2 is so because of some other end, then E_1 must be higher in political science's hierarchy of ends or goods than E_2. Hence achieving E_2 must be the best means to achieving E_1. Achieving E_1, then, involves already having achieved E_2, whereas the converse does not hold. In an obvious sense, then, E_2 must be less complete than E_1, since it is a *part* of achieving E_1. That is why the very existence of incomplete ends is made clear by the fact that some ends are means to others: "Though apparently there are many ends, we choose some of them—for example, wealth, flutes, and instruments generally—because of something else; hence it is clear that not all ends are complete" (*NE* I 7 1097^{a}25–27).

The case described in [2] involves an end E_1 that—while choiceworthy—is never worth choosing for the sake of something else, and an end E_2 that is choiceworthy both for its own sake and for the sake of E_1. Here E_2 is less complete than E_1, since E_1 must be higher in political science's hierarchy of ends than E_2, so that achieving E_1 again has achieving E_2 as a part. The end described in [3], since it is always worth choosing for its own sake, but never for the sake of something else, must be the topmost good in the hierarchy, and so, for parallel reasons, must be the most complete one. Since this topmost good is happiness, it follows that happiness must be the most complete of goods: "the best end or good is evidently something complete, so that if one thing alone is complete, it will be the good we are looking for, and if more than one, the most complete of them" (*NE* I 7 1097^{a}28–30).

As completeness is allied with the telic hierarchy introduced by the identification of happiness with the end of political science, so telic *self-sufficiency* or the self-sufficiency of an end is allied with completeness: "The same conclusion [that happiness is the best good] also appears to follow from considerations of self-sufficiency, since the complete good seems to be self-sufficient. . . . We take what is self-sufficient to be what all by itself makes a life (*bion*) choiceworthy and in need of nothing, and we think happiness is like this" (*NE* I 7 1097^{b}6–16). Now the sort of human life a self-sufficient end or good makes choiceworthy and in need of nothing might be *some* particular sort of human life or *any* sort of human life at all. That it must be a human life of a particular sort becomes clear later on when complete happiness is identified with contemplation in accord with theoretical wisdom (*NE* X 7 1177^{a}16–17). For once that identification is made, Aristotle goes on to say that happiness "will also need external prosperity, since we are human beings; for our nature is not self-sufficient for contemplation, but needs bodily health too, and the availability of food and other kinds of service" (*NE* X 8 1178^{b}33–35). The implicit contrast is with some other beings whose nature *is* self-sufficient for contemplation, and so for complete happiness. These beings, not surprisingly, are the gods, whose lives consist essentially in the activity of contemplation alone, and so are self-sufficient for it (*Met.* XII 7 1072^{b}26–27, 9 1074^{b}34–35). In order for happiness all by itself to make a *human* life choiceworthy and in need of nothing, that life needs other things:

> Happiness obviously also needs external goods to be added . . . , since we cannot or cannot easily do noble actions without resources. For in many actions, we use friends, wealth, and political power, just as we do instruments. Besides, deprivation of some things—such as high birth, good children, beauty—mars our blessedness, since we do not altogether have the stamp of happiness if we are terribly ugly, of low birth, solitary, or childless, and have it still less, presumably, if our children or friends are thoroughly bad, or good but dead. (*NE* I 8 1099^{a}31–^{b}6)

Moreover, the life must last long enough to count as complete, since "one swallow does not make a summer, nor does one day; nor, similarly, does one day or a short time make us blessed and happy" (*NE* I 7 1098^{a}18–20).

When the happiness in question is of the incomplete or second best sort constituted by activity in accord with practical wisdom and the virtues of character (*NE* X 8 1178^{a}9–23), its dependence on external goods is quite substantial. When it is of the very best sort, constituted by contemplation in accord with theoretical wisdom, its dependence on them is much less. That is why contemplation is more self-sufficient than practical activity and has a better claim to be complete happiness than practical activity (*NE* X 7 1177ª12–27). Where lifespan is concerned, on the other hand, contemplation and practical activity are in the same boat. That is why a human being's complete happiness will be contemplation, only if the contemplation "receives a complete span of life, since nothing incomplete belongs to happiness" (*NE* X 7 1177ᵇ25–26).

An end's *choiceworthiness* is so related to its self-sufficiency that each illuminates the other: "We think that it [happiness] is the most choiceworthy of all goods, not counted together with others—counted together with others it would clearly be more choiceworthy with even the least of goods, since what is added becomes an increase of goods, and the larger of two goods is always more choiceworthy" (*NE* I 7 1097ᵇ16–20; also *NE* X 2 1172ᵇ28–32). Because contemplation that receives a complete span of life is self-sufficient, it can all by itself make a human life choiceworthy and in need of nothing, without the aid of even the least additional good. Eternal contemplation can make the life of the gods that way, after all, and their life consists entirely of it. To be sure, a human *life* needs to be augmented with external goods if it is to be apt for such happiness, but the *happiness itself* needs nothing. If the addition to it of even the least good increased its choiceworthiness, and so that of the life to which it was added, this would not be so. Hence it must already be the most choiceworthy end or good.

Two Types of Happiness

When Aristotle specifically reengages with happiness, he compares theoretical wisdom to practical wisdom to see which is best and most complete. The criteria of completeness, self-sufficiency, and so on, used as aids to finding the definition of happiness, are now redeployed for this new purpose, as are other similar criteria that have emerged in the subsequent discussion. The virtue of understanding, which is our best and most divine constituent and the one with which we are most of all to be identified, is theoretical wisdom (*NE* X 7 1178ª2–8). Activity in accord with it is the most continuous one of which we are capable, also the most pleasant, the most self-sufficient, the most leisured, and the only one choiceworthy for itself alone (*NE* X 7 1177ª19–ᵇ4). Practical wisdom (which involves the virtues of character), by contrast, is the virtue of the merely human compound of body and soul (or deliberative part and desiring part), and one with which it would be absurd to identify (*NE* X 7 1178ª3–4). Activity in accord with it is not the most continuous activity of which we are capable, nor the most pleasant, nor, since it needs many external goods, the most self-sufficient, nor the most leisured, since the politics and wars within which it occurs are trouble zones, nor choiceworthy for itself alone, since we engage in it also for the sake of an additional end. Thus theoretical wisdom emerges as the best virtue (*NE* X 7 1177ᵃ13), and activity in accord with it, provided it receives a complete span of life, as complete happiness (*NE* X 7 1177ᵇ24–26).

Because contemplation is complete happiness, practical wisdom, in prescribing with the aim of furthering happiness, must prescribe for its sake (*NE* VI 13 1145ᵃ6–9) and with something like its maximization in view, since "the more someone engages in contemplation, the happier he is, not coincidentally but in accord with his contemplating" (*NE* X 8 1178ᵇ29–31). Unlike a god, however, a human being needs friends and other external goods if he is to have a happy life; he cannot survive on a diet of contemplation alone (*NE* X 8 1178ᵇ33–35). Hence "insofar as someone is human, and so lives together with a number of other human beings, he chooses to do the actions that are in accord with virtue [of character]" (*NE* X 8 1178ᵇ5–7). These actions are prescribed by the most architectonic practical science, after all, and so are the ones that best further his contemplative goal. Besides, they contribute directly to the happiness of life: "the life in accord with the other kind of virtue [practical wisdom and virtue of character] is happiest in a secondary way, because the activities in accord with this virtue are merely human" (*NE* X 7–8 1178ᵃ9–10).

To be practical wisdom, then, a state of the calculative or deliberative part of the soul must be appropriately correlated with virtue of character and must have something like the maximization of contemplation as its end or target. Although, in its architectonic form as political science, this state has control over all the crafts and sciences, other factors relevant to its goal are largely matters of luck: "some goods must be there to start with, whereas others must be provided by the legislator. That is why we pray that our city will be ideally equipped with the [external] goods that luck controls, since we assume that luck does control them" (*Pol.* VII 13 1332ᵃ28–31). Even if such prayers are answered, blight and famine, plague and earthquake, bellicose neighbors may leave little or no time for contemplation, and so can prevent practical wisdom from achieving its goal. What they cannot so readily prevent is the exercise of practical wisdom itself, or the incomplete happiness it constitutes. A virtuous person may not be blessed or happy if luck deals him a sufficiently savage blow, but he won't be wretched either, since he will avoid the vice in which true wretchedness consists. Happiness may be "difficult to take from us" (*NE* I 5 1095ᵇ26), especially in comparison with external goods, but it remains true all the same that we are blessed with it, if we are, only "as a human being is" (*NE* I 10 1101ᵃ20–21).

Virtue, Function, and Happiness

The fact that happiness is complete and self-sufficient, and so maximally choiceworthy, argues for its being the best good, but it doesn't yet tell us clearly enough what happiness is. It is with the aim of providing the requisite clarity that the human function (*ergon*) is introduced (*NE* I 7 1097ᵇ22–25). A thing's function is intimately related to its nature, form, essence, and end. For something's nature is "its end—that is, what it is for the sake of" (*Ph.* II 2 194ᵃ27–28), as too is its function, since each thing with a function "exists for the sake of its function" (*Cael.* II 3 286ᵃ8–9). Hence if something cannot perform its function, it has no more than a name in common with its functional self: "If the whole body is dead, there will no longer be a foot or a hand, except homonymously, as one might speak of a stone 'hand' (for a dead hand will be like that); but everything is defined by its function and its potentiality; so that in such condition [that is, dead] they should not be said to be the same things but homonymous ones" (*Pol.* I 2 1253ᵃ20–25; also *Mete.* IV 12 390ᵃ10–13).

Aristotle attributes functions to parts of bodies and souls, to instruments or tools of various sorts, and to human beings, insofar as they play certain sorts of roles. Thus a "a flute-player, a carpenter, and every craftsman" has a function, since he has a characteristic activity or type of action that he does, namely, playing the flute or doing woodwork (*NE* I 7 1097ᵇ25–26). With the exception of human beings (*NE* I 7 1097ᵇ27–28), he seems not to attribute functions to whole animals. But this seems to be of little consequence. For if human beings have a set of life activities that are essentially characteristic of them, so do lions, tigers, and bears. But where there is a characteristic activity, there is a function, whose actualization has that activity as its internal end, and where there is a function there is a virtuous state ensuring that the activity is done well (*NE* I 7 1098ᵃ7–18).

Instead of arguing directly that human beings have a function, Aristotle treats the uncontroversial fact that craftsmen have "certain functions and actions," and that bodily parts, such as eyes, hands, and feet do (*NE* I 7 1097ᵇ28–33), as making it absurd to think that they do not have one. The first thought seems to be that if in his roles as craftsmen of various sorts a human being has a function, he must also have a function of a more general type that suits him to play those roles, and to adapt himself to the rational principles and norms of the associated crafts and other choice-relevant sciences. The second thought seems to reach the same conclusion by something like the reverse route: if each part of the human body has a function, the whole of which they are the parts must also have one, to which each of theirs contributes, so that its function explains theirs.

Whatever the human function turns out to be, then, it must be something we can intelligibly think of as explaining the functions of the parts of the human body, and how it is that human beings can be craftsmen, subject to the rational principles or norms of their craft. These are the requirements that shape Aristotle's search:

> [1] What, then, could this [human function] be? For life (*zên*) is evidently shared even by plants, while what we are looking for is something special. Hence we should set aside the life (*zôên*) of nutrition and growth. Next would be some sort of perceptual life; but this too is evidently shared by the horse, the ox, indeed by every animal. [2] There remains, then, some sort of practical life of what possesses reason, [3] one part in that it obeys reason, the other in that it possesses it and engages in understanding. [4] Since this [practical sort of life], too, is spoken of in two ways, we must take the one [spoken of] in accord with activity, since it seems to be so called in the fuller sense. (*NE* I 7 1097^{b}33–1098^{a}7)

Two Greek words correspond to the English word "life"—*zôê* and *bios*. *Zôê* refers to the sorts of life processes studied by biologists, zoologists, and other scientists (including psychologists and theologians): growth and reproduction are such processes, as are perceiving and understanding. Hence *zôê* is [4] ambiguous, meaning either the potential to grow, reproduce, perceive, or the process or activity of growing, reproducing, perceiving, and understanding (*Protr.* B79–83). *Bios* refers to the sort of life a natural historian or biographer might investigate—the life of the otter, the life of Pericles—and so to a span of time throughout which someone possesses *zôê* as a potentiality: "The good and the bad person are least distinct while asleep, which is why happy people are said to be no worse off than wretched ones for half their life (*bios*)" (*NE* I 13 1102^{b}5–7). Hence, in the conclusion of the function argument, we are reminded that a *zôê* will not be happiness for a human being unless it occurs "in a complete *bios*" (*NE* I 7 1098^{a}18–20).

What is characterized as *praktikê* in [2] is the a *zôê* of what possesses reason, which might lead us to think that what is being referred to is a peculiarly practical as opposed to theoretical or contemplative rational activity. What is *praktikê*, however, often includes what is theoretical or contemplative, rather than excluding it (*Pol.* VII 3 1325ᵇ16–21). [3] seems intended to remind us of just this. Rational activity, it tells us, is twofold—that of the part that obeys reason and that of the part that possesses reason autonomously. The part that obeys reason is the desiring part. But when we consider it [4] as actively obeying reason, it also involves the activity of the calculative subpart of the part that possesses reason autonomously. The twofold activity of what possesses reason isn't [a] nonrational active desiring and [b] practical thinking, therefore, but rather [c] active desiring in accord with practical thinking or deliberation and [d] theoretical thinking or contemplation. It is the distinction between [c] and [d], indeed, that paves the way for the disjunctive conclusion of the argument as a whole: "the human good turns out to be activity of soul in accord with virtue, and, if there are more virtues than one, in accord with the best and most complete" (*NE* I 7 1098ᵃ16–18). For the most complete virtue is theoretical wisdom, which is the virtue of the scientific part, and is responsible for theoretical thinking or contemplation, while the less complete one is the amalgam of practical wisdom and the virtues of character, which is the virtue of the calculative and desiring parts, and is responsible for practical thinking or deliberation.

When Aristotle elsewhere employs the notion of a function for more general philosophical or scientific purposes, as we saw, he associates a thing's function with its essence, its virtues or excellences with what enables it to complete its function well, and its end or target with its function completed in accord with those virtues. Since the essence of a kind of thing must be special to it, it might be that in assuming the function of human beings is also special to them, he is simply relying on this nexus of doctrines, some elements of which—such as the connection between function and virtue—appear elsewhere in the function argument (*NE* I 7 1098ᵃ8–12). If this were his reason for thinking that the function of a thing must be special to it, however, it is surprising that he doesn't say so. Moreover, the supposedly uncontroversial examples he gives of things that have characteristic activities suggest a somewhat different explanation. Having the potentiality to become a practitioner of a craft or skill does seem to be something special to human beings: "it is special to a human being to be capable of learning grammar, since if something is a human being, it is capable of learning grammar, and if it is capable of learning grammar, it is a human being" (*Top.* I 5 102ᵃ19–22). Hence the human function might be special to human beings because it is presupposed, in the way we explored, by potentialities that are special to them.

The implicit argument by elimination that Aristotle uses in [1–2] to identify the human function with rational activity of a sort presupposes his own account of the soul (*NE* I 13). But whichever account we appeal to, rational activity of some sort will surely emerge as best fitted for the double explanatory duty the human function must perform. For the crafts and choice-relevant sciences are rational enterprises, and the parts of the body, since they can be moved in accord with their norms, are arguably adapted by nature to subserve and further their ends and goals:

> Just as every instrument is for the sake of something, the parts of the body are also for the sake of something, that is, for the sake of some action, so that the whole body must evidently be for the sake of some complex action. Just as the saw is there for the sake of sawing, not sawing for the sake of the saw, since sawing is a certain use [of a saw], so the body, too, is somehow for the sake of the soul, and the parts of the body for the sake of those functions for which each is naturally adapted. (*PA* I 5 645ᵇ14–20)

That is why [2] the human function, as a rational activity of the soul, is something additional to all the functions of the bodily parts (*NE* I 7 1097ᵇ32–33).

Once the human function is identified with a type of rational activity, the conceptual or analytic connection between a thing's functions and its virtues is used to legitimate the introduction of these virtues:

> If, then, the function of a human being is activity of the soul in accord with reason or not without reason, and the function, we say, of a certain sort of thing is the same in kind as that of a good thing of that sort, as for example in the case of a lyre player and a good lyre player, and this is so unconditionally in all cases, when we add the superior achievement that is in accord with the virtue to the function (for it belongs to a lyre player to play the lyre and to a good one to do so well)—if all this is so, if a human being's function is taken to be a sort of life (*zôên*), and this life to be activity of the soul and actions that involve reason, and it belongs to a good man to do these well and nobly, and each thing is completed well when it is in accord with its proper virtue—if all this is so, the human good turns out to be activity of the soul in accord with virtue, and if there are more virtues than one, in accord with the best and most complete. (*NE* I 7 1098ᵃ7–18)

The investigation of happiness then focuses on the various candidate virtues governing rational activity, with the aim, finally, of discovering which of them is most complete. Once we know that, we will have the clearer account of what happiness is—or what its essence is—that readies it to be a scientific starting-point.

The Human Function

In one way it is easy to say what the human function is: it is activity of the soul and actions that involve reason. It is when we try to be more specific that we run into difficulties. For there seem to be three possibilities for what such activity could be. It could be: contemplative activity involving reason of the sort that theoretical wisdom completes or perfects; practical activity involving reason of the sort that is completed or perfected by practical wisdom and the virtues of character; or some sort of activity involving reason that all of these virtues together somehow complete or perfect. If human happiness just were contemplation in accord with theoretical wisdom, the human function would have to be contemplation alone, since whatever the human function is, it must—if the function argument is to succeed—be whatever is completed or perfected by the best and most complete virtue. At the same time, the human function is supposed to be special to human beings. Yet contemplation is not special to them, since God and the various heavenly bodies also have it as their characteristic activity.

In the *Protrepticus*, we find Aristotle apparently confronting this problem in an interesting way, unparalleled in his other works:

[1] When each thing completes in the best way that which—not coincidentally but intrinsically—is its function, the thing in question must be said to be good too, and the virtue by which each thing can by nature accomplish this should be deemed to have the most control. [2] What is composite and divisible into parts has several different activities, but what is by nature simple and does not have its substance in relation to something else must have one controlling virtue intrinsically. [3] If then a human being is a simple animal and his substance is ordered in accord both with reason and with understanding, he has no other function than this alone, namely, the attainment of the most rigorous truth about the beings. [4] But if he is naturally cocomposed of several potentialities, and it is clear that he has by nature several functions to be completed, the best of them is always *his* function, as health is the function of the doctor, and safety of a ship's captain. We can, however, name no function of thought or of the understanding part of our soul that is better than truth. Truth, therefore, is the function of this part of the soul that has most control. [5] But this it attains in accord with unconditional scientific knowledge, or rather in accord with what is scientific knowledge to a higher degree [than anything else], and of this the end that has most control is contemplation. For when of two things one is choiceworthy for the sake of the other, the latter is better and more choiceworthy, precisely because the other is choiceworthy for it, as, for example, pleasure is more choiceworthy than pleasant things, and health than healthy ones, since

the latter, we say, produce the former. Than theoretical wisdom (*phronêsis*),[10] however, which we say is the potentiality in us that has most control, nothing is more choiceworthy, when one state is discerned in relation to another, for the part that has knowledge (*to gnôstikon meros*), whether taken separately or jointly, is better than all the rest of the soul, and its virtue is [a sort of unconditional] scientific knowledge [namely, theoretical wisdom]. (B63–67)

[1] reprises doctrine familiar from the function argument, making plain what is implicit there, that a thing's function is what the virtue with most control completes or perfects. [2] contrasts two kinds of beings: a simple being—God—who has only one function (implied in [3]), and so only one virtue with most control; and a complex being, which has many parts. If a human being were a simple animal, his function would be "the attainment of the most rigorous truth," and so [5] his one virtue would be the theoretical wisdom ensuring such attainment. But [4] he isn't a simple animal. Instead, he has many potentialities and functions to be completed, and so (by implication), many virtues too. Nonetheless, it is the best of these functions that is *his* function, so that the virtue of his that has most control, like the virtue of the simple being, is theoretical wisdom.

It is not the case, however, that God's virtue and that of a human being are on a par. An easily missed difference between [2] and [5] shows why. Because God is simple, and so has only one function, he has only one virtue that has most control. Because he does not have his substance in relation to something else, he has this one virtue *intrinsically*. A human being, by implicit contrast, has his substance in relation to God, since he depends on him. So, though he does have the same maximally controlling virtue as God, he does not have it intrinsically. Moreover, the happiness that consists in activity in

10. The *Protrepticus* identifies human beings above all with their understanding (B62), which is the only divine constituent in them (B108–110). Its virtue or excellence, which is variously called *phronêsis, sophia,* or *philosophia,* is the one whose activity is identified with happiness (B68, 91–95). At the same time, a kind of *phronêsis,* recognizably akin to practical wisdom, is distinguished from a kind of *sophia,* recognizably akin to theoretical wisdom, and assigned a subsidiary value and role (B27). Implicitly acknowledging that *phronêsis* and *sophia* are doing this sort of double duty in the account, some fragments speak of "theoretical" *sophia* (B29) or "theoretical" *phronêsis* (B46), contrasting these with their practical varieties. Theoretical *phronêsis,* which seems to be identical to theoretical *sophia,* is the special possession of the philosopher, who "alone lives with his eye on nature and the divine" (B50). The *phronêsis* under discussion here is clearly theoretical wisdom.

accord with this virtue is not something he has intrinsically, either: "our well-being is in accord with something different, he is himself his own well-being" (*EE* VII 12 1245ᵇ18–19). Hence the same must be true of his function, which when actualized has that activity as its internal end (*Met.* IX 8 1050ᵃ21–23). A human being's function, then, while in one way not special to him, since it is God's function also, is special to him in another way, since it is possessed in a special way, different from the way God possesses it.

Besides, [4] explicitly allows that a human being has many functions to complete, and so many virtues. That the best of these functions has a special role, and is distinctively his, does not change this fact. In subsequent sections, Aristotle elaborates on its implications:

> Hence the function to which this virtue [theoretical wisdom] pertains is not that of what we call the individual virtues [of character], since it is better than all of them, as the end produced is always better than the science that produces it. Nor is every virtue of the soul related in the way [unconditional scientific knowledge is] either to the human function or to happiness. For if it [unconditional scientific knowledge] is productive, its products will be different from it (as, for example, the craft of house-building produces a house but is not part of a house), but theoretical wisdom (*phronêsis*) is part of the virtue of the soul and of happiness; for happiness, we say, either comes from it or is it. According to this argument too, then, it [theoretical wisdom] cannot be a productive science, since the end must be better than what causes it to come into being, whereas nothing is better than theoretical wisdom (*phronêsis*), unless it is one of the aforementioned things [that is, happiness or one of its parts]—but none of these is different from the function to which it pertains. Hence we must say that this type of scientific knowledge is theoretical or contemplative (*theôrêtikên*), since its end cannot be to produce anything. The activity of theoretical wisdom (*to phronein*) and contemplation (*to theôrein*), therefore, are the function of the [human] soul, and of all things it is most choiceworthy to human beings, just as sight, we think, is to the eyes, since one would choose to have sight even if nothing additional to it and different from it were to come about because of it. (*Protr.* B68–70)

The function human beings share with God is not just one they possess in a different way than he does (in relation to something else rather than intrinsically) but one that is differently supported in them than in him. For he, being simple, has no need of the virtues of character, any more than he does of family, friends, external goods, or a political constitution (*NE* X 8 1178ᵇ8–18). A human being, by contrast, as a political animal whose understanding is incarnate, does need of all of them in order to contemplate and be happy.

Types of Completeness

The adjective *teleion*, which derives from *telos* ("end," "goal"), is discussed in the following entry in Aristotle's philosophical lexicon:

> [1] We call [*part-whole*] complete that outside which not even one part (*morion*) is to be found, as, for example, the complete time of each thing is the one outside of which there is no time to be found that is part of that time, and [2] we also call [*value*] complete that which, as regards virtue or goodness, cannot be surpassed relative to its kind, as, for example, a doctor is complete and a flute-player is complete when they lack nothing as regards the form of their own proper virtue. . . . Moreover, virtue is a sort of completion, for each thing is complete and every substance is complete when, as regards the form of its proper virtue, it lacks no part of its natural extent (*megethous*). [3] Again, things that have attained a good end are called (*end*) complete; for things are complete as regards having attained their end . . . which is a last thing. . . . And the last thing for the sake of which [something is done] is also an end. (*Met.* V 16 1021ᵇ12–30)

When Aristotle speaks of virtue as being complete, he often means that it is [1] *part-whole* complete. In the *Eudemian Ethics*, for example, he identifies complete virtue with virtue as a whole, incomplete virtue with its parts: "life (*zôê*) is either complete or incomplete, and similarly virtue, since in the one case it is whole (*holê*), in the other a part (*morion*)" (*EE* II 1 1219ᵃ36–37). There and in the *Magna Moralia* he also identifies complete virtue with the amalgam of practical wisdom and the virtues of character he calls *kalokagathia* or noble-goodness (*MM* II 8 1207ᵇ20–27, *EE* VIII 3 1249ᵃ16–17). In both, he identifies happiness with activity in accord with complete virtue in a complete life (*MM* I 4 1184ᵃ35–ᵇ9, *EE* II 1 1219ᵃ38–39). At the same time, he acknowledges the existence of practical wisdom as a virtue of thought, not of character, characterizes it as inferior to theoretical wisdom, and recognizes the contemplative activity that theoretical wisdom perfects or completes as of the greatest possible import to happiness (*MM* I 34 1197ᵇ3–11, *EE* VII 15 1249ᵃ24–ᵇ25). What he does *not* do is explain how all these claims can be consistent with one another.

The *Nicomachean Ethics* might seem to inherit this problem. For there, too, general justice is "the complete use of complete virtue" (*NE* V 1 1129ᵇ31), not "a part (*meros*) of virtue, but virtue as a whole (*holê*)" (*NE* V 1 1130ᵃ9). Yet theoretical wisdom, which is also "a part (*meros*) of virtue as a whole (*holês*)" (*NE* VI 12 1144ᵃ5–6), is not a part of general justice or its use. For "the virtue of understanding is separate" from the virtues of character and practical wisdom, which are virtues of the hylomorphic compound of soul and body (*NE* X 8 1178^{a}9–23), just as understanding is separate from the compound itself. Thus the problem implicit in the *Magna Moralia* and the *Eudemian Ethics* now seems right out in the open.

In all three ethical treatises, virtues are divided into those of character and those of thought, but once the (full) virtues of character are shown to be inseparable from practical wisdom, this distinction fades in prominence, and the distinction between the complete virtue of the merely human hylomorphic compound of body and soul on the one hand and the virtue of the fully human or divine constituent in us in accord with which we contemplate on the other gains prominence—implicitly in the *Magna Moralia* (II 3 1199^{b}38–1200^{a}5) and *Eudemian Ethics* (VIII 1 1246^{b}32–33), explicitly in the *Nicomachean Ethics* (*NE* X 8 1178^{a}16–22). Thus in the *Nicomachean Ethics*, happiness is no longer activity in accord with complete virtue but is activity in accord with the best and most complete virtue. Moreover, theoretical wisdom is the virtue of the best thing and the one with most control, so that its activity is complete happiness (*NE* I 7 1098^{a}16–18, X 7 1177^{a}12–17). Thus it is now recognized as a more complete virtue than full virtue of character. Yet the sense in which it is more or most complete cannot be a matter of [1] part-whole completeness, since, again, full virtue of character is not part of theoretical wisdom. Instead, it seems that the completeness it possesses to the greatest extent is something more akin to [2] *value* completeness, so that theoretical wisdom is more value complete than full virtue of character, because relative to the kind *virtue*, it cannot be surpassed in value.

While theoretical wisdom may be more value complete than full or complete virtue of character, it is apparently less part-whole complete than human virtue as a whole, which includes both of them (*NE* VI 12 1144^{a}5–6). In the case of virtues, in other words, it might seem that the two sorts of completeness can come apart. It is signal, therefore, that while the *Eudemian Ethics* seems not to distinguish *complete* virtues from *whole* virtues, the *Nicomachean Ethics*, while it recognizes human virtue to be a whole, of which theoretical wisdom and full or complete virtue of character are both parts, never characterizes it is as complete. Full virtue of character is *a* virtue, as are its constituents, practical wisdom and the individual virtues of character. It is something with which activity can be in accord. The same is true of theoretical wisdom. Human virtue as a whole, by contrast, is not *a* virtue, *a* state, or something with which activity can be in accord: for activity in accord with theoretical wisdom is leisured, while activity in accord with full virtue is unleisured (*NE* X 7 1177^{b}4–26). Hence it is not something that is even a candidate for being a complete virtue, let alone the most complete one. The *Nicomachean Ethics* avoids a problem in the conception of a complete virtue present in the *Magna Moralia* and *Eudemian Ethics*, then, in a way that might reasonably be taken to suggest an awareness of its existence.

A problem similar to the one we have been exploring in the case of the virtues arises, too, in the case of ends or goods. The *Magna Moralia* is explicit that that thing "is better for the sake of which the rest are." Nonetheless, it uses this fact not to define telic completeness or the completeness of ends, as the *Nicomachean Ethics* does (I 7 1097ª30–34), but to establish the superior value of goods that are ends over that of goods that are not ends but are nonintrinsically valuable means to them (*MM* I 2 1184ª3–7). The relative value of ends, on the other hand, is established by a kind of completeness that is part-whole:

> Among ends themselves, the complete is always better than the incomplete. A complete end is one whose attainment leaves us not still needing anything in addition, whereas an incomplete one is one whose attainment does leave us needing something in addition. For instance, if we attain justice alone, there are many things we need in addition, but when we attain happiness, there is nothing additional we still need. This, therefore, is the best end we are searching for, the complete end. The complete end, then, is the good and the end of the [other] goods. . . . But the complete end, unconditionally speaking, is nothing other than happiness, it seems, and happiness is composed of many goods. . . . For happiness is not something separate from these, but is these. (*MM* I 2 1184ª7–29)

The conclusion reached is that happiness "cannot exist apart from external goods, and they come about as a result of good luck" (*MM* II 8 1207ᵇ16–18). Nonetheless, happiness does not consist in these goods but "in actively living in accord with the virtues" of character (*MM* I 4 1184ᵇ35–36), in a life complete (*MM* I 4 1185ª1–9). Implicitly, then, the distinction is recognized between goods that are parts of happiness and those that are necessary or enabling conditions of it, as in the *Eudemian Ethics* (I 2 1214ᵇ26–27). Since the many goods of which happiness is composed are the activities of the various virtues of character, this again leaves the relationship of *theoretical wisdom* to happiness in an unstable situation—now because of how happiness is being conceived. In the *Nicomachean Ethics*, this instability is removed by recognizing two different types or grades of happiness, one incomplete, constituted by activity in accord with full virtue of character, another complete, constituted by activity in accord with theoretical wisdom.

The *Nicomachean Ethics* recognizes that if activity in accord with theoretical wisdom is to constitute complete happiness, it must receive "a complete span of life" (*biou*) (*NE* X 7 1177ᵇ25) or must occur in or throughout "a complete life" (*biô[i] teleiô[i]*) (*NE* I 7 1098ᵃ18). What it doesn't do is explain what a complete life is or what makes it complete. The *Eudemian Ethics* refers to the "life with most control" (*biou tou kratistou*) (*EE* I 3 1215ᵃ4–5), emphasizes the importance of ordering "one's life (*bion*) in relation to some end" (*EE* I 2 1214ᵇ10), and replaces *bios* with *zôê* in requiring happiness to be "activity of a complete life (*zôê*)" (*EE* II 1 1219ᵃ38–39) but is equally silent about what makes a *bios* or *zôê* complete. In spelling out what a complete life is, the *Magna Moralia* stands alone:

> Since, then, happiness is a complete good and end, we should not overlook the fact that it will also exist in what is complete. For it will not exist in a child (since a child is not happy) but in a man, since he is complete. Nor will it exist in an incomplete time, but in a complete one, such as that of a human life (*bioi*). For it is correctly said among the masses that a life's happiness should be discerned in its longest time, since what is complete should exist in a complete time and a complete human being. (*MM* I 4 1185ᵃ1–9)

As in the case of virtues and ends, then, the completeness attributed to lives is part-whole completeness.

The completeness assigned to a life in the *Nicomachean Ethics*, by contrast, cannot be of this part-whole variety, since the demands attributed there to virtue are plainly inconsistent with it:

> The good [virtuous] person does many things for his friends and fatherland, and will die for them if he has to, since he will sacrifice money, honors, and goods of competition generally in procuring what is noble for himself. For he will choose intense pleasure for a short time over mild pleasure for a long one, and a year of living (*biôsai*) nobly over many years of indifferent life, and a single action that is noble and grand over many insignificant actions. (*NE* IX 8 1169ᵃ18–25)

It may be true, of course, that a happy life is *presumptively* of normal length, and so is part-whole complete—just as long as it is recognized that a shorter life can also be happy, provided its shortness is compensated for in some way.

In characterizing one sort of compensation, Aristotle again appeals to the notion of completeness. A virtuous person, he says, who has suffered many great strokes of bad luck will not quickly become happy again, but "if it happens at all, it will take a long and complete period of time in which he achieves grand and noble things" (*NE* I 10 1101ª12–13). Again, this sort of completeness, while clearly some sort of measure of life extent, cannot be that of normal life expectancy or part-whole completeness. The sort of life (*bios*) to which a natural life expectancy belongs, indeed, is primarily a biological life: elephants and plants also have life expectancies in this sense. An individual human being's life, however, is the sort in which a biographer or a dramatist might also take an interest, and a *biographical* life can be a success—can be worthwhile and in need of nothing—even if it isn't of normal length. One way it might be so is by containing, like the life of a great hero, "a single action that is noble and grand"—that is to say, an action of the sort the *Iliad* or *Odyssey* is built around, "an action that is unified, and a whole as well, whose parts, consisting of the events that happen, so constructed that the displacement or removal of any one of them will disturb and disjoint the whole" (*Po.* 8 1451ª32–35). Such a life may in a way be part-whole complete, but what is really important is that by achieving a good end it is [3] *end* complete.

Whether we consider virtues, ends, or lives, then, Aristotle seems to move away from thinking of their completeness in part-whole terms and toward thinking of it in telic terms. The reason he does so, in the case of virtues and ends, seems to be the tension that otherwise results in how to include theoretical wisdom among the virtues. Where life itself is concerned, the reason seems to have more to do with the virtues themselves and the demands they make—demands that cannot be made subservient to a formula, of the sort provided in the *Magna Moralia,* for how long a virtuous or happy life must be.

8

THE HAPPIEST LIFE

Since practical wisdom includes political science, it shares its status as most architectonic. Yet there are limits even to its control. Practical wisdom "does not control either theoretical wisdom or the better part, any more than the craft of medicine does health; for it doesn't use it, but sees to its coming-into-being: it prescribes for its sake, therefore, but not to it" (*NE* VI 13 1145ᵃ6–9). To think otherwise would be like thinking that political science "rules the gods, because it prescribes with regard to everything in the city. (*NE* VI 13 1145ᵃ10–11). For while political science does indeed enact laws concerning the distribution of priesthoods, the location of temples, and other things pertaining to the public worship of the gods, these are for the sake of the gods, ensuring their proper honor and worship, not laws to which the gods themselves are subject (*Pol.* VII 9 1329ᵃ27–34, 10 1330ᵃ11–13). Similarly the divine constituent of the soul (the scientific part) and its virtue (theoretical wisdom) do not operate in accord with practical wisdom's pre-scriptions, but rather these prescriptions are for their sake. True, practical wisdom (or its component political science) "uses the other practical sci-ences" (*NE* I 2 1094ᵇ4–5), but what that means is that it uses them to further happiness, which just is the activity of theoretical wisdom. It doesn't use theoretical wisdom itself, since it doesn't use *it* to further anything. In this regard, practical wisdom is like medicine, which does not issue prescrip-tions to the already healthy, or use health to further some additional end, but rather prescribes to the sick to see to it that health comes-into-being in them.

Theoretical wisdom is a state of the soul's scientific part. Hence to see to its coming-into-being, practical wisdom must arrange for its acquisition by some group in the city it supervises, and then arrange for those in the group to have the leisure necessary to actualize their acquired state in active contemplation, throughout a life that is sufficiently long to count as complete. In the case of the best kind of city and constitution described in *Politics* VII–VIII, the implication seems to be that *all full citizens* should have access to happiness, so that all should acquire and, to the extent possible, exercise theoretical wisdom. There seems to be no question of restricting theoretical wisdom to some intellectual elite, or to those who are actual or future political leaders, or heads of households. Aristotle does, of course, restrict membership of the class of unconditional or full citizens of the best city, but the way he does it shows him to be entirely unconcerned about issues of this sort.

Because a city must be a self-sufficient community, it needs a "multitude of farmers to provide the food, as well as craftsmen, soldiers, rich people, priests, and people to discern what is necessary and what advantageous" (*Pol.* VII 8 1328^{b}20–23). It is from these groups that the unconditional citizens must be selected. One way constitutions differ, indeed, is by making the selection in different ways: "in democracies everyone shares in everything, whereas in oligarchies it is the opposite" (*Pol.* VII 9 1328^{b}32–33). So the task is to determine how in ideal circumstances the selection should be made:

Since we are investigating the best constitution, the one that would make a city most happy, and since happiness cannot exist apart from virtue . . . , it evidently follows that in a city governed in the noblest manner, possessing men who are *unconditionally just*, as opposed to being just given certain assumptions, the citizens should not live the life of a vulgar craftsman or tradesman. For lives of these sorts are humble and inimical to virtue. Nor should those who are going to be citizens engage in farming, since leisure is needed both to develop virtue and as regards political actions. But since the best city contains both a military part and one that deliberates about what is advantageous and makes judgments about what is just, and since it is evident that these, more than anything else, are parts of the city, should these tasks also be assigned to different people, or are both to be assigned to the same people? This is evident, too, because in one way the tasks should be assigned to the same people, and in another they should be assigned to different ones. For since the prime time (*akmês*) for each of the two tasks is different, in that one requires practical wisdom and the other physical strength, they should be assigned to different people. On the other hand, since those capable of using and resisting force cannot possibly tolerate being ruled continuously, for this reason the two tasks should be assigned to the same people. For those who control the hoplite weapons also control whether a constitution will survive or not. The only course remaining, then, is for the constitution to assign both tasks to the same people, but not at the same time. Instead, since it is natural for physical strength to be found among younger men and practical wisdom among older ones, it is advantageous and just to assign the tasks to each group by reference to age, since this division is based on merit. Moreover, the property should belong to them. For the citizens must be well supplied with resources, and these people are the citizens. For the class of vulgar craftsmen does not participate in the city, and nor does any other class that is not "a craftsman of virtue" (*tês aretês dêmiourgon*). This is clear from our basic assumption. For happiness necessarily goes along with virtue, and a city must be called happy not by looking to just a part but by looking to *all the citizens*. It is also evident that the property should be theirs, since the farmers must either be slaves or non-Greek subject peoples. (*Pol.* VII 9 1328ᵇ33–1329ᵃ26)

The phrase "a craftsman of virtue" is borrowed from Plato, who uses it to characterize the work of the philosopher rulers in drafting the constitution of his own best city, Kallipolis:

The philosopher, by associating with what is orderly and divine [that is, the Platonic Forms] becomes as divine and orderly as a human being can. . . . And if he should come to be compelled to make a practice—in private and in public—of stamping what he sees there into the people's characters, instead of shaping only his own . . . he will [not] be a poor craftsman of temperance, justice, and the whole of popular virtue (*dêmiourgon . . . tês dêmotikês aretês*). (*Republic* VI 500d)

It is hard to believe that Aristotle would use this phrase were he not also planning to educate *his* ideal citizens in philosophy. But that is a small point on which we have no need to lean.

The primetime for a man's hoplite service is that of his body, which is somewhere between the ages of thirty and thirty-five, while the primetime for that of his soul or his potentiality for thought is forty-nine or fifty (*Pol.* VII 16 1335ᵇ32–35, *Rh.* II 14 1390ᵇ9–11). Until the age of forty or so, then, male citizens lack the experience necessary for practical wisdom and deliberative office, and thereafter possess it. Yet, though full virtue of character is something they can develop only in middle age, all are presumed capable of developing it. No elaborate tests are countenanced, as they are in Plato's best city, to segregate the future philosopher rulers from other citizens equally mature, but less gifted in, for example, mathematics. A political scientist aims at "happiness for himself and for his fellow citizens" (*NE* X 7 1177ᵇ14), not for the happiness of some narrower few. As an end additional to the unleisured activities of the virtues of character themselves, such happiness must be contemplative in nature.

The mature citizens of the best city are all unconditionally just, which involves their possessing full virtue of character. Moreover, all of them are happy, which involves their also possessing theoretical wisdom. But theoretical wisdom cannot be acquired except through lengthy education and experience (*NE* II 1 1103ª14–17). Hence the natural place to begin an investigation of how practical wisdom arranges more specifically for theoretical wisdom's acquisition is with the discussion in *Politics* VII–VIII of the education that the best city and constitution provides.

Educatedness

A community could not really be a city, Aristotle thinks, if it did not educate its citizens in virtue, since it is by means of education that people are unified and made into a city (*Pol.* II 5 1263ᵇ36–37, III 9 1280ᵇ1–8). Consequently, education should be suited to the constitution and provided to the citizens by it, so that it is communal or public rather than private (*Pol.* I 13 1260ᵇ15, VIII 1 1337ª14–26). Although most of the discussion of education in the best city concerns that of (future) male citizens, communal education is also provided to girls and women (*Pol.* I 3 1260ᵇ13–20, VII 16 1335ᵇ11–12). Since women's virtues of character are different from men's, part of their education must also be different. Just how different it will be when these virtues are no longer the issue is hard to say. Women cannot have unconditional practical wisdom and virtue of character, since the deliberative part of their soul lacks authority (*Pol.* I 13 1260ª12–13). The scientific part, on the other hand, seems unaffected by this difference. So, perhaps, women are capable of acquiring theoretical wisdom, or some close approximation to it. Aristotle does not explicitly rule it out, but he doesn't discuss it either.[1]

Education from infancy to early adulthood seems to have four stages:

[1] The first concerns the treatment of infants, and their informal training up to the age of five (*Pol.* VII 17 1336ª3–ᵇ35). The emphasis here is on diet, on the shaping and conditioning of the body, and especially on the use of leisure appropriate to free citizens.

[2] From age five to seven, children observe the studies they will later learn for themselves (*Pol.* VII 17 1336ᵇ35–37).

---

1. Among the students in Plato's Academy, where Aristotle spent twenty years, Diogenes Laertius (III 46, IV 2) lists two women, Lasthenia of Mantinea and Axiothea of Phlius, citing Dicaearchus, one of Aristotle's pupils, as a source of his information. Hence Aristotle cannot have been ignorant of the existence of women philosophers.

[3] From seven to fourteen, their education includes lighter gymnastic exercises (*Pol.* VIII 4 1338^{b}40–42).

[4] From fourteen to twenty-one, the first three years are devoted in part to "other studies," and the next four to arduous physical training combined with a strict diet (*Pol.* VIII 4 1339^{a}5–7).

Much of what is included in [1–4] falls under the rubric of the "education through habituation" provided by physical trainers and coaches, which precedes "education through reason" (*Pol.* VIII 3 1338^{b}4–7) and helps lead to habituated virtue. The "other studies" mentioned in [4] are not explicitly identified. They could be restricted to reading, writing, music, and drawing (*Pol.* VIII 3 1337^{b}24–25), but then the only thing that children would be taught in [3]—a period of seven whole years—would be light gymnastics. This is sufficiently implausible in its own terms, and a sufficiently large departure from common Greek practice that we would expect Aristotle to acknowledge it as an innovation and defend it carefully. The fact that he does neither suggests that he is intending to follow tradition and include reading, writing, drawing, and music in [3], not [4]. A promised discussion of a kind of education that sons must be given "not because it is useful or necessary, but because it is noble and suitable for a free person" (*Pol.* VIII 3 1338^{a}30–34) is not a part of Aristotle's works as we have them. Nonetheless, what we do have contains some clues as to the nature of such studies. We know, for example, that music and drawing are both to be taught in part because they are free subjects and contribute to leisure (*Pol.* VIII 3 1338^{a}21–22, 1338^{b}1–2). We also know that a free person must have theoretical knowledge of various aspects of wealth-acquisition (*Pol.* I 11 1258^{b}9–11). [4] seems a plausible location for some level of training in these subjects.

Aristotle also sometimes refers to what he calls "a well-educated person" (*pepaideumenos*)—someone who studies a subject not to acquire scientific knowledge of it but to become a discerning judge:

Regarding every branch of theoretical knowledge and every line of inquiry , the more humble and more estimable alike, there appear to be two ways for the state to be, one that may be well described as scientific knowledge of the subject matter, the other a certain sort of educatedness. For it is characteristic of a person well educated in that way to be able accurately to discern what is well said and what is not. We think of someone who is well educated about the whole of things as a person of that sort, and we think that being well educated consists in having the capacity to do that sort of discerning. But in one case, we consider a single individual to have the capacity to be discerning in practically all subjects, in the other case, we consider him to have the capacity to be discerning in a subject of a delimited nature—for there might be a person with the same capacity as the person we have been discussing, but about a part of the whole. So it is clear in the case of inquiry into nature, too, that there should be certain defining-marks by reference to which one can appraise the manner of its demonstrations, apart from the question of what the truth is, whether thus or otherwise. (*PA* I 1 639ᵃ1–15)

A person well educated in medicine, for example, is capable of discerning whether someone has treated a disease correctly (*Pol.* III 11 1282ᵃ3–7), and the "unconditionally well-educated person," who is well educated in every subject or area, "seeks rigor in each area to the extent that the nature of its subject matter allows" (*NE* I 3 1094ᵇ23–1095ᵃ2).

Since a well-educated person is discerning, he knows who is and isn't worth listening to on any topic, and so is free from intellectual enslavement to self-proclaimed experts. He is also free from the sort of intellectual enslavement that is often the lot of the narrow specialist, whose imagination is often straitjacketed by the one thing he knows too well. A well-educated person has studied all the "free or liberal sciences," but he has done so only "up to a point" and not so assiduously as "to lower the mind or deprive it of leisure" (*Pol.* VIII 3 1337ᵇ17). Presumably, then, the citizens of the best city, who are all free and well-educated people, must be trained in these subjects at some stage, if not as part of [4], then later in their lives: "the young," notoriously, are not "an appropriate audience for political science" (*NE* I 3 1095ᵃ2–3).

That there must be public education in philosophy generally, and not just in ethics or political science, is certain, since philosophy is required for leisure and education in it is needed to make a city good (*Pol.* II 5 1263ᵇ37–40, 7 1267ᵃ10–12). Besides, since theoretical wisdom is at least part of the *sophia* of which *philosophia* is the love, it must be education in *philosophia* that leads to *sophia*'s acquisition, and so to the happiness it constitutes. But theoretical wisdom is theology, which is the most rigorous form of scientific knowledge, and—since it is of the most estimable things—the most estimable. Yet even in the case of the most estimable sciences, among which the "philosophical sciences" (*Top.* I 2 101ᵃ27–28) are surely to be counted, Aristotle distinguishes, as we saw, between being well educated in them and having scientific knowledge of them. The "true political scientist . . . must somehow know about the soul," he tells us, but he should "acquire theoretical knowledge of it" only to the extent adequate for his legislative ends, since "more rigorous knowledge would presumably take more effort than his purpose requires" (*NE* I 13 1102ª7–26). Since political science is a branch of practical wisdom, and the same state as it, the practically wise—and so fully virtuous—man must be in the same boat. What is true of psychology, then, should also be true of theology. Yet how can it be, when complete happiness consists in having the most rigorous scientific knowledge of it?

Philosophy

Aristotle sometimes applies the term *philosophia* to any science aiming at truth rather than action: "It is also right that philosophy should be called scientific knowledge of the truth. For the end of theoretical science is truth, while that of practical science is the result (*ergon*) [of action]" (*Met.* II 1 993ᵇ19–21). In this sense of the term, all the broadly theoretical sciences count as branches of philosophy, and *philosophia* is more or less equivalent in meaning to *epistêmê*. *Philosophia* also has a narrower sense, however, in which it applies exclusively to sciences providing knowledge of starting-points. Thus "natural—that is, secondary, philosophy" has the task of providing theoretical knowledge of the starting-point of perceptible substances (*Met.* VII 11 1037ª14–16), whereas "the determination of the unmoving starting-point" of natural substances "is a task for a different and prior philosophy" (*GC* I 3 318ª5–6). Since there are just "three theoretical philosophies, mathematical, natural, and theological" (*Met.* VI 1 1026ª18–19), theological philosophy must be primary, mathematical philosophy tertiary (although it is not, I think, ever referred to as such).

Besides these theoretical philosophies, Aristotle occasionally mentions practical ones, such as "the philosophy of human affairs" (*NE* X 9 1181ᵇ15). It is among these that his own ethical writings belong:

Everyone holds that what is just is some sort of equality, and up to a point, at least, all agree with what has been determined in those philosophical works of ours in which we draw distinctions concerning ethical matters; for justice is [a matter of giving] something to someone, and it should be something equal to those who are equal, it is said, but equality in what and inequality in what should not be overlooked, since this involves a puzzle and political philosophy. (*Pol.* III 12 1282ᵇ18–23)

Since puzzles—especially those about starting-points—are the provenance of dialectic and philosophy, it seems that political philosophy, like its theoretical fellows, should be primarily concerned with the starting-points of political science, and with the puzzles to which these give rise.[2] A well-known description of general methodology suggests that this is how Aristotle conceives not just political philosophy but philosophy generally:

> As in the other cases, we must set out what appears true and, having first gone through the puzzles, in this way prove all the reputable beliefs . . . or if not all of them, most of them and the most authoritative, for if the difficulties are resolved, and the reputable beliefs preserved, that will be adequate proof. (*NE* VII 1 1145^{b}2–7; also *Met.* III 1 995^{a}27–^{b}4)

Many of his writings are recognizably engaged, in any case, with working out definitions of various scientific starting-points, showing these to be in accord with reputable beliefs, and using dialectic or aporematic philosophy to solve puzzles about them. It is in relation to the starting-points of the philosophical sciences, indeed, that dialectic is particularly useful (*Top.* I 2 101^{a}25–^{b}4).

In its early stages, at least, the education that practical wisdom provides to citizens in the best city overlaps with the habituation designed to cultivate in the young the habits of being pleased and pained correctly that will lead them to form true beliefs about the noble and just things that the subject matter of ethics comprises. Once such habits are acquired, the task remains of explaining why the beliefs these habits support are true by demonstrating them from the appropriate starting-points (*NE* I 4 1095^{a}30–^{b}8). This is a task for the practical sciences, whether political or ethical. By showing that the various conventionally distinguished virtues of character are mean states that help us complete or fulfill our function well, for example, political science shows that they are genuine virtues, and provides a demonstration (or the raw materials for a demonstration) of them, by revealing their relationship to its own starting-point—happiness. In the

---

2. Since starting-points are ultimate reasons why, the following text might also be cited in this regard: "In every line of inquiry, there is a difference between what is said philosophically and what is said unphilosophically. That is precisely why even political scientists (*tôn politikôn*) shouldn't regard as irrelevant to their work the sort of theoretical knowledge (*theôrian*) that makes evident (*phaneron*) not only the fact, but also the reason why. For in every line of inquiry this is how the philosopher proceeds" (*EE* I 6 1216^{b}35–39).

process, it explains why they are worth having, and why the beliefs they help sustain are true. Once political science has accomplished this task, it falls to political *philosophy* to give us clear understanding of the starting-point by solving the relevant puzzles. Political science and the related philosophy, then, are what transform habituated virtue into full virtue and practical wisdom, by providing them with understanding of the target or end they further: "to those who form their desires and act in accord with reason," knowledge of political philosophy[3] will be "of great benefit" (*NE* I 3 1095ᵃ10–11), since it is through "habits, *philosophy*, and laws" that cities are made virtuous or good (*Pol.* II 5 1263ᵇ39–40).

The focus of the various philosophies on starting-points is indicative of their reflective or higher-order status—their being not so much science as *meta*-science. Hence it is by reflecting on first-order sciences generally that primary philosophy begins, seeking insight not so much into the subject matter of each one as into the structure of the whole of the reality—the beings as such or qua being—these sciences collectively characterize and explain:

> We are seeking the starting-points and causes of beings, and, clearly, qua beings. For there is a cause of health and of good condition, and the objects of mathematics have starting-points, constituents, and causes, and in general every science involving understanding or that shares in understanding deals to some extent with causes and starting-points, whether more rigorously or more simply. But all these sciences mark off some being, that is, a genus, and investigate it, but not as a being in the unconditional sense or qua being, and for the essence they give no argument whatsoever, instead, starting from it— some making it clear to the senses, others assuming the essence as a hypothesis—they then demonstrate the intrinsic attributes of the genus, either in a more or in a less strictly necessary way. It is evident from this induction, therefore, that there is no demonstration of the substance or essence here, but some other way of making it clear. Similarly, they say nothing as to the existence or nonexistence of the genus they investigate, and this is because it belongs to the same thought to make clear the essence, and whether or not it exists. (*Met.* VI 1 1025ᵇ3–18)

What induction reveals is that the familiar special sciences, each of which deals with a single genus, are all to some degree demonstrative in structure,

---

3. The political science under discussion here is called "political philosophy" at *NE* V II 1152ᵇ1–3.

have essences as their starting-points, and give no arguments for these or demonstrations of them. Hence they "say nothing" about the existence of the genus of beings with which they deal. Induction also reveals that the special sciences fall into three distinct types: natural, mathematical, and theoretical, these being distinguished by the kinds of essences that serve as their starting-points, and whether or not they involve matter. These types are not genera, however, since natural and mathematical beings, for example, belong to multiple genera.

Although theorems of mathematics are usually special to some branch of it, such as arithmetic or geometry, there are also "certain mathematical theorems of a universal character" (*Met.* XIII 2 1077^{a}9–10):

> That proportionals alternate might be thought to apply to numbers qua numbers, lines qua lines, solids qua solids, and times qua times, as used to be demonstrated of these separately, although it is possible to prove it of all cases by a single demonstration. But because all these things—numbers, lengths, times, solids—do not constitute a single named [type] and differ in form from one another, they were treated separately. But now it is demonstrated universally: for what is supposed to hold of them universally doesn't hold of them qua lines or qua numbers, but qua this [unnamed] type. (*APo.* I 5 74^{a}17–25)

That proportionals alternate is a theorem of universal mathematics, but its universality is open to challenge, since lines, numbers, and so on belong to different genera. For the tight unity of the definitions that are scientific starting-points makes it "necessary for the extreme and middle terms in a demonstration to come from the same genus" (*APo.* I 7 75^{b}10–11). Consequently, transgeneric demonstrations seem to be ruled out: "it is impossible that what is proved should cross from one genus to another" (*APo.* I 23 84^{b}17–18). Yet even though the explanation of why the theorem about proportionals holds "in the case of lines and of numbers is different, qua such-and-such an increase in quantity, it is the same" (*APo.* II 17 99^{a}8–10). What the theorem does hold of, in other words, are *quantities* (*Met.* XI 4 1061^{b}19–21). *Quantity*, however, is not a genus, since it is unified only analogically: "Of the items used in the demonstrative sciences some are special to each science and others common, but common by analogy, since they are only useful in so far as they bear on the genus falling under the science. Proper, for example, that a line is such-and-such, and straight so-and-so. Common, for example, that if equals are taken from equals, the remainders are equal" (*APo.* I 10 76^{a}37–41). It is an analogically unified *category*, therefore, that serves as the ontological correlate or truth-maker for theorems of universal mathematics (*APo.* I 32 88^{b}1–3).

The status of universal natural science is similar:

> It is the same with universal natural science as with universal mathematics. For universal natural science provides theoretical knowledge of the attributes and starting-points of the beings qua moving or changing, and not qua beings, whereas the primary science, as we have said, deals with the subjects [of the universal sciences] qua beings and not qua something else. For this reason, both universal natural science and universal mathematics should be regarded as parts of theoretical wisdom. (*Met.* XI 4 1061^{b}27–33)

There must be theorems of universal natural science, then, that, like those of universal mathematics, require distinctive analogically unified ontological correlates. These are what are needed to explain change generally:

> The causes and starting-points of different things are in a way different, but if we speak somehow universally, that is, analogically, in a way they are the same for all. For we might raise the puzzle about whether the starting-points and constituents are the same for substances and for relations, and similarly in the case of each of the categories. . . . As we usually say, in a way they are, and in a way they aren't. For example, the constituents of perceptible bodies, presumably, are as *form*, the hot, and, in another way, the cold, which is the *privation*; and, as *matter*, that which, primarily and intrinsically, is potentially these; and these things are substances, and also the compounds of them, of which they are the starting-points. . . . But since the constituents present in a thing are not its only causes, but also something outside it, that is, the moving or efficient cause, it is clear that while starting-point and constituent are different, both are causes; and that which moves or halts is a starting-point and a substance. It follows that by analogy there are three constituents and four causes and starting-points; but the constituents are different in different things, and the primary cause of movement is different for different things. . . . Moreover, besides these there is that which as first of all things moves all things. (*Met.* XII 4 1070^{a}31–^{b}35)

The upshot for universal natural science is that the ontological correlates or truth-makers for its theorems are not species or genera, but beings that, as a type, are characterized in terms of analogical unities: the three fundamental constituents (matter, form, privation) and the four analogically characterized causes (material, formal, final, and efficient) (*Met.* XII 5 1071^{a}29–1071^{b}2).

Once the fundamental constituents and starting-points of the various universal sciences have been identified, it falls to the associated philosophy to give an account and—where appropriate—a demonstration of them. Matter, form, the various causes are among philosophy's topics, therefore, but so too are the other transgeneric or transcategorial attributes: being and nonbeing, unity and plurality, likeness and unlikeness, sameness and difference, equality and inequality, priority and posteriority, whole and part (*Met.* IV 2 1003ᵇ22–1004ᵃ25). It is because all beings share in these that the various transgeneric principles or axioms hold of them. Since substantial beings are the kind on which all the other kinds (qualitative, relational, quantitative, and so on) depend, the same branch of philosophy deals with both:

> We must state whether it belongs to one science or to different ones to provide theoretical knowledge about the axioms (as they are called in mathematics) and about substance. It is evident, of course, that it does belongs to one science, and indeed, the philosopher's as well, to investigate them. For these hold of all beings and not of a certain genus, separate and distinct from the others. Everyone uses them, it is true, because they hold of being qua being, and each genus is a being. But each uses them to the extent he needs them, that is, so far as the genus extends about which he presents his demonstrations. Hence, since it is clear that they hold of all things qua beings (for being is what all things have in common), it follows that it also belongs to the one who knows being qua being to provide theoretical knowledge of the axioms. That is why none of those who investigate a special area undertakes to say anything about whether they are true or not. Neither geometers nor arithmeticians do so, though some students of nature do. This is not surprising, since they were the only ones who thought they were investigating the whole of nature and of being. But since there is someone still higher than the student of nature, since nature consists of only one type of being, the investigation of these axioms must fall to the student of what is universal, the one who provides theoretical knowledge of primary substance. Natural science is also a type of wisdom, but it isn't primary. (*Met.* IV 3 1005ᵃ19–1005ᵇ2)

The implication that primary or theological philosophy investigates these matters is one we should for now simply register.

The transcategorial axioms, which serve as starting-points of the universal sciences, also have a starting-point, since the principle of noncontradiction is "a starting-point even of all the other axioms" (*Met.* IV 3 1005ᵇ33–34). For though the other logical axioms, such as the law of excluded middle, which are "the starting-points of a syllogism" (*Met.* IV 3 1005ᵇ5–8), also apply to beings as such, noncontradiction is the most secure of them:

> The one whose subject matter is the beings qua beings must be able to discuss the most secure starting-points of things. This person is the philosopher. And the most secure starting-point of all is one we cannot think falsely about.

For this sort of starting-point must be known best (since it is invariably what people don't know that they make errors about) and must be unhypothetical. For a starting-point we must possess in order to understand anything at all about beings is not a hypothesis, and what we must know in order to know anything at all is a starting-point we must already possess. Clearly, then, this sort of starting-point is the most secure of all. And what it is we must next say, namely, that it is impossible for the same thing to belong and not to belong to the same thing at the same time and in the same respect. (*Met.* IV 3 1005^{b}10–20)

The reason noncontradiction has this special secure status is that we cannot think falsely about it but must "always . . . think truly" (*Met.* XI 5 1061^{b}35–36). This does not mean that we cannot sincerely deny it or say we don't believe it, since "what one says need not be what one supposes to be true" (*Met.* IV 3 1005^{b}25–26). What it does mean is that a demonstration of the principle of noncontradiction to someone who denies it cannot, except perhaps in cases of confusion, constitute his primary reason for believing it, since there is no reason more basic than it. For a demonstration "is not related to external argument, but to the one in the soul, since a syllogism isn't either, for one can always object to external argument, but not always to internal argument" (*APo.* I 10 76^{b}24–25).

As a starting-point of all sciences, the principle of noncontradiction cannot be unconditionally demonstrated, since no science can demonstrate its own starting-points: "There is no unconditional demonstration of such things. . . . For it is not possible to deduce this from a more reliable starting-point, yet it must be possible to do so, if indeed one is to demonstrate it unconditionally" (*Met.* XI 5 1062^{a}2–5). Nonetheless, it can be demonstrated "by refutation" (*Met.* IV 4 1006^{a}11–12) or "against someone" (*Met.* XI 5 1062^{a}3):

I distinguish demonstration by refutation from demonstration. For in attempting to demonstrate [the principle of noncontradiction], one might be taken to be assuming what is at issue, but if someone else [the denier of the principle] is responsible [for the assumption], it will be a refutation [of him], and not a demonstration. The starting-point for all such [demonstrations by refutation] is not the demand that the opponent speak of something either as being or as not being (for this one might take as assuming what is at issue) but the demand that he signify something both to himself and to another. For he must do this if he says something. For if he does not, no statement is [possible] for him, either in response to himself or to anyone else. But if he does grant this, there will be a demonstration [by refutation against him], since something will be definite once he grants this. But the one responsible [for the starting point] is not the one who demonstrates but the one who allows [this to take place]; for eliminating statement he allows statement. Furthermore, in allowing this, he has allowed that something is true independently of demonstration, so that not everything will be F and not-F. (*Met.* IV 4 1006ª15–28)

The *say-or-signify-something requirement* is the starting-point common to all demonstrations by refutation of the principle of noncontradiction. If the denier satisfies this requirement, *he* takes on the responsibility that allows the philosopher to escape the charge of assuming what is at issue. Hence the denier, in complying with the say-or-signify-something requirement, must unwittingly reveal his commitment to noncontradiction: "To demonstrate to an asserter of opposites why he speaks falsely one must obtain from him something that is equivalent to 'the same thing cannot both be and not be at one and the same time,' but which does not seem to be equivalent to it" (*Met.* XI 5 1062ª5–9). Whatever the say-or-signify-something requirement amounts to, and in whatever way Aristotle's use of it to defend the principle of noncontradiction is supposed to work, one salient point is uncontroversial: the principle itself is not an outré one, uncovered through specialized scientific research, but one we all already accept, even if confusion leads us to deny that we do.

A second principle with a status comparable to that of noncontradiction is the principle that natural beings are subject to change (*Ph.* I 2 185ª12–13). Because this principle is a transgeneric starting-point of universal natural science, a defense of it "is not a contribution to natural science" (*Ph.* I 2 184ᵇ25– 185ª5) but belongs instead (since the principle does not apply to all beings as such) to secondary or natural philosophy. Hence natural philosophy should provide a demonstration—or demonstration by refutation—of it. The following, whether intended as such or not, seems a plausible candidate:

Even if it is truly the case that being is infinite and unchanging, it certainly does not appear to be so according to perception; rather, many beings appear to undergo change. Now if indeed there is such a thing as false belief or belief at all, there is also change; similarly if there is imagination, or if anything is thought to be one way at one time and another at another. For imagination and belief are thought to be changes of a sort. (*Ph.* VIII 3 254ª24–30)

As someone can deny the principle of noncontradiction in words, so he can deny that natural beings are subject to change. To do so internally, however, seems impossible, since the denial of it itself involves self-conscious change.

As a product of confusion, the demand to have it demonstrated that natural bodies are subject to change shows not intellectual probity but lack of discernment:

> To investigate this at all, to seek an argument in a case where we are too well off to require argument, implies poor discernment of what is better and what is worse, what commends itself to belief and what does not, what is a starting-point and what is not. It is likewise impossible that all things should be changing or that some things should always be changing and the remainder always at rest. For against all these, this one thing provides sufficient assurance: we *see* some things sometimes changing and sometimes at rest. (*Ph.* VIII 3 254ª30–ᵇ1)

In the case of the principle of noncontradiction, too, the demand for a demonstration is a bad sign:

> Some people demand that we demonstrate even this, but their demand is due to lack of education. For we lack education if we do not know what we should and should not seek to have demonstrated. For it is generally impossible to demonstrate everything. . . . But if there are some things of which we must not seek a demonstration, these people could not say what starting-point is more appropriately left without demonstration than this one. (*Met.* IV 4 1006ª5–11)

To grasp such fundamental starting-points, then, we do not need specialized training in a science, just the discernment that comes with being well educated. To defend them against skeptics, of course, one needs to be dialectically or philosophically proficient, but such proficiency is what leads the well-educated to a clear understanding of them in the first place, free of the intellectual knots that unsolved puzzles constitute.

Contemplation

Theology, which is the science dealing primarily with God, is God's own science (*Met.* I 2 983ª5–10). And what God does in theologizing is actively contemplate or understand his own essence, which—since it involves no matter—is identical to his understanding of it. This essence, however, which is what he grasps or touches in active theologizing, is simple and incomposite: if it weren't, he would not be essentially an activity, complete at every moment, but "would undergo change in [understanding] the parts of the whole" that his essence consisted in (*Met.* XII 9 1075ª5–6; also XII 7 1072ª30–32). Consequently, theology cannot have the inferential complexity characteristic of most demonstrative sciences. As God's essence is simple, so theology is simple, too, since it is a science whose one starting-point is its only theorem. The perfect mesh of theology with its simple subject-matter is thereby assured.

A second of Aristotle's thoughts about theology, as we saw in passing, is that it is identical to primary philosophy:

> The most estimable science must deal with the most estimable genus of beings, so that the theoretical sciences are more choiceworthy than the others, and it [theology] than them. . . . Now if there were no substances besides those constituted by nature, natural science would be the primary science, but if there is an unmoving substance, the science of it would be prior and would be primary philosophy. (*Met.* VI 1 1026ª21–30)

The problem is that the identification of theology with primary *philosophy* seems to confuse a science with the philosophy that deals exclusively with its starting-points. Of course, this may just be a case of imprecise expression, as when the political scientist is referred to as "the political philosopher" (*NE* VII 11 1152ᵇ1–2) or when natural philosophy is referred to as "natural science" (*Met.* XI 7 1064ᵇ10). The peculiar nature of God, and so of his science, shows that no confusion need be involved. God is his own starting-point, his own cause. Moreover, he always and eternally has clear understanding of himself, and so of theology. Hence he does not need primary or theological *philosophy* to clarify his understanding by solving the puzzles that muddy it and knot it up. In his case, theology itself fulfills primary philosophy's function. In our case, of course, things are different. Our understanding of theology is darkened by puzzles, so that we do need primary philosophy. In the limit, however, that need evaporates even for us. For the most exact scientific knowledge of theology comes only at the end of the dialectical process that renders our understanding clear and puzzle free. In the end, then, when we become truly well educated, primary philosophy is replaced by theology in our case too.

We might analogize this conclusion to a more familiar one. In some versions of Christianity, complete happiness consists in the eternal, untrammeled vision of God, which is achievable by anyone, once they have accepted

Christ as their savior and been cleansed of their sins, since all have in their immortal souls a spark of the divine. There is no one, as a result, too intellectually humble to see God. Aristotle doesn't go that far, but he is recognizably traveling a parallel road. Each human being has understanding, which is something divine. It is darkened by incarnation and by puzzles, which prevent it from seeing clearly. In certain sorts of human beings with the right natural assets, incarnation seems not to be an absolute handicap (*EE* VII 2 1237ª3–9); puzzles alone are the problem. And these a good general education can often resolve. In the case of theology, the distinction between being well educated in it and having scientific knowledge of it, like the distinction between theology itself and theological philosophy, breaks down or is overcome. To be sure, the liberal education, in which dialectic and philosophy figures so prominently, may still seem much too demanding to expect of all free citizens, since it bears too close a resemblance to the philosophy that experts have now made their own. This may be true, but we can at last see why Aristotle thought it wasn't, and why his well-educated free citizens do not compromise their status as such when they acquire, in becoming theoretically wise, the most rigorous form of scientific knowledge: "we do not seek theology because of its usefulness for something else, but rather just as a human being is free, we say, when he exists for his own sake and not for someone else's, so this is the only one among the sciences that is free or liberal, since it alone exists for its own sake" (*Met.* I 2 982ᵇ24–28; also *Protr.* B25, 30, 43).

Life for a human being is twofold, as we saw, consisting in *bios*, or biographical life, and *zôê*, the life activities that take place within it. In the case of God, on the other hand, *bios* just is the life activity of contemplation to which he is identical:

> And life (*zôê*) too certainly belongs to him [God]. For the activity of understanding is life (*zôê*), and he is that activity; and his activity is intrinsically life (*zôê*) that is best and eternal. We say, then, that God is a living being (*zôê*) that is eternal and best, so that continuous, eternal life (*zôê*) and duration belong to God, since it *is* God. (*Met.* XII 7 1072ᵇ26–30)

The more of the life activity of contemplation our *bios* contains, therefore, the more like God's it is in its happiness (*NE* X 8 1178ᵇ21–32). In its best form, such activity consists in theologizing, since that is the most rigorous and most excellent kind of scientific knowing. That is why the *Nicomachean Ethics*, whose focus is on virtues or excellences of thought, mentions no form of theoretical activity besides the very best sort in connection with the contemplative life: it is as perfectionistic about it as it is about practical wisdom. Elsewhere, the picture is somewhat different:

> Among the substances constituted by nature, some never for all eternity either come-to-be or pass-away, while others share in coming-to-be and passing-away. Yet, as it happens, our theoretical knowledge of the former, though they are estimable and divine, is slighter, since as regards both those things on the basis of which one would investigate them and those things about them that we long to know, the perceptual appearances are altogether few. Where the plants and animals that pass-away are concerned, however, we are much better off as regards knowledge, because we live among them. For anyone willing to take sufficient trouble can grasp a lot about each genus of them. Each type of theoretical knowledge has its attractions. For even if our contact with eternal things is but slight, all the same, because of its esteem, this knowledge is a greater pleasure than our knowledge of everything around us, just as even a chance, brief glimpse of those we love is a greater pleasure than the most rigorous view of other things, however many or great they are. On the other hand, because we know more of them and know them more fully, our scientific knowledge of things that pass-away exceeds that of the others. Moreover, because they are nearer to us and because their nature is more akin to ours, they provide their own compensations in comparison with the philosophy concerned with divine things. . . . For even in the theoretical knowledge of animals that are disagreeable to perception, the nature that crafted them likewise provides extraordinary pleasures to those who can know their causes and are by nature philosophers. . . . For this reason we should not be childishly disgusted at the investigation of the less estimable animals, since in all natural things there is something marvelous. (PA I 5 644^{b}22–645^{a}17)

As in the *Ethics*, a glimpse of the divine remains the best kind of theoretical knowing. The difference is that now the extraordinary pleasures offered by the vaster scientific knowledge of the sublunary realm are also part of the picture.

It is in discussing pleasures, indeed, that Aristotle acknowledges an obvious fact about our nature:

> It is clear that a pleasure arises in accord with each sense, since we say that sights and sounds are pleasant, and it is clear, too, that it arises most of all when the sense is in the best condition and is active in relation to an object of which the same holds. When both the perceptible object and the sense that is doing the perceiving are like this, there will always be pleasure—at any rate, as long as the producer [of the perception] and that in which it is produced are both present. . . . Hence as long as the intelligible or perceptible object is as it

should be and likewise what is discerning or contemplating it, there will be pleasure in the activity, since as long as the thing being affected and the one producing the affection remain the same, and in the same relation to each other, the same thing naturally arises. How is it, then, that no one is continuously pleased? Or is it because of getting tired (*kamnei*)? After all, continuous activity is impossible for everything human. So no continuous pleasure arises either, since it accompanies the activity. The fact that some things delight us when they are novelties but later delight us less is due to the same thing. Initially, thought is aroused and intensely active regarding them, as happens with our sight when we focus intensely on something, but later the activity is no longer like that but becomes unfocused, so that the pleasure is dimmed as well. (*NE* X 4 1174ᵇ26–1175ᵃ10)

The tiredness that explains why we cannot be continuously pleased might be the sort a good night's sleep relieves, which is what *kamnein* usually signifies. The immediate mention of novelties, however, suggests that boredom rather than fatigue may be the issue—especially since the reason no activity pleases us for long isn't simply that our batteries wear down:

> One and the same thing is never always pleasant because our nature is not simple but also has in it a part of a different sort, in that we are mortals, so that the action of one part is contrary to nature for the other nature in us, and when they are equally balanced, what we are doing seems neither pleasant nor painful. For to something with a simple nature the same action would always be most pleasant. That is why God always enjoys a single simple pleasure. For there is activity not only in movement but in nonmovement, and pleasure lies more in rest than in movement. "In all things change is sweet," as the poet says, but this is because of some sort of badness. For just as a human being who is easily changed is a bad one, so too is a nature that needs change, since it is neither simple nor good. (*NE* VII 14 1154ᵇ20–31)

Usually, the fault line in human nature seems to coincide with the divide between action and contemplation, between the merely human practical life of politics and the truly human or divine contemplative life. Now, however, it has opened up within the contemplative life itself. Not even theologizing, it seems, will continuously charm us. At some point boredom or tedium will set in, and we will crave the delights of contemplating something else, something closer to home. *Historia Animalium* offers plenty of examples to choose from.

The focus on theoretical wisdom, as the very best kind of contemplation of the very best intelligible object, makes the task that practical wisdom faces seem somewhat simpler than it is, suggesting that by maximizing the time we spend theologizing, it will make us happiest. It would be truer to say, it seems, that it will do so by giving us as much theologizing as we can tolerate, and as many contemplative alternatives to it as we may need. This doesn't quite turn the dazzling brightness of theory into nature's green, but it makes the contemplative life look much less monochrome.

The education that practical wisdom provides to citizens of the best city must already include sufficient exposure to the special sciences to enable the induction that leads to the universal sciences and their associated philosophies, since only in that way can theoretical wisdom be reached. It might seem that with this enrichment of the contemplative life comes a need for something closer to firsthand expert scientific knowledge of the special sciences themselves, rather than reflective, meta-level, secondhand knowledge of their starting-points. Consequently, it is of some importance that even in the case of the special sciences, it is those who "can know their causes and are by nature philosophers" who get the extraordinary pleasures they have to offer. It may be less the narrow specialist who is being described, therefore, than the well-educated person, who sees the beauty even in naked mole rats or other unattractive living things because he has had a clear-headed glimpse of the divine, and so can see that "all things (even swimming creatures, flying creatures, and plants) are jointly organized, though not in the same way, and are not of such a character that one thing has no relation to another, but there is some relation between them, since all are jointly organized in relation to one thing" (*Met.* XII 10 1075^{a}18–19)—which is, of course, God. What distinguishes "those doctors who pursue their craft more philosophically" is that their search for the "primary starting-points of health and disease" leads them to begin by considering nature in general (*Sens.* 1 436^{a}17–^{b}1; also *Juv.* 21 480^{b}22–30). It can hardly be an accident, in any case, that Aristotle's longest paean to well-educatedness forms a preface to a biological treatise, suggesting that the treatise itself is a contribution to the very thing praised therein.

One sort of simplification the *Nicomachean Ethics* engages in when portraying the contemplative life is a result of its focus on the *virtues* whether of character or thought, since this has the effect of making the star of the contemplative show—the most virtuous or excellent kind of contemplation—look like the entire cast. A second sort of simplification is caused by its focus on the question of what activity in accord with what virtue *happiness* is, which tends to make the contemplative components of the leisurely life look like the leisurely life as a whole. This has the further effect of overheightening the contrast between the leisurely contemplative life and the unleisurely political life that supports it. When we appropriately correct for these simplifications, we see—to put it provocatively—that the best political and contemplative lives are not so much two separate lives as distinct phases of the same life.

As Aristotle conceives of it, political activity is already a step up from productive work, since, as activity in accord with practical wisdom and full virtue of character, it is choiceworthy at least in part because of itself. Unleisured, productive work, by contrast, is choiceworthy only because of the additional ends that are its products. Engaging in it, therefore, or in certain sorts of it anyway, such as farming or the vulgar crafts, unfits one to be a free citizen of many constitutions, including the best one. Leisure for a productive worker may well just be time off from work. This, no doubt, is how we conceive of it ourselves. We are at leisure when our time is our own to do with as we please. Aristotle's view is different: we are at leisure not when we are, as we say, doing nothing, or doing as we please, but when what we are doing is choiceworthy because of itself. Much practical activity is, in that sense, already somewhat leisurely, even if, because it also has an additional end, it is also somewhat unleisurely.

The reason leisure shouldn't consist exclusively of playing games or amusing oneself is that amusement is choiceworthy for the sake of relaxation, and relaxation isn't something choiceworthy for its own sake but only because the pains and exertions of unleisure require it:

> Happiness is not found in amusement, since it would be absurd indeed for the end to be amusement, and our life's labors and sufferings to be for the sake of amusement. For we choose almost everything, except happiness, for the sake of something else, since it is the [unconditional] end. To work hard and toil [just] for the sake of amusement, however, appears a silly and entirely childish thing to do. Rather "play to be serious," as Anacharsis puts it, seems to have it right. For amusement is a form of relaxation, and it is because we cannot toil continuously that we need relaxation. Relaxation, then, is not an end, since it occurs for the sake of activity [in accord with virtue]. (*NE* X 6 1176^{b}27–1177^{a}1)

Nonetheless, because, as political animals, we do have to engage in unleisurely practical activities, the best city "should permit amusement, but be careful to use it at the right time, dispensing it as a medicine for the ills of unleisure" (*Pol.* VIII 3 1337^{b}35–42). Amusement is a bridge, in other words, between the unleisurely life of politics and the leisurely one—included in the latter only because of its connection to the former.

A free person should be educated in drawing, in part because it helps him better discern the quality of a craftsman's work, so that he is not "cheated when buying and selling products," but also as a leisured pursuit that enables him to better "contemplate the beauty of bodies" (*Pol.* VIII 3 1338ᵃ41–ᵇ2). He should also be educated in reading and writing, because "they are useful for making money, managing a household, acquiring further learning, or for many political activities" (*Pol.* VIII 3 1338ᵃ15–19), but also, no doubt, because they too can be leisured pursuits: Aristotle's own love of books was legendary. Finally, he should be educated in *mousikê*, a combination of poetry, dance, and music proper, which was a staple of traditional Greek education, solely because it is a leisured pursuit, "appropriate for free people" (*Pol.* VIII 3 1338ᵃ22–23). We are already a long way, then, from thinking of the leisured life as consisting of contemplation alone.

Within that life, moreover, a variety of different virtues have roles to play:

Since it is evident that human beings have the same end, both individually and collectively, and since the best man and the best constitution necessarily have the same defining-mark, it is evident that the virtues suitable for leisure should be present in both. For . . . peace is the end of war, and leisure of unleisure. Now, some of the virtues useful in relation to leisure and passing the time fulfill their function during leisure, while others do so during unleisure. For many necessities must be present in order for leisure to be possible. That is why it is appropriate for our city to have temperance, courage, and endurance. For as the proverb says, there is no leisure for slaves, and people who are unable to face danger courageously are the slaves of their attackers. Now courage and endurance [are useful] in relation to unleisure, philosophy in relation to leisure,[4] and temperance and justice in relation to both, but more so in relation to peace and leisure. For war compels people to be just and temperate, but the enjoyment of good luck and the leisure that accompanies peace tend more to make them arrogant. Much justice and much temperance are needed, therefore, by those who are believed to be doing best and to be enjoying all the things regarded as blessings—people like those, if there are any, who live in the Isles of the Blessed, as the poets call them. For the more they live at leisure amid an abundance of such goods, the greater will be their need for philosophy,

4. Philosophy, which must be theoretical wisdom here, since it is exclusively useful in leisure, is also theoretical wisdom in the following passage: "if any want to enjoy things through their own' selves (*di' hautôn*), they should not look for a cure beyond philosophy, since all other pleasures require [other] human beings" (*Pol.* II 7 1267ᵃ10–12). For it is the theoretically wise person, who is able—"and more able the wiser he is"—to engage in contemplation "even by himself" (*NE* X 7 1177ᵃ32–34).

temperance, and justice. It is evident, then, why a city that is to be happy and good should share in these virtues. For it is ignoble to be unable to make use of good things, but it is even more ignoble to be unable to make use of them when we are at leisure—to make it plain that we are good men when working or at war, but slaves when at peace and leisure. (*Pol.* VII 15 1334ª11–40)

The mention of good luck and arrogance strongly suggest that the use temperance and justice (and so practical wisdom) have in leisure concerns external goods, since it is these that luck controls, these whose possession in abundance arrogance commonly accompanies: "The type of character produced by wealth lies on the surface for all to see. Wealthy men are arrogant and insolent, being psychologically affected by the acquisition of wealth, for they seem to think that they possess every good thing, since wealth is like a standard of value for all of them, and so it seems as if there is nothing it cannot buy" (*Rh.* II 16 1390ᵇ32–1391ª2). Add to this the fact that abundant external goods are positive hindrances to contemplation (*NE* X 8 1178ᵇ3–5) and something like the following picture is suggested. As human beings whose lives are not self-sufficient for contemplation, we must live together with others in a city, where—if we are lucky and our city is the best possible—abundant external goods will be available (*Pol.* VII 13 1332ª28–31). For unless we possess an abundance of such goods, we cannot exercise all the virtues of character—generosity and magnanimity being obvious examples. When we are at leisure, some of these virtues, such as courage and endurance, are inactive, while others, temperance and justice, are active. Since these are inseparable parts of full virtue of character, however, all must be possessed together with practical wisdom, if any are. We must be fully virtuous and practically wise, it follows, not just when involved in unleisurely activities but also when involved in leisurely ones.

The best human life, then, has an unleisured part, consisting of practical political activities, and a leisured one, consisting of contemplative activities of various sorts, as well as other activities of a noncontemplative sort, such as relaxing amusements. The organization of all these into a single life-structure that best furthers the contemplation of God is a task for practical wisdom and political science:

What is most choiceworthy for each individual is always this: to attain what is highest. . . . A political scientist must . . . particularly look, therefore, to those things that are better and those that are ends. . . . But reason and understanding are our natural end. Hence they are the ends the training of our habits should be organized to further. . . . Supervision of desire should be for the sake of understanding, and that of the body for the sake of the soul. (*Pol.* VII 14–15 1333ª29–1334ᵇ28; also *Protr.* B17–30)

Since every telic system—including cities and human beings—is identified most of all with the constituent in it that has most control (*NE* IX 8 1168ᵇ31–32), and a life with the structure described is clearly such a system, there is good reason to call it the contemplative life, since contemplation is the end or target that controls it. When Aristotle says that the "contemplative life" is the one "we shall examine in what follows" (*NE* I 5 1096ª4–5), then, he is arguably describing the *Nicomachean Ethics* as a whole.

If abundant external goods are not to hinder contemplation, we must not overindulge in them, or become involved in the sort of competition for them to which greed gives rise. We need temperance, therefore, which pertains to the private use of such goods, and justice, which pertains to their fair and equal distribution. Leisure time itself is also a sort of good, of course, which needs to be used temperately and justly for the same reason. Theoretical wisdom—philosophy—is needed in this regard, too, because it is only if we have experienced contemplation for ourselves that we can grasp as a practical truth that *it* is what complete happiness consists in. That is why, having provided a theoretical argument in support of contemplation's claim to be complete happiness, Aristotle insists that the proof of the pudding, where a practical treatise like the *Ethics* is concerned, lies ultimately in the eating:

> These sorts of considerations do carry some conviction; but the truth in practical matters must be discerned from the things we do and from our life, since these are what have the controlling vote. Hence when we examine everything that has been previously said, it must be by bringing it to bear on the things we do and on our life, and if it is in harmony with what we do, we should accept it, but if it conflicts, we should suppose it mere words. (*NE* X 8 1179ª17–22; also II 4 1105ᵇ10–18, X 1 1172ª34–ᵇ1)

This is what gives the virtues of character a more intimate role to play even within those leisurely activities that are strictly contemplative. In the case of the gods, contemplation always appears as the happiness it really is. This is not so for us: to experience contemplation *as happiness*, we must have the virtues of character, since it is they—and they alone—that make our target, and our suppositions about it, correct. Without the virtues of character, therefore, even if we did engage in contemplation of God, we could not possibly see it as what all by itself made a life choiceworthy and in need of nothing. Other activities in which we found much greater pleasure and satisfaction might seem far stronger contenders. We would then be entirely justified from the practical point of view in dismissing Aristotle's arguments to the contrary as mere words. For human beings, then, if not for gods, it is impossible to have theoretical wisdom without also having practical wisdom and the virtues of character.[5]

In the best city, practical wisdom is something all the male citizens achieve when, at around the age of forty, they have acquired an experienced eye to complement their theoretical knowledge. But one does not need to have been brought up in the best city to be practically wise. Even an oligarchy or a democracy, provided it isn't too extreme, can provide someone with good enough habits to make him an adequate student of noble and just things, once he is old enough. At the beginning of his ethical studies, he will already have a grasp of the pertinent facts, a grasp of what the noble and just things are, since this good habits can provide unaided. What he does not have is an explanation of these things. That is what, by the end of his studies, he will have acquired. He will have seen how and why noble and just things further happiness.

In the best city, practical wisdom is ideally placed and rules everything, but it can get by with much less:

> Even though no one can be blessedly happy without external goods, still we should not think that to be happy we will need many of them and large-scale ones. For self-sufficiency does not depend on excess and neither does action, and even someone who does not rule land and sea is capable of doing noble things, since even from moderate resources we can do the actions that are in accord with virtue. Indeed, this is plain to see, since many private individuals seem to do decent actions no less—in fact, even more—than those in political power. Moderate resources are adequate, since someone's life will be happy if it accords with virtue. (*NE* X 8 1179^{a}1–9)

Aristotle's own will reveals that he had a sizable estate, including houses in Chalcis and Stagira, significant capital, a domestic partner, two children, a number of slaves, a large library, and a wide circle of friends.[6] Adequate

---

5. Contrast David Charles, "Aristotle and Modern Realism," in *Aristotle and Moral Realism*, ed. R. Heinaman (Boulder, Colo.: Westview, 1995), p. 159 n. 19, representing what is surely the majority opinion.

6. The will, as preserved in Diogenes Laertius V 11–16, is printed and discussed in Ingemar Düring, *Aristotle in the Ancient Biographical Tradition* (Göteborg: Studia Graeca et Latina Gothoburgensia, 1957), pp. 13–79.

resources, one would suppose. When he was seventeen, there was the Academy, where he spent twenty years studying under the greatest philosopher there has ever been, himself perhaps excepted. No doubt, the best city would do much better, but adequate training in philosophy the Academy surely provided. Later in life, there was the Lyceum, and the company of distinguished colleagues and coworkers, his friend Theophrastus prominent among them. That Aristotle had practical wisdom by the time he composed the *Ethics* seems a safe assumption, then, given his own account of what it takes to acquire it. That he nonetheless somewhat lamented his exclusion from active participation in politics—he was a metic or resident alien in Athens, not a citizen, and as such was debarred from holding office, participating in the assembly, serving on a jury, owning land, or building a house—is something we can, perhaps, infer from the fact that the best life, as he describes it, involves ruling a city as one of its free and unconditional citizens.[7]

Since Aristotle can hardly have thought the contents of his own works on ethics mere words, it follows—though the inference is seldom drawn—that he must have known (or thought he knew) *from the inside* that contemplating God does indeed make life worth living and in need of nothing. This could not be true, of course, unless he had experienced its life-transforming powers for himself, and lived accordingly. He was a philosopher, after all, living a philosophical life. Not just that, he was confident enough others would agree with him that he proposed a simple test—as simple in some ways as the one he proposed for the principle of change. As we can just see that things change, and so need no elaborate proof that they do, so we can—when the muddles and puzzles left unsolved by an adequate upbringing are cleared away by a good education in philosophy—just *see* that contemplation of God is happiness. If we can't, the words of the *Ethics* will be just that—words with no practical significance.

What God is, we know: as *hê noêsis noêseôs noêsis*, he is an active understanding precisely of understanding itself—a form of reflexive conscious awareness. Having no other content, he is just that: active reflexive awareness that is otherwise objectless. As in accord with his own science, theoretical wisdom, his awareness is a kind of scientific knowledge, indeed the most rigorous kind. Hence he understands himself exactly as he is. As an unim-

7. See D. Whitehead, "Aristotle the Metic," *Proceedings of the Cambridge Philological Society* 21 (1975): 94–99, and Martha C. Nussbaum, *The Fragility of Goodness* (Cambridge: Cambridge University Press, 1986), pp. 345–353.

peded active contemplation of the best thing, he is happiness itself, the most pleasant pleasure. As a life activity, he is a form of life—a way of being alive. When we contemplate God, therefore, and our understanding—so far as it can—engages in the active understanding that he is, it, too, is an active reflexive awareness, which, while otherwise objectless or contentless, is wholly veridical, wholly pleasant, wholly and happily alive. From the inside, then, from the point of view of the subject experiencing it, it is a state of consciousness of a sort familiar from the writings of the great religious mystics, in which both subject and object disappear from an awareness that yet remains fully and truly attentive, fully alive and joyous.[8] Insofar as we have any experience-based evidence of what a beatific state is like, this one surely approximates to it. Were we to experience it, then, there is some reason to think that we would agree that it is bliss indeed, blessed happiness unalloyed.

What we experience on the inside, however, has to mesh with what we know on the outside. The God we experience as a Zen-like state of consciousness must also be the most fundamental starting-point of all, the prime mover. To explain how this could be true would be to retrace our steps through Aristotle's works, following the paths that lead him to the conclusion that nothing but *hê noêsis noêseôs noêsis* could play these ultimate ontological and epistemological roles. So let us take a shortcut. Imagine the world without consciousness in it, without conscious life. It is a world, isn't it, without value or significance, without *eudaimonia*? The good is always good in relation to someone (*DA* III 7 431ᵇ10–12). Now think about how little idea we have of how to put consciousness into a world except by putting it in direct and whole. We have no compelling story of how it could emerge from nonconscious processes, though we may be confident that there must be one. Combine those thoughts, and neither Aristotle's strange God nor his role in the happiest human life should seem quite so strange.

The shortcut, however, is no substitute for the rough road. Unless we travel it, we cannot grasp as God—as the ultimate starting-point—what awaits us at the end of our journey. To see God as the solution, we must first untie the knots in our understanding that darken our vision:

8. As David Bradshaw, *Aristotle East and West: Metaphysics and the Division of Christendom* (Cambridge: Cambridge University Press, 2004), pp. 153–277, convincingly argues, Eastern Christianity, as developed by the Greek Fathers (especially St. Dionysius the Areopagite, St. Maximus, St. John of Damascus, and St. Gregory Palamas) takes Aristotle's thought in this more "mystical" direction, while St. Augustine and St. Thomas Aquinas take it in the more "rationalist" one, familiar in the West.

Those who wish to be free of puzzles must first go through the puzzles well; for the subsequent puzzle-free condition (*euporia*) is reached by untying the knots produced by the puzzles raised in advance, and it is not possible for someone who is unaware of a knot to untie it. A puzzle in thought, however, reveals a knot in its subject matter. For thought caught in a puzzle is like people who are tied up, since in either case it is impossible to make progress. That is why one must have studied all the difficulties in advance, both for these reasons and because those who inquire without first going through the puzzles are like people who don't know where they have to go, and, in addition, don't even know whether they have found what they were inquiring about, since the end is not clear to them. But to someone who has first gone through the puzzles it is clear. (*Met.* III 1 995ᵃ27–ᵇ2)

The bright-adapted eyes we acquire when the puzzles are solved, we may be assured, will no longer be "as the eyes of bats to the blaze of day," but instead will at last see clearly "the things that are by nature the most evident of all" (*Met.* II 1 993ᵇ9–11).

INDEX OF PASSAGES

ARISTOTLE

GENERAL INDEX

Abortion, 152n17
Abstraction, 85–86, 89
Ackrill, J. L. 188n42, 232n7
Action (*praxis*), 40–50, 55–57, 140–144;
   as conclusion of a syllogism, 169–178.
   See also Activity
Activity, 7–8, 140–142; contemplation as,
   264–270; God as, 14–16, 205–211;
   happiness as, 161, 171–173, 226–234;
   human beings as, 211–216; pleasure as,
   146–147; substance as, 200–205; un-
   derstanding as, 16–19, 52–55, 138–139
Actualization, 7–8, 200–205y
Adequacy, 107
Admit of being otherwise, 77–79, 131,
   143; and deliberation, 165, 180
Adultery, 119, 153
Alexander of Aphrodisias, 157n23
Amusement, 270
Anaxagoras, 13, 51, 213n9
Anger, 85
Annunciation vs. assertion, 41–42, 66–68
Anscombe, G. E. M. 189n43
Aphrodite (Venus), 217
Aporematic, 61–63, 147, 161, 188, 192,
   225, 257
Appearance, 27, 39–40; and animal
   movement, 20–21; in deliberative per-
   ception, 182–183; in science, 60–61,
   267; and understanding, 43–50, 55,
   206–211
Aquinas, 174n38, 276n8

Architectonic, 90, 99, 108, 136, 142, 149–
   150, 151, 160, 164, 167, 174, 185, 188,
   215, 232–234, 250
Aristocracy, 106, 108, 110–111
Aristotle, 274–275
Assertion. *See* Annunciation
Astronomy, 60–61, 85, 86, 89, 91, 218
Attribute, 195–200; special, 72n18, 158
Automata, 19–24
Avoidance. *See* Pursuit
Axiom, 58, 62, 261
Axiothea of Phlius, 253n1

Barnes, Jonathan, 19n12, 80n22
Beere, Jonathan, 2n1
Being (*einai*), difference in, 150–151
Being qua being, science of, 256–264
Belief, 48–49, 131; reputable (*endoxon*), 62
Blood, 4, 22–23, 44–45
Bodéüs, Richard, 218n15
Body, primary. *See* Ether
Bolton, Robert, 61n4, 62n6
Bordt, Michael, 15n10
Bos, A. P., 8n4
Bradshaw, David, 14n9, 276n8
Broadie, Sarah, 142n10, 187n42, 212n7,
   213n8, 216n11
Brown, Lesley, 111n9
Brunschwig, Jacques, 157n22, 158n24
Builder, 14, 20, 102, 166, 200
Burnyeat, M. F. 32n3, 141n9, 211n6
Bywater, I., 128n17, 182n39

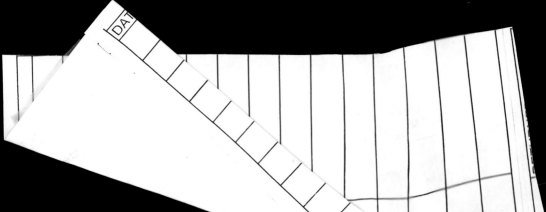